Danny Dorling is the Halford Mackin[...] University of Oxford. His previous boo[...] [...] and *The Equality Effect*. With others, he created the website worldmapper. org, a digital collection of demographic maps.

Further praise for *Slowdown*:

"A spellbinding book that will almost certainly make you reconsider what you thought was happening in and to the world, and then think again about where we might be heading." Juliette Powell, author of *33 Million People in the Room*

"Blinded by a cult of progress, many of us can't see the slowdown that Dorling makes clear. A true public intellectual, he shows that, if we survive, life will be slower—and possibly better." Paul Chatterton, author of *Unlocking Sustainable Cities*

"Dorling's optimism is infectious as he brilliantly explores the huge challenges of a slowing pace of growth while the world transitions to a new 'normal' of stable and then shrinking populations." Vicky Pryce, author of *Women vs Capitalism*

"Powerful, thought-provoking, and timely. Professor Dorling brilliantly exposes how spiralling work intensity, alongside bumper profits and freedoms for capital, cannot sustain people and planet. From stronger unions to a greener economy, he compellingly shows how we can choose a more hopeful and humane future." Frances O'Grady, General Secretary of the Trades Union Congress

"In this counterintuitive and eye-opening book, Dorling explodes the prevalent myth of acceleration and shows a beneficial slowdown is already happening—and needs to happen." Vanessa Baird, co-editor, *New Internationalist*

"An incredibly insightful and inspiring analysis showing that an increasingly slowing pace of economic and population growth can go hand in hand with greater human progress, planetary responsibility and refocusing on the things that really matter in life." Dimitris Ballas, University of Groningen

ALSO BY THE AUTHOR AND HIS COLLEAGUES

Geography

Inequality and the 1%

The Atlas of the Real World

Injustice: Why Social Inequality Persists

The Equality Effect: Improving Life for Everyone

Finntopia: What We Can Learn from the World's Happiest Country

Population 10 Billion: The Coming Demographic Crisis and How to Survive It

OWN

the end of the great acceleration—
and why it's a good thing

updated edition

danny dorling

illustrations by kirsten mcclure

Yale UNIVERSITY PRESS/NEW HAVEN & LONDON

Yale University Press books may be purchased in quantity for
educational, business, or promotional use. For information, please e-mail
sales.press@yale.edu (U.S. office) or sales@yaleup.co.uk (U.K. office).

Set in Minion type by Newgen North America.
Printed in Great Britain by Clays Ltd, Elcograf S.p.A.
Illustrations by Kirsten McClure.

Library of Congress Control Number: 2020947077
ISBN 978-0-300-24340-6 (hardcover : alk. paper)
ISBN 978-0-300-25796-0 (paperback : alk. paper)

A catalogue record for this book is available from the British Library.

This paper meets the requirements of ANSI/NISO Z39.48-1992
(Permanence of Paper).

10 9 8 7 6 5 4 3 2 1

To Bob Hughes (1947–2019): activist, academic, friend, and
one of the five co-signatories of the 2003
No One Is Illegal Manifesto

CONTENTS

ACKNOWLEDGMENTS

With thanks to my father, David Dorling, who is now very happy spending most of his days sweeping the leaves and feeding the birds in his woodland garden, who kindly corrected and revised the first, second, and third drafts of this book. And to my mother, Bronwen Dorling, who always told me I could do anything I put my mind to, and that whatever I did would be okay. Alison Dorling has been more realistic as to my limitations, but always enthusiastically sure that this project was worthwhile. Robbie, Izzy, and Sol Dorling tolerated a particular obsession that lasted from when the oldest was just a teenager to when the youngest achieved that status and the oldest became an adult and got his first proper job.

My thanks especially to Anthony Caira-Carnell in Australia who, despite the severe effects of his hemophilia, suffering the legacy of the NHS infected blood products scandal, and being sixteen thousand kilometers away, very kindly offered to read all the final drafts, commented in brilliant detail on where I was going round in circles, and still kept a clear head. My heartfelt thanks are also owed to Karen Shook and Claire Hann, both of whom read and improved every draft chapter after I had amalgamated so many other people's thoughts and edits and did so to a standard beyond that which I could ever do. Susan Laity then smoothly took over production of a complex book with many illustrations and introduced me to Robin DuBlanc, the most thoughtful and courteous copyeditor I have ever had the pleasure to (electronically) meet. Books like this are the product of a large team of people, not of individual minds, despite being marketed as such.

I am also especially grateful to Kirsten McClure, who designed the style of converting the timelines in the book to the graphics you see here and redrew all of them from my crude Excel sheets. So many others also helped and commented. I am grateful to Qiujie Shi and Tomoki Nakaya for help on statistics on China and Japan, respectively; and again to Qiujie for all her work producing a huge number of additional timelines using many different data sets that are now all on this book's website (and available to all for free). And I thank Lorenza Antonucci, Ben Ayre, Aniko Horvath, Carl Lee, John McKeown, Khadija Rouf, Simon Ryde, Craig Twyford, Tara van Dijk, and others (I should have kept a list), who kindly commented on earlier versions of various chapters, as I slowly tried to untangle a mass of thoughts, opinion, and bits and pieces of evidence into this book and became somewhat tiresomely obsessed to find that almost every subject I looked into was showing some evidence of slowdown.

I am very grateful for the thoughts of the undergraduate science students of the University of Cambridge, who first heard me present these ideas in February 2019; to the postgraduate students at the London School of Economics, who commented on the first drafts of the timelines in March of that year; to all those who commented after I gave my first public lecture on this topic at the Oxford Martin School in May 2019; and to the London Universities Economic and Social Research Council–funded PhD students for their views, given in June 2019.

Finally, I must thank above all Joe Calamia, my editor at Yale University Press, without whom this book would probably have proceeded a great deal more slowly, and very possibly not at all. He is patient, calm, and very kind. I think he'll fit in well to the new future.

SLOWDOWN

to worry

imaginatively

The country's fertility rate—the number of expected babies per woman—
fell to 0.98 in 2018, according to the latest government data released on
Wednesday.

—*Song Jung-a in Seoul, South Korea, 28 August 2019*

Over the past 160 years our numbers have doubled and doubled and almost doubled again. Never before have we seen such a huge rise in human
population in so few generations. Never again will we. Today our population growth is slowing down. In 1859 Charles Darwin wrote of "the numerous recorded cases of the astonishingly rapid increase of various animals in a state of nature, when circumstances have been favorable to them
during two or three following seasons."[1] Using examples ranging from minuscule seedlings to giant elephants, he discussed the very rare cases in
nature when exponential population growth occurred in a species. In fact,
the best example he could have picked would have been that of his own
species, humans, who at that time were just beginning their own unprecedented, exponential, worldwide increase in numbers.

Today slowdown (a word first used in the 1890s, meaning to go forward more slowly) affects far more than our rate of population growth. It
affects almost every aspect of our lives. Our current slowdown represents
a huge challenge to the expectation of acceleration, and a step into the unknown. To what extent are our current belief systems (economic, political,
and otherwise) built on assumptions of rapid future technological change
and perpetual economic growth? Accepting that a slowdown is upon us

will require us to shift our fundamental view of change, innovation, and discovery as unalloyed benefits. Will we be able to accept that we should stop expecting ceaseless technological revolutions? The possibility that we might not sensibly be able to do so is itself frightening. What mistakes will we make if we assume that slowdown is unlikely and new great shifts lie just around the corner? What will happen if things stay much the same as they are now while the rate of change simply slows down?

Imagine that you have spent your life on a speeding train and you suddenly feel the brakes being applied. You would worry what was about to happen next. Now imagine that not just you but all the people you know—as well as their parents, grandparents, and great-grandparents, as far back as anyone can remember—have all lived on that very same speeding train, and that the train has been accelerating for virtually all of their lives. For you, hurtling forward at breakneck speed is comfortingly normal, but now you can begin to feel the slowdown, a new and frightening feeling. However, because the train is still rushing forward, people all around you are still talking of acceleration—the increasing pace of change—although in reality the train is no longer going ever faster. Something has changed. Out of the window the landscape is going by less quickly; everything is slowing down. An era is ending.

The great acceleration that has occurred in recent generations created the culture in which we live. It created our current expectation for a particular kind of progress. By "us" I mean the large majority of older people now living on Earth, those who have for the most part seen their health, housing, and workplaces improve compared to what their parents and grandparents experienced. I mean those who have witnessed education being extended, those who have seen both absolute poverty and immiseration recede during their lifetimes. I am thinking of those who now have a sense that their children's generation will not be much better off than they are now, those who are feeling a new sense of slowdown.

It is because we have so few examples of slowdown to draw on from the past couple of centuries that we find our times especially confusing today. However, slowing down is a very good thing—and the alternative is unimaginably bad. If we do not slow down, there is no escape from imminent disaster. We would wreck our very home, the planet we live on. We need to slow down because we have nowhere else to speed to without catastrophic consequences. Slowdown means we need not fear the nightmare scenario of worldwide famine depicted at the end of Paul and Anne Ehrlich's 1968 book *The Population Bomb,* in which they concluded of India that its people should be allowed to starve: "Under the triage system [suggested by them] she [India] should receive no more food."[2] This kind of concern and brutal conclusion were rife in the recent past. Images of out-of-control acceleration became commonplace. For instance, Joel E. Cohen, a mathematical biologist, wrote in 1992:

> Back in 1970 Ansley Coale, a demographer at Princeton, observed that the population of the United States had increased by half since 1940. At that growth rate, he calculated, the US population would reach a billion shortly before the year 2100. Within six or seven more centuries we would reach one person per square foot of land area in the United States, and after about 1,500 years our descendants would outweigh the Earth if they continued to increase by 50 percent every 30 years. We can even calculate that, at that rate of increase, our descendants would, in a few thousand years, form a sphere of flesh whose radius would, neglecting relativity, expand at the velocity of light.[3]

Ansley Coale was making his calculations just a year or so after the point when what he was measuring ceased to accelerate any further. By the early 1990s we began to worry less about acceleration. It was then that we began to realize that continued acceleration was no longer possible.

Slow down.

Now take a step backward.

Look at what is happening all around you.

It is New Year's Day 2019. I have just listened to an early-morning radio discussion about how, if we humans planned a trip to the planets of Uranus and Neptune this year and began working on that plan straightaway, we could get a spaceship there by 2043. It would take almost a quarter of a century just to see those planets up close.

We are trapped by time—and space. It simply takes too long to get to anywhere else. We are stuck here, on Earth, for (hopefully) a very long time to come. Fortuitously, human population growth began to slow down dramatically in the late 1960s (ironically, around the very same time as the first human walked on the moon). There is now nowhere where the population is any longer accelerating. Deceleration has become the norm, and today in much of Europe, the Far East, and in large parts of the Americas, total human population numbers are falling.

A slowdown in population does not necessarily mean immediate stability, but rather stability to come. It is most likely that a century from now the average number of children in a family will be fewer than two. Slowdown means that within a century the new global norm will be a slowly shrinking total planetary human population. This would also mean a continuously aging population for many decades to come, but the rate of aging will itself also slow in the near future as the rise in human life expectancy slows down.[4] The age of the world's oldest person has not increased in the past twenty years.[5]

Of course, as the slowdown progresses, there will be shocks and many surprises which, by definition, are entirely unpredictable; but it is now sensible to admit that the process has begun. Understanding that to be true requires looking at the recent past and present very differently from how we have become accustomed to viewing our times. But first, we must consider what continuing to speed up would look like.

SEEING THE GREAT ACCELERATION

There are many ways in which change can be shown, but if you want to really see the detail of change—and what is changing within the change itself—that is best done by viewing a timeline. The method used in this book is unusual, employed only very rarely in Western social science.[6] However, it is a remarkably effective way of showing how large a total is while simultaneously highlighting how that total is also changing, over both very short periods of time and—most important—overall. Furthermore, timelines drawn as they are drawn in this book allow the second derivative of change, the change in the rate of change, to also be appreciated. The short appendix at the end of this book gives more details of how these particular graphs can be both drawn and read.

Isaac Newton and those of his time who understood rates of change could easily have comprehended the method that is used to make the timelines shown in this book, which are statistical graphs. The first known statistical graph dates back to 1623, just a few decades before Newton was born.[7] What is new today is how widely we share the understanding of such concepts, which in the past very few were allowed to be taught. Because of this wider and wider sharing, the rate of growth in discovery also initially rose rapidly. As it rose, until recently, we were changing how we think more quickly with every human generation—with new graphs, new mathematics, new physics, entire new academic disciplines, with science as a truth to replace the old gods—with new everything.

The example timeline drawn in figure 1 shows the population of an imaginary country, Nosuchland, which was home to 100 million people in the year 1950 and then experienced an increase in that number by 2 percent a year every year thereafter. Japan had a population of about that size in 1950, and was growing at that rate that year. In the first year, the population of Nosuchland rises by 2 million people to 102 million. Even at this apparently modest rate of change, the total population grows rapidly, and after thirty-five years it has doubled; by 1985 there are 200 million people living in our imaginary country and the annual increase has grown to 4 million a year (2 percent). Just twenty-one years later, in 2006, the population has tripled, reaching 300 million and growing at a huge 6 million a year. The timeline simply plots the size of the population against the absolute rate of change in that size. The relative rate of change, a percentage, is always 2 percent. In contrast, the absolute rate of change, a number of people, keeps rising as 2 percent of a growing population is always rising. The pendulum drawn on the timeline illustrates the speed of change as it moves away and to the right.

On the timeline in figure 1, constant acceleration appears as a straight line, with the gaps between the years, between the circles on the line, becoming progressively wider and wider over time. This is what is crucially different about this way of showing change. Drawn in this way, on a timeline, we are able to see the speed at which change is happening by allowing growth to appear as literally being faster when the actual amount of change is greater. The pendulum shown at the bottom of the figure is largely decorative. On all the figures in this book it highlights the very first and very last two points in time shown, the rates of change at those two times, and hence the change in the rate of change between those two time points.

The pattern shown in figure 1 is what used to happen before 1970 in more affluent countries. But today changes like this are increasingly rare, usually found only following a war or a similarly devastating catastrophe, or in the poorest of places where there is currently little else that is getting better and much that is still becoming worse: less fair, more brutal, more desperate. In contrast, in a real place, like Japan, actual annual population growth slowed from 2.0 percent in 1950 to 1.0 percent in 1958, rising again to 1.5 percent in 1973, falling back to 1.0 percent in 1977, 0.5 percent in 1986, and first actually decreasing in 2012.

There are very few countries in the world today that have a population trajectory anything like the one depicted in the timeline shown in figure 1. However, when I was born (over half a century ago), almost all countries

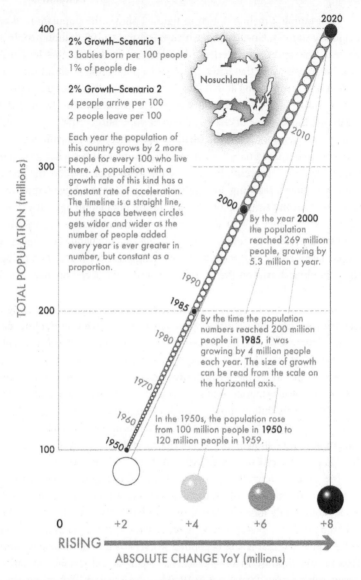

2% Growth—Scenario 1
3 babies born per 100 people
1% of people die

2% Growth—Scenario 2
4 people arrive per 100
2 people leave per 100

Nosuchland

Each year the population of this country grows by 2 more people for every 100 who live there. A population with a growth rate of this kind has a constant rate of acceleration. The timeline is a straight line, but the space between circles gets wider and wider as the number of people added every year is ever greater in number, but constant as a proportion.

2020

2010

2000

By the year **2000** the population reached 269 million people, growing by 5.3 million a year.

1990

1985

1980

By the time the population numbers reached 200 million people in **1985**, it was growing by 4 million people each year. The size of growth can be read from the scale on the horizontal axis.

1970

1960

In the 1950s, the population rose from 100 million people in **1950** to 120 million people in 1959.

1950

TOTAL POPULATION (millions)

400

300

200

100

0   +2   +4   +6   +8

RISING →

ABSOLUTE CHANGE YoY (millions)

1. Population of an imaginary country, 1950–2020 (accelerating at 2% per year). This is a hypothetical example of very simple constant acceleration. Note that "YoY" is shorthand for "year on year."

were on that kind of trajectory of around 2 percent population growth (give or take a percentage point) and, through my birth, I was unwittingly adding to the collective nightmare to come—or so many people feared at the time.[8] I was born in 1968. In that year, many of the small cohort of people who had access to the most recently acquired knowledge thought that the imaginary country shown in this timeline reflected their own grim future.

In 1968 those who looked could see only the section of the graph from 1950 to 1968, and then imagined the rest. A year later, in 1969, when a couple of men landed on the moon, it was as if we were about to literally step off the planet, because those men had just done that. No wonder the Ehrlichs in *The Population Bomb* were arguing for an exodus from Earth that would allow the lucky few to escape the global famine to come. But just fifty years later, everything has changed.

A child born today can expect to live to see the world's human population shrink—with no disaster needed to bring that about. If there are huge disasters in the future in which millions die, that would probably result in a subsequent acceleration of total population growth, not a permanent reduction. We can predict with ever-growing certainty that if we manage to avoid such colossal disasters, then for the first time in human history, the species will very soon naturally decline in number. We have entered the slowdown.

BACK TO NORMALITY

In many ways, slowdown will take us back to what was normal before the great acceleration. To give just one example, prices could begin to stabilize worldwide. There is no need for inflation in a more stable future. Our grandchildren might find that a beer costs the same when they are sixty years old as it did when they had just turned twenty-one. In that world they may well not be able to make great amounts of money simply by "investing." Most of the gains from investment in the past came from taking money from the future larger population. For instance, I may have borrowed money to build a house that I believe will be worth more in the future, but if the population in the future is smaller, then my house may never rise in price. My speculation may fall flat. I will not profit greatly in the future, but also—and vitally—other people will not be ripped off.

Great economic inequalities are very hard to sustain during and following a population slowdown. It becomes much more difficult to make money out of a shrinking and aging population. People may also become savvier as things change less, and it could become harder to fool them with an ever-increasing and more complex stream of the "latest" and "newest" consumables, especially if the slowdown in technical innovation means there is, in fact, less of real novelty on offer.

Sales tactics that worked only because of accelerating social, economic, political, and demographic change—because of the ever-expanding market—will no longer bring the same rewards during, and especially following, the slowdown. This is partly why tech companies now throw so many more advertisements at us every day. Those who market goods that are not much needed, that you might be persuaded to think you need but that do not increase your well-being, are becoming ever more desperate as we all become collectively wiser.

We have to stop seeing stagnation as an ill. Slowdown means our schools, workplaces, hospitals, parks, universities, palaces, and homes will stagnate, no longer transforming as much as they have changed for each of the past six generations. It means more durable goods and less waste. Social and environmental problems that we currently worry about will not be problems in the future. We will, of course, have new problems—including ones we cannot even imagine right now.

Slowdown is itself a very new problem. There is no easy way of predicting its implications, as we have no past model of slowdown beyond the few countries today that are among the first to have started to slow down. We have to use the experiences of those places to give us clues. All that we can be certain of is that the slowdown has begun. In fact, it began some while ago. As we take notice of the slowdown, at some point it will become a cause of great concern. Humans always worry and probably always will.

It may help to offer an analogy. Three hundred years ago, people had a lot of things to worry about. These problems included the fear of burning in the fires of hell if they did not live a religiously correct life. Many people still have that worry, but not as many of them as before, and the fear is arguably not as keenly felt as when almost everyone believed, and many tentative nonbelievers felt it safer to hedge their bets. We built many churches in the newly growing cities of the Western world to mitigate the particularly acute risk of burning (forever) in hell. At the very same time, the church builders ran economies based on slavery or the indirect profits of slavery.

Slavery was not abolished in the United States until 1865, after the end of the American Civil War, in Britain and its dominions not until 1883, and in Brazil not until 1888. With so much profit flowing back to Europe, the incentive to formally end slavery was low. Long before then, most slaveholders and those they enslaved would have found it hard to believe that one day slavery would be mostly illegal (even though indentured labor still exists, and modern-day slavery is rife). Nor would it have been believed, not very long ago, that in the future churches and chapels would be mostly empty, with many converted into homes or nightclubs.

Despite all the changes that we have experienced, we still find it hard to imagine how different things could be. Especially if that difference in the future is the slowing down of change.

The way in which fears change is a telling consideration when observing the differences between the generations. Which of the fears that appear entirely rational to us today will not worry us in the slightest in the future? Climate change could be one such. This is not because climate change is not real or extremely serious, but because it is the paramount change of our times, mostly caused by our behavior over the past half-dozen decades. In future we will no longer pollute the air as we do today. What we do not know now is how long it will take us to get to that future. The longer we take, the more serious are the consequences.

It can take a couple of human generations, around fifty years or more, to fully adapt after it becomes obvious that we need to change. But when we are confronted with the need to do so, we do regularly adapt and alter our behavior. Because we are also very impatient animals, we don't recognize how much we can change and indeed already have changed. For us, change always seems to be far too slow in coming, and we are easily frustrated. But we adapt quickly to new circumstances, and so we will likely adapt well to slowdown.

Humans will always fret. It is in our nature. We evolved to be the hunted as well as the hunter. Our peripheral vision is wide because those who could see who or what was coming survived more often. Consider how we had no idea two hundred years ago that an invisible by-product of the burning of coal, carbon dioxide, would stay in the air for so long and not be quickly reabsorbed, with such a huge and toxic effect. Inevitably there will be something else we are doing today that will also have terrible repercussions of which we have as yet no conception at all. We are only animals, after all. As one well-known thinker once put it, it's a wonder humans can even feed themselves.[9]

We once feared nuclear winter, and the coming of the next "natural" ice age. A few years ago, I made a list of many calamities that have been the focus of our fears over the past century. My favorite was the "killer bees" invasion once prophesied to sweep across California. As a child I heard stories about bees that came straight from the movies. The 1974 film *Killer Bees*, which starred Edward Albert and Kate Jackson, was quickly followed by *Swarm* in 1978, and in 2011 we were alarmed by *1313: Giant Killer Bees!*[10] Bees seem to be more closely linked to the end of time than most other species. Today we worry about there being too few bees to pollinate our crops.

Slowdown is not an end of history or the coming of salvation. We are not heading toward a utopia, although life for most people may be less precarious, with better housing, education, and less onerous work than in the recent past. We are heading for stability. Stability may be a little boring, like Pittsburgh, Stockholm, Kyoto, Helsinki, Ottawa, or Oslo, especially if you are hankering after excitement and bright lights. However, we will definitely come up with new things to be afraid of. A great deal of this fear will be very helpful because it will be protective; worrying is how we make ourselves safe. But we so often worry about the wrong things: about our children falling out of trees, for instance. Tree climbing is far safer than you might imagine.[11] Our worries are so often about the dangers of the past, without us realizing it. We have developed an innate fear of heights, but we're less concerned by large metal objects moving at speed because, until we invented cars, few such objects threatened us.

Try to imagine what your descendants might worry about in 2222—when the global human population has been falling for many decades and economic equality is high, and when the planet is no longer warming up but may even be starting to cool as the current interglacial warm period slowly begins to end. At some point before that year, sea levels will become more stable than they are today, although much higher than now. Power sources will be secure and largely nonpolluting. AI (artificial intelligence) will have turned out to be useful—but still very artificial and not that intelligent. In this future we should all be well fed, but fewer of us will be too fat. What will we worry about then? It will definitely be a great worry—whatever it is! To be human is to worry imaginatively—to always be searching for utopia, but to fear disaster.[12]

A slowdown is upon us, and this is something to be very thankful for. The alternative—an ever-growing total human population, ever more economically divided societies, ever-greater consumption per head—would be a catastrophe. Without both population growth and material economic growth, capitalism—the economic system we have become so used to that we cannot imagine it ending—transforms into something else. Something far more stable and sensible. Whether people will be happier or not in that future world is impossible to know. They might more often come to see that you cannot find happiness through acquiring more possessions and more exotic experiences. There is so much we cannot know. But we should at least recognize that the slowdown is upon us and can now be found in so many surprising areas.

It is less and less the case that we are all being rapidly hurled into an unknown future; but we are only just emerging from the dense fog of our roller-coaster past, and are now beginning to see the clouds parting as our journey slows. There are good seasons to come, but not fertile seasons in which our numbers, inventions, and aggregate wealth grow exponentially; in fact, our numbers will very soon stop growing at all. The past few generations have seen great progress as well as great suffering, including the worst of all wars in terms of fatalities, genocides, and the most despicable of all human behaviors—including the planning and construction required for the mass nuclear annihilation of our species.

It may take us some time to accept that we now face a future of fewer discoveries, fewer new gizmos, and fewer "great men." But is this such a bitter pill to swallow? We will also see fewer despots, less destruction, and less extreme poverty. And we will never again worship the "creative destruction" that twentieth-century economists so stupidly lauded at the height of the great acceleration. That was the bizarre idea that everything got better as firms went bust because only firms that deserved to go under did so. This nihilistic rhetoric was logical according to their weird (but at the time mainstream) survival-of-the-fittest theory of corporate evolution.

Given that we are still being taught that scientists keep on discovering great things at an ever-accelerating rate, it will initially be very hard for many people to accept what they might at first see as the gloomy prospect of slowdown. But progress is all relative, and it is progress itself—in the form of female emancipation—that is most clearly powering the slowdown. Progress toward stability was driven not by the achievements almost entirely ascribed to men and their wonderful inventions, but by the choices that women first made once they had won just a little of the freedom to work, vote, and plan the size of their families.

THE DECLINE

What does a slowdown look like? Let's begin again with our example of a country of 100 million people in 1950 and an annual growth rate of

2 percent. This is exactly the same starting population we saw in figure 1, and exactly the same starting rate of population growth as in that example: 2 percent. However, let's reduce that growth rate by subtracting a tenth of a percentage point a year, so that in the second year the annual population growth is 1.9 percent, and by the twentieth year (1970) the growth rate is 0 percent.

The number of people who would be living in this imaginary country by the year 1952 would have been 102 million multiplied by 1.019. The number of people in the year 1973 would be 123 million times 0.997. Instead of the straight line that you saw in figure 1, you now see a curve. The population of the imaginary country peaks at 123 million in 1970 and next drops back to 100 million by 1991, falling further to 45 million by 2015. It is because of the reality of slowdown such as this that almost all the other timelines in this book depict curves sloping backward in one way or another, not continued exponential growth. Figure 2 shows what the most dramatic slowdown looks like.

The circles, each representing a year in the timeline (each being centered on an exact point in time mid-year) are, by 1970, all equally spaced apart rather than moving further and further apart as time progresses. Change each year appears to be very similar to the year before and after. But the rate of change is itself slowly changing. After 1970 the circles begin to move progressively closer together. This becomes obvious if you consider how the population will head toward zero but never quite reach zero, given the formula for change imposed in this imaginary scenario. The circles also become smaller and smaller after 1970 as the population of this imaginary country falls.

The timeline shown in figure 2 is the mirror-image dystopia to the first timeline of this book. Figure 1 illustrated a population accelerating ever upward. Figure 2 shows a population that will soon die out altogether: not a slowdown but an extinction. This is the plot of the 1992 story *The Children of Men* (adapted into a film in 2006), set in a fictional England in 2021.[13]

In figure 2, the population is hurtling toward extinction. Fewer children are being born every single year, and finally none at all. As people die they are insufficiently replaced, even via immigration. There are simply not enough people. This is what a fatal decline looks like. When the number of people and the annual rate of change are plotted simultaneously, it becomes obvious how such a trend plays out. This is what we would see

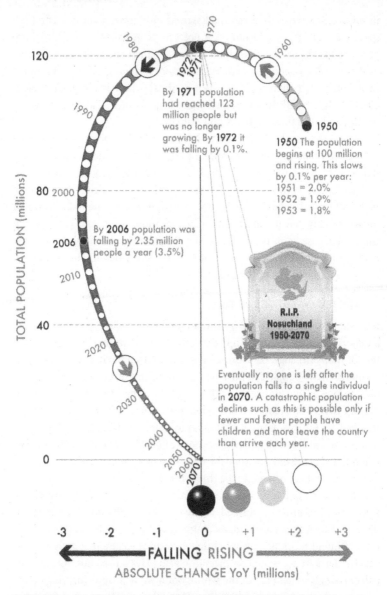

120 ——

1980 *1970*

1972
1971

By **1971** population
had reached 123
million people but
was no longer
growing. By **1972** it
was falling by 0.1%.

1960

1990

● **1950**

1950 The population
begins at 100 million
and rising. This slows
by 0.1% per year:
1951 = 2.0%
1952 = 1.9%
1953 = 1.8%

TOTAL POPULATION (millions)

80 2000

2006 By **2006** population was
falling by 2.35 million
people a year (3.5%)

2010

**R.I.P.
Nosuchland
1950–2070**

40

2020

Eventually no one is left after the
population falls to a single individual
in **2070**. A catastrophic population
decline such as this is possible only if
fewer and fewer people have
children and more leave the country
than arrive each year.

2030

2040

2050
2060
2070

0

-3   -2   -1   0   +1   +2   +3

◀━━ **FALLING** RISING ━━▶

ABSOLUTE CHANGE YoY (millions)

**2. Population of an imaginary country, 1950–2070 (initially rising but thereafter
decelerating).** This is a hypothetical example of population acceleration transforming to
deceleration.

if, on average, we each always had significantly fewer than two children; moreover, fertility would not even need to be as low if every year more people chose to leave this imaginary country than chose to arrive. Such a decline has happened before in human history, albeit involving thousands of people rather than millions, such as those who left the great ancient cities along the Silk Road: Loulan (Krorän), Niya (or Caḍota), Otrar (or Farab), and Subashi (in what is now Xiniang).

You will almost certainly never have heard of the places just listed, or even the city-states they were once a part of, because they were all abandoned and now exist only as ruins. In recent decades they have yielded up archaeological wonders and so we know their names again. There will be many other such places yet to be discovered. Building a new silk road will uncover many, but it will not result in ever more traffic and goods being traded, because soon there will be fewer consumers, especially fewer naive consumers. Everything eventually always slows down. The pendulum included in figure 2 is settling toward zero.

THE BEGINNING OF THE END

It is odd that we so rarely worry about population decline, given that today a majority of people on Earth live in places where, for many years and often for many decades, on average people have been having fewer than two children. Many people can have two children, and just a few have none or one, as long as low numbers of others have three or more children, for the average to be well below two. We often find such simple mathematics hard to grasp, and this is partly why it takes time for our fears to catch up with reality and for us to imaginatively generate new fears to replace the old. We still often fear the old demons, the ones that our parents had good reason to fear but that are no longer the threat they once were.

Soon, even in the very poorest countries, people will no longer necessarily starve or grow up stunted. Many who live in the poorest regions of the world currently have as many children as they do only because of high rates of infant mortality, meaning that they must ensure that at least a few survive. Lack of access to contraception also plays a part, but now only in a decreasingly small part of the world. Soon we will stop worrying about whether we, in total, have enough food, and then worry much more about whether what we are eating is good for us, and soon we will all be eating far less meat.

Soon our descendants (or other people's descendants) will look back at how we are now and ask why we could not see the transformation that was under way. But, in our defense, it is worth remembering that when you are on a speeding train and the brakes are suddenly applied, you feel that you are being thrown forward. It is only when you look back that you see you are no longer moving forward as quickly as before. This book looks back.

the slowing down
of almost everything

Greece's economy is, and will remain, in a slowdown until at least July
[2019] . . . after losing some 25 percent of its annual gross domestic product
between 2009 and 2017.

—*OECD, as reported in China, 25 January 2019*

The young man in the old village on the Greek island of Chios appeared far
calmer than most of his generation. He had left Athens to settle where his
grandparents, great-grandparents, and countless previous generations of
his family had lived. Athens was too hot, too crowded, too busy, too frantic.
Vassilis and his wife, Roula, moved away from Greece's sprawling capital
in 2006, before there was any sign of the economic crisis that would soon
engulf the city, to a place where life moved far more slowly.

There were numerous magazine articles published about Vassilis,
Roula, and their family because at the time such a move was rare. The im-
plicit question in each of the articles was why a young man and woman
might want to slow down and move to somewhere where the key activity
is (slowly) bringing in the mastic harvest. Their friend Ilias Smyrnioudis,
who manages the local factory that takes in the harvest, explained that for
him it was because "he enjoys his job and the fact that he can go swimming
in the sea every day."[1] Ilias has a PhD in molecular biology. He could be
working in a pharmaceutical lab in the Swiss Alps. Instead he has chosen, like Vassilis and Roula, a cheaper, slower, less damaging life. One that
gravitates around mastic.

UNDER THE MASTIC TREE

Most of the commercially harvested mastic trees in the world are found on Chios, which lies in the Aegean just a few miles off the Turkish coast. A Mediterranean lifestyle is today seen as the epitome of living calmly and slowly, with a diet that is thought to help people live longer and more healthily. In fact, the Mediterranean lifestyle is not slow; rather, Europe, and especially northern Europe, for a time, for a few centuries, became exceptionally fast.

Legends say that Homer was born on Chios. Homer himself may be the product of fable, not a single individual. Many scholars believe that the *Iliad* and *Odyssey* are the work of generations of storytellers and poets rather than of one bard. In antiquity Chios is thought to have had a population of around 126,000, many more than the 52,000 people living there today.[2] We are so used to population growth and acceleration that we easily forget that growth is not inevitable, and that eventually everywhere on Earth will at some point have fewer people living there than at some particular point in the past. In fact, it is deceleration, not acceleration, that is inevitable. Chios was just one of the first places where deceleration happened. The Scottish Highlands are another example, as are Ireland, the lost cities of the Silk Road mentioned in Chapter 1, and the ghost towns and gold rush settlements of North America and Australia.

Sitting at what was the crossroads of the world, near the only point where three continents meet and on one of the world's earliest principal trading sea-lanes, Chios was repeatedly invaded and conquered. However, its greatest depopulation was very recent. Urbanization, and in particular the markedly rapid growth of Athens, drew the young to the mainland, to bright lights and opportunity. It drew them toward the great acceleration.

The slowdown began as a trickle. In Athens, "Roula and Vassilis were typical workaholics, working for large information technology companies."[3] Holidays abroad to more tranquil places eventually led to a yearning to slow down. The pair left the crowded capital behind and moved to Chios, where Vassilis's grandparents had lived, and began to farm mastic and olive trees. In 2007 they set up Masticulture, an ecotourism company. Within a decade, the *Lonely Planet Guide to Greece* would rank it among the top ten green choices for responsible vacations to the country. "Meet the locals and eat the produce of local farmers and fishermen, see how the mastic is harvested, sea-kayak around the beaches," invites Masticulture's promotional material. What it should add is: "Get a glimpse of the future." It may look not that different from the distant past, except that levels of comfort are much higher. Maybe, given its location, there will one day again be 126,000 people sustainably living on Chios?

People need breaks from boredom. Ecotourism provides one such break, although the more often people undertake such vacations relatively locally, rather than traveling great distances, the more ecological it will be. Choosing travel that offers us a better understanding of the world is one of the things we should expect to continue as we slow down. Hopefully we will also start traveling more slowly and be in less of a rush all the time. In the future, if you are traveling to Chios to learn about mastic, you will be able to take your time getting there, as you should live in a world that becomes less demanding of your time.

A mastic grove may be at its most productive when thirty years old. In July you clear the ground under each tree and sprinkle a layer of calcium carbonate on the hard soil. Next you scour the bark so that the mastic resin seeps out, as the trees try to heal the wound. The resin drops to the ground in beads, which can be up to the size of small bricks, but mostly the drops are tiny. They harden after a week, and can then begin to be collected and painstakingly cleaned. The finished product is used in everything from drinks to natural remedies, from chewing gum to toothpaste.

When and where stability comes, every day may start to seem like the one before. The news will no longer report a series of crises one after another. Our perpetual sense of fear and uncertainty may be replaced by a nagging feeling that life is static. In the past, it was partly the boredom associated with rural living that made growing cities so enticing. There were also times when it was no longer possible to live peacefully in a village, such as on Chios or in many other places worldwide, because invaders came and brought destruction. Then the invaders promoted the more obsequious locals to the role of landlords and began the process of enclosure. Slowly but surely the villages died, and the cities on the mainland swelled. But that was then.

Stability does not mean always staying the same. Populations are likely to gently oscillate up and down each generation, more slowly shifting in size after gradually falling for some time following the peak. The echoes of baby booms will reverberate for far longer than a century into the future, even when much else has begun to settle down. In such a scenario, migration, not mortality or fertility, becomes the major driver of change. Even migration becomes less common when so much has settled down. A great deal of current migration is driven by not knowing. People do not know that the roads are not paved with gold in the cities that were once so far ahead of their times. Times change, but the stories change more slowly. Mass migration is driven by turmoil, war, famine, pestilence, or some other great instability. With slowdown, such migration too should slow. Who would want their very few children to move to the other side of the world?

People will still move around in the future, of course. In a less frantic and more logical world, they should have much more time to do so. But they won't be moving to where the work is and away from a place that has become unproductive. As so many have written so often, there is no need for us to spend so much time producing so much that is of so little real worth. We will have more leisure time, but all that time will have to be used sustainably—hence the ecotourism boom. In the future most tourism will be ecotourism, just as most paint in most countries is now unleaded paint.

So what happens as a population stabilizes? On a conventional graph, such a situation looks like the damping of an oscillating spring or pendulum. Given the way the curves are drawn in this book, an ever so gradual trend of approaching stability looks like a spiral moving inward.[4] When we calculate the amplitude of this oscillation given in the example below, we find that it is 31.4 years. This is the average age at which many people become parents in Europe today, but only in a few places yet in the United States (such as San Francisco). The average age of first parenthood is already much later than 31.4 years in Tokyo.[5] Such a pattern is created if children tend to have fewer or more children than their parents, but grandchildren have roughly the same number as their grandparents.

STABILIZATION

Begin again with a country of around 99 million people in 1950, but with a very stable population that is only slowly changing. At first there is just a little population growth, as people live longer and the population grows to just over 99.3 million because of that increased longevity. However, fewer babies are being born, so when the old do die, the population drops in the 1970s, and that reduction accelerates to its fastest rate in 1980. But then (perhaps following some government fertility initiative to encourage people to have more children) the birth rate rises a little, and there is a demographic echo from earlier times that means the death rate falls, as relatively fewer people are elderly because fewer were born eighty years earlier.

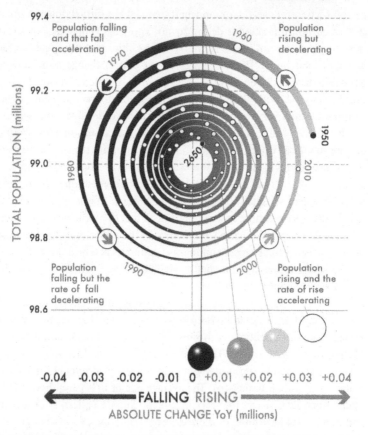

3. Population of an imaginary country, 1950–2650 (the miraculous spiral). This is a hypothetical example of population acceleration and deceleration both slowing down over time. Absolute change is in millions of people per year.

In figure 3, by 1980, the population has dropped to 98.98 million, but the rate of change has also fallen to losing (net) only 32,000 people a year because of deaths outnumbering births, helped by a little net in-migration, so that by the year 2000 the population is rising again by 14,000 people (net) a year and by 2010 it is almost back to 99 million. This is terrible, say the fictional politicians of this fictional country, trying to curry favor among a population that might otherwise notice that the politicians' friends keep on taking most of the dwindling profits from their businesses. You might well view the fluctuations involved here as trivial, but hardly any current population debates in the world today are really about the actual magnitude of the numbers involved.

The cycle depicted in the fictional timeline in figure 3 repeats and repeats, each time settling a fraction nearer equilibrium than before. It repeats because a great many children were born around 1880 in this imaginary country, and they are mostly dying in their eighties in the 1960s or in their nineties in the 1970s. These old people had fewer children themselves, but their grandchildren, born around the year 1950, are slightly more numerous, and when they begin to have children in their late twenties and thirties this helps to slow down the population decline, and the great-grandchildren contribute to the rise. Migration balances this all out; more migrants settle in the periods in which fewer people were born twenty or thirty years earlier. More people leave if they are born in a large birth cohort, as there are fewer opportunities for them at home.

Families' average number of children fluctuates slightly, generation by generation, in this imaginary country (the third and last to be presented in this book before we begin to look at real data). However, partly because this imaginary country is affluent and partly for the reasons just given, when people have fewer children, more migrants will arrive than leave a generation later. The migrants become, in effect, the children who were not born in this country, often at times when fertility rates in the country were low. Over time these annual and generational fluctuations reduce, so that soon in an average year population numbers go up or down by fewer than ten thousand people, or around 0.01% of the total population. Such stability is unknown today, but is very possible in the future. However, to achieve such a perfect spiral would require a certain megalomaniacal level of migration control, with an exact number set every year. That will, hopefully, never happen. Who, for instance, would be so stupid as to propose controlling immigration to "tens of thousands" or think that building a wall would prevent migration?[6]

The spiral timeline drawn here has the same shape found in the chamber mollusk called nautilus and in the patterns of spiral galaxies.[7] Peregrine falcons are said to take off in flight along the path of this spiral and to swoop down on their prey to almost exactly this pattern, as it is the most efficient flight path to take.[8] This is what a very well-controlled slowdown would look like. However, no one is controlling the slowdown we are currently living through, so we never see anything even roughly as neat as this in any of the data we have. What is shown here is a completely steady trend toward a steady state but, at any point in time within it, it looks nothing like that. That is why it is often difficult to see a slowdown.

THE PADDY FIELDS OF SHIMANTO

Chika was a shop manager in Osaka, Japan. Her husband, Takeshi, was a driver. The couple, in their late thirties, felt there was nothing much wrong with their lives, but after a holiday to much quieter Tasmania in Australia, they decided they wanted to slow down. It was when they saw something very different that they realized they did not like what they had, and that the speed of life in Osaka did not suit them. Osaka, like all Japanese cities, is a very safe place to be. I once visited the poorest quarter of Osaka alone, in daylight; my Japanese host told me not to be so stupid as to think that I needed a guide. It was safe, but life was frantic, noisy, and unsettling. Chika and Takeshi wanted to live somewhere slower.

Osaka is Japan's second-largest city, with almost 20 million people living in the wider metropolitan area. It is also one of the liveliest cities in the country, according to the *Economist*, which documented Chika and Takeshi's decision.[9] In May 2017, accompanied by their two very young children, they moved to Shimanto on the smallest of the four main islands of Japan. They settled in the south by the coast with the intention of making their living through farming. Chika said: "It is a risky choice, but we are happy."

Like Greece, whose population peaked at 11.3 million in 2010, Japan has been shrinking, falling from a peak of 128 million people in 2011. The fastest rate of population decline has been in rural areas, and so the arrival in Shimanto of a young—by Japanese standards—couple and their children became a news story. Chika and Takeshi arrived in the Kleingarten community of twenty-two basic houses built next to allotments. The prefecture of Kochi that the community sits in experienced peak population in 1955. By 2015 it had fallen by almost a fifth, to just 728,000 people.

Chika and Takeshi are not unusual. In 2015, some 45 migrants from elsewhere in Japan arrived in Shimanto, then 73 in 2016, and 139 in 2017. By 2017, some 33,165 people were making inquiries about relocating there, a threefold rise in just four years. It is no longer only the old who are looking to retire to somewhere more peaceful, but also some of the young who want a different way of life.

This stream of people heading to the countryside can never become a river, as then the countryside would become a city. However, these new streams are a part of what is necessary for the slowdown toward a new stability to take place. In many of the richest countries on Earth, the countryside has become underpopulated. A few more pioneering people need to return to stabilize its population. Increasingly, some of them will also be working in (hopefully relatively local) ecotourism businesses that will provide respite for some of the majority of the world's people who live in densely packed cities. But even those cities will become less and less densely packed as each family is, on average, a little smaller than the last.

The new impetus in Japan to move to the countryside springs from imagining a better work-life balance, finding cheaper housing, and escaping the rat race, but also from the growing reassurance that you will no longer be alone if you wish to slow down. It is becoming more normal to admit to dreaming of another way. Thankfully, more people settling in the countryside will also help the work-life balance for everyone else by providing places to go to rest in addition to reducing pressure on housing in the city a little faster than fertility decline alone will do, and helping to puncture the myth that the rat race is essential for the ever-rising growth that capitalism currently requires.

In Japan, the government is encouraging the young who are keen to leave the city. That is not yet the case in Greece, but it is not hard to imagine such encouragement beginning across much of rural Europe soon, which is why economists talk about these things in their most popular magazines. The *Economist* article ends: "After living there for three years, Naofumi Takase, who is 31, is planning to start a bed-and-breakfast business. Mayu Kase, 22, who left her job as a hotel receptionist in Chiba, an area east of Tokyo, wants to open a cake shop. 'I love it here,' she says." For her new business to work, many people from the city will have to come and visit—and eat cake.

From anecdote to data, from data to anecdote—this is how we learn. The slowdown can be seen only with data. It is about what is happening to billions of people, but it can be understood at a human scale only through anecdote. We have very little feeling for a group much larger than the few dozen people we know well. Without the data I would have to rely solely on anecdotes, a few interviews undertaken with a few people I had selected to talk to, who might well tell a story of the great acceleration of our times. But that story would be false. The data show why this is. It is almost impossible today to find data that suggest any great acceleration is under way; instead, almost all the data point toward slowdown, and so I have picked these particular stories to illustrate what that slowdown might mean in practice.

The future rural idyll will depend on urban tourism, not self-sufficiency, but if that tourism is well spread out, it need not spoil the idyll. It could even help to make reality more like the myth.[10] Slowdown does not require a significant move of younger people to the countryside. It requires the countryside to stabilize, for its population pyramid to stop becoming ever more top heavy, ever older. The slowdown began in some of the most affluent parts of the world. In the poorest parts of the world, many rural populations are still growing rapidly, and migration to urban centers is causing cities to become enormous. But there are now enough signs of how this too will soon change, and the best guides are the places that are already slowing down the most.

In many rural areas of the United States and Europe (so not just in Japan, Korea, China, and Oceania), there have been falling numbers of young children in many rural communities for decades. After leaving school in the countryside, the would-be parents often moved away in search of the better jobs available in towns and cities. For couples, even if one adult in a pair could get employment with a reasonable income in a rural area, his or her partner was unlikely to be able to. This matters more in more unequal countries such as the United States and the United Kingdom, as high income inequality means that, for a huge section of today's working-age adults, two incomes are essential. Poorer workers are now paid too little for one income to be able to support a family.

"Village life" is not that attractive to young people, apart from the few who do not want to leave home. Once the option of moving to a city became available, millions did so, partly to be free of community observation and control, and partly because they had no other choice when tractors came to the farm and replaced much manual labor. In much of the rich world, rural depopulation began long before agricultural mechanization, with the advent of enclosure (the consolidation of small farming plots into larger farms owned or run by just one family). Retirees who don't want the bustle of big cities but don't wish to be completely isolated will find some villages attractive, but a village in which everyone is retired is likely to have no shops, no services, no children, and no heart.

Some young idealists yearn for an isolationist life, one's own little "sustainable" homestead out of reach of the big bad world. By definition this life can involve only individual families or very small community groups, and thus will never be an option for large segments of society, short of following an unimaginable catastrophe in which billions die. Of those who do make such a move, few live in a commune for more than a decade. Most progress to life in increasingly larger villages, and that is why sustainable "alternative living" homesteads are so rare. Of all those seeking Arcadian bliss, very few succeed in making it work. Many dream of it, but very few are able to stick to a choice that requires adopting the living standards of previous centuries. The future will be one in which people are ever more interconnected, not more isolated. For the vast majority of us, our future is urban.

The future being described here, the one imagined in these pages, is generated from current trends that began with a change that can be traced back to half a century ago, to something that started to be common in the late 1960s. Back then, everything changed, but it was "too early to say." Now, however, we can say. All around the world in the late 1960s, young people began to behave very differently. This is demonstrated later in this book in terms of the abrupt reversal in the acceleration of global population growth around that time, but there was much else to see that, in hindsight, suggests more and more strongly as we move further away from those years that a widespread slowdown began in the very late 1960s.

What happened in the 1960s? One Chinese politician suggested an answer. Zhou Enlai was born in 1898. In February 1972, just before his seventy-fourth birthday, Zhou, who was then the first chairman of the Chinese Communist Party, had a conversation with Richard Nixon. The American president asked Zhou for his view on the significance of the French Revolution of 1789. Famously, Zhou is said to have replied: "It's too early to say." However, as a diplomat in attendance later explained, it was almost certainly the case that Zhou misunderstood, assuming Nixon meant the dramatic student uprising in Paris in 1968. He would have been right. Just four years after those events it certainly was too early to say what the impact of 1968 had been. In hindsight, the students were just one of many small parts in a far greater play that was only just beginning. It was the start of the slowdown, but as to why then and there, it might still be too early to say.

What can sometimes look like turmoil is, in fact, the reaction to something not changing. The lives of the students of '68 were not changing. They were not becoming parents, at least not at the ages that their parents had, and among them were agitators, just a few years older, who were also not encumbered by having to look after babies. They knew the world of politics was out of control. They were horrified by the war in Vietnam and by the fear that their parents might propel the world into a third world war. Some of them were dreaming of an idyll—a simple life—that could not be achieved in the way they might have wished it.

By having fewer children and having them later than their parents had done, and because their children in turn had fewer children—often none, one, or at most two—the sixties generation brought about a great change. Not so much because they were marching, protesting, and demonstrating, but because so many of them were not replicating the lives their parents had lived. Although in 1968 all eyes were on the youthful protesters in Paris and their counterparts in the United States and other centers of affluence and excess, 1968 and the years around then were actually a worldwide turn of events, as the timelines later in this book demonstrate.

Before we consider this global shift and when it might have begun, the last of this series of fictional timelines needs to be introduced as it is through concentrating on the rate and direction of change in greater context that a shift becomes apparent. It is very easy to fail to see that a spiral is a spiral. Figure 4 shows what figure 3 looks like when conventionally drawn, with time on the horizontal axis and population on the vertical axis. Now imagine that most of the graph is missing. You are living in the year 2020 and all you can see is the great sweep up to the 1960s, followed by the subsequent fall in population as people had fewer children, and then a rise in the past quarter-century as more migrants arrived than departed. If that were all you could see, you would hardly think that you were looking at a picture of stability. You might well say that "immigration is out of control." Whether immigration is seen as out of control or not is never about the absolute numbers involved, but is always a question of rhetoric and political perspective.

People can easily think immigration is out of control both because they have too little information ("It is too early to say") and because they are not looking at the information in the clearest way. By 2020, in the hypothetical graph shown in figure 4, the rate of growth due to inward migration is slowing rapidly; but, of course, the population of this fictional place is still rising. The press and politicians, obsessed by absolute numbers and generally confused by rates of change (the first derivative), talk of a crisis based on the idea that the country has too many people, because (they say that) too many people are arriving. The media never, and commentators hardly ever, talk about the second derivative: the change in the change that is occurring.

SLOWING DOWN IS HARD TO SEE

Begin again with a country of just over 99 million people in 1950. What you are seeing, compared to what else is possible, is a very stable population that is changing only very slowly. However, figure 4 may not appear that way to you, and you now have to imagine that you have only this one pattern to see. The longer and alternative histories are not all available to you. It is especially important that you are also not looking at the longer context, at what happened before. Instead, you are looking just at this one short slice of time in this particular way. The past is cut off to the left; the future is unknown on the right. You just have the heights of seventy-one circles to compare, with a line drawn between them.

You and your friends construct a story about what the graph drawn in this way shows. When you look at it this way you do not say: At first there is just a little population growth as people lived longer and the population grows to just over 99.3 million. Instead you say: At first there was rapid population growth following the baby boom after the Second World War. However, by the mid-1960s this had slowed, contraception use became widespread, and an earlier larger birth cohort—those born around the time of the First World War—began to die, at first just a few in early old age. By the 1980s and 1990s, far more of those earlier war babies were reaching the end of their lives; the generation born between the wars had been smaller and so it had fewer babies. The population of this country fell from around 99.3 million in 1970 to 99 by 1980, and was just 98.7 million by 1990. The decline was accelerating dangerously, by 300,000 in just a decade. At this rate there would be no one left in a few centuries, especially if the decline sped up.

The story you and your friends construct sounds very plausible. It is peppered with dates linking particular events to the patterns shown in the graph; it connects the mechanisms whereby people are born to trends in conception and contraception, and it connects these trends in turn to what appear to be the changes in slope on the graph; it weaves in a story of older generations, not shown in the time frame depicted here, and thus the echoes of their lives are also reflected in the picture. However, there is a problem. There are no intrinsic changes of slope in the graph; there appear

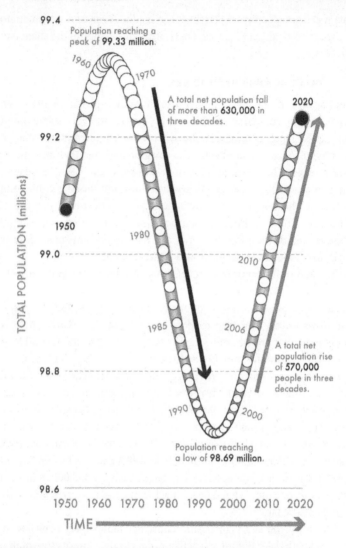

99.4

Population reaching a
peak of **99.33 million**.

1960

1970

A total net population fall
of more than **630,000** in
three decades.

2020

99.2

1950

1980

2010

99.0

2006

A total net
population rise
of **570,000**
people in three
decades.

1985

98.8

Population reaching
a low of **98.69 million**.

1990

2000

TOTAL POPULATION (millions)

98.6

1950 1960 1970 1980 1990 2000 2010 2020

TIME

4. Population of an imaginary country, 1950–2020 (conventional depiction). This is a
hypothetical example of increasing stability that looks like great change.

to be only because of the way it has been drawn. The data in this timeline are identical to that shown in figure 3. This is simply the same miraculous spiral. Nevertheless, we have started telling this story in a particular way, so let's continue.

By the 1990s, with the population falling so rapidly, and so few youngsters having been born, there were too few people to carry out the low-waged jobs typically described as "low-skilled": cleaning workplaces, picking fruit in the fields, serving in cafés. Immigrants began to arrive from the poorer former colonies of the empire that this country had once been a part of. They undertook the jobs that the children who were never born in the 1970s might have done. Slowly the population decline was halted: there were fewer older people available to die; the immigrants themselves began to have children, and more began to arrive from elsewhere, especially from the East, from newly opened-up countries whose citizens had not been permitted to enter our fictional country until very recently. But they came (it was said) in too large a number and "swamped" the local population. They did not fully assimilate, unlike all those earlier immigrants that the old claimed they were friends with now.

By 2011 the population was rising quickly again, to over 99.01 million people—far too many for the crowded island this imaginary country inhabited. By 2015, 100,000 more were added. The year after, there was a referendum on proposals for immigration control that might reduce immigration, and by 2020, when numbers reached an "unsustainable" 99.23 million, the future looked less precarious, but still dominated by unstoppable future growth.

This conclusion, of course, is rubbish, because it is based on looking at a section of the timeline of the diminishing spiral drawn in another, more conventional way. But look at the figures on the vertical axis. The fluctuations involved are tiny—just as population growth rates today in the United Kingdom and United States are tiny. The rhetoric around out-of-control inward migration is ridiculous, but it can be read as convincing by those with little feel for numbers and, seen from 2020, the line still appears to be heading quickly upward.

PHASE PORTRAITS

A pendulum swings from side to side. To us it appears to move most slowly just as it approaches the outer reach of its arc, almost touching its first asymptote. For those of us who are observing it in a particular way, it is moving most quickly at the point when it is briefly hanging vertically downward. Then its speed slows down again as it approaches its second asymptote, the other side, where it hovers for a fraction of a second, the smallest possible fraction of a second, and then, slowly at first, begins to retrace its path. We see it like this because of the kind of beings we are, but there are other ways of seeing the same swing: seeing the potential energy build up as its speed slows down, or seeing the pendulum as tracing the path of a spiral when its speed is plotted alongside the position of the pendulum. The speed or "first derivative" of position is the rate of change, and change is all about time.

The "tick-tock, tick-tock" sound that we reflexively associate with the passage of time came into being in 1656, when Christiaan Huygens invented the pendulum clock.[11] Today it is said that his pendulum increased the accuracy of mechanical clocks from being perhaps fifteen minutes awry to being out by, at most, just fifteen seconds a day.[12] Prior to his invention, clocks often had only an hour hand! Huygens grew up in what was to become the Netherlands and in what was, at the time, the most powerful center, economically and politically, in the world. The wealth that the Dutch secured through a new kind of mercantile trade enabled the sons of the wealthy to play with clocks and with mathematics. Huygens helped to make the measure of time so much more accurate just at the point when a great acceleration was beginning. It was an acceleration in thinking, in cooperation, in invention, and in wealth. It spread from The Hague and Amsterdam to London with the invasion of England, which the English still call the Glorious Revolution of 1688. Revolution means change.

Within a century of Huygens's invention, English carpenter and clockmaker John Harrison was producing marine chronometers, designed to be so accurate that they could be used to determine precise longitude when out in the ocean. To achieve this required losing or gaining less than a second a year in error. Today the accuracy of timekeeping is so high that there is little more to be achieved. As a student at Newcastle University in the 1980s, I once met a "time lord" whose job it was to ensure that the very early internet kept time to a fraction of a nanosecond. He rode a Harley-Davidson and worked in the sub-basement of Claremont Tower (I am ashamed to admit I was most impressed by his motorbike!). Today our measurements are so accurate that we can now tell when time itself slows down or speeds up due to time dilation, but even that little-known process was predicted by Einstein and first measured as long ago as 1938.[13]

How did we travel so very quickly, in just 282 years, from first measuring time with only rough accuracy with a pendulum to understanding that time itself was not constant? You can take six steps forward from 1656, each spanning forty-seven years, and marvel at the fact that at each step our measurement of time improved by at least one order of magnitude. We went from losing up to a minute a day to just a few seconds a day to a few seconds a week, a month, a year to just a second or so a year, and then by 1938, once quartz crystals were being used, our measuring of time became accurate to just a third of a second a year. In our era, the atomic clocks we use are so accurate that we have to slow them down to take into account the slowing spin of the Earth around its axis.

Your smartphone, even with the aid of its lightweight columbite-tantalite (coltan most probably from the Congo) capacitors, doesn't measure the time especially accurately. Instead, it regularly asks the time of a central server to correct itself. That server itself constantly talks to others on the network to keep everything in check, all of them serving each other. There will still be a few time lords in a few universities keeping a check on the times of their special central servers. It was only as recently as the early 1970s, when Zhou Enlai and Richard Nixon were discussing the significance of the French Revolution, that the very first computer servers were beginning to talk to one another, not long after the start of the Advanced Research Projects Agency Network (ARPANET) funded by the U.S. Department of Defense. It can sometimes feel as if everything around you is accelerating because so much is going on, but another way of seeing these more recent developments is looking at them as part of a process of visible acceleration that began around 1656. In many ways the rate of innovation since the invention of ARPANET has slowed down. We are simply more aware now of so much going on. How much more have we learned about keeping time and about time itself since the late 1960s? Everything that accelerates eventually decelerates.

Seeing time differently requires an imaginative leap. You have to imagine yourself stepping outside of time itself, looking down or up at what it is you are thinking about while you are no longer within it. Instead of seeing time as something that simply progresses, and where you are always at a point in time that is always moving forward at exactly the same speed, you have to imagine that you are an observer detached from space and time itself.[14]

Leaps of the imagination are called leaps because they are not easy to do, but once made they can appear obvious, intuitive, even pedestrian. The idea that time moves forward steadily as we place one foot in front of the other is easy to imagine. The idea that we travel faster through time as we begin to run makes sense (even though we don't speed up time). The idea that we cannot run faster and faster forever should also be obvious. Somehow, we have convinced ourselves that when it comes to innovation and technology, unending progress is feasible, or it is at least feasible for some time to come. It takes a leap of imagination to realize that we are slowing down.

The term *phase space* is attributed to a trio of mathematicians and physicists all working at the same time. Ludwig Boltzmann, the Austrian grandson of a clockmaker, devised his famous formulae with the use of phase space thinking.[15] Henri Poincaré, the French polymath, created a mathematical map, initially to look at planetary orbits and how they subtly altered over time. At around the same time, in a paper published in 1873, the American scientist Josiah Willard Gibbs introduced the idea of phase diagrams. They were all thinking like this because of the times and places they were living in. Today the place that has slowed down the most is Japan and the most recent development of phase diagrams is now occurring there.[16]

A phase space is an area within which all possible values of the variables considered can be plotted. There is a point within the space that represents every state that is possible. Figure 1 and figure 2 are maps of a phase space. If you assume that population can never be infinite, then all the possible levels and changes in population numbers can be drawn upon them. In contrast, figure 4 does not show a phase space because it can show only a limited period because time is one of its axes.

A phase portrait is a picture that demonstrates actual possible trajectories within a phase space.[17] In this book the timelines are phase portraits all drawn in the same way, depicting just two of the very simplest measures of each object on each timeline. The position of the object, its current value, is always shown on the vertical axis, so that the higher up a point is, the larger is the value being shown, and the lower down, the smaller it is. The object might be the number of people living in a place in a year or the amount of support for a political party in a month or the value of gold on a single day, but whatever is being presented, the higher up a point is in each diagram, the more of it there is. The lower down the point is, the less there is of what is being measured: fewer people, less support, or a lower price for gold that day—just to give a few examples.

In the phase portraits or timelines shown in this book, the horizontal axis is used to plot velocity, the rate of change in what is being measured. How quickly is the population growing or falling each year? By how much is support for the political party rising or declining each month? What is the daily amount of growth or decline in the value of gold? When a dot is drawn far to the right, its value is rising quickly; when it is drawn at any point on the vertical axis, it is neither rising nor falling. When it is drawn far to the left it is falling quickly. At the left or right edges, change is fast, and nearer to the center it is slower.

Finally, the dots are connected together by curves. The curves connect dots next to each other in time. Curves are used because otherwise the wrong impression is given, that of the rate of change suddenly altering at the points at which the change is measured. The Bézier curves used here are designed to smooth out what is seen so that the points of measurement are simply points on a curve and are not, usually, points with special significance. What matters most is the overall shape of the curves that can be seen and what that might signify as to whether we are slowing down today or not. The points on the curves are drawn as circles sized by the value being shown on the vertical axis and labeled by dates—years, months, or even days—which allows the phase portraits to show time, change, and rate of change simultaneously. But it is always the shape of the curves that matters most and how that shape is changing, not any particular single event. As a result, these diagrams are particularly useful for answering questions like "How did we get here?" and "Where is it all heading?"

Each of the images in this book is a portrait of a single series of statistics. Each shows both the value of that series at specific points in time, and how quickly that value has been changing. Time is automatically compressed when there is little change and expanded during periods of great change, making it easier to understand the long-term perspective. There are an unlimited number of subjects that can be portrayed in this way, and only a very small selection is shown here. Just as few things are completely new, this method of looking at change is not really new; it is just using a different perspective. Please see the appendix for more on that perspective and especially if you are thinking of drawing these yourself.

Part of what is so hard in trying to understand what is going on today is that each of us has such a very short time to try to learn so very much— much more than anyone in generations before ours had to try to learn. That is just one of so many implications of the great acceleration in information that we have been living through. Slowdown may make learning easier, if a little less exciting. If we are entering a period of fewer discoveries, at the very least we can try to better piece together what has already been discovered, and what has recently befallen us.

LOOKING IN FROM OUTSIDE

Today we teach children about deceleration using the pendulum. Search for "phase portraits" in Wikipedia and one of the many diagrams you are shown is Krishnavedala's illustration of the movement of a pendulum. It is redrawn here in figure 5. All we know of its original author is that he or she uploaded this image on 29 November 2014 and asked to be remembered for this. The illustrator gave only one name: Krishnavedala (which may be a concatenation of Krishnatej Vedala).[18]

The first image in figure 5 is the pendulum as you might usually view it, swinging from side to side. Its furthest extent to the left is marked by the number 1. As it swings to the center, pulled by gravity, it accelerates and reaches the point marked by the number 2 at its greatest speed. It continues then upward to point 3, decelerating now until it appears to hover for the tiniest fraction of a second at number 3, its most rightward extent, before falling back again to point 4, which is also point 2, except that the pendulum is now going in the opposite direction. Then it begins to slow again until it reaches point 1. This pattern is then repeated again and again, but not quite (given air resistance and friction at the pendulum's pivot) ad infinitum. In the appendix to this book figure 74 shows the phase portrait of the pendulum slowing down.

The right-hand image in the diagram in figure 5 shows the same pattern of change, but now plotted against time. It also depicts velocity as well as position. It shows how the velocity of the pendulum is zero at points 1 and 3 and highest (but opposite in direction) at 2 and 4. The pendulum is accelerating when its velocity is rising and slowing down between 2 and 3, and 4 and 1, when its velocity is falling. The end of the timeline, furthest to the right, perfectly fits the start, furthest to the left, to show how this pattern repeats. Moreover, in contrast with the first diagram, it is now clear how the rate of change in its position itself changes. The first diagram shows only position.

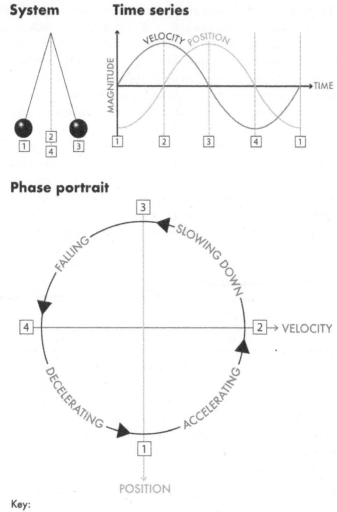

5. Three different ways of describing the movement of the perpetual pendulum. (Adapted from an illustration in the Wikipedia entry "Phase Portrait," probably by Krishnatej Vedala, accessed 7 September 2019, https://en.wikipedia.org/wiki/Phase_portrait#/media/File:Pendulum_phase_portrait_illustration.svg.)

The final of the three diagrams, shown at the bottom of figure 5, takes time off any axis. This phase portrait of the pendulum is a circle around which the pendulum is swinging anti-, or counter-, clockwise. Deceleration toward its highest position on the circle, which is furthest right in real space (number 3), occurs after a slowdown between points 2 and 3. A pattern like this in a phase portrait is a pattern of deceleration because velocity is declining, although position is still rising, just less and less at each point in time. The phase portrait allows the state of the pendulum to be more clearly divided into four sectors (starting at 1): accelerating and rising; still rising but decelerating (slowdown); falling and accelerating backward; and finally decelerating but still falling. Slowdown is where humanity is today.

The advantage of phase portrait depiction is that it forces you to concentrate on the change in the change. The pendulum may still be rising to the right as it slows down, but what matters most for seeing where it is going is to understand that it is slowing down. It will clearly soon be falling back. To worry that something is rising while it is decelerating is foolish. The point at which you do not know if it is the swing of a pendulum, or not, is when it is accelerating. The phase portrait helps you to think ahead.

A phase portrait can be theoretical, as in the case of figure 5 in which the pendulum moves in a vacuum and there is no friction at its imaginary perfect pivot, but with real data it can also be used to highlight what actually happens when the pendulum does not circle around and around forever (figure 74 in the appendix illustrates that). Friction in its bearings and the resistance of the air mean that, unpowered, the pendulum on each swing never quite gets out as far as before. Its maximum velocity on each swing is a fraction less than on the swing before. If we were to draw the circle for many thousands of interactions, we would gradually see it shrink in size to a point, the point at which the pendulum no longer moves. It is, in fact, a spiral. Like most things in life, the pendulum is slowing down.

3

debt

a decelerating sign of the slowdown

> Student debt continues to grow, albeit more slowly than in previous
> years. About 66 percent of [U.S.] college students graduated last year
> carrying debt.
>
> —*Annie Nova, reporting for CNBC, 20 September 2018*

A less snappy title for this and the next two chapters would be "Exceptions that prove the rule—debt, data, and environmental degradation—the three areas of human life where we think we are not yet slowing down (but we either are or will have to)." This is the first chapter of the book to look at real data, and it concentrates on one of the very few phenomena that are still thought to be showing signs of growing at a high, or even exponential, rate: these rare marvels tend to interest us the most and often worry us greatly because they look as if they are out of control. They are also included here, early on, because you probably are already wondering how they fit into a book about slowdown. I start with the hardest of cases in the hope that you will be less inclined to skip it!

It makes sense to begin with the exceptions when looking at the changing shape of our societies. As economic inequality in income begins to fall in most countries of the world, we need to ask what is now becoming the more serious issue.[1] Today most things are settling down, but some things are still rising out of control, almost always as a legacy of some past event, decision, mistake, or ignorance.

Wealth inequalities, and with them huge inequalities in debt, continue to rise long after income inequalities fall. Information continues to spew forth long after the ability to produce and process such information has peaked (hence the abundance of fake news at the start of the age of slow-down). The pollution caused by economic growth, growth that has long since slowed down, continues to have great effect, above all in increasing the temperature of the planet.

Debt is the opposite of wealth. Without an increasing concentration of wealth, there could not be growing debt. Without the belief that those who hold the most wealth deserve it and are entitled to unearned income from it—which ultimately comes from receiving debt interest—wealth would not continue to grow as fast as it does. As wealth grows, most of us become, on average, poorer. Information, insofar as it is recorded, explodes in quantity in the wake of rises in the ability to produce and store it, but as we become swamped by it we do not necessarily become more clever or better informed.

Because a slowdown is a deceleration, not a fall, we do not easily recognize it occurring. The slowdown occurs unhurriedly, in some cases over the course of several generations. We are today still tuned to look for what is new, exciting, and different, and to expect continued rapid social progress, coupled with danger and frequent unanticipated change. We can predict that the weather a few weeks from now will probably be similar to the weather today, until the season changes. But after that, the weather changes completely.

That time is upon us. The favorable seasons for human expansion, ever-greater technological innovation, and a rapid geographical reordering of where we live are coming to an end, slowing down and stabilizing. This is nothing to be scared about. There will still be change, just not as dramatic. Those favorable seasons—which were far from universally beneficial—could not last long. Although, of course, it's true that most of us are alive as a result of the enormous population explosion and the recent great acceleration.

Favorable seasons for a species are those in which its population size increases rapidly. Such seasons tend to be rare. In the case of humans, that population increase was also associated with a transformation of what it meant to be human. For most people on Earth, the favorable seasons did not begin until around 1900. We migrated to cities, became taller and cleaner, better educated—but perhaps also greedier. Much has to change rapidly if we are to survive well in our new numbers. The strongest case for this need for change is made when we look at what has yet to fully slow down.

The fact that these examples of acceleration are rare highlights how, in almost every other aspect of our lives, we are no longer experiencing rapid change, at least not the kind our parents or grandparents lived through. This chapter begins with the issue of student debt in the United States and in the few other countries that have allowed it to balloon in recent years. The rise in student debt followed the rise in university student numbers. The latter is a good thing: without such an expansion in student numbers there would be very few people who could understand a book such as this one. But rising student debt was and is not a necessary corollary.

RISING STUDENT DEBTS

With debt we have an example of something that we are led to believe is not slowing down but is growing at an accelerating rate. Student debt is highest of all in the United States, then the United Kingdom, and then possibly Canada, Chile, or South Korea. Its invention and then rise was largely the product of economic slowdown, corruption, and ineptitude in these countries which, fueled by political malice, led in turn to policies that increased economic inequality. A highly unequal country, or one that is becoming more unequal, may tolerate the introduction of high student loans, but only for a short time. They are simply not sustainable.

A key part of understanding that student loans are unsustainable is recognizing that we need to change our thinking from believing we are living in an age of acceleration to seeing that so much is decelerating. If everything were still accelerating, if inflation were ever rising and future salaries were going to be huge, then large debts would become small debts and could easily be paid off in future. This argument is not wild speculation. It is already possible to see that student debt growth is slowing down in terms of the overall size of borrowing.

The rate of growth in U.S. student debt peaked in July 2009, but the debt itself is still growing. If we were able to estimate total global student debt in the minority of countries where high fees are charged to a large number of young adults for university education, we would no doubt see that it is still growing internationally, just as other forms of debt rise in total. But the curbing of the accelerating growth of U.S. debt is an intriguing pattern here, and the curbing began at exactly the point that the global financial crisis started. Although, as the epitaph at the start of this chapter illustrates, that slowdown began to be newsworthy only a decade later.

U.S. student debt growth rates have declined, and they have not declined because there are fewer younger people who could go to university, or because U.S. universities are charging less for their courses. Between 1969 and 1979, the number of degrees awarded by U.S. universities rose from 1.27 million a year to 1.73 million, or by 43 percent.[2] During the next ten years to 1989, which was mostly the era of President Ronald Reagan, this number rose to 1.94 million, or by just 12 percent. In the 1990s the annual total of degrees being awarded rose to 2.38 million annually, and so by 23 percent in the decade to 1999. In the twenty-first century, the number accelerated to 3.35 million, or a rise of 41 percent, from 2000 to 2009, and to 3.55 million by 2010 and 3.74 million by 2011, but then the growth halted. There were fewer degrees given out in 2017 than in 2016: the number of young people going to university in the United States who have been awarded a degree has most recently been shrinking.

Student debt in the United States continues to grow not only because of the interest charged on it, but also because more and more students are unable to pay off their loans. Every year, tuition fees rise higher, even as graduates discover that well-paid jobs do not materialize as they had for their parents. However, even before the numbers of young people opting for university study in the United States fell, a deceleration started in the rise in the debt. As I write, this has been going on for at least ten years. While both nationally and internationally debt continues to rise as the wealth of the super-rich grows, the most recent get-rich-quick schemes have been the first to stumble. Eventually student debt will be a thing of the past: not only will it continue to be practically nonexistent in most of mainland Europe and China, it will disappear from everywhere else in the world that tried this one-generation speculative financial trick on the young.

The timeline in figure 6 shows that student debt in the United States rose from $481 billion to $1,564 billion in just twenty-two years; but also that the rate of debt growth within that time period slowed, with the July 2009 turning point easy to see.

Research reported by the Federal Reserve Bank of St. Louis has revealed calculations of outstanding U.S. student loans held by those giving out this credit in the same way since January 2006 across all of the United States. By 2007 some $401.9 billion had been lent to 22.6 million students in the form of federal family education loans, averaging $17,783 in outstanding loans per former student.[3] Couple that with a further $106.8 billion in direct federal loans to a further 7 million students, and with Perkins Loans and other smaller lending, and the total by the first quarter of 2007 was around £510 billion, rising by around $15 billion a quarter, or by 11 percent a year.

From 2006 to 2011, just five years, the number of students accessing the federal loans system had risen from 28.3 million to 38.3 million. The

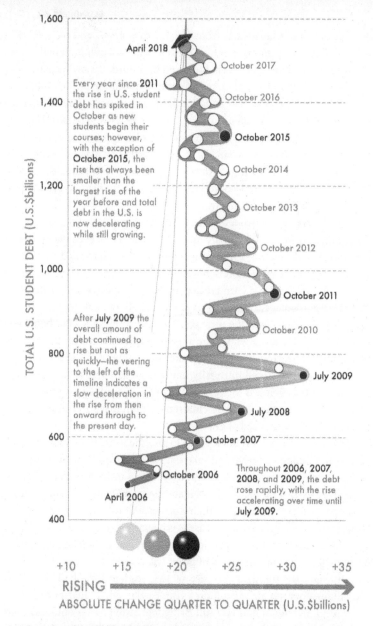

April 2018

October 2017

Every year since **2011** the rise in U.S. student debt has spiked in October as new students begin their courses; however, with the exception of **October 2015**, the rise has always been smaller than the largest rise of the year before and total debt in the U.S. is now decelerating while still growing.

October 2016

October 2015

October 2014

October 2013

October 2012

October 2011

October 2010

After **July 2009** the overall amount of debt continued to rise but not as quickly—the veering to the left of the timeline indicates a slow deceleration in the rise from then onward through to the present day.

July 2009

July 2008

October 2007

October 2006

April 2006

Throughout **2006, 2007, 2008,** and **2009**, the debt rose rapidly, with the rise accelerating over time until July 2009.

TOTAL U.S. STUDENT DEBT (U.S.$billions)

1,600

1,400

1,200

1,000

800

600

400

+10   +15   +20   +25   +30   +35

RISING

ABSOLUTE CHANGE QUARTER TO QUARTER (U.S.$billions)

6. U.S. student debt, 2006–18 (billions of dollars). (Data adapted from Board of Governors of the Federal Reserve System [US], "Student Loans Owned and Securitized, Outstanding [SLOAS], 2018Q2," retrieved from FRED, Federal Reserve Bank of St. Louis, accessed 28 December 2018, https://fred.stlouisfed.org/series/SLOAS.)

average debt per student rose from $18,233 to $24,757, and the total debt owed to the federal authorities by 2011 stood at $948 billion. It had almost doubled while student numbers had risen by a third. By any measure, this growth could rightly be called "out of control." However, as the timeline in figure 6 shows, the peak year and month of acceleration—July 2009, when loans rose by $30 billion in just one quarter—had already passed. Had this rate of increase (in the rate at which loans were being given out) continued, then very soon the debts would have far exceeded all other kinds of debt in the United States. Their growth rate had become unsustainable, and for that very reason we should have known that student debt could not continue rising as it had indefinitely.

The debts of recent students are far greater than those of older students. Part of the way in which loans are made palatable is that each generation of students is told that those who come after them will have to borrow even more. They will be even more screwed: tuition fees will be even higher for them, their debts will be even greater, and they'll be competing with more and more graduates for jobs that pay salaries high enough to pay off their debt. "Don't worry" was the message: it might be bad for you, but it will be even worse for those who come after you, and so you will do relatively better. Of course, students who were the children of the richest adults did not need a loan to attend university in the United States, so they were the least screwed of all. It was the very wealthy who conspired to rig the system against all those other people's children—children with aspirations—by encouraging loans instead of grants.

The U.S. student loan book tends to rise the most in October of each year as new students arrive and take out new loans. But this was not the case in 2009, nor in 2011. By 2012 the extra 1.8 million students new to the system (net) were matched by an additional $100 billion lent to all attending university or added to their outstanding interest in just that one year. But by 2012 this rate of increase was beginning to decline each year as the growth in student numbers slowed rapidly, and even fell at one point. Nevertheless, the outstanding debt never fell.

During 2018 the quarterly rise of U.S. student debt had slowed to $20 billion a quarter, or $80 billion a year. By the fourth quarter of 2018 it stood at $1.56 trillion and was still rising, but rising by less and less each year. At that point, the average student in the United States aged under twenty-five owed the federal government $14,753. Those aged twenty-five to thirty-four owed $35,553. Their debts had risen by far more than they were able to pay off. By age thirty-five to forty-nine, the average debt for former students was even higher: these were people who had had to borrow far less because they attended university at a time when tuition fees were lower, but, due to mounting interest charges, each of them now owed an average of $38,593. Among those aged fifty to sixty-one the average debt had fallen only to $37,828, and for yet older borrowers it was still $34,316. At least federal student loans are canceled with death.[4]

The U.S. student loan debt is still rising, but more slowly than before. It has to, to keep up the pretense of some rationality in a system that clearly is far from rational. Elsewhere, in the United Kingdom, for instance, total student debt is still accelerating with, as yet, no sign of deceleration in sight. But it will slow down. It has to, especially as the two leading opposition political parties in the United Kingdom are opposed to its existence, the Labour Party and the Scottish Nationalist Party.[5] Nothing accelerates forever.

AUTOMOBILE DEBT

So, student debt in the United States is still rising, but that rise is decelerating. What about car purchase debts? Debts can easily be created when something that someone has to have, like an education or a home, can be acquired only through borrowing money. In countries where education is provided free at the point of delivery, funded through general taxation, there is little scope to make money out of the desire and need to go to school or university. It is only where and when open and fair access to education is denied that young people, following advice from their families who cannot pay the fees upfront, feel compelled to borrow to give themselves a better chance later in life.

In most of the world, most people do not have cars. Even in some very rich countries car use is now reducing. Japan is the best example. As long ago as 2014, it was clear that the number of motor vehicles per Japanese household had been falling for many years and was soon set to fall below one vehicle per household.[6] In contrast, and remarkably, the U.K. census in 2001 showed that many households had more motor vehicles than people old enough to drive in the household.

A well-ordered affluent society slows down. It relies more and more on public transport, as well as cycling and walking, rather than under-occupied, extravagant, congesting, and polluting private cars. It will have some very fast trains, but relatively few people will need to use them regularly. There is no particular need to have to travel so far and so fast (or even more slowly), often on your own, steering your own tonne of metal and glass. Those who do not realize that we are slowing down often talk of exciting futures in which we will all be speeding around town in robot-driven cars. Other than it being another good way to get fat quickly, what else is there to recommend about that vision of the future? Why not organize life so that it does not involve so much unenjoyable traveling?

The United States of America is the country of acceleration. It is the place that made things bigger, better, faster, larger, longer, higher, and greater than anywhere else. What folly that appears to be today; but such folly is no reason to take pleasure in the ill fortune of that place of excess. Whichever country had been the richest country in the world at the time of greatest human acceleration, the 1950s and 1960s, would have been the place to have invented the largest barbecues, the most grotesquely large food servings, the weightiest body mass indices, and the most enormous and fuel-guzzling cars. The United States even propelled a few white men to the moon at enormous speeds to show how great America was, and how much money it was prepared to spend to boost the national self-confidence that had been dented by the USSR's own space program.[7]

Today it is very hard to live in the United States without a car, usually necessary to get to work, school, or shopping areas. For the homeless, their car, or someone else's discarded car, is somewhere to sleep. Many years ago, the American automobile industry became a debt industry. Cars were sold like dreams, they were curved like dreams, and they embodied the American dream of freedom on the open road.

By 2003 the amount of debt associated with the purchasing of cars in the United States stood at $622 billion, or about $5,600 per household. By 2018 it had roughly doubled to $1.27 trillion, or about $10,400 per household. However, although the national automobile debt is still rising, just as with growing student loans, it is no longer rising as quickly as it once was. The United States is still a very long way away from achieving what Japan has achieved, becoming a country where every year in recent years fewer and fewer cars are driven on the roads. Without more public transport initiatives, the United States will probably not match Japan's achievement, but the deceleration in this area of American debt suggests that the tide is turning.

For almost all of the twentieth century, one of the greatest causes of rising private debt in the rich world was the need and desire to purchase a new car. Old cars can be driven for longer than many of their owners drive them today, but the car industry needed people to buy and drive new ones. When people did not have the savings to do so, the industry invented a new kind of loan, one that was secured on the car itself, so that you could drive a car long before you could afford to buy it.

Debt and desire are often thought to go together, but debt is possible only where there is credit, and credit is available only where there is enough greed and surplus wealth. Wealth has to be corralled into the hands of a few for debt to be greatly expanded. The more wealth that is held by just a few people, the more money there is to be lent out to others. Under circumstances of both great economic inequality and rising population, private banks are permitted to create money as new debts. The owners of those banks, and also their highest-paid employees, benefit the most. For everyone else, prices rise and their debt grows.

You might think that it is not possible to have new cars without enormous—and rising—automobile debt. However, the situation is the same as in the case of student debt; millions of people in other countries of the world now attend university without incurring huge debts. You might think it is not possible for most people to have a reasonable existence without having to take out a loan to buy a car, but the United States is the exception in this matter rather than the rule.

Umpteen people's debt is one other person's asset. It is that person's source of income. This one person will often already have huge wealth, usually enough to last long after their death, but they always seem to want more. Greed is addictive and can be all-consuming. By lending other people the money to buy a car, and charging interest on all their loans, the very wealthy can see their assets grow while they do nothing. Those other people have to drive the cars they have borrowed money to buy in order to get to work to make the money they need to repay all their other loans. Most of them will never be able to save any significant sum. This system would not work if they could save, as then they would not choose to get into debt.

Rich individuals can lend indirectly. For instance, they lend to the federal government, buying up part of the U.S. national debt, and in doing so some of their money is, in turn, lent to university students as federal loans. Those students who pay back their loans with interest should, so the theory goes, more than offset those who fail to, and so the federal government can afford in future to pay back the rich individual, with interest added. But eventually such a giant Ponzi scheme has to fail, because only a tiny minority can ever be rich if we live our lives this way.

The rich may not have realized the long-term folly for them of lending money to people to get an education and learn how the world works better than the rich understand, people who are usually so focused on short-term profit maximization.

Some say that a national economy based on debt is essential if pension funds are to grow for the minority of people who have decent private pensions, but a debt-based economy has no mechanism for providing adequate pensions for all. Most people in an unequal affluent society enter their old age in a state of modest to acute poverty, looking forward to a retirement of even greater poverty. So how could such a system ever come to be in a country in which the majority supposedly rules? Why, in the home of the free, are so many weighed down by so much debt? The answer may partly be a belief in future acceleration, a belief that is now being undermined.

The U.S. debt-based economy appeared to do well in the 1950s and 1960s because of injections of cash from abroad. American industry was then at the height of its power and success. Behind it stood the all-powerful American military. A Cold War raged across the planet; in fact, it was a hot war in many poor countries, especially those that were seen as being of U.S. interest. The United States made more money from people in the rest of the world than it spent buying their goods and services. It was when this state of affairs began to end that the reality of the precarious situation of the majority of Americans became more and more visible.

Since the 1930s, the majority of cars purchased in the United States have been bought on credit, and the amount that was borrowed and the number of cars sold rose and rose almost every year afterward until it reached a peak in 1978 of almost 15 million vehicle sales.[8] The recession of the early 1980s brought about a dip in sales, but there were 16 million sales in 1986, followed by another dip until a late 1990s rise up to 17 million, reached in 2000. Then the annual total fell dramatically, to just over 10 million in 2009, with the coming of the great recession.

Car sales in the United States started to recover after the great recession but only slowly, not again reaching 17 million a year until 2016, and they are now shrinking once again.[9] The ten-year period between 2003 and 2013 was one of great turbulence for the American car-loan industry. But take a step back and you can begin to see that what was once seen as the great U.S. acceleration in cars and lending is now also clearly slowing down—and has been for some time.

Although car loans are still rising in the United States, they are rising more slowly than before. America is full of many old cars that could be made to work for longer before they are trashed. There is great scope for the current slowdown to continue. But for it to continue, the United States has to start to move away from its love of the car. In just fifteen years, from 2003 to 2018, outstanding car loans in the country rose from $622 billion to $1,238 billion, but within those years there was an almighty crash. The Federal Reserve publishes quarterly statistics on the amount of money Americans have outstanding on their car loans. In most years (since at least the late 1970s) this balance has risen, and before 2003 it was generally growing faster and faster each year as the number of cars Americans purchased grew and the price of those cars rose. At the same time the number of Americans of driving age was also growing, but their ability to purchase cars without debt was not, so the amount of car debt in the United States did not just grow, it accelerated up to the dizzying heights of $622 billion by 2003.

In the early 2000s, U.S. car debt was rising by an average of $25 billion a quarter, or $100 billion a year. An extra billion (net) was being added every three days to the car-debt mountain. As old debts were being paid or written off, even larger new debts were being taken out or extended. But then, at the end of 2004, there was a shock to the system. The price of gasoline had been steadily rising throughout 2003. The peak year of worldwide growth in demand was 2003–4, when demand grew by 3.4 percent in a single year.[10] At the end of that year fewer people bought new cars. Lending fell again in early 2005, then recovered for a few months before falling again at the end of 2005. It cycled round on the timeline in figure 7, recovering during the year to fall again at the end of 2006, and then at the end of 2007, and then it fell continuously from mid-2008 all the way through to mid-2010, each and every quarter. By this point the banks were themselves crashing and unable to underwrite the loans that the car companies wanted to give out.

By the start of 2011, total lending was no higher than it had been at the end of 2003. It was not until mid-2013 that the growth in U.S. car loans had returned to the rate that had been normal a decade before. But by then, something else had changed fundamentally.

Each second quarter from 2015 onward saw a smaller growth in car loans in the United States than the second quarter before it, and all were much lower than Q2 2005—which had been the height of the previous acceleration. The timeline in figure 7 slopes to the left. It is zigzagging toward the year in which car loans will reach their peak. We cannot know when that will be, but we can see the trend. Another oil-price shock is very possible

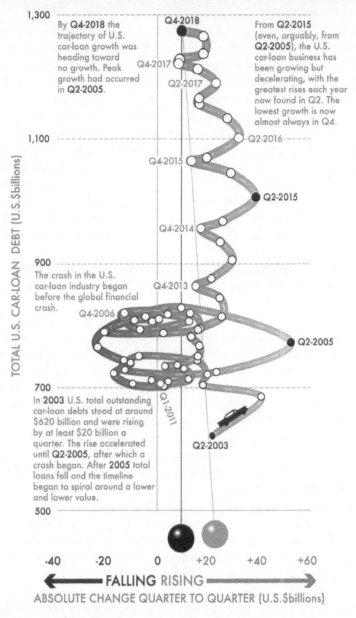

TOTAL U.S. CAR-LOAN DEBT (U.S.$billions)

1,300

By **Q4-2018** the trajectory of U.S. car-loan growth was heading toward no growth. Peak growth had occurred in **Q2-2005**.

Q4-2018

Q4-2017

Q2-2017

From **Q2-2015** (even, arguably, from **Q2-2005**), the U.S. car-loan business has been growing but decelerating, with the greatest rises each year now found in Q2. The lowest growth is now almost always in Q4.

1,100

Q2-2016

Q4-2015

Q2-2015

Q4-2014

900

The crash in the U.S. car-loan industry began before the global financial crash.

Q4-2013

Q4-2006

Q2-2005

700

Q1-2011

In **2003** U.S. total outstanding car-loan debts stood at around $620 billion and were rising by at least $20 billion a quarter. The rise accelerated until **Q2-2005**, after which a crash began. After **2005** total loans fell and the timeline began to spiral around a lower and lower value.

Q2-2003

500

-40   -20   0   +20   +40   +60

◄—— **FALLING** RISING ——►

ABSOLUTE CHANGE QUARTER TO QUARTER (U.S.$billions)

7. U.S. car-loan debt, 2003–18 (billions of dollars). Note that in the three months to Q1-2019, debt rose by 0.5 percent, 0.7 percent to Q1-2018, and 0.9 percent to Q1-2017. (Data adapted from Federal Reserve Bank of New York [US], "Quarterly Report on Household Debt and Credit [HHD_C_Report_2018Q3]," retrieved from the Center for Microeconomic Data, accessed 28 December 2018, https://www.newyorkfed.org/micro economics/databank.html.)

in the meantime; but in the medium term, the trend in U.S. car loans is toward deceleration. The loans are still rising, but by less than before.

By the second quarter of 2018 U.S. car loans were rising by just $18 billion in the quarter of fastest growth, and by only $8 billion or $9 billion in the two quarters before that. While most Americans remain relatively poor, and a few are staggeringly rich (with a dwindling number being in the middle), we can expect loans to remain the main means by which Americans are able to buy a car. It will not be until wealth inequality in the United States begins to subside that car loans will become less essential.

A century ago Americans purchased their Model T Fords before they were allowed to drive them. They placed a deposit with a Ford dealer and then made weekly installments until the full purchase price was achieved, and then they drove off with their car and with no outstanding debt. There is no need for debt to be used to enable people to get around. Bicycles can be purchased without debts, and cities can be planned so you do not need a car to get to work. As more people around the world begin to live in better planned cities, fewer will need cars. Public transport can be made affordable and cars can be bought with savings by the older rural minority who need a car, as is the case in Japan today. One day automobile debt in the United States will also largely be a thing of the past.

The interest currently being paid on over $1.2 trillion of debt may actually be less than that which was being paid in 2003 on just over half that debt, because interest rates have fallen so much, but U.S. interest rates are now rising slightly once again. In the long run, borrowing makes no sense for assets that are depreciating in value. Rising interest rates should also deter borrowers if they can find any other way to travel.

U.S. HOME-LOAN DEBT

Everywhere you look in the world there are loans, but the loans in the United States are larger than anywhere else. For young people in America student loans are still rising, but the speed of that rise is slowing down, albeit only slowly as the total continues to grow larger and larger. Automobile loans in the United States are still rising as well, but that rise is also slowing down, a little more quickly than student loans. Next in terms of the magnitude of what Americans borrow for is the most essential loan of all, the loan you need to take out to obtain any security of tenure in the country today—the mortgage needed if you are to buy a home. In America, you have a secure place to live only if you buy. If you rent, you can be moved on, even if you have enough money to pay the rent.

In many countries there is a choice between renting and buying. Rents are regulated by the state, usually the local government, and are not allowed to increase quickly or to be set at a level that is too high for the quality and size of property being rented. Tenants have a right to stay in their home if they pay their rent. In the best-organized of the world's affluent countries, if a landlord wants to take back possession of a property, he or she must offer the tenant financial compensation, and if it is not enough, then the tenant can choose to carry on renting and living there. It is, after all is said and done, a home. A home is much more than mere property.

It is often when secure renting is not an option that the prices of houses and apartments can skyrocket. Today in most states of the United States, tenants have very few rights. Rents can be increased at the whim of the landlord, and so tenants can be easily evicted simply by raising their rent. The quality of rented property can be abysmal, and the rent can be significantly higher than the mortgage for an equivalent property. Those who can buy try to. However, for most people being able to buy means being able to borrow to buy, and that depends on their credit history. Furthermore, the interest rate at which they are lent money in the United States can vary both over time and by who they are and where they live—even though redlining is supposed to be illegal today.[11] People have individual credit ratings.

Buying a home in the United States is not like buying a home in much of Europe, where mortgages with interest rates fixed for as long as two decades or more are common. Buying a home is better than renting, but still often perilous, as if you fail to make each mortgage payment the lender can take possession of your home and evict you. The rich in the United States avoid this peril by buying in cash with the money they have made, often interest received directly or indirectly from lending to those who are not rich. When there is great economic inequality, trying to be or stay rich often appears the best aim to have. But only a small minority can ever be rich.

It is not that difficult to build a house or an apartment; human beings have been doing it for a very long time. It is, however, hard to control speculation and inflation. Just after the Second World War, in 1949, all outstanding U.S. mortgage debt, including the borrowings of landlords as well as those of households, stood at only $54 billion.[12] By 1953 it had more than doubled, to $112 billion. It doubled again to $227 billion by 1960, and again to $450 billion by 1969. It hit $1 trillion in 1977, $2 trillion in 1984, $4 trillion in 1992, and $8 trillion in 2002. It rose every quarter from 1949, without exception, until the second quarter of 2008, and then it fell for twenty successive quarters in a row, right through to the third quarter of 2013. Something fundamentally different had just occurred: a system of housing finance that had appeared to work well for over six decades had crashed.

But in truth, the housing system in the United States had been working well only for a minority of Americans, and especially well for those rich enough to buy more than one home. There is almost no social housing in the United States, or housing managed and rented out at affordable rates by local government or charities. Almost everyone who cannot buy has to rent privately. Many who can buy have trouble paying the mortgage every month. If you lose your job, become ill, or split up from your partner, it is especially hard to continue to make the payments. A huge number of people have spent years paying off part of their mortgage and still do not end up owning a home. Others have had to take out interest-only loans because they were deemed ineligible for a repayment mortgage. As the price of housing rose and rose in the late twentieth and early twenty-first century, the majority of Americans lost out, especially the young and the poor.

The money we pay for our homes has very little connection to the cost of building them. Nor is it much related to any rule of supply and demand. The demand for homes did not suddenly fall in 2008, but the supply of money that could be borrowed in order to buy homes did collapse at that time. We are often told that the value of a home mainly reflects the value of the land it is built on, but that is also a chimera. The value of land in the United States did not suddenly degrade in 2008. There never was some mystical intrinsic land value that was holding up prices; instead, the housing market was a game being played by a few people lending more and more money to a much larger number of people who needed somewhere to live. House prices reflected the money supply for mortgages. The lenders were pushing up prices. They lobbied government to give borrowers tax incentives in order to make what they were doing appear less predatory. They preyed on the fears and needs of the many who had to borrow to be able to have a home. When slowdown comes, it is a sign that such a system is beginning to end.

Various debt issues, which are usually treated in isolation, are profoundly interconnected. The money required to make a car is not reflected in the cost of a car today. Most of the cost is the payment required to service the debt needed to buy the car. After that, you are paying for the profits of the car manufacturers and for the cost of the advertising and marketing needed to convince you and many others that a new car is worth so very much to you that you will be willing to take on even more debt. You are also buying status in what is effectively a bidding war. After that, if the car is manufactured in the United States, then you are paying the wages of car workers, but most of those wages will go on things like high housing costs, the costs of the workers' own cars, and the help they may try to give their own children to get an education. People have to be paid highly in the United States because housing and so much else is so expensive. All this acceleration was related and, for a period, it was self-perpetuating and reinforcing.

For most university degrees, the money actually needed to provide the services required to teach a student is trivial. They need a seat to sit on, a desk to work at occasionally, and access to a library (although students will make far more use of the internet than books these days). The costs of the wages of the professors mainly reflect the cost of housing in the local area and, of course, the costs of their transport to get to work. If they have to travel by car, then they need to be paid a little more. However, most of the huge fees that students in the United States pay to attend university each year do not go on the wages of teaching staff, or on the running costs of university libraries. The fees go instead on what were (until very recently) the sharply rising salaries of senior university managers and the high costs of constructing trophy buildings, as well as the cost of all that advertising that universities undertake to make it appear that such high fees are worthwhile.

A large number of people in the United States do not make goods, such as cars; they do not teach; and they are not constructing homes. Instead they are middlemen involved in the financing and arranging of all the activities that we used to do well without so much intervention. There are now lawyers embedded in every organization, along with accountants, investors, and consultants—bureaucracy, in other words. They all increase the costs of everything they touch—until at some point, the bubble bursts.

You cannot keep ratcheting up prices forever, lending out more and more. While house prices were appreciating, many bankers did not mind to whom they lent. They either collected interest or repossessed an asset that was almost always worth far more than the loan. Eventually, shortly after 2005, a very large number of households, rather than just the usual continuous trickle, began to default on their mortgages.[13]

In 2006 and 2007 bankers became warier of lending, the real price of borrowing money rose, fewer people were able to borrow, housing prices fell, bankers then became even more wary of lending on assets that were depreciating in value, and a downward spiral began to take shape. Goods becoming cheaper is normally considered good news, but house prices falling became a disaster for the economy in those countries reliant on rises, revealing how their economic system was structurally flawed.

All debts are connected. A university degree, a car, a home: these are all things that should not put people in debt for most of the rest of their lives. In much of the world they do not, and in living memory in the United States and the United Kingdom they did not. When debts are allowed to grow too high, individuals and then entire households become unable to repay. The value of the assets they are buying reduces when others are unable to borrow enough to buy them. University degrees are deemed to have less worth when they become commonplace; people stop buying new cars so frequently because it no longer makes them look so good; and the inflated prices of homes fall.

The proportion of mortgages in the United States that were taken out by house owners (rather than landlords) increased in recent years, as landlords sold off property that was falling in value and reduced their exposure to debt. In the great majority of cases, their tenants were evicted to "facilitate" the sale. When a ship is sinking, those most in the know jump first. Those looking to lend money are becoming more and more desperate to do so as they find fewer and fewer safe people and places to lend to. That is one inevitable outcome of the great deceleration in a system predicated on perpetual growth.

Home loans in the United States in total rose from $4,942 billion to $9,140 billion in just the fifteen years from 2003 to 2018; but, again, the rate of growth is now slowing down (see figure 8). The 2008 great economic recession is what your eye is first drawn to, but see what the figure shows before and after that. Look at the slope of the timeline in 2006, 2007, 2017, and 2018. It moves leftward both well before and long after that economic crash.

The Federal Reserve of New York publishes quarterly figures on home loans. Its most recent series began in 2003 when the total mortgage debt of U.S. households stood at just below $5 trillion. As house and apartment prices both rose, as more were built to be purchased with debt, and as the population of the United States continued to rise, mortgage debt continued to grow and grow, at first at an accelerating pace.

The acceleration dampened a little in early 2004, but by the autumn of that year outstanding U.S. household mortgage debts had passed the

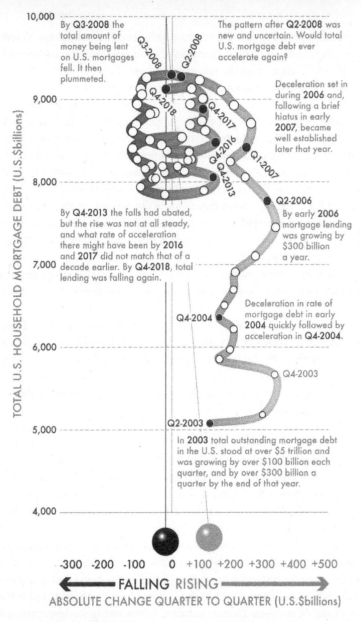

By **Q3-2008** the total amount of money being lent on U.S. mortgages fell. It then plummeted.

The pattern after **Q2-2008** was new and uncertain. Would total U.S. mortgage debt ever accelerate again?

Deceleration set in during **2006** and, following a brief hiatus in early **2007**, became well established later that year.

By **Q4-2013** the falls had abated, but the rise was not at all steady, and what rate of acceleration there might have been by **2016** and **2017** did not match that of a decade earlier. By **Q4-2018**, total lending was falling again.

By early **2006** mortgage lending was growing by $300 billion a year.

Deceleration in rate of mortgage debt in early **2004** quickly followed by acceleration in **Q4-2004**.

In **2003** total outstanding mortgage debt in the U.S. stood at over $5 trillion and was growing by over $100 billion each quarter, and by over $300 billion a quarter by the end of that year.

Q3-2008
Q2-2008
Q4-2018
Q4-2017
Q4-2016
Q1-2007
Q4-2013
Q2-2006
Q4-2004
Q4-2003
Q2-2003

TOTAL U.S. HOUSEHOLD MORTGAGE DEBT (U.S.$billions)

10,000
9,000
8,000
7,000
6,000
5,000
4,000

-300 -200 -100 0 +100 +200 +300 +400 +500

⟵ **FALLING** RISING ⟶

ABSOLUTE CHANGE QUARTER TO QUARTER (U.S.$billions)

8. U.S. mortgage debt, 2003–18 (billions of dollars). (Data adapted from the Federal Reserve Bank of New York [US], "Quarterly Report on Household Debt and Credit [HHD_C _Report_2018Q3]," retrieved from the Center for Microeconomic Data, accessed 28 December 2018, https://www.newyorkfed.org/microeconomics/databank.html.)

$6 trillion mark. More households were taking out larger loans, much larger than the ones that other people were paying off, to the tune of around $200 billion net a quarter being added to the national mortgage bill. During 2005 the increases in U.S. mortgage debt grew, the acceleration increased, and the $7 trillion mark was passed in the autumn of that year. By spring 2006 over $300 billion was being added each quarter, and the $8 billion threshold was breached in autumn 2006. Growth in new loans slowed slightly then, but accelerated for one final burst upward in spring 2007. The $9 trillion mark was reached in autumn 2007, but by then a fundamental change was afoot.

The overall rate of growth in lending had already clearly begun to fall in late 2007; and for subgroups of the population it had fallen earlier. The overall rate fell for nine successive quarters through to autumn 2010. Even with the very first quarter of falls, it became clear that a crisis had begun. In hindsight that crisis could be seen to have started earlier than was widely reported and long before the great crash of 2008. However, previous apparent slowdowns in the rise of lending had all been reversed. This included the deceleration after the fourth quarter of 2003, the third quarter of 2004, and the second quarter of 2006. Recent history had provided no sure model of what might happen next. Previously, lenders who had reined in their lending tended to lose out financially on the subsequent rise in indebtedness. So the "smart money" had carried on being doled out, until the great crash began. Only then did it become obvious that having lent so much was not so smart after all.

Interest rates were slashed to try to ensure that more households did not default on loans that they could not afford to repay unless those interest rates shrank. Total lending fell below $9 trillion in the third quarter of 2009, and below $8 trillion in the first quarter of 2013. This was not a slowdown, it was a crash. Housing prices plummeted, the number of households borrowing money fell, the number of people extending their mortgages grew smaller, and people across the United States began to pay off debts faster than they took them out. The scope for the relatively few very rich people to get richer and richer by lending more and more money at high rates of interest to the millions of less well-off people dwindled.

The first apparent recuperation of the housing market at the end of 2010 collapsed during 2011. The second, in early 2012, similarly fell back. The third, during 2013, appeared to be more sustained, but again collapsed in 2014. A fourth in 2015 appeared slightly stronger, and lending crept up to $9 trillion again by the third quarter of 2018; however, by now the average quarterly rises were just a fraction of what had been normal before, oscillating between only $50 billion and $100 billion a quarter, with the ever-present possibility of a further collapse.

By 2019, America's mortgage brokers were left asking whether this was a semi-permanent hole into which their industry had fallen, or whether they should expect to see a great escape take place and lending resume its ever-upward trajectory. Nobody could give them the answer to their conundrum. The one thing we can be sure of is that a huge slowdown has occurred. What is far harder to determine is whether a fundamental shift in trajectory has really taken place. For that fundamental shift to happen, to be solidified, requires political change—or an even greater crisis to occur to force such a political change.

The U.S. government needs to stop enabling lenders to lend so easily at such a high rate of profit making. People need to begin to collectively solve their housing problems without having to resort, so often, to borrowing from the rich. All of this requires far-reaching political change: namely, undertaking the building of social housing allocated on the basis of need rather than ability to pay through disposable income, bringing in effective rent regulation in the private sector, and imposing more stringent regulations on banks and other mortgage lenders. We need to escape from a situation in which people are prepared to pay "anything" to secure a home, and "anything" is whatever the lenders think they can get away with (without serious payment default). If none of these changes take place, then another debt bubble will grow, for a few years at least.

U.S. NATIONAL DEBT

Debt is one aspect of life that is too often wrongly assumed to be not just continuing to rise, but also accelerating. This view is a hangover from a time when that was indeed the case. The wealth of most of the world's rich rose greatly in the decades before the First World War. Those years were also, and consequently, years of rising debt for others. Debtors' prisons had become common in Europe in the eighteenth and nineteenth centuries. In contrast, they were largely phased out in the United States during the middle of the nineteenth century, when that country was at its most economically equitable: federal debtors' prisons were eliminated in 1833.

The extent of debt within a country is often very closely associated with the concentration of income and wealth in that country. When the majority of people have very little, and especially very little savings, they are far more likely to have to rely on debt. At the same time, when a few people find themselves with great wealth, it will lose value if they do not invest it. Investments almost always create debt for others. At times and places of great equality, people are able to invest in their own homes and businesses without having to borrow from others to do so. But as Europe, and then the United States, became more and more inequitable in the latter half of the nineteenth century, debts rose. Before then many people were extremely poor, but they did not have debts. Only a few better-off people acquired debts, but gradually having debts became the norm. Debts also rose for the government during wartime, as a government cannot rely on taxation alone to raise enough money, quickly enough, to pay for a war, especially a war that goes on for a long time. Debts also rose for many people in the industrial slump and great depression that followed the First World War.

In North America, across all of Europe, and elsewhere, especially in Japan, there was a great increase in economic equality following the Second World War. The first two decades of postwar reconstruction were achieved by taxing the rich instead of borrowing from them. More equitable societies are more efficient and tend not to rely on debt as much as very economically unequal societies do. However, after a few decades of growing equality, many people became used to what they had achieved and did not defend it well enough from those who prefer inequality. In the United Kingdom and the United States, from the 1970s onward, with great acceleration during the 1980s, debts rose as income inequalities increased and wealth inequalities began to spiral upward. Those debts also included huge increases in national public government debt.

It is only possible for debt to rise in an accelerating manner because people with money think they can make more money by lending or pretending to lend. Money can be made in all kinds of ways; it can, for example, legally be created out of thin air by private banks if those banks are sanctioned by governments to do so.

As the number of people living in a country rises, and the number of people alive in the world rises, more money has to be created to avoid deflation. But in many countries in recent decades, most of that new money has gone to the few who already have the most. They then lend it out to other people. If those others can make more from their investments than their debt repayment costs, they too can become rich. However, that profit can be made only at the expense of others, who often get into debt to buy what is being produced. This is a cycle that eventually has to break, and always does at some point. It may appear as if huge levels of debt have always been with us, but the continued obligation to reward those who have managed to gain control of the most money is seen as normal only during a time of acceleration, or when a population has been tricked into believing it is their religious or civic duty to pay chattels to the rich church or king.

Sovereign governments can, should they wish, create money for themselves. There are numerous ways in which this can be done, from printing more notes to simply issuing their central banks greater funds. Governments can also rack up debts. The most famous and largest sovereign debt in the world is that owed by the U.S. government. For many decades that debt was not only rising, its rise was accelerating. Despite this, there have been periods when the U.S. national debt rise decelerated. It did so from 1991 to 2000 and is doing so again as I write. The total U.S. national debt actually fell in value, briefly, in the years 2000, 2013, 2015, and 2017. In most years, though, the U.S. national debt was rising rapidly, but it's inaccurate to think that this is inevitable: not only does such debt not always accelerate, it can also fall and has fallen more often in the past ten years than at any other time in recent U.S. history.

In 1835 the United States had no debts. It had paid them all off that year. Debts rose during the American Civil War and during both world wars, but tended to be paid down afterward. However, from the early 1970s onward, the U.S. government chose to raise less money in taxation and more through borrowing. In particular, top tax rates were reduced from nearly 70 percent on very high incomes in the 1970s to 50 percent in the 1980s, to as low as 25 percent in the early 1990s, and in recent years they have stood at about 35 percent.[14] By borrowing from the rich, rather than taxing the rich, the U.S. government got itself into huge debt. It also borrowed greatly from abroad. In effect, when the United States could no longer afford to pay for goods from China, it began to borrow money from China to buy those goods! This is a trick that can work for a while, but not for very long; and it is a reaction to not accepting slowdown.

The interest rate that the U.S. government agreed to pay on its debt rose to above 10 percent a year in the early 1980s, at the very same time when it was taxing the rich the least.[15] It has since fallen to as low as half a percent during the current financial crisis, but has been rising again more recently; it stood at 2.25 percent at the start of 2019. So the United States continues to borrow huge sums of money, but it will not pay back so much more in the future, not unless interest rates are raised greatly again. The battle over whether the U.S. government taxes or borrows is a political battle. Debt itself is a political battle, and always has been.[16]

Today we think that debt will be with us forever, including national public debt. But just as it rose from zero only within the past two centuries, so too can it shrink back to zero again. Debt is not some natural phenomenon. Debt is a human-made construction. It is a political decision. The first signs that debt might fall in future would be debt falling in our own times, and we have seen this happen much more often in the past ten years than in the fifty years before then. Today, no form of debt is still accelerating upward. Much debt is still rising, but rising more slowly than previously. However, for debt to fall steadily will require a change in our collective political beliefs—and a reimagining of what is seen as "sound economics."

In recent years, academic publication after publication has explained that we cannot continue to live with debt as we do, and that "our creation of money through loans/debt, where the interest is never created, means that there is always more debt in the system than the ability to repay it."[17] Bankruptcy and other forms of defaulting on loans are the only way in which the total amount of debt in the world can be reduced.

When we see the rate of growth of the U.S. national debt slow, that slowdown often means that other forms of debt for other entities or individuals has risen. For instance, we try to fund many pension schemes in rich countries through debt. The pension firms make "investments," which are often simply loans, in the mistaken belief that a smaller future younger population will somehow pay back that money with interest. This was possible only when the world population was growing. Ultimately debt will have to shrink, just as the number of people on our planet will shrink as we all have fewer children. Many of our current economic problems are caused by how slowly we are adapting to the population slowdown that began in the late 1960s.

Debt is the hangover of the great population acceleration, especially of the great rise in adults born before the late 1960s. The U.S. national debt rose from $321 billion to $21,516 billion in just fifty-two years (1966–2018), but again the rate of growth is now slowing. We tend not to see that because we are so in awe of just how rapidly the debt, until recently, grew; but it does not always grow steadily and it is very unlikely to do so in future.

Why did the U.S. national debt not grow in size smoothly? In the late 1960s it was growing by around $50 a year for every $1 million of national debt. In 1968, that figure fell to $20 a year more for $1 million being borrowed by the government. By 1971 the debt stood at $400 billion. The federal government was borrowing around $40 billion more a year, only $10 billion more each quarter. You can hardly see that change at all, given the scale of the graph in figure 9.

During the 1970s the U.S. national debt rose quickly, at about twice the rate it had been growing during the 1960s. The greatest acceleration came in 1974, when debt rose hugely in just a few successive quarters. By the end of 1974 the U.S. government was borrowing an additional $14 billion each quarter, $23 billion by the end of 1975, or $150 for every $1 million it had already borrowed that year. By 1976 the U.S. national debt stood at $600 billion, and the rate of acceleration slowed a little, but the $700 billion milestone was passed in 1977, $800 billion was reached in 1979 and then, during 1980, national debt acceleration was growing again and $30 billion extra was being borrowed every quarter. At that rate it should be no surprise that the total national debt passed $900 billion in 1980 and $1 trillion in 1981. With Ronald Reagan in the White House, the greatest-ever acceleration in the nation's debt was well under way. Reagan did not like taxation, but he liked spending money, especially on the military. The only way to square that circle was to increase the size of the debt—which, coincidentally, also served to enrich the affluent who had money to lend to the government.

The 1980s were the decade of U.S. national debt. It soared upward to $1.5 trillion in 1984, passing $2 trillion in 1986. The fastest relative rate of growth in the U.S. national debt was reached in late 1982 when an extra $185 was being added every year for every $1 million that had been borrowed. After that point, the quarterly additions would grow and grow, but as a proportion of the outstanding loans they would never grow quite as quickly again. The outstanding debt passed $3 trillion in 1990, and $4 trillion in 1992. It then grew more slowly, and there was a deceleration during Bill Clinton's second term in office. It took until 1996 to reach $5 trillion, 2002 to reach $6 trillion, 2004 to make it to $7 trillion, 2005 to reach $8 trillion, and 2007 to touch $9 trillion. It leapt to $10 trillion by the third quarter of 2008 in the biggest leap it would ever make.

In 2008 financial Armageddon struck. The banks needed rescuing, and the only way out, if you choose not to tax the rich, is yet more national debt. Much more national debt. In the first quarter of 2008, "just" $131 billion more was borrowed, in the second $294 billion, in the third $604 billion, and in the fourth $551 billion. For a few months in late 2008 the debt was growing at almost the same high relative rate that it had under Reagan, at around $170 extra a year for every $1 million already borrowed. However, so much had already been borrowed that this was a much larger amount of money. The national debt after 2007 was rising by $1 trillion a year. From $8 trillion in 2005 to $21 trillion in 2018, that's $13 trillion in thirteen years—rising rapidly, but it is now not rising quite as rapidly, or as rabidly, as before.

With the slope of the timeline trend shown in figure 9 now leaning strongly to the left, even the national debt was no longer rising as quickly as before. To reiterate, as this is now over a decade ago, in absolute terms the greatest acceleration was in quarter 3 of 2008, when the national debt grew by $604 billion in just three months. This was greater than the quarter 4 2015 high point of $557 billion in the same short space of time. However, these later years were also the years in which there were quarters when the total national debt fell. As pointed out above, when smoothed over a year, the relative rises in the 1980s were, in fact, even greater than the relative rises in 2008 or 2015. We are no longer seeing U.S. national debt rise as it rose under Ronald Reagan in the 1980s or during George W. Bush's presidency from 2001 to 2009. Republican presidents appeared to have been committed to getting their country into greater and greater debt.

The great rise in debt was partly what fueled the great acceleration. From the beginning of the British, French, and Dutch East India Companies, over four hundred years ago, through to the global spread of American banks today, debt has been used to expand trade, power, and privilege. It is a trick that works better and better when the number of potential debtors rises higher and higher. Those who have put others in their debt usually claim that they have made investments and that these investments are their property, property they have a right to, even though that property might be another human being's home, means of transport, or even education.

The movement of all the major American lines of debt toward the central axis of the timelines in the four figures in this chapter suggests that an end is in sight to the long, checkered, and at times near continuous rise in the overall size of debts. Admittedly, this is just within the most indebted

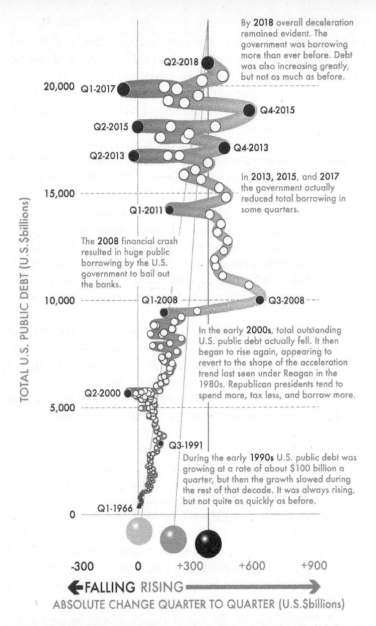

By **2018** overall deceleration remained evident. The government was borrowing more than ever before. Debt was also increasing greatly, but not as much as before.

Q2-2018

20,000 Q1-2017

Q4-2015

Q2-2015

Q4-2013

Q2-2013

In **2013**, **2015**, and **2017** the government actually reduced total borrowing in some quarters.

15,000

Q1-2011

The **2008** financial crash resulted in huge public borrowing by the U.S. government to bail out the banks.

10,000 Q1-2008   Q3-2008

In the early **2000s**, total outstanding U.S. public debt actually fell. It then began to rise again, appearing to revert to the shape of the acceleration trend last seen under Reagan in the 1980s. Republican presidents tend to spend more, tax less, and borrow more.

Q2-2000

5,000

Q3-1991

During the early **1990s** U.S. public debt was growing at a rate of about $100 billion a quarter, but then the growth slowed during the rest of that decade. It was always rising, but not quite as quickly as before.

Q1-1966

0

TOTAL U.S. PUBLIC DEBT (U.S.$billions)

-300   0   +300   +600   +900

← **FALLING** RISING ⟶

ABSOLUTE CHANGE QUARTER TO QUARTER (U.S.$billions)

9. U.S. public debt, 1966–2018 (billions of dollars). (Data adapted from the U.S. Department of the Treasury, "Fiscal Service, Federal Debt: Total Public Debt [GFDEBTN]," retrieved from FRED, Federal Reserve Bank of St. Louis, accessed 29 December 2018, https://fred.stlouisfed.org/series/GFDEBTN.)

state in the world—the land of acceleration—which is itself now slowing down. To see why the rate of growth of debt is decreasing in just this one country, out of so many countries, requires looking at a series of other trends, not just within the United States but worldwide.

Carlo Pietro Giovanni Guglielmo Tebaldo Ponzi arrived in the United States in 1903 from Italy. If you are interested in Ponzi schemes and where such flights of fancy can lead, look him up. In a fast-changing world, many of his schemes initially worked; but none worked for very long. In a world of slowdown there should be fewer chances of any of the schemes of such gamblers getting off the ground. The only reason we know Ponzi's name is that his many schemes failed in his lifetime, often spectacularly. The names of others who got rich in just as dubious ways, but stayed rich, are not yet held in such low esteem. We should not be surprised if, in future, they are remembered with ridicule. It all depends on how the unrepayable debts of the young are unraveled.

4

data

the deluge of less and less that is new

Think about it: The pace of change has never been this fast, yet it will never be this slow again.

—*Justin Trudeau, Davos Address, 23 January 2018*

Ridiculous generalizations are repeatedly made concerning the pace of change. We are creating more data than ever, we are told: more information, more knowledge, all swelling in volume at unfathomable rates. Of course there is some truth in this claim, but nevertheless we have not, in the past few decades, actually discovered significantly more information than over the course of all the rest of human history. What has happened is that people now have the means to duplicate and preserve information in a way that is unparalleled in modern history, but this phenomenon mirrors the introduction of new forms of duplication in the past. This time the quantity is much larger, but the shock is not necessarily any greater than before.

The first form of duplication was storytelling. No one can know how long it took after language developed before the tradition began, but it is still through the telling of stories that we mostly learn and pass on information. You are reading a story now, one I have constructed from hearing, seeing, and reading other stories. This book is an attempt to refashion one particular (and in many ways rather familiar) tale: the account of how fast the human world is changing. The story was the first form of data, transmitted inefficiently, always evolving, and spreading—duplicating and growing—as many people heard it told and a few embellished it. In antiquity, and in many places until very recently, a story was lost unless at least one of those who heard it remembered it and passed it on.

Writing preserved stories more reliably. We know a lot more about the history of writing than the history of storytelling. Thanks to the few very ancient relics of written language that have been preserved through the ages, we still know some very old stories. The epic of Gilgamesh, a mixture of mythology and history relating to a Mesopotamian king who lived in the twenty-first century BCE, has been largely pieced together from many clay tablets created as far back as 1800 BCE. This story cycle contains tales very similar to the accounts of the Garden of Eden and Noah's flood in the Hebrew Bible. The written word enabled the preservation of both truth and myth.

Writing allowed for the more certain storage and transmission of larger quantities of information, and it ensured far less adulteration of the original data. As with almost everything that we can think of measuring, the use of writing at first accelerated after it was developed. More people learned to read, more people learned to copy script, and an explosion in written material followed. But it was a process that relied on the arduous labor of huge numbers of scribes, and because of the labor-intensive means of production, there were understandable limits to how much could be written down and also how much would survive.

Then as now, the tendency of the powerful few to hold sway over the many led to controls on the generation of, access to, and spread of information. If you were a ruler, you generally preferred to have very few subjects who were able to read and write. However, once writing could be mechanically duplicated, there was much greater access to written material, which made it easier for more people to have the opportunity—and the desire—to become literate.

Printing by means of pressing began a long time before Johannes Gutenberg's movable-type machine was developed around the year 1440. The most efficient writers in the distant past were Chinese, who were able to quickly paint a single character that stood for an entire word. In the ninth century CE, Chinese monks used wood blocks coated with ink to make multiple copies of books. Monks in Korea used movable metal type in 1377 to print Buddhist sayings.[1] In these cases, the first use of the new technology was to share the oldest stories. Religious texts were the first to be reproduced in bulk, including the Buddhist Diamond Sutra (with an 868 CE Chinese version being the earliest complete example of a dated printed book), the Jikji (a Korean Buddhist document) in 1377, and subsequently the Christian Bible in Europe.

The leaps, bounds, and troughs of the great growth of data over time echo those of debt, and the two phenomena are intricately linked. Without written records, it is hard to keep a tally on debts. Without the printing press, it is not possible to mass-produce notes that say, "I promise to pay the bearer on demand the sum of . . ." in such a way that they are not easily forged. A bank note, first widely used in China in the eleventh century CE, is a note of debt. In a world before telegraph wires and then computers, international finance was underwritten by the shipping of bars of gold around the planet, by the careful keeping of ledgers, and by the quaint presumption "My word is my bond."

The computer can be seen as one more in a series of intrinsically similar innovations: from language to storytelling to writing to printing. It would be interesting to consider how many billions of human lives had been lived between each of these developments. It is possible that the number between each is not very different. From our vantage point, these innovations look as though they are increasingly closely packed together, but that is only when we measure time in terms of years rather than the number of human lives. The rate of innovation per person may well be static. But that is hard to quantify because the number and significance of innovations are nebulous.

Today we associate rising quantities of information, of exponentially growing data, with the advent of the computer, but we should see it instead as part of a longer process of knowledge growth and information sharing. Computers are no longer new. When I was a young student, old lecturers would bore us with detailed accounts of the paper punch cards they used to store data. I remember, as a graduate student, being amazed that the entire company share registry of the United Kingdom required only a little more than one hundred large magnetic tape reels, and even more amazed that I was allowed to write a program to read them all and make a list of the addresses of the people who had the largest amount of share wealth, along with what the mean and median local share wealth was of everyone (by individual postcode) in the entire country.

Perhaps I am not enamored of the notion of out-of-control data growth because for a very long time I have had more data than I could ever know what to do with, and I long ago stopped worrying about how my data are stored. As a PhD student I carefully guarded the four hundred floppy discs that contained the data I used for my PhD thesis. I had no other backup.

Today, being old-fashioned, I carry a very small data stick in my wallet that holds all the data I have ever analyzed and everything I have ever written. If I were more up to date, I suppose I would use the cloud, but I don't quite trust it. Everything, including my data stick, is backed up on each of my computers, and today it appears that hard discs hardly ever fail.

The first floppy disc was produced when I was three years old—computer discs are an old technology. Today floppy discs are obsolete, and increasingly hard discs are joining them. When we say that the amount of data we can store, or the amount of data we have, is spiraling up and up, we may well be remembering our younger days. When journalists have to answer the question of how much data there might be in the world, they almost inevitably write something like this: "Nobody really knows because the volume is growing so fast. Some say that about 90% of all the data in the world today has been created in the past few years. And as mobile phone penetration is forecast to grow from about 61% of the global population in 2013 to nearly 70% by 2017, those figures can only grow."[2]

There is no reason to think that data production will "only grow," and there are many reasons to think it will not. For a start, the growth in the global population of humans is itself slowing down. The number of human beings would have to rise and rise exponentially in the future if we were to continue to create data at a rate such that 90 percent of it is always so new that it is just a few years old. Or we would have to delete more and more of what we have only recently collected to ensure that the vast majority is always new. The proportion of people who have a mobile phone obviously cannot rise above 100 percent, and there are also limits to the number of selfies and videos any one individual can create.

For some time to come, companies may well collect and store information in such inefficient ways that despite there being fewer than 8 billion of us on the planet, we have already stored at least the equivalent of 8 billion bytes of information per person on computers. Although most of this information might not be about people, it will include everything from remotely sensed imagery to scanned photographs of ancient art. It has all been collected by people and for people. Currently there is enormous duplication. By 2020, it is estimated that 1.7 megabytes of data will be created every second for every person on Earth.

In 2018, according to *Forbes* magazine, there were "2.5 quintillion bytes of data created each day at our current pace, but that pace is only accelerating with the growth of the Internet of Things (IoT)."[3] A quintillion is 10^{18}, and a byte is a very small piece of information that can take up to 256 forms, rather like a letter in a word. Each letter you read here is stored as a byte on the computer I am typing this on.

Given all the estimates floating around, we may believe we are collectively writing a very long story equivalent to 8 billion letters in length for everyone living on the planet every month of the year. Most of these data are, of course, obsolete or redundant when it comes to their information content, let alone what they might mean in terms of advancing human knowledge. Most of it will be a copy of something recorded many times over in many other places.

If we are to get to grips with whether the amount of information in the world really is growing exponentially, then we have to distinguish between useful, not very useful, and completely useless data. Most data are virtually useless, and most of the rest are of little real use. Even when we look at the data that are of the most use to most people around the world—say, the information carefully gathered by Wikipedia's unpaid army of volunteers—only a tiny fraction of it will be frequently used, and there will be many Wikipedia articles that are hardly ever read by anyone.

Leaving aside the fact that not everything published by Wikipedia is useful, we can use the growing size of this online encyclopedia to estimate the growth in useful information over time. Think of Wikipedia as a minuscule drop in the information ocean, albeit a more valuable drop than most. Next, suppose that Wikipedia takes up a fixed fraction of the more useful subset of the 2.5 quintillion bytes of data created every day. In other words, presume that a fixed part of the data deluge is being created to make additions to Wikipedia. If this is the case, then we should expect Wikipedia itself to be growing rapidly in size, more rapidly with every extra individual who gets his or her first smartphone or computer and becomes potentially one more person who might contribute something to the world's most widely used database. However, Wikipedia's growth is not accelerating; in fact, it is slowing down in terms of both the number of entries added each year and the size of new entries.

If claims of an exponential growth in data were correct, the slowdown in the growing size of Wikipedia would suggest that not only is the rest of the data held on computers in the world growing more and more rapidly than recognizably useful data such as Wikipedia's, but a greater share of what we are storing is likely to be little more than rubbish—in other words, information that would have been thrown out if it were stored on paper. If you think a lot of what is on Wikipedia isn't of great value, you may prefer not to think about everything else we're shoveling into the planet's digital landfills!

WIKIPEDIA

I could have chosen many different examples of data sets to examine, but it would have been hard to come up with one that you're more likely to use yourself and to be familiar with than this one. Wikipedia was a good idea. A very good idea. So good that many thousands of people almost instantly spotted how useful it was within a few months of its creation (see figure 10). In just nineteen years, the number of Wikipedia articles grew from 19,700 to 5,773,600.

Wikipedia was launched on 15 January 2001, with no central power controlling its content or growth. Within less than a month, by 12 February 2001, 1,000 articles had been added; 10,000 were published in just over six months, the milestone of 100,000 was passed during 2003, and 1 million in March 2006.[4] At this point its growth was exponential, but within a year that rate of growth had slowed. Why?

According to Wikipedia itself, "The number of regularly active editors on the English-language Wikipedia peaked in 2007 at more than 51,000, and has since been declining." An article published in 2013 suggested: "The main source of those problems is not mysterious. The loose collective running the site today, estimated to be 90 percent male, operates a crushing bureaucracy with an often abrasive atmosphere that deters newcomers who might increase participation in Wikipedia and broaden its coverage."[5] But that suggestion does not explain why Wikipedia's slowdown began in 2007, rather than 2006 or 2008.

There are many other explanations for the slowdown in the growth of Wikipedia; in fact, the most plausible explanations are also very possible. Could it be that by 2007, most of the very obvious entries had already been written and the proportion of entries that were more trivial was growing? The very smooth trend in Wikipedia's initial remarkably rapid growth, followed by its slower deceleration, tends to support such an explanation. Perhaps it is the case that many people, worldwide, are very interested in between 1 and 2 million things and that, after that number is reached, each additional million entries are generally of less interesting content than the previous million were. The encyclopedias of the past had far fewer than a million entries.

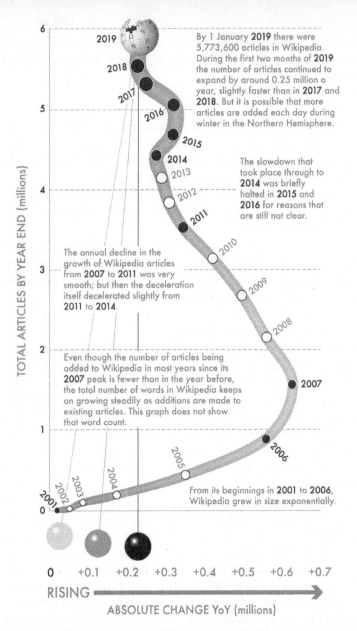

By 1 January **2019** there were 5,773,600 articles in Wikipedia. During the first two months of **2019** the number of articles continued to expand by around 0.25 million a year, slightly faster than in **2017** and **2018**. But it is possible that more articles are added each day during winter in the Northern Hemisphere.

The slowdown that took place through to **2014** was briefly halted in **2015** and **2016** for reasons that are still not clear.

The annual decline in the growth of Wikipedia articles from **2007** to **2011** was very smooth; but then the deceleration itself decelerated slightly from **2011** to **2014**.

Even though the number of articles being added to Wikipedia in most years since its **2007** peak is fewer than in the year before, the total number of words in Wikipedia keeps on growing steadily as additions are made to existing articles. This graph does not show that word count.

From its beginnings in **2001** to **2006**, Wikipedia grew in size exponentially.

TOTAL ARTICLES BY YEAR END (millions)

0   +0.1   +0.2   +0.3   +0.4   +0.5   +0.6   +0.7

RISING

ABSOLUTE CHANGE YoY (millions)

10. Articles in Wikipedia, 15 January 2001–1 January 2019. (Data adapted from "Wikipedia: Size of Wikipedia," *Wikipedia*, accessed 24 February 2019, https://en.wikipedia.org/wiki/Wikipedia:Size_of_Wikipedia.)

A second change can be seen in the trend that occurred in 2015, when Wikipedia's growth rate briefly accelerated again. It is possible that people had started assuming that they would find a Wikipedia entry for anything and everything they thought was important or interesting, and so those who could edit (and computer literacy was increasing quickly back then) added more "stubs" to make the existing gaps apparent, and other people coming across the stubs were invited to do something about it via a notice on the page itself. This is just one of many possible explanations for the 2015 anomaly in Wikipedia's slowdown.

At some point, when the history of Wikipedia is written, all the possibilities will be explored in much greater detail. The most interesting of these explanations may concern what happens next. Will Wikipedia become set in stone, like a holy text? Might future "editions" be merely slight revisions of what has been laid down within the past two decades, following increasingly standardized formats? Or will Wikipedia continue to evolve, if the attention of those who might become editors is not lured away to other, more glamorous platforms or projects?

The count of internet users online worldwide was doubling annually around the years that the growth of Wikipedia peaked. The World Wide Web was new and especially exciting. Wikipedia was one of its most exciting parts—a major attraction along what we initially called "the information superhighway."

In recent years the growth of all the information available on the internet has slowed, increasing in content now by only around 10 percent annually. The growth of the internet as a whole also has to inevitably decelerate over time. To give an analogy, when the car was invented, the building of roads smooth enough to easily drive on grew exponentially too, doubling and doubling again in length in just a few decades in its early years. Wikipedia is today a part of both the attractions and the new roadway that is the internet; its early years of exponential growth are now over.

OLD DATA

Is what we see with Wikipedia simply what we see with any new innovation? At first the innovation takes off and then it inevitably slows down; but measuring progress in this way does not tell us much if we are doomed always to see the same patterns. Fortunately the answer to that question is no. We often see an innovation begin, stumble, rise, appear to succeed greatly, then appear to be failing, then rise up again. However, the vast majority of innovations never even achieve this pattern: they fail very early on; and so most of us never hear of them.

So let's go back in time, from the computer back to the printing press. How did the number of new titles grow when books could be printed using movable type? By 1500, the retail price of books had halved since the introduction of the printing press just a few decades earlier. By 1600 books were ten times cheaper, measured against the average wage, and by 1680 they were twenty times cheaper. Interestingly, the price of producing and purchasing books did not fall much in real terms after that, at least not by the 1870s, which is when the particular historical data source I am relying on here ends.[6] Consistent data sets over long periods of time are rare because of changes in what precisely is recorded. Today, most consistent data sets go back only a few decades, and often are only reliable for specific countries.

Books are not easy things to count. According to the United Nations Educational, Scientific and Cultural Organization (UNESCO): "A book is a non-periodical printed publication of at least 49 pages, exclusive of the cover pages, published in the country and made available to the public. . . . A title is a term used to designate a printed publication which forms a separate whole, whether issued in one or several volumes."[7]

UNESCO used to produce a time series to show how many new books were being published each year per person per country, but in recent years the organization's statisticians have become more and more concerned about the validity of the data they can amass. The spread of the internet means that billions of people can, if they so choose, produce a book and also find some way of making it available to the public—even if only in digital format. However, the rise of the internet and changes in fashion over buying and owning books have led to a decline in the need for printed copies of books, just as printing ended the need for manuscripts to be copied by hand. Fifty years ago, few people questioned the assumption that we would need an almost unlimited rise in the number of copies of new books for an increasingly educated world population. How quickly our predictions can turn out to be wrong.

Very rapid increases in the availability of data and information have happened many times before, and not just in our age. For instance: "In the year 1550 alone, for example, some 3 million books were produced in Western Europe, more than the total number of manuscripts produced during the fourteenth century as a whole."[8] If we consider only new book titles rather than actual copies of books (most of which in Europe were initially copies of the Bible), then the speed of change is not quite so fast. This is because new books have to be dreamed up and written by a person or people before they can be mass-produced. The idea that books need not all be factual but could be works of fiction was also something that needed to grow in popularity for the number of new titles to rise greatly.

In Europe, the greatest rise by far in the production and consumption of books during the seventeenth and eighteenth centuries was in the country we now call the Netherlands. The areas being considered here are what was previously called the United Provinces, and when it came to the sale of locally produced books these areas included the Low Countries and parts of present-day Belgium (Leuven and Antwerp). By 1600, a new book was being produced per year for every six thousand people alive there, doubling to two by 1650 and four by the 1740s. So let's think about the changing geography of the growth in storytelling before taking a closer look at book production in the Netherlands, from the time of the advent of the printing press through to when William of Orange sailed for England in 1688. By that year, Great Britain was producing the second greatest number of books per person after the Netherlands, and Germany the third most.

Human language first evolved in Africa. Many of the oldest recorded stories were first told in Asia, traveling from there around the world, including into the Americas. Writing's origin has been traced back to where continents meet: in Mesopotamia and Egypt (at the junction of Asia and Africa) five millennia ago; and from where the two Americas meet (Mesoamerica) over two millennia ago. A very different kind of writing may also have begun independently far away from all these places: in China, over four millennia ago, where a large number of humans had established a settled society. Writing was most needed at points of greatest trade, and it required stability to evolve and survive.

The explosion of print publishing was European. This was despite the continent having been the least prolific in the production of ancient stories. Printing with wood blocks was carried out much earlier in China, but there was no later impetus for a great expansion of printing there. In contrast, in Europe, the early experiments with printing coincided with the accumulation of wealth, the growth of debt, religious turmoil, and then the invasion and conquest of the New World, beginning in 1492, which suddenly made Europe the geographical center of the known world.

In a way it seems only fair, geographically speaking, that the internet should have originated in America. Every continent has its key part to play in the great story of stories, the longest lasting, that have been repeatedly told, possibly starting in Australasia. Arguably, it is also apt that the internet began in the U.S. Department of Defense: information growth is strongly linked not only to monitoring debt but also to the planning and carrying out of war. The rate at which information is released, controlled, and created often has more to do with war than we might think. The story of the ups and downs of book publishing in the Netherlands is a story punctuated by wars.

OLD BOOKS

In less than two centuries, from 1500 to 1688, the number of new books published in the Netherlands grew from 41 to 395 per million people annually. The figures given here are averaged over a decade so that we are not too distracted by very short-term fluctuations in the overall pattern.

At first the number of new titles rose quickly, from forty-one per million residents a year in the 1500s to forty-nine per million in the 1510s. But then, in 1520, a public burning of newly printed books was carried out in Leuven. This was followed by the burning of another four hundred books in Antwerp. These included the works of Martin Luther, which were being confiscated from bookshops and set alight before they could even be sold. In 1521 a mass book burning took place in Utrecht, and in 1526 Amsterdam's first burning of printed books was recorded.[9] These events started a tradition of burning that went on for decades, which (along with many other factors) held back the expansion of publishing in the Netherlands until the 1570s and 1580s.

With the formation of the Dutch Republic in the very late 1570s, book production accelerated again, then slumped in the 1620s. Production rates fell partly because population growth was outstripping the growth in new book printing, but the change was also due to the resumption of the war with Spain in 1621 after a long truce. Nevertheless, the printing of new volumes when compared as a ratio to the population of the local area accelerated again with the Dutch conquest in Brazil and as the Dutch East India Company grew in wealth and power. Dutch book production decelerated with the advent of the 1660s war with England, when there was a decade-long slump in the number of new titles being printed each year. Then in the 1670s the rate of new book publication grew once again. Figure 11 shows three periods of slowdown and three of acceleration.

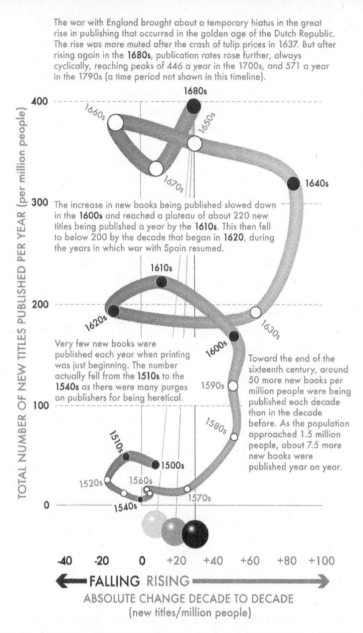

The war with England brought about a temporary hiatus in the great rise in publishing that occurred in the golden age of the Dutch Republic. The rise was more muted after the crash of tulip prices in 1637. But after rising again in the **1680s**, publication rates rose further, always cyclically, reaching peaks of 446 a year in the 1700s, and 571 a year in the 1790s (a time period not shown in this timeline).

The increase in new books being published slowed down in the **1600s** and reached a plateau of about 220 new titles being published a year by the **1610s**. This then fell to below 200 by the decade that began in **1620**, during the years in which war with Spain resumed.

Very few new books were published each year when printing was just beginning. The number actually fell from the **1510s** to the **1540s** as there were many purges on publishers for being heretical.

Toward the end of the sixteenth century, around 50 more new books per million people were being published each decade than in the decade before. As the population approached 1.5 million people, about 7.5 more new books were published year on year.

TOTAL NUMBER OF NEW TITLES PUBLISHED PER YEAR (per million people)

400

300

200

100

0

1680s
1660s
1650s
1640s
1670s
1610s
1620s
1630s
1600s
1590s
1580s
1510s
1500s
1520s
1560s
1540s
1570s

-40   -20   0   +20   +40   +60   +80   +100

⟵ **FALLING** RISING ⟶

ABSOLUTE CHANGE DECADE TO DECADE
(new titles/million people)

11. New book titles published in the Netherlands, 1500–1680. (Data adapted from *Our World in Data*, https://ourworldindata.org/books, which used Jonathan Fink-Jensen's "Book Titles per Capita," 13 December 2015 data set, http://hdl.handle.net/10622/AOQMAZ, which gives access to IISH Dataverse V1.)

The particular timeline in figure 11 is interesting because it illustrates in a very simple way how the rise of a new technology can be punctuated by particular events. This method of highlighting the rate of change as being *just as important* as the level attained at any one point makes the slowdowns that did occur much more evident. A change you would have described from looking at a standard graph as going "a bit up and down" becomes more clearly a major event.

In figure 11 your eye is drawn to the three times the line crosses the vertical axis and moves to the left, to the brief eras when fewer new books were printed in a particular decade, or series of decades, than immediately before. In recent decades, trends such as these have usually been drawn on graphs as the "best fit" straight line. If that didn't work, the graph's author might change his or her technique to drawing two straight lines that supposedly showed "when the trend changed." However, trends do not usually go in straight lines. What is notable here is when the trend changes from speeding up to slowing down. These shifts are clearly visible on these phase space timeline graphs—the points at the farthest right or farthest left are highlighted. Such points, the actual points when the trend changes, are hardly detectable on a standard graph, one that has time as one of its axes.

The timeline in figure 11 for 180 years of Dutch publishing also highlights how the periods of growth were all quite strong. In the thirty years after the 1570s, book production grew by an additional fifty new titles a year. As mentioned above, the timeline uses a decadal average to smooth out briefer fluctuations. The total number of new books being printed a year thus went from fifty to two hundred per million people in only thirty years. At the start of that thirty-year period, one person could have read all the books that had ever been printed in the Netherlands. By the end of that three-decade period, that would have been impossible.

It is worth remembering that the hiatus in publication growth at the start of the seventeenth century was still a period in which two hundred new books were being printed each year. It is rather like the hiatus in the expansion of Wikipedia that we see today. It was a hiatus because the number of new books was not growing faster than before, but there were still so many new books being printed a year that unless you were able to read one complete book in a day, almost every day, you could not possibly read everything that was new, let alone everything that had been published. But you could very probably read everything of significance—if you were able to read, were rich enough to buy books, and had the time and energy for all that reading.

Literacy had to spread for ever-increased book production to continue to be profitable. The religious belief that a person must be able to read the Bible had a great effect on the initial acceleration of printing in Europe, but at first not all souls were seen as equal. Literacy tends to rise generation by generation as a wider and wider section of society becomes seen as needing to read: first men and then a few women of the upper and then middle class, are routinely taught to read, and occasionally write, for pleasure—not just for spiritual edification or for the purposes of business. People also began to specialize in what they read. Leonardo da Vinci (1452–1519) could be a polymath partly because when he was a young man what had recently been printed, or made available in handwritten manuscript form, was not an impossibly large quantity of information.

It was during the seventeenth century that specialization in publication grew. It was not just that so many new discoveries were being made in this age, but also that knowledge of these discoveries could begin to be more widely disseminated then because the means of dissemination, printing, was becoming cheaper and more widespread by the decade. That dissemination itself then led to more innovation. At some point around 1650, a new title was being printed every day in the Netherlands for every million people living there—and that was just in that one single country, albeit the richest country in the world at the time.

PEAK BOOK

What we have seen with Wikipedia, we also see with any successful new innovation. At first the innovation takes off, users rise, sales or hits rise, and then inevitably that rise slows down, but the trend can have many false slumps on its rocky road upward. Both the early growth of book publishing and its later evolution illustrate this phenomenon. But eventually—or even very quickly—all new technologies become either old or obsolete. Eventually, almost everything is obsolete.

Unless you're using a Kindle or listening to this in your car or as you walk, what you are currently holding in your hand is now a very old technology. It is not yet obsolete because you (and hopefully a few more people) are still using it. By looking at the historic timeline record of book production, from when printing began up to the present day, we can perhaps form a better view as to whether books are heading toward obsolescence or just experiencing another slump. You can view the timeline in figure 12 below and make up your own mind on that question. But what the timeline does certainly show is that we have reached at least a temporary period of "peak book"—that is, if the record of the Netherlands is more widely applicable.

We are constantly being told of the wonders of new technologies that will change our world forever. We don't always remember all the old ones about which this promise was made and then failed to materialize. If you are British and of my age, you might just remember the Sinclair C5, a tiny, battery-powered, sit-down, one-person road vehicle that failed to transform the world of automotive travel. One reason it failed is that drivers don't tend to feel very safe when traveling very low down on a road, sandwiched in between standard-sized cars and trucks. Then again, if we decide to make roads safer and create separate lanes for bicycles and electric buggies or souped-up wheelchairs, perhaps the Sinclair C5's time might then finally arrive?

To sell new technologies, we deploy a whole battery of marketing departments, public relations firms, and advertising conglomerates. Universities are encouraged to take a stake in their staff's "start-up" and "spin-off" firms. Innovation hubs are created. Business incubators are incubated. In the few years that I have spent working at the University of Oxford, I have met more affluent young master's students convinced that they will become successful entrepreneurs than in all the rest of my adult years combined. As you might have gathered by now, I am a bit of a skeptic. I don't think these young people are especially creative. I do think that an unusually high proportion of the postgraduate students at the University of Oxford come from families with sufficient money to kick-start their children's dreams, which leads them to seek more funding for schemes that mostly, inevitably, will fail. We rarely realize that for every idea that worked, millions of others were tried and failed. We also often fail to recognize how frequently amazing and complex collaborative inventions, such as languages, now die.

Make a list of the ancient technologies that you use today. You may choose to begin with the wheel or with woven cotton and wool. How much of what is in your life was invented a millennium or more ago? The letters you are reading now were. When I was a child, my father read *The 22 Letters* by Clive King to me. It was a children's book about how adults were beginning to discover the ways in which things had been discovered in the very distant past. At the time he was reading it, innumerable languages were disappearing around the world as the last person to speak those tongues died. At the same time, writing in an enormous variety of languages was shrinking to writing in just a few dozen languages, those few used by almost everyone who writes today. New publications in other languages are increasingly just translations.

How many old technologies do you use? What was the technology used to build the home you live in? Do you live in an apartment with an elevator, and if so do you consider elevators an old technology? The elevator made living high up in the sky possible. A few steam-powered ones were introduced around 1850, and the first electric one around 1880. What has been the greatest innovation since then that alters the home you live in? You might say the television, but it was invented not long after the elevator. The modern-day versions of these technologies are smoother, safer, flatter, and more widespread. But the elevator still just takes you up floors of buildings so you can avoid the stairs, and the television still just enables an image to be shown on a screen.

How many fairly new technologies are you reliant on? Ones that were new when your parents were the age you are now? I find it hard to leave the house without my mobile phone, but I have felt that way for thirty years (ever since I had such a phone). I find it harder to remember the inventions that we thought were the next big thing, the must-have gadgets that we no longer use. There are an enormous number of them. Hundreds of thousands of patents are taken out every year. Just think of all the drugs that were invented in the past that are no longer prescribed, or that have been found to be very harmful due to side effects that were only later discovered.[10]

And how many very new technologies do you use? You may wear a Fitbit. Do you think you might still do so in a decade's time, or will it go the way of the sweatband? Are you an "early adopter," and if so, does that mean you have spent a lot of money on things that turned out not to be as useful as you initially thought? Do you keep your old Filofax as a memento of your youth, or are you younger and have no idea what I am talking about? Do you ask Alexa what the weather will be today or to play you a song or to read out an entry from an old dictionary when you ask her: "What is slowdown?" Or do you have no idea who Alexa is? If you are reading this in China you will almost certainly never have heard of her. She is a virtual electronic assistant marketed by the mega-firm Amazon from late 2014 onward, based on 1960s science fiction that it took half a century to turn into a product.

Discoveries are always being made, but perhaps not at the same speed, or in the same quantity or quality, as was previously the case. Some claim that the peak years of innovation were the 1930s. Much more recently, unraveling the human genome has been miraculous, but it is now well known that it did not live up to all its promises in terms of what such a discovery would immediately give us—although it has shown us that some widely held ideas were naive. There are not specific genes for specific talents. And despite all that has been achieved, we are still trying to work out how famine, war, pestilence, and disease can be avoided. Despite our flurry of new discoveries, some very old problems remain largely unsolved.

There are many very large industries whose purpose is to convince people that everything is getting better and better. The industry in which I work (research) spends a great deal of its time telling anyone who will listen about the ever-increasing inventiveness of academics in making new drugs, machines, software, and—above all—discoveries. That so much of this is hype is not because humans are becoming less creative, or because universities are more stultifying places to work in than they once were. There was never a golden age, even if we did invent a few more very useful things than was usual in the 1930s, when we began to really work out what could be done with electricity.[11] Our problem today is that the majority of the easy wins have already been won. There are now so many more millions of people searching for the next big thing, but lately such things come along rarely, suggesting that there are fewer to find.

Before books could be printed with movable type, the scope for learning was greatly limited. Once ideas could be spread via printed pages, once more and more people were permitted to learn to read, once the rules about who could have an opinion were relaxed and old religious orthodoxies were reined in, discovery upon discovery ensued. Printing led to the discovery of electricity, transistors, the zipper, paperclips, Velcro, washing machines, penicillin: all the stuff that makes our lives brighter, easier, simpler, neater, quicker, cleaner, and safer than before. Each and every one of these depended on the spread of books to inform those who would invent.

How we think of ourselves changed with printed books, and how we entertained ourselves too. The novel (a new story), in place of the old tales, was invented and flourished. Books that presented arguments from different points of view were possible only after the prohibition on "heresy" was relaxed. These books hinted that it was possible that the Earth was not at the center of the universe, although it was still possible to revere some almighty Being. As Charles Darwin wrote in the *Origin of Species,* what we now call evolution "makes the works of God a mere mockery and deception."[12] He was not doubting the existence of a supreme deity, just the "mysterious ways" in which God was said to have worked.

Considering the importance of books in feeding our imaginations, one response to learning that there has been a slowdown in the rates of increase in the writing and publication of new books might be to think that the rate of innovation has slowed. However, it is more likely that the number of people who want to read yet more books is slowing, and that younger people in particular may be less interested in books than older people were. When books were all we had in the way of information, they were all-important.

My father read *The 22 Letters* to me because he enjoyed books, he especially enjoyed reading to young children (he still does), and he wanted me to enjoy books too. However, he now has a house full of informative books that are increasingly obsolete and are mostly not used. My own children, at the age I was when I was read to, would not tolerate a story as long as *The 22 Letters,* especially a story that didn't involve wizards. They have so many other ways to access information, not least because the television and the computer and the telephone have all been combined into one device roughly the same size as a flint hand ax used to be. It comfortably fits in your palm or pocket and connects you to almost everything.

NEW BOOKS

What will my children read to their young children? If we are truly slowing down, then they will read to them as I did, and as their mother did far more diligently than I. If we are slowing down, then children in future will still be read to at night by their parents, not by a machine pretending to be a parent. Because reading to a child is about far more than simply passing on information. Maybe a child's story in the future will include an aside that in the four hundred years from 1600 to the millennium, the number of new book titles published in the Netherlands grew almost twentyfold, from 168 to 3,219 per million residents per year. Now that rise is not just slowing, but the total number of new titles published each year is falling. By 2020, that future story will reveal, it looked as if the number of new stories was in decline. Are we running out of new stories?

The beginning of the story of Dutch books that I recounted above ended, for the purposes of that tale, in 1680, because up until then the trends were relatively simple. There was growth, punctuated by the occasional slowdown. After the 1680s, book production appeared to stabilize in the Netherlands at around four hundred to six hundred new titles per million people per year. It was no longer accelerating, nor was there even much growth, but a steady state had been achieved.

During the steady publication years, the Netherlands had been at the peak of its domination of European trade. In 1670, some 568,000 tonnes of goods were traded from Dutch ports. Analysis of these records shows that this was more than the combined trade of all the merchants of France, England, Scotland, the Holy Roman Empire, Spain, and Portugal at that time. The Netherlands had become hegemonic. Amsterdam sat at the crossroads of commerce, the most important maritime trading hub of that era, between the grain-producing northern Baltic States (and Poland) and the rest of Europe, where the greatest demand for food lay. From the south of Europe and further afield, spices, sugar, silk, wine, and silver were shipped back to the Netherlands in exchange for foodstuffs.[13]

Books were just a minuscule part of international trade. The majority were probably produced for the domestic Dutch market. The growing wealth that trade had brought to those who could gain the most advantage from it allowed for the initial acceleration and then continued growth of book publishing in the richest places on Earth until a steady state of great affluence was achieved.

There were ups and downs. Looking beyond the initial 180-year story, the 1720s were a low point for Dutch publishing as the national economy slowed down while nearby Britain's grew. The 1860s, in contrast, were a high point, as Dutch cities grew more quickly, along with literacy. As the timeline in figure 12 shows, however, there was no new clear pattern. Something of a plateau had been reached. But then, not long after 1900, production began to slowly grow again.

By 1900 more than seven hundred additional new book titles were being printed per million people per year in the Netherlands, and then more than eight hundred extra per year each decade as compared to the decade before. But in the 1930s, there was a slump, which continued, owing to the Second World War, into the 1940s; but in the postwar period there was enormous acceleration. After 1945, the Netherlands was a dream market for publishers, and this state of affairs lasted right through until the early 1980s. More new titles were published in the twentieth century, per person, than in all the preceding centuries of publishing in the Netherlands combined.

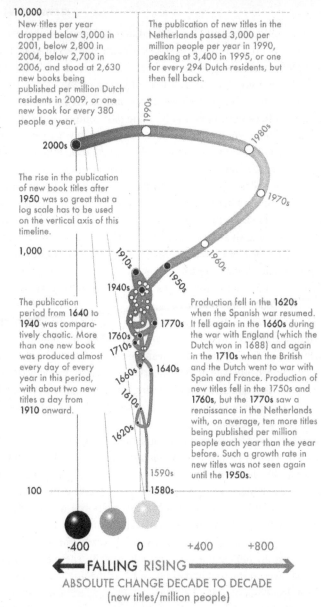

TOTAL NUMBER OF NEW TITLES PUBLISHED PER YEAR (per million people)

10,000

New titles per year dropped below 3,000 in 2001, below 2,800 in 2004, below 2,700 in 2006, and stood at 2,630 new books being published per million Dutch residents in 2009, or one new book for every 380 people a year.

The publication of new titles in the Netherlands passed 3,000 per million people per year in 1990, peaking at 3,400 in 1995, or one for every 294 Dutch residents, but then fell back.

1990s

1980s

2000s

1970s

The rise in the publication of new book titles after 1950 was so great that a log scale has to be used on the vertical axis of this timeline.

1,000

1910s

1950s

1940s

1960s

The publication period from 1640 to 1940 was comparatively chaotic. More than one new book was produced almost every day of every year in this period, with about two new titles a day from 1910 onward.

1770s

1760s

1710s

1660s

1640s

1610s

1620s

Production fell in the **1620s** when the Spanish war resumed. It fell again in the **1660s** during the war with England (which the Dutch won in 1688) and again in the **1710s** when the British and the Dutch went to war with Spain and France. Production of new titles fell in the 1750s and **1760s**, but the **1770s** saw a renaissance in the Netherlands with, on average, ten more titles being published per million people each year than the year before. Such a growth rate in new titles was not seen again until the **1950s**.

1590s

1580s

100

-400   **0**   **+400**   **+800**

← FALLING RISING →

ABSOLUTE CHANGE DECADE TO DECADE
(new titles/million people)

12. New book titles published in the Netherlands, 1580–2009. (Data adapted from *Our World in Data*, https://ourworldindata.org/books, which used Jonathan Fink-Jensen's "Book Titles per Capita," 13 December 2015 data set, http://hdl.handle.net/10622/AOQMAZ, which gives access to IISH Dataverse V1.)

The timeline in figure 12 is a little different from those that precede it. A log scale is used on the vertical axis because the rate of growth was so very high from the 1950s to the 1990s and then the rate of decline so large again most recently. This timeline is a semi-log plot, the vertical (ordinate) scale is logarithmic, while the horizontal coordinates (the abscissa) are not. Such graphs have been drawn only in the past century and a half, at first very infrequently. We have accelerated so quickly in what we understand, in how we count, in how we draw graphs even, that we find it very hard to accept that we are now slowing down. The slowdown is new.

In the post-Gutenberg world, humans progressed quickly from printing words with moving type to printing images and designing new ways of plotting data about the world around them. In the 1970s, the Netherlands had become an almost completely literate society, and a decade later, most Dutch people were well off enough to be able to buy books routinely, sometimes many books. Book buying was no longer just the preserve of the middle class; more and more books were purchased that would never be fully read—coffee-table books.

However, by the 1990s the number of new titles being published in the Netherlands had stopped rising overall, and by the 2000s the total was clearly falling. This fall does not mean that fewer Dutch people read new books today. Most people in the Netherlands can also read at least one language other than Dutch, so an increasing number might be reading books printed in German or English, and almost everyone can read online, which also leads to less book buying.

Production of books in the Netherlands fell slightly in 1981, but then recovered. It fell in 1986 and 1989, but only by 1 percent, and each time for just a year. But then it fell by 3 percent in 1996 and 6 percent in 1997. All these annual changes are smoothed out in the timeline here, but had you been working in book publication in those years you would have known about the staff layoffs, the market contractions, and the worry. The fall in 2003 was 6 percent, the rise in 2004 was 5 percent, but then there was a 7 percent fall in 2005 and a 4 percent fall in 2009. These transient details are not shown on the timeline in figure 12, as the line represents changes between decades, not years. Furthermore, looking at the long-term trend, it is clear that these changes had been a long time coming, given the overall direction of change moving toward deceleration in the 1970s. The particular year in the 2000s in which the falls came may well have been somewhat random, but in hindsight it had been on the cards for a long time.

Never say never, of course: the publication of new book titles in the Netherlands could rise again. But when you factor in the advent of the internet, it would not be at all surprising if 1995, when 3,402 new book titles were published in the Netherlands for every million people living there, was a peak that will never be surpassed. After all, that is one new book being published per year for every 296 people living in that country. Many of the new titles may be slightly altered reprints, translations, and books intended for export, but all the same, just how many books can a person read in a year—or even buy with every intention of reading but never quite getting past the first chapter? Everything has to come to a peak at some point, including the number of book titles published per year per million people.

SLOWING TECHNOLOGY

The deluge of new data and new ideas is now slowing down. This was one aspect of human life that in the 2010s, when I began writing this book, I had expected to still be accelerating in our current decade. But however I measured it, from Wikipedia page entries to Dutch books to so much else that I cannot include in these few pages, I have found no time series concerning data that is now still rising exponentially (see www.dannydorling .org). Everything appears to be decelerating, even if still often going faster than before. It is just now speeding up more slowly.

The efficiency of the microprocessor is the oldest trope, resulting in endless debates about whether Moore's 1965 law (the doubling of the maximum number of components in an integrated circuit every two years) has finally come to an end. During 2018 those speculating suggested that "it's time to start planning for the end of Moore's Law, and that it's worth pondering how it will end, not just when."[14] I could have looked at the efficacy of machine learning and noted that in 2019 "a systematic review shows no performance benefit of machine learning over logistic regression for clinical prediction models."[15] If machine learning and artificial intelligence are viewed as the future for predictive analytics, then according to this systematic review by epidemiologists, there is a problem. We should at the very least begin to worry about whether we are being misled in general as to what is just around the corner as far as the much-trumpeted new era of artificial intelligence is concerned.

There is huge resistance to being told that technology is no longer improving as fast as it used to. If you need much more evidence than can be fit into this book to find my argument convincing, you are not alone. Some people argue that we are not tuned to look for the new. They say that things are still changing rapidly but we just cannot see this; we assume that we are looking straight ahead to a plateau future. They say that we can't necessarily see the upward curve of progress ahead of us because we lack the imagination to do so. That might be true given our past of great stability, where not much changed from generation to generation, but in recent generations there has been a great acceleration and so arguably we have instead become used to that.

We may well be tuned, long term, to cope well in a world in which less and less changes. We could be well adapted for the stability that is already upon us. However, before we accept that things are no longer speeding up, many of us may clutch at every future small technological discovery as a great advancement. One day I hope I will not have to type words on a QWERTY keyboard, but that day should already have come. That keyboard was designed for slowdown—to actually slow down typists' speed so that the levers of old typewriters did not jam.

A few friends of my age whose hands have also been worn out by too much typing now use voice recognition to dictate their ideas, rather like how businesspeople used to dictate to their secretaries. But something quicker than speaking was once possible. When I was young an ingenious five-button mouse was invented. When you placed the five fingers of your right hand over its five keys, thirty-two combinations were possible, enough for all twenty-six letters, space, period, comma, and so on. The speed at which you could type with little training was amazing, as just the slightest depression of a couple of fingers produced a letter without the need to first locate the correct key. Allow your left hand to be used on another such mouse, and some thirty-two "shift keys" could come into operation: bold, italic, underline, change case, change size, subscript, accents, and so on. But the idea never took off, and the Quinkey is no longer available for purchase.

It is easy to underestimate the power of tradition and to see exponential improvements in innovations when they are not always there. Similarly, it is easy not to realize that future technological advances can be expected to help reduce the catastrophic climate-transforming effects of some of our behavior.[16] Technological breakthroughs could well help to get us to where we will soon need to be, but they are most likely to be the enhancements of old technologies, such as batteries, and not the inventions of new ones, such as teleportation.

It is often claimed that technology continues to accelerate even in the face of numerous examples of slowdown as well as examples of when innovation was deliberately avoided. Moore's law may have come to an end, but then parallel computing means that does not matter, and computers will continue to become ever faster and faster as they couple together more and more processors. Some Moore's law advocates on Wikipedia suggest that by 2025 it will most clearly be accepted as having faltered. Others say it already has and the speed of processor advancement was fastest in the period 1975–84.[17] What is rarely pointed out is what the extra processing power is being used for. There are clearly diminishing returns. Fantasists suggest (as always) that truly clever artificial intelligence is just around the corner. So far image and voice recognition represent most of what can be claimed as its successes. Both are simply advanced forms of pattern recognition.

It is also worth noting that the processors charted in the classic Moore's law diagram (easily googled) showing continued acceleration in processor speed since the 1970s were in the 1980s mostly mass-market general-purpose processors.[18] Those created subsequently have often been more specialized processing chips. Furthermore, most of the processors lie above the line of exponential speed-up in the early period and below it since 1990. The line is curving downward. Moore's law has, in reality, not been a law for many decades. If we want to see real technological progress, we should look at the recent historical trajectory of communication: letters, telegrams, telephone, email, Skype, social media networks. Determine what is very innovative and what is not, and ask whether we are still moving as rapidly forward now. Being able to send a letter was once revolutionary. Being able to flash a message on a friend's phone is what children now do (and adults tend not to).

Today even our washing machines can talk to one another. But why would they? Will data be transmitted between washing machines using 5G technology—or will it always go from one washing machine to some central control hub? If our washing machines are connected to one another in the brave new Internet of Things—then can we expect them to revolt?![19] The washing machine itself was a great leap forward. Getting washing machines to talk to one another is not. But of course there are still leaps to be made.

The total quantity of data being amassed by space telescopes may still be accelerating, but is ever-greater resolution quite the same as producing the first lens that allowed detail on the moon to be viewed, or hearing the first buzz from the first radio telescope? One day soon we will view little holograms of our loved ones as we talk to them across the ether, but that is not much more magical than being able to hear their voices for the first time from across the Atlantic—in fact, it will likely seem much less magical.

The world's knowledge is no longer locked up in a few dusty, elite-access-controlled libraries. New ideas are being generated all the time, but in aggregate they are not quite as new or as frequently profound as those that most of our parents, grandparents, and great-grandparents experienced.

When it comes to information and technology, my children have access to little that is much different from what I had access to as a child. Mine is the first generation to be able to say that for many years. For my children it is all far more convenient and works far more smoothly, but they were not among the first to be able to send an email or stand in a field and make a telephone call—I was. Selecting a track to listen to on Spotify or being able to choose a movie to watch on demand is not quite so mind-blowing as the technological changes in the 1970s and 1980s were for me—for them, it is just normal, because for them this is now commonplace. They have what billions of others have—a common technology. No longer are our children standing on the edge of acceleration looking forward into the utterly unknown.

5

climate

industry, war, carbon, and chaos

> For way too long the politicians and people in power have got away with not
> doing anything at all to fight the climate crisis and ecological crisis. But we
> will make sure that they will not get away with it any longer.
>
> —*Greta Thunberg, 22 April 2019*

One day in August 2018, a schoolgirl in Sweden started a school strike. At
first it was hardly a strike. It was only her. Her parents tried to stop her, but
she persisted. She went and stood alone outside the parliament in Stockholm on a Friday holding a banner and began the Skolstrejk för Klimatet
(School Strike for Climate). She returned the next Friday, and the Friday afterward. Initially her classmates were not interested in joining: "Passers-by
expressed pity and bemusement at the sight of the then unknown 15-year-
old sitting on the cobblestones with a hand-painted banner."[1] On 13 March
2019, Greta Thunberg was nominated for the Nobel Peace Prize.[2]

In April 2019 she took the train to London to address climate change
protesters there. Almost one thousand had been arrested by the end of the
Easter weekend for blocking roads and bridges in the capital city of the
United Kingdom. In the summer of 2019, still aged sixteen, as she was when
she explained the situation very simply in London in April, Greta Thunberg crossed the Atlantic: "It took 13 days and 18 hours for the Malizia II to
complete the journey from Plymouth, England across the North Atlantic,
past the Azores, to New York City."[3] At the time of writing, Greta Thunberg
was taking her message across the Americas.

So how did this story begin?

THE EARLIEST HUMAN-MADE CARBON EMISSIONS

Everything is connected. The growth of the debt-fueled capitalism that encouraged greater and greater production and consumption is connected to the spread and acceleration of knowledge. The growth and spread of data and new information enabled innovations to be both imagined and disseminated at a faster and faster rate, faster than ever before. Principal power sources changed from wind, water, and carbon-neutral wood to coal and coke and then to oil and gas. The cost of paper fell as production was mechanized and more and more books could be printed, as long as there were more and more people willing and able to read and buy them, and enough trees from which to make the paper.

But let's go back to a time when very few people could read and write, and when we were just beginning to learn how to produce more and more (and yet more) of what was most coveted. Early on, long before most households had a single book, items made of iron were in great demand. The origins of the great acceleration lie a long way in the past. The spark that began this particular fire may well have been lit by a much earlier crossing of the Atlantic in 1492, but the fire smoldered slowly at first. Even three centuries after global geopolitics and economics were turned on their heads by the joining of the Old and New Worlds, observers from another planet, measuring the chemical composition of our air, would hardly have noticed that anything had changed.

It is estimated that in the year 1750, the total amount of CO_2 being released each year into the atmosphere as a result of what little industrial activity was then taking place around the globe was just 1 percent of a billion metric tonnes.[4] A great deal of that activity was the smelting of metals, principally iron. By 1791, the worldwide tally of human-made carbon emissions rose to 2 percent of a billion tonnes, 3 percent by 1802, 4 percent by 1810, and 5 percent by 1816, when modern industrialization was still just beginning. Philip James de Loutherbourg's 1801 painting *Coalbrookdale by Night* looks quaint today, especially when compared to later industrial vistas of mile upon mile of furnaces and factories. However, even that early glimpse of the dawning industrial era was likened to a vision of hell. Coalbrookdale, a small village in Shropshire, England, was the site of Europe's first sustained coke-fired blast furnace for the production of iron.

By 1816, iron had been made in bulk in coke-fired blast furnaces in Europe for just over a century, but at first only in a few, typically isolated places near iron ore and coal mines. Relatively small amounts of coal were required to fuel the furnaces. The fact that in the 1790s as much carbon was added annually to the atmosphere worldwide as in the forty years before is the first measurable sign of acceleration in emissions due to the rapidly growing use of coal and other fossil fuels by these emerging industries. At this time, it was mainly European, predominantly British, industry that was growing rapidly. So rapidly, in fact, that as much pollution was added in the eight years to 1810 and in the six to 1816 as had been added worldwide by industrial activity in the whole decade of the 1790s. In sixty years annual worldwide carbon pollution had increased more than sixfold, and the acceleration was ongoing.

If imaginary alien visitors had been monitoring the planet with a very sensitive scientific instrument, they would just barely have been able to discern the change to the composition of the air around the planet two centuries ago. It is important to bear in mind that at the time, they would not have been able to tell the difference between that first large rise in carbon dioxide in our air and the emissions that a single large volcano could have produced. Had they been able to determine the source of most of the pollution, they could have seen that it was then from mainly English and other European activity, although it is unlikely that they could have discerned what had caused the rise, or even understand such political subtleties that still matter so much to us, such as the knowledge that the Netherlands (most of what had been the United Provinces until 1795) had lost its dominance of the control of trade, and dominions, to the United Kingdom.

Far away from Europe and a few decades earlier, a few farming colonies, thirteen in all, had been fighting for their independence from the British in North America. While their gaining independence was annoying to the British, it did little to alter the initial speeding up of European industrialization and growth of the great acceleration of carbon emissions. No one then could predict that in the future it would be the United States that would become the greatest emitter of CO_2 that the world has ever seen.

It is not easy to grasp the extent to which the demand for industrial products, products that were produced using energy derived from fossil fuels, exploded during the nineteenth century. Populations were growing, especially and fastest in Europe, where there was already the greatest effective demand—in other words, demand backed up by the ability to pay. That ability to pay was itself backed up by the profit Europeans were just beginning to extract from their rapidly growing overseas empires.

All across Europe—not just in the United Kingdom, as British textbooks tend to suggest—new methods were invented or imported for extracting yet more coal from deeper seams, pumping water more quickly out of mines, blasting iron ever more efficiently, and spinning wool and cotton in mills powered by steam that was created by burning coal instead of being driven by the significantly lower power of waterwheels. In 1825 the world's first public railway to use steam locomotives was in operation in England, and it was fueled by coal. At the same time, the first steam-powered ships began to carry cargo along the largest rivers of the United States.

Coal became king. Mines multiplied. Mills, blast furnaces, and steam engines spread like animals in the midst of a population explosion. So much coal was being produced that more and more could be used. In some places coal became cheap enough for it to be used to heat homes. Ships exporting the goods made in the industrial areas proliferated, including ships that carried coal. As all that coal was burned, the carbon within it was converted into carbon dioxide that spread up, out of the chimneys and into the air—more, so much more almost every single year that passed than the year before.

For every metric tonne of solid carbon (coal contains 50 to 80 percent carbon) that has been burned, 3.664 metric tonnes of carbon dioxide have been created. Each carbon atom weighs just three-quarters as much as a single oxygen atom. Combine two atoms of oxygen with one of carbon, during combustion, and you create something that is 3.664 times heavier than the carbon content of what you have taken out of the ground in the first place. However, carbon dioxide's density is so low that it occupies a permanent volume around four hundred times that of the original carbon. Initially this pollution was in such comparatively low amounts that it was virtually negligible across the planet as a whole. Today, combined with other fuel waste and other sources of greenhouse gases, carbon pollution has become the most concerning international issue of our times.

Our imaginary alien visitors would likely know well the nature of carbon and oxygen atoms and how they combine. Yet looking down on Earth from their fictional spaceship two centuries ago, they may not have spotted the human beings. We were still quite an insignificant species, one of many that had spread all the way around the Earth. A few of the walls we had built, our canals, a dozen pyramids, and some of the land we had cleared of trees would have been more obviously visible than the people scurrying about in what would have looked like mostly aimless meandering. The vast majority of humans at this time were clustered into villages surrounded by a few tilled fields or rice paddy fields and many weeds. A significant number were still hunting and gathering from the wild.

Quite understandably, and forgivably, for centuries people assumed that almost all of the air pollution they were creating would somehow eventually dissipate. A few imaginative souls began to wonder whether this might not be the case, but it would be many decades after the early days of the industrial era being described here before any real hint would emerge of the gigantic problem that polluting the planetary atmosphere had created. After all, it was only around 1900 that we were beginning to work out how atoms worked and what they might weigh, let alone how the combination of one carbon atom with two oxygen atoms could create a greenhouse effect that would surround the entire planet and result in such potentially devastating climate change. For us, before that happened, the planet we live on was almost as unimaginably large as atoms were unimaginably small. It is asking a great deal of the human imagination to link these submicroscopic particles and a molecule of CO_2 to such a huge macroscopic event as global warming.

By 1836, human activity was releasing 0.1 billion metric tonnes of CO_2 a year worldwide, 0.2 by 1852, 0.3 by 1859, 0.4 by 1864, 0.5 by 1868, 0.6 by 1872, 0.7 by 1877, 0.8 by 1880, and 0.9 by 1882. The gaps between these years shortened from sixteen to seven, to five, to four, then widened to five in the 1870s, and then shortened to three and then just two years by 1882. In hindsight, we now know that the long economic depression from 1873 to 1879 coincided with the first measurable hiatus in our overall pollution of the planet. In the United States, that depression began with fears that too much debt had been accrued by the (coal-powered) railway companies in the form of speculative investments that were prone to failure, and rail mania subsided.

Steam trains belched out smoke, as did the steel mills in which the metal for the tracks and the engines was being made. Nevertheless, even given how unpleasant the visible smoke was, it was in fact the invisible permanent pollution, rather than the smoke, that worries us so much more today. At the very same time, in Europe, the Vienna stock exchange crashed in 1873, again over fears that too much money had been lent (or "invested") in the new coal-powered industries. Pollution levels dropped when debt/investment reduced, but still no one knew that pollution would not dissipate. How could they know? Maybe they thought it floated out into space, or was absorbed by the oceans. But most probably they never thought about it at all. "They" were my great-grandparents, and this was not very long ago.

The long economic depression of the 1870s slowly subsided. Even during that depression, more carbon was being burned as fuel each and every year, worldwide, than the year before. It was just that the rate of acceleration in production and pollution had diminished. In 1878 an arc lamp was installed in the picture gallery of William Armstrong's Cragside home in Rothbury, Northumbria, England. In 1880 the first incandescent domestic lamp was installed there.[5] Armstrong was then one of the richest people in the world. Few of his contemporaries would have imagined that, within a century, it would be common for most people in Britain to live in a home—a home they owned—lit by hundreds of electric lights of one kind of another, all more impressive than Armstrong's.

What made it possible for both industry and later home ownership to spread so quickly was debt. The availability of debt to drive both production and consumption was clearly linked to the speed in the growth of overall air pollution. By 1884, over a billion metric tonnes of human-created CO_2 was being emitted annually worldwide. This was the first time that industrial and other uses of fuels together with shifts in humans' use of land had brought about such a change.[6] Then, after 1884, everything, literally almost everything people did, sped up. Still, almost no one thought it might be a problem. Why would they?

It took only seventeen years, between 1884 and 1901, for the world to move from generating an additional billion metric tonnes of CO_2 a year to producing 2 billion metric tonnes, with the doubling largely the result of the activities of transport and industry. Those seventeen years were very eventful, and the rise was no longer as steady as it had been, but what matters most was that in the course of just seventeen years, emissions grew by as much, annually, as they had grown in all the years, decades, and centuries of human industrial production prior to 1884. Then, in just nine years from 1901 to 1910, emissions from industry and fuel use grew even faster, with 3 billion metric tonnes of carbon dioxide being added to the air around the planet each year. The first two of my grandparents were born. This was recent history. For any patiently watching aliens quietly observing us and measuring the atmosphere, this was when things started to get really interesting.

Our emissions of carbon into the air within the course of the last century is an example of what an enormous acceleration looks like. The kind of acceleration that you would feel if you were in a rocket taking off from Earth, fired vertically upward (which itself would take enormous amounts of fuel). Yet, even in these early years of CO_2 emissions growth, there was the occasional period, of twelve months or a little more, when the total emitted was a little less than the year or years before. Human activity was now key to the change in CO_2 emission levels; volcanoes no longer mattered greatly. Because worldwide human economic activity began to fluctuate wildly, those pollution levels were not always rising steadily. Business cycles, troughs, and peaks were especially important in determining when emissions grew most quickly, or more slowly, and those trends depended in turn on the growth of debt, trade, and new technology.

Chapter 3 of this book began by considering more recent debt—housing, automobile, and student debt. However, at first it was the debt monies provided to nascent industry through investments that allowed that industry to grow so quickly. Those debt monies came from the profits made by rapidly growing world trade within the era of colonialism. It was only long after 1910 that mass mortgage debt could even be imagined as a possibility, and could contribute greatly to the increase in consumption and pollution. Before then, the majority of people living in cities rented their home and, unlike us, they tended not to fill up their rented homes with countless possessions that all would have had to be manufactured, and many of which—once connected to mains electricity—could later also use up even more carbon-based fuel. My grandfather once told me a story of sitting as a young boy on the coal barge that his grandfather steered through the canals (which preceded the railways) of Yorkshire in his job as a bargeman. My grandfather's father had once operated the steam pump that would draw water out of the local mine. None of them had many possessions, despite their lives revolving around the extraction of black gold (coal).

Before 1910, the capacity of the masses to buy consumer goods was very limited. Not least because the vast majority had so little storage space. Most people purchased little more than the food they needed, the clothes they would wear until they wore out, and only a very few luxuries. Most people lived in homes that were not connected to an electricity supply. When we think about today's debts, they are often of an entirely different type. Credit cards came into existence in the 1950s, with their rise to ubiquity coming later, in tandem with the rise of computing. Similarly, in the first decade after the Second World War, the notion that more than just a tiny proportion of high school students would go on to university was seen as utopian. Federal student loans, backed by government, were invented in the United States in 1958, following advice from the economist Milton Friedman. Margaret Thatcher introduced student loans into the United Kingdom in 1989. In the rest of the world, however, the expansion of education without debt was normal. It has been the countries most enamored by debt that expanded debt-based production the most and polluted so much so early.

So much is different today from when my grandfather and his grandfather were alive, but it is not quite as utterly different or as rapidly changing as we so often claim it is. Today we live with the illusion of rapid and continuous wholesale technological change. This rate of technological change is slowing, just as the rate of growth of Wikipedia is now steadily declining. We often find such arguments unconvincing because we have become accustomed to believe and repeatedly tell the very opposite story.

In 1968 the first Boeing 747 airplane taxied down a runway. It is still the mostly widely used airplane in the world, guzzling up fuel as it takes off, and using up the majority of its fuel within the first third of its journey, going on to land with very little left so as to maximize fuel-weight efficiency. Those airplanes are a very fast and efficient way to pollute. Orville and Wilbur Wright had only just begun to take to the skies at the time we are still considering here, first flying together as a pair in 1910. It was an age in which it would have been almost impossible to imagine a world with millions of people flying within just a few decades; such was the rate of acceleration that recent generations have since lived through. This may be why it became so hard to imagine that there would be so little innovation in flying in the fifty years after 1968 compared to the fifty before. We are still not very good at these acts of imagination. We are not yet ready to contemplate slowdown.

The idea of innovation slowing down is a story that we are as yet rarely told. Today we are told that artificial intelligence (AI) is our future, and there are widespread claims that if computers just become fast enough and are programmed well enough—or begin to program themselves well enough—they will rapidly be able to think like we do, as well as we do, in the way that we do, and ultimately better than we do. I can clearly remember being told this as a child in the 1970s, at the time when I first programmed a computer. The rate of progress in artificial intelligence has been remarkably slow since then. In my PhD thesis in the 1980s, I mischievously referred to it as being as slow as a sea slug because that was the only creature that had been partially successfully emulated then using a computer. No one has, as yet, even created an artificial robot pet that realistically behaves like the actual animal, let alone artificial humans. The rate of technological progress before the 1970s was remarkably rapid. But the rate afterward has been surprisingly slow.

It is not because we are especially great thinkers that humans are so hard to emulate. It is because we are animals, not machines, that it is so difficult to create an artificial mind. We think in very strange ways. Not necessarily good, quick, or clever ways, just strange ways. Thus, a computer can be programmed to recognize number plates, then text, then words. It can "machine learn" to translate between languages, especially if it is given enough source texts that have been carefully translated by experts working for the countries of the European Union (which is why Google Translate works best for European languages). But a computer cannot be made to deeply understand why it is wrong to let other people go hungry, or to care for the long-term consequences of its actions. A computer cannot worry about climate change like a fifteen-year-old Swedish girl can. William Armstrong's gravestone in the churchyard at Rothbury bears the epitaph: "His scientific attainments gained him a world wide celebrity and his great philanthropy the gratitude of the poor."[7] No mention is made of how he actually made his money, which was through the manufacture and selling of arms. And artificial intelligence is as far away today from emulating the human concern for such immorality as it was when it was first invented.

This morning I asked Alexa, the robot in my kitchen: "Why is it wrong if people go hungry?" She replied, "Humm, I don't know that one." Google it and you might find an economist telling us whether it is or is not economically sound to allow people to go hungry (and tragically one has probably made the calculations). The machine never actually knows intuitively if something is morally wrong. You need to be human to know, and to *not* care requires treating other people as less human—which, remarkably, some humans can do. Explaining all that to an artificial intelligence engine, and not simply having it parrot your words back to you, would be very difficult.

INDUSTRIAL EMISSIONS PRIOR TO WORLD WAR I

At the start of the twentieth century, fuel and industry CO_2 emissions globally were growing so rapidly that by 1910 they had reached 3 billion tonnes per year. Ten times more per year was being emitted than in 1859, just half a century earlier. If you were living in that age, the change you would see within your lifetime would have been staggering. A rise such as this one would be impossible today. It took another ninety-six years, almost a century, for a similar tenfold increase to take place again—but we are getting ahead of ourselves. So let's think back to the start of the great acceleration and ask why it didn't begin earlier.

When a technology is very new it almost always accelerates at first. The burning of fossil fuels, initially coal and sometimes carbon in the form of coke, was very rare many centuries ago. It was far easier to cut and burn wood than to dig out coal. Wood is not a fossil fuel. The growing of new trees absorbs as much carbon from the atmosphere as the burning of old ones creates. When trees are not burned, most of the carbon in the wood is stored in the rotting trunks and some of that might eventually, after many tens of hundreds of millions of years, become coal and oil.

Industrial coke burning began in China over a millennium ago, on a small but significant scale. Writing on the production of iron and steel in eleventh-century China, and the use of bellows to increase the heat in furnaces fueled by coke (made from coal instead of charcoal made from wood), the historian William McNeil observed: "Even if the separate techniques were old, the combination was new; and once coke came to be used for smelting the scale of iron and steel production seems to have surged upwards in quite extraordinary fashion."[8] Table 1 shows the rate of iron production in the key part of China McNeil refers to. It demonstrates how there was no inevitability that the current acceleration in pollution could only have happened recently; it could easily have started almost a millennium earlier.

Table 1. Production of Iron in China

Year	Tons
806	13,500
998	32,500
1064	90,400
1078	125,000

Source: William H. McNeil, *The Pursuit of Power* (Chicago: University of Chicago Press, 1982).

Thus the worldwide fossil fuel–powered Industrial Revolution could well have begun in China during the Song Dynasty in the eleventh century CE, but in the twelfth century production of iron and steel fell. The costs of transporting these metals had become higher when the canal trade was interrupted by war, and political upheaval led to a drop in demand from the capital city. Invaders from Manchuria disrupted production, and a century later Genghis Khan's army swept over the most prolific iron-producing region. Production was subsequently restricted largely to efforts to "equip the Mogul armies with armor and weapons" (not unlike William Armstrong's main use of iron all those centuries later for the manufacture of armaments).[9] Weapons of war often play a key role in the rise or fall in iron production. The previous mini-acceleration ended when the Yellow River broke through its dikes in 1194 and forged a new path to the sea, following on from previous extensive floods in 1034 and 1048. We humans have known great catastrophes many times in our history; we are just not that good at remembering them, especially when they happened in far-away places and times.

At any point in the seventeenth and eighteenth centuries, similar political and environmental fates could have destroyed the nascent Industrial Revolution in Europe, but they did not. The timeline depicted in figure 13 shows the annual additions to CO_2 in the atmosphere each year from 1750 to 1910, but what mattered most for global warming was not that, but the cumulative total. Carbon tends to stay in the atmosphere indefinitely, until it is taken up by plants and trees or absorbed by ocean plant life. There are other sources of increased human-made emissions to consider as well, but carbon is by far the most important. Furthermore, the more that forests are cut down, the less CO_2 is absorbed back from the air.

It is estimated that by 1807 there were 1 billion metric tonnes of CO_2 in the atmosphere that were the product of human use of fossil fuels. That doubled to 2 billion by 1827, 4 billion by 1847, 8 billion by 1862, 16 billion by 1877, 32 billion by 1892, and 64 billion by 1908. The gaps between these years fell from twenty to fifteen, and then rose only slightly to doubling in sixteen years. That sixteen-year period included two of the great economic downturns of the U.S. economy (see table 2). Despite such recessions, however, overall industrial pollution did not slow down. It just rose less quickly than it otherwise would have.

The 1870s slump in production is but a mere dent in the timeline shown in figure 13. The effects of the economic depression of 1882–85 are

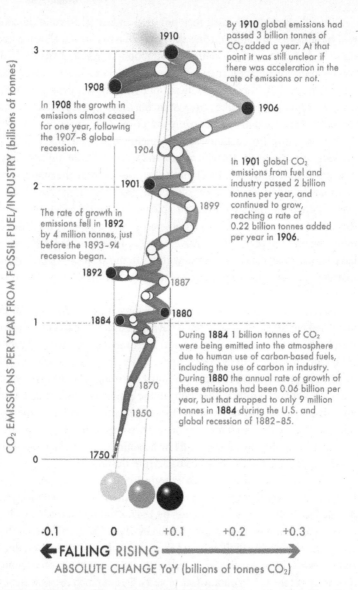

3

By **1910** global emissions had passed 3 billion tonnes of CO_2 added a year. At that point it was still unclear if there was acceleration in the rate of emissions or not.

1910

1908

In **1908** the growth in emissions almost ceased for one year, following the 1907–8 global recession.

1906

1904

In **1901** global CO_2 emissions from fuel and industry passed 2 billion tonnes per year, and continued to grow, reaching a rate of 0.22 billion tonnes added per year in **1906**.

2

1901

1899

The rate of growth in emissions fell in **1892** by 4 million tonnes, just before the 1893–94 recession began.

1892

1887

1880

1

1884

During **1884** 1 billion tonnes of CO_2 were being emitted into the atmosphere due to human use of carbon-based fuels, including the use of carbon in industry. During **1880** the annual rate of growth of these emissions had been 0.06 billion per year, but that dropped to only 9 million tonnes in **1884** during the U.S. and global recession of 1882–85.

1870

1850

1750

0

CO_2 EMISSIONS PER YEAR FROM FOSSIL FUEL/INDUSTRY (billions of tonnes)

-0.1   0   +0.1   +0.2   +0.3

← **FALLING** RISING ➡

ABSOLUTE CHANGE YoY (billions of tonnes CO_2)

13. Global fuel/industry CO_2 emissions, 1750–1910. (Drawn from data adapted from the Global Carbon Project, "Supplemental Data of Global Carbon Budget 2018" [version 1.0], Global Carbon Project, https://doi.org/10.18160/gcp-2018.)

Table 2. Major recessions in the United States before 1929

Downturn	Months	Business activity
1873–79	65	−33.6%
1882–85	38	−32.8%
1893–94	17	−37.3%
1907–8	13	−29.2%
1921–22	18	−38.1%

Source: Victor Zarnowitz, *Business Cycles: Theory, History, Indicators, and Forecasting* (Chicago: University of Chicago Press, 1996).

far more evident. (The 1883 eruption of Krakatoa, a giant volcano in what is now Indonesia, will also have added a few hundred million tonnes of carbon to the atmosphere.) Similarly, the 1907–8 depression following the bankers' panic of 1907 is also clear in its effect. But outside of these economic depressions, pollution just grew and grew more and more quickly up until a few years before the First World War broke out.

WAR AND DISEASE CHANGE EVERYTHING

From 1910 to 1960 the trend in CO_2 emissions from industrial and fossil fuel activities was at first erratic and then, from 1946 onward, remarkably steady, always rising outside of periods of war. In searching for the causes, it's worth noting that this period saw not only mass electrification, but also acceleration in automobile manufacturing.

Mass production of motor vehicles began in 1901 and then grew rapidly with the opening of the first Ford automobile factory in 1913. The United States dominated car production worldwide from the beginning. By 1961 it was producing almost half of the world's new cars, 5.5 million annually. Germany produced 1.8 million, the United Kingdom and France 1 million each, Italy 0.7 million, Canada 0.3 million, Japan 0.25 million, Australia 0.18 million, Russia 0.15 million, and Sweden 0.11 million.[10]

It is quite common—but mistaken—to assume that as the number of people in the world rises, carbon pollution into the atmosphere will rise in tandem. Some people even think that by having fewer children they will somehow reduce overall pollution. The truth is that if you bring up a child to campaign to reduce pollution, you will have a far greater positive effect than had you remained childless. What actually happened in the historical record is that a very small proportion of the world's population swiftly became more polluting at particular times and in particular places. Look closer, and we see that within only a small number of countries the majority of the additional pollution was being caused by the consumption of a few particular goods that were initially available only to the wealthiest. Cars, for example, not only required a very large amount of fossil fuel to produce, they also ran on fossil fuels. It is hard to think of a consumer item better designed to maximize CO_2 emissions than the early automobile.

At first there were very few cars, and even fewer trucks. The world's population grew, between 1900 and 1913, from 1.56 billion to 1.79 billion, an increase of 15 percent.[11] At the same time, carbon emissions from industry and fossil fuel use grew from 1.96 billion metric tonnes a year to 3.46 billion metric tonnes, up by 77 percent. Most young adults in the world in 1913 lived a life very similar to that which their parents had lived. They worked on the fields near to their village and sowed crops with a plow that might, if they were lucky, be pulled by a horse or an ox. They planted rice or maize as it had been planted for centuries, by hand. If they were very lucky, the bicycle might come into common use where they lived. They were not consuming more and more fossil fuel, or vastly more iron or steel. They certainly were not running their own internal combustion engine in their own gas-powered vehicle. They did not even have electric lights, because their home and village had no electricity supply.

From 1913 through to 1920, world population grew by 4 percent to 1.86 billion people. The First World War, terrible as it was, was a minor event when considered on a global population scale. It was confined to Europe and resulted in about 0.04 billion deaths, mostly of weakened soldiers dying some weeks or months after they were wounded. The influenza pandemic of 1918–19 added a further 0.05 billion to deaths during those years. Had these two apocalyptic events not occurred, we might have expected a total of 1.95 billion people alive in 1920, worldwide, and population growth in that scenario would have risen by 9 percent over those seven years. However, the postwar baby boom of 1919 would not have occurred, so the later actual rise might well have been less. Nevertheless, the world's population grew by 70 million people from the start to the end of these seven years. By how much did pollution grow? The answer: it fell! Pollution can fall even when population rises and vice versa.

Between 1913 and 1920, annual global CO_2 emissions dropped by 1 percent. The greatest fall had been in 1919, during and in the immediate aftermath of when the deadliest outbreak of influenza the world has ever known spread and the number of young adults fit enough to work in industry was severely reduced. The number shrank through illness more than through death, and because people buy much less when they are not well and earning, demand fell. The flu pandemic hit the young particularly hard, which might help explain why global carbon emissions fell by 14 percent between 1918 and 1919, but then rose by 16 percent the next year after most of the sick had recovered. Influenza had a far greater effect on industry, production, and consumption than the First World War.

From 1920 to 1940, the world's human population rose from 1.86 billion people to 2.30 billion, or by 23 percent. Global carbon emissions from industry and fuel use rose over the same period from 3.42 billion tonnes a year to 4.76 billion, or up by 39 percent, rising much more than population growth. Again, these two number series are linked only in the very weakest of ways. Pollution was rising the most in the parts of the world in which the number of people was rising the least—namely, the industrialized countries. Per head it is quite possible that pollution may have fallen in some of the poorest countries of the world at this time. The vast majority still had no electricity and no cars, and were living lives very similar to those of their parents, often in countries that had been created only in the preceding few decades. Their villages were now seen as part of a country with all the newly imposed, and initially very crude, institutions of a state; and they were rarely the greatest beneficiaries.

The political disruption of colonization had the effect, across most of the human world, of disrupting the previous relative population stability. The populations of the poorest countries of the world were about to grow rapidly. That huge population growth came after pollution by industry and fossil fuel use had exploded among that minority of the human population that was the wealthiest—and becoming yet more wealthy. It is very important to know this and to continue to bear it in mind. The key point here is that it was not a greater number of people that resulted in a greater amount of pollution, it was the result of what a very few people chose to do. The choices made by an even tinier few with power and authority also brought us world war.

The Second World War was completely different from the 1914–18 war as far as emissions of carbon into the atmosphere were concerned. The 1939–45 conflict was an industrial war, won by the quantity of bullets, bombs, tanks, ships, submarines, and aircraft that could be produced. It was also a truly world war, affecting the majority of the globe. Global carbon emissions had peaked at 4.2 billion metric tonnes a year in 1929, but following the worldwide economic depression that began in that year, they then fell. Emissions did not recover to 1929 levels until 1937. The planet's population was growing year on year in this period, but as pollution has so little to do with total population numbers and so much to do with the wealth and behavior of the most affluent, the continued growth in global human population had no impact on the worldwide pollution levels of the 1920s and 1930s.

The depression of the 1930s meant that fewer cars could be purchased and thus fewer were produced, and less fuel was used to run cars. The banking crash of 1929 had dried up the supply of credit and hence the production of debt. The demand for steel used to make cars fell and less fuel was needed to power the production lines. Fewer luxury household goods were made and purchased. There was a general decrease in industrial production in the most affluent countries after the great economic crash. Protectionism rose, global trade fell, and with that pollution fell. With fewer goods being made, less fuel was needed to power the old steamships to transport those goods, or the new diesel-engined oceangoing vessels that were beginning to replace them.

The Second World War and the rearmament before it caused a boom in global military production and military consumption, and a 4 percent rise in pollution in 1939 alone, which more than doubled to a 9 percent rise the following year. However, the subsequent wartime reduction in consumption of everyday goods, and especially luxuries such as cars in the richest countries in the world, resulted in yet another slowdown in pollution. Global carbon pollution, despite global war, rose by only 3 percent in 1941, 1 percent in 1942, 4 percent in 1943, and then fell by one percentage point in 1944 and by a massive 16 percent in 1945 when the military war effort largely ceased. Carbon pollution rates have never fallen by anything like that amount ever again since that year. In the year in which the largest worldwide baby boom of all time began (1945), carbon pollution from industry and fuel use fell the most. It cannot be said loudly enough or enough times over: it is not more people that causes more pollution, but what a few especially profligate people choose to do.

So what happened after 1945–46? The postwar world rapidly became a more equitable one, at least within the richest of countries. Better-paid workers in the United States could begin to buy cars; their counterparts in Europe could start to dream of buying cars. Certainly more cars were being made, and once all the rich families had a car, or two or three, production continued to expand because the improvement in wages achieved by trade unions meant more families could afford a car.

The automobile was in this era still a luxury item even in the richest countries. There was little need to have a car. The vast majority of people walked, cycled, or took public transport to work. Towns and cities had expanded so that homes were near to workplaces, and public transport was at its most extensive. The railway network in the United Kingdom would grow to its greatest extent during these years. (Much of it would be shut down in the 1960s as increased car use made many railway lines appear inefficient, but that is to jump too far ahead.) From this period the story now changes so quickly and with so many complex twists that it is hard to narrate it in a linear fashion.

After the Second World War, despite growing equality within the rich minority of countries, the human world rapidly became more inequitable with respect to the gap in consumption rates between the planet's rich and poor countries. In the rich countries, population growth slowed rapidly after the 1945–46 baby boom, but consumption of goods per family rose significantly. In the poorer countries, which were and continue to be the majority of the countries of the world, consumption hardly rose at all, but their populations began to grow rapidly. This was attributable to political disruption and the imposition of major changes in those countries that subverted the checks and balances that had ensured relative population stability. Being colonized has some very long-lasting detrimental effects; changes that began with colonization continued right through to the 1980s and 1990s, when the structural adjustment policies of the World Bank and International Monetary Fund led to a further population boom in Africa (as explained further by figure 25 in Chapter 7 of this book).

A Cold War was now beginning to be waged around the world, in which the United States (to a greater extent) and the USSR (to a lesser extent) would seek to control the political choices of the peoples of almost all other countries. That control included supporting dictators across Latin America who happily saw the poor further impoverished. There is nothing quite like poverty and instability to encourage population growth. Apart from anything else, people have more children because they know some of them will die. The Cold War period included the transformation of China from a feudal to a communist state, which initially contributed to huge Chinese population growth as the old ways were abandoned and new ways were imposed. In times of great uncertainty and turmoil, the only insurance policy available to the poor is having more children to look after them. However, communism soon brought much greater stability, and in one generation the number of children each woman had fell from six to two. The communist government, despite this great achievement, and probably partially unaware of it, then decided to instigate a dramatic and drastic further population slowdown through its official one-child policy. Population growth is the subject of the seventh and eighth chapters of this book, especially concerning China.

INTO THE SWINGING SIXTIES

Global fuel and industry CO_2 emissions grew most rapidly during the 1950s, rising to 9.4 metric tonnes a year by 1960. Between the year of my parents' birth, 1942, and when they turned eighteen, an additional 123 billion metric tonnes of CO_2 were added to the atmosphere—more than had been placed there by humans over the entire period spanning the very first European industrialization in the early eighteenth century right through to 1930.

From 1940 to 1960, Earth's human population rose from 2.3 billion to 3 billion, or by 32 percent (see table 3 for 1951–60). Annual global carbon emissions from industry and fuel use rose over the same period from 4.8 billion metric tonnes a year to 9.4 billion: by 98 percent, or three times as much as the numbers of people grew. The 1910–60 emissions timeline shown in figure 14 illustrates how it is possible to have oscillating stability and then a doubling in emissions, even as world human population growth steadily rises. It also shows us that something fundamentally changed after 1945.

In 1945 annual emissions were falling and stood at only just a fraction above 4 billion metric tonnes of CO_2 a year, a level that today we would, as the unfortunate phrase has it, kill for. Then in 1946 and 1947, emissions grew by almost half a billion metric tonnes each year. The war economy of all the industrialized nations was being reprogrammed into a peacetime production machine. America's military-industrial complex was just taking its current shape, and so the United States managed to sustain both its military manufacturing and its emissions, while at the same time creating a huge industrial base for its increasingly affluent and equitable home market of consumers, as well as for export to a world in which it was the greatest military power. Production dipped briefly in 1948, in the year before the U.S. business cycle was approaching its October 1949 trough.[12]

Table 3. World annual population growth, 1951–60 (and U.S. share)

Year	World population (billions)	Annual growth (%)	People worldwide per U.S. resident (number of people)
1951	2.6	1.7	16.6
1952	2.6	1.8	16.6
1953	2.7	1.8	16.6
1954	2.7	1.9	16.7
1955	2.8	1.9	16.7
1956	2.8	1.9	16.7
1957	2.9	2.0	16.7
1958	2.9	2.1	16.8
1959	3.0	1.9	16.8
1960	3.0	1.5	16.8

Source: Angus Maddison Estimates: http://www.ggdc.net/maddison/oriindex.htm.
See also Angus Maddison, *Contours of the World Economy, 1–2030 AD: Essays in Macro-Economic History* (Oxford: Oxford University Press, 2007).

Then the American economy began to grow again. The United States was, at this time, all-important to the production of global emissions. It was not worldwide practices that mattered; it was the business practices of the United States.

Production surged upward again, hitting a new annual high of almost 6 billion metric tonnes of CO_2 annually in 1950 and achieving an unprecedented peak acceleration rate of 0.64 billion metric tonnes more than the year before. Then there was a short slowdown before growth in production resumed in the year after the May 1954 business cycle trough, and again in the year after the April 1959 trough. The small undulations of the U.S. economy produced large global changes in pollution rates. Global population levels mattered hardly at all in this. What mattered most was what was being made and consumed by the tiny fraction of the planet's population that was the richest.

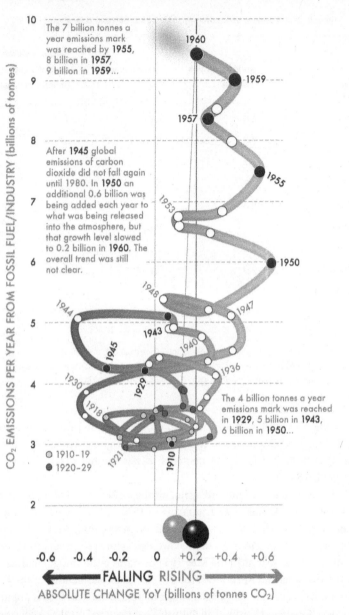

The 7 billion tonnes a year emissions mark was reached by **1955**, 8 billion in **1957**, 9 billion in **1959**...

After **1945** global emissions of carbon dioxide did not fall again until 1980. In **1950** an additional 0.6 billion was being added each year to what was being released into the atmosphere, but that growth level slowed to 0.2 billion in **1960**. The overall trend was still not clear.

The 4 billion tonnes a year emissions mark was reached in **1929**, 5 billion in **1943**, 6 billion in **1950**...

CO₂ EMISSIONS PER YEAR FROM FOSSIL FUEL/INDUSTRY (billions of tonnes)

○ 1910–19
● 1920–29

-0.6   -0.4   -0.2   0   +0.2   +0.4   +0.6

◀━━ **FALLING** RISING ━━▶

ABSOLUTE CHANGE YoY (billions of tonnes CO₂)

14. Global fuel/industry CO₂ emissions, 1910–60. (Drawn from data adapted from the Global Carbon Project, "Supplemental Data of Global Carbon Budget 2018" [version 1.0], Global Carbon Project, https://doi.org/10.18160/gcp-2018.)

By the 1950s most of the richest people in the world were living in the United States. In 1950, worldwide, only one person in every 16.6 lived in the United States, but collectively they were responsible for by far the largest share of global carbon emissions, and that was mostly due to just the actions of the wealthiest people in the world's largest superpower, those who controlled most U.S. businesses. Global population grew from 2.5 billion people to 3 billion during the decade that followed (see Table 3).

The acceleration in the worldwide human population reached a peak annual growth rate of 2.1 percent briefly in 1958. It would later hit that peak once again, this time for the four years from 1968 through to 1971 inclusive. However, that global population growth was essentially insignificant as far as carbon pollution was concerned. What mattered was what was happening in the United States, and to a lesser extent Europe and Japan, where industry was being rebuilt or newly introduced.

Even by the end of the 1950s, half of all the new cars in the world were being produced in the United States. At the beginning of that period one country was producing the majority of cars and making the majority of the world's steel, despite being home to less than a sixteenth of the global population. Oil wells were being sunk wherever oil could be found. Coal, the previous key source of global pollution, was no longer so dominant. A slightly "cleaner" way of emitting even more carbon into the atmosphere had been found with the proliferation of gasoline, diesel, and later jet engines. Meanwhile, in a remote corner of the United States, on the island of Hawaii, a time series of atmospheric measurement would begin to take shape that would later be used to prove the key link between human emissions and global atmospheric concentrations of CO_2.

Way back in the 1950s, within living memory of a very large number of people today, almost nobody knew what would soon transpire. You could look at the timeline in figure 14 that ends in 1960 and even imagine a slowdown coming, especially if you concentrate on the period from 1950 to 1960. However, a slowdown it was not to be. Had we known at that time the damage that this pollution would cause, it could have been much easier to deal with. Sadly, we equated industry with progress and greater production with rising living standards. The car was seen as a symbol of freedom and the airplane as a means of adventure. Traveling faster and further was to be admired. In September 1959, the Soviets' unmanned Luna 2 spacecraft landed on the moon and the news was received in awe.

CARS, ACCELERATION, AND ATTRIBUTION

The emission of yet more and more CO_2 into the atmosphere, leading to climate change and thus global warming, is still accelerating, but it cannot continue to do so indefinitely if we are to survive well (or—logically—even if we don't prosper) as a species. It is the only major exception to the general rule that most aspects of human life are currently slowing down. We have yet to slow down our carbon emissions, or even the rate of growth of those emissions. That rate of increase of the growth itself has begun to abate. That first possible twist in this foreboding tale can be seen on figure 15's timeline. What it shows is something that is only just becoming evident.

According to the estimates being used here, the cumulative total of CO_2 that had amassed in the Earth's atmosphere as a result of our industrial and other fossil fuel–based activities had risen to 128 billion metric tonnes by 1928, 256 billion by 1955, 512 billion by 1976, and 1 trillion by 2000.[13] During 2015 it surpassed 1.5 trillion metric tonnes. These figures tell us something shocking, but they will tell us something even more useful if we measure the length of the gaps in time to the next doubling.

The amount of CO_2 we added annually to the atmosphere from industry and fossil fuel use worldwide doubled in twenty-seven years, from 1928 to 1955. It doubled again in the next twenty-one years to 1976, and then again in the twenty-three years before the year 2000. The rate of doubling is finally just beginning to slow, although no one is likely to take much comfort in that fact. The situation today would be far worse if the "time to double" statistic had not, finally, begun to lengthen to twenty-three years. That lengthening began in 1976, in the years in which the price of oil more than quadrupled in a short time. This resulted in the smallest of slowdowns in the exponential rise in emissions—a slowdown in the rate of acceleration of the growth in emissions—but not in the growth in global emissions themselves.

Many people think it is too late. We continue to emit more carbon into the atmosphere every year than we did the year before, occasionally much more. This is enormously more than natural processes such as plants, forests, and ocean absorption can mitigate. As we do this we now become more and more sure that the planet will simply heat up faster and faster. We now think of the relationship between the amount of carbon in the atmosphere and the warming up of our Earth as being linear, such that when one quantity rises so does the other, in direct proportion—but we do not yet know if that will always be the case. There may be feedback loops

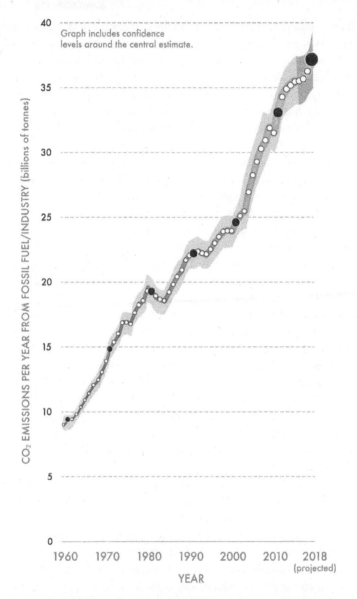

15. Global fuel/industry CO$_2$ emissions, 1960–2018 (conventional graph). (Redrawn from data in Corinne Le Quéré et al., "Global Carbon Budget 2018," *Earth System Science Data*, 5 December 2018, 2141–94, https://www.earth-syst-sci-data.net/10/2141/2018/.)

that come into play in future and bend the line upward or downward into a curve. However, linearity has been the case, so far, for my entire lifetime.

We do know that we had to double and double and double again the amount of carbon we were emitting before we finally saw the temperature changes that we are now experiencing. That doubling took remarkable tenacity. We had to desperately want to produce more and more goods. Or at least a small minority of us had to want to do that. We had to be willing to sit in mile upon mile of traffic jams, and a small number of us had to want to fly so much and so often so as to fill the skies with planes traveling in all directions. We fueled all this with debt, with investments that were borrowed, with cars bought on installment plans, with holidays purchased with credit cards. The ultimate driving force behind all of this was greed. Above all the greed of those who stood to become the most rich most quickly by investing their wealth—lending to others, providing the means and the money to fly overseas, to buy cars, and later spending huge sums lobbying to prevent public transport systems from being built and local holidays from being encouraged.

So how did we manage to achieve that doubling of the quantity of artificially added CO_2 in our planet's atmosphere, that huge amount emitted by industry and fossil fuel use that took place between the years 1955 and 1976? How on Earth did we ramp up the output of what was supposedly needed to burn so much coal and oil, so much gas, that we added as much in just those twenty-one years as we had added in all of recorded and estimated human history before that? For the answers, we must look at the development of the production line and the oil well, but also at the free-market ideology that would be used to justify any behavior—as long as it made money.

The discovery of what we thought were vast reserves of oil provided the fuel for yet more power plants, industry, and transport: so much more, so very quickly. The mechanization of coal mining made it possible to exhaust seams of that ancient compacted geological store of carbon faster than we had ever before dreamed of. The building of gasometers and the laying down of vast pipelines made the transportation and storage of coal gas, and then natural gas, both economically feasible and practically possible. Millions of poorly insulated homes and offices could be heated by gas, for as long as the gas supply was still plentiful.

All this dramatic increase of carbon being pumped into the atmosphere occurred almost entirely due to the activities of those who lived in the richest countries of the world. It was our homes that were first heated so well. It was our driveways on which at first one and then two cars would so often and now so normally sit. It was we who began to routinely expect to be able to have more and more that was new and to throw away the old before it was worn out. It was we who first began to fly in such large numbers to a place in the sun for a holiday. It was not the growth in the numbers of poor people in the world that burned up all this carbon.

In 1961 almost half of the 11.4 million cars produced in the world were produced in the United States. Production in that country increased by 55 percent over the course of the 1960s, even as production elsewhere began to grow at an ever-faster rate. By 1971, 26.5 million cars were being produced a year worldwide, and almost all of those that had first rolled off the production line in 1961 were still running on a road somewhere ten years later, creating far more CO_2 through their continual use than through their initial production.

By 1971, the United States' share of global car production had fallen to just over a third, or by 8.6 million cars a year, but it was still producing 2 million more a year than it had a decade earlier. Germany produced 3.8 million cars by 1971, double its 1961 output. Japan produced 3.7 million, a fifteen-fold increase on its 1961 total. France was turning out 2.7 million cars a year now, the United Kingdom and Italy 1.7 million a year each, Canada 1.1 million, and next Russia, which made "only" 0.5 million cars per annum in 1971. Whenever anyone tells you that it was too many people in the world that led to the doubling of carbon in the atmosphere, it is worth informing them just how short the list is of those countries that most contributed to that pollution.

Of course, it wasn't just cars that were responsible for our runaway CO_2 emissions. It was the building of motorways. It was the growth in the number of trucks and the amount of freight, and it was the increased production of meat that also produced other greenhouse gases. It was the use of so much more concrete than ever before. Producing a tonne of cement creates a tonne of CO_2. It was the airplanes, and the ships. It was the mass production of what had once been exclusively luxury goods. It was the growth of fashion, music, vinyl (made from fossil fuel); it was the package holiday, the automatic coffee maker and the idea some had that they might want to own their own trouser press.[14] Almost all of these goods, we were repeatedly told by advertisements, had become superseded by something newer and supposedly better, yet another must-have. It was the get-rich-quick attitude of a new kind of financier. It was, as ever, the availability of debt, but now much more debt, as we had found a new way of defining money so that banknotes no longer needed to be backed up by actual deposits of gold. The gold standard was officially ended by the United States in 1973, the dollar floating completely free in October of that year, allowing an explosion of debt. Textbooks gave us almost no warning of what was to come, because this had not happened before—at least not quite like this. However, above all, it was the car that most typified the age. In Britain, the prime minister, Margaret Thatcher, said in 1986 that a man older than twenty-six traveling by bus could count himself a failure—he should be driving a car.

By 1981 worldwide automobile production had risen again, but only slightly, to a total of 27.4 million vehicles a year rolling off the various production lines around the globe. The contribution of the United States to car production, if not yet car consumption, had finally fallen. Its production in the early 1980s shrank not just relatively but also absolutely, to 6.3 million new cars a year, significantly fewer than Japan's 7 million. German production had declined slightly, but the country was still producing almost 3.8 million cars annually. Similarly, France's output had dropped only slightly to 2.6 million. Production in Russia, in contrast, had almost tripled to 1.3 million. Italy was the next most productive, but had experienced a 26 percent fall in output to 1.3 million. That was nothing compared to the United Kingdom's drop of 45 percent to just under 1 million, only one hundred thousand more cars a year than the number produced by Spain, whose production had grown by 89 percent in the same ten years. Although that local detail is of no global consequence; what does matter is that these were all affluent nations and so by the 1980s they were still producing and consuming the bulk of most new cars worldwide—and emitting the lion's share of carbon into our ever more polluted atmosphere.

Almost all the additional carbon that has been artificially added to our atmosphere over the course of recent centuries has been added by the activities of the United States, Europe, and Japan. The carbon may have been extracted from oil fields in the Middle East, and a few more vehicles might actually have been driven in Africa than before, but those vehicles were almost all made by people in the rich world, who also drove the vast majority of them worldwide. The global pollution acceleration was still dominated by purchasing power, not numbers of people. The global share of world population living in the rich countries was falling rapidly, but their share of pollution was still rising as more and more people drove. Many families now had two cars.

By 1991, annual global car production was rising again, to 35.3 million cars a year. As production increasingly shifted overseas, the United States' share had fallen to less than a quarter of the total. Japan still ranked first, the United States second, Germany third, and France fourth, but Spain was now in fifth place, well above the United Kingdom. South Korea, a new contender, squeezed into ninth place, alongside an almost completely ignored China, which registered the production of just eighty-one thousand cars in 1991 and so earned itself a new entry, coming in at twenty-sixth in the global league table.

Zoom forward another ten years, to 2001. By then some 40.1 million new cars were being built each year, most in Japan, then Germany, and only 12 percent being made in the United States in third spot. Fourth was France, fifth South Korea; Brazil had risen to eighth; Mexico thirteenth, China fourteenth, and India fifteenth. Finally, and long after the greatest rates of pollution growth had been achieved, some of the world's most populous countries were entering the very lowest ranks of the industrial production and pollution tables.

Jump forward another decade. By 2011 52 million new cars were being produced annually. A fifth of these were made in China, which now made the most by far, then the next most in Japan, then Germany, with the United States dropping to fourth. South Korea was still fifth, but India was now sixth and Brazil seventh. Jump a further five years to 2016, with 56.6 million new cars a year, and almost a quarter now come from China, just 7 percent from the United States and 3 percent from the United Kingdom. Only by the very end of this very long period, only in the very last few years, have we seen any significant contribution to global CO_2 pollution from automotive production in the most populous countries of the world, and even then so many of the cars produced in these countries are intended for export to the rich, less populous countries.

The figures in figure 15 on global fossil fuel emissions (due to industry, transport, electricity production, and domestic uses such as heating and cooking) were presented to the world by the scientists who had estimated them on 5 December 2018 in the form of a conventional graph with an error band added.[15] The tick up at the very end appeared especially dramatic when colored in red, although it is worth noting that the final year's data were provisional. The year 2018 had not even ended at the point when the graph was released.

It is very hard to see, especially when a time trend is presented as it is in figure 15, whether there is any particular pattern to the moments when the trend rises less, or even falls, and those other points at which it accelerates.[16] The full paper that this conventional graph is taken from and its associated data sets are all available via open access.[17] This is the data source from which all the trends shown so far in this part of this chapter have been derived. It is all exactly the same data, just looked at in a different way. Compare figure 15 to figure 16, which shows the identical data, but drawn in the way that is usual in this book and highlighting the key climate change world conferences.

RECESSIONS, DEPRESSIONS, INDUSTRY, AND CARBON

The era in which CO_2 pollution around the world grew to 37.1 billion tonnes of CO_2 a year is our own. It is most if not all of the lifetime of anyone reading this book. Once you know how we ratcheted up production and pollution the next question you begin to ask is, How can we quickly reduce it again? To answer that, one of the best clues can be found in the most recent fluctuations in overall total world carbon pollution.

What, if anything at all consistent, explains the perturbations seen in the timeline of CO_2 emissions due to industry and other fossil fuel use from 1960 to 2018 shown in figure 16? Emissions grew each year in the 1960s. In half these years they grew by even more than the year before. By 1970 annual CO_2 emissions had reached the dizzying heights of 15 billion metric tonnes a year, up from 10 billion just ten years earlier. Then a slowdown ensued, and by 1974 fewer metric tonnes of carbon were being emitted than the year before, for the first time in a very long time. By 1976 it looked as if business as usual had returned, but then the economic recession of the early 1980s brought about global falls in industrial and other fossil fuel emissions. Not just in 1980, but also in 1981 and 1982.

Among the very small group of people who at the time had an inkling that growing carbon emissions might be storing up a huge problem, some of them might, had these estimates been available at that time, have drawn some comfort from what appeared to be a deceleration beginning around 1969 and looking fairly well established by 1980. However, the statistics for the late 1980s would have quashed such optimism. The fall in emissions in 1992 could have rekindled it briefly, but that was just an association with the early 1990s global economic recession, which passed quickly. The final hiatus in the global rise, in 1998, was associated with a price rise in oil the previous year that saw it hit just over $40 a barrel, before oil prices fell to their lowest levels since just after the Second World War a year later in 1999.

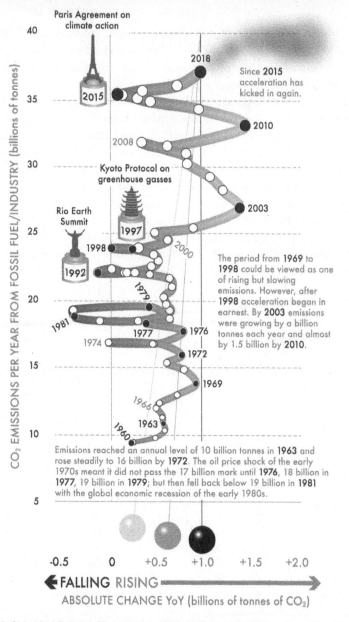

16. Global fuel/industry CO$_2$ emissions, 1960–2018 (timeline). (Drawn from data adapted from the Global Carbon Project, "Supplemental Data of Global Carbon Budget 2018" [version 1.0], Global Carbon Project, https://doi.org/10.18160/gcp-2018.)

When oil prices rise, car companies cut their production, and thus in 1998 only 37.3 million new cars were made worldwide—down from 38.5 million. The car production numbers recovered, rising to 38.8 million in 1999 and then 40.7 million in 2000. The tally fell briefly with the dot.com bubble crash (and the associated minor credit crunch) in 2001, when emissions also briefly stalled; however, car production regained strength in 2002 to 41.2 million and in 2003 to 41.7 million before slowing again, but only briefly before falling sharply in 2008 and dramatically in 2009 following the worldwide economic crash. Production most recently recovered again before falling in 2015 and then rising again. Car production is just a tiny part of all industrial and other fossil fuel–related emissions but, interestingly, it tends to wax and wane along with overall emissions trends.

Note how much can change in such a short time. Table 4 shows how in just fifteen years China went from producing almost no cars to accounting for one-quarter of total worldwide production. It shows the United States'

Table 4. Cars manufactured worldwide (millions) and percentage of industry share by country, 1961–2016

	1961	1971	1981	1991	2001	2011	2016
Cars worldwide	11.4	26.5	27.4	35.3	40.1	52.0	56.6
China	0%	0%	0%	0%	2%	19%	23%
Japan	2%	14%	25%	28%	20%	14%	14%
Germany	16%	14%	14%	13%	13%	11%	10%
United States	48%	32%	23%	15%	12%	6%	7%
India	0%	0%	0%	1%	1%	5%	5%
Spain	0%	2%	3%	6%	6%	4%	4%
South Korea	0%	0%	0%	3%	6%	6%	4%
Mexico	0%	1%	1%	2%	2%	3%	4%
Brazil	1%	1%	1%	2%	4%	4%	3%
United Kingdom	9%	7%	3%	4%	4%	3%	3%
Remainder	23%	29%	28%	27%	30%	26%	23%

Source: Bureau of Transportation Statistics, *World Motor Vehicle Production, Selected Countries* (Washington, DC: U.S. Department of Transportation, 2017), accessed 9 September 2019, https://www.bts.gov/content/world-motor-vehicle-production-selected-countries.

production possibly stabilizing after its massive postwar losses of market share up to 2011. It shows the U.K. car industry dropping from 9 percent of the global total to 3 percent, from well over half of German production in 1961 to less than a third. In addition, it may possibly show a slowdown in the rate of increase in the production of new cars overall. The growth rate and absolute rise that took place in the 1960s is yet to be exceeded, but that is currently cold comfort in a rapidly warming world.

On 8 October 2018 the Intergovernmental Panel on Climate Change (IPCC) produced a special report on global warming.[18] The report confirmed that if the additional carbon added to the atmosphere could be kept below 420 gigatons of CO_2, then there was a 66 percent chance of keeping global temperate rises below 1.5 degrees Celsius. At the current rate of emissions, that total would be breached by 2030. If the rate of emissions were to continue to increase as it has been doing since 2015, then that limit will be exceeded earlier. In contrast, if action is taken now, the date by which that limit was breached could be delayed. It is unlikely that it will not be breached, although since that 2018 report was released, at first one, then hundreds, then thousands, and then hundreds of thousands of schoolchildren around the world have begun to protest very regularly—demanding action. Perhaps we should not have been as surprised as we were when they first took to the streets in such numbers—it is they who have the most to lose. As I write in the autumn of 2019, climate and ecological protests are one of the few things not slowing down—along with the global rise in surface temperatures.

6

temperature

the catastrophic exception

Sharp and potentially devastating temperature rises of 3C to 5C in the
Arctic are now inevitable even if the world succeeds in cutting greenhouse
gas emissions.

—*UN Environment Programme, Nairobi, 13 March 2019*

Almost everything is slowing down apart from one thing: the rise in
temperature of the air around us. Even the rate of growth of CO_2 emissions
has, within most people's living memory in some years and in some places,
been slowing, if not the total amounts of emissions themselves. Most things
we think of as still accelerating are—at the very least—slowing down, if not
yet actually falling. As shown in the previous chapters, this includes the
amount of useful information we have amassed; the size of the debts we
take on; the number of books we buy (and in fact the quantity of almost
everything we now buy is now often less, in weight, than it was a few years
ago); and, most important of all, the number of children we have. But the
temperature keeps rising.

Global air temperatures appear to rise almost in direct proportion to
what we put into the atmosphere around us, and if we want them to stop
rising we urgently need to get to the point where we put no more in than
is naturally taken out—and we need to do that very soon. We are currently
a long way from reaching that point. However, before you conclude that
nothing else matters and all the other slowdowns in human life are unimportant, consider just how much we have learned about temperature
and climate in such a short time. Consider how little we really knew until

relatively recently about what turned out to be the most significant story of all. This chapter is about that story of temperature and of human learning, thinking, and adaptation.

It takes a generation to learn, *really* learn. During the course of your lifetime, you will mostly believe what you were taught at school. All that knowledge sank into your brain at just the right time in your life to get stuck there. You can try to update your knowledge, of course; you can read books like this. But whether you accept or reject most of what is said in this particular book—or any other book, for that matter—will depend as much on what you were taught to believe when you were young as on how convincing the words on these pages are. That is just how we are wired.

Our wiring is largely set in place during our childhood. For most of our history it was very efficient to be taught as a child through observation and instruction. Recent generations have seen enormous changes over their lifetimes. Before then nothing much changed during a single lifetime—wars and other disasters happened, but there was very little progress. Although we did not have schools for most children before the great acceleration, what we learned as children from the adults around us was usually useful and correct for the rest of our lives.

The introduction of mass schooling was part of the great acceleration, but even that did not keep pace with the rate of change, schools often teaching children things that turned out to be untrue later in their lives. (When I was at school in England in the 1980s I was taught that an ice age was overdue.) Unfortunately, the idea that older adults know the information a child needs is not useful when what is known alters radically. It will be the children of today who will fundamentally change things. The interesting question is just how quickly they will achieve this.

In the previous chapter we considered only emissions, not their effects. Excessive emissions from early European industrialization in the more distant past did have a cumulative effect, but much of the tiny amount of CO_2 originally released by these first industrial activities will have been reabsorbed into the oceans and mitigated through the ongoing recycling by plant life on land. The dramatic increases in human-created CO_2 emissions have occurred only in recent decades, but of course we have been polluting the atmosphere for far longer than that. The greatest effects of rising pollution would be expected to come long after the initial pollution levels had risen. This is why there is currently such widespread popular and political debate about climate change, because we have already put such huge quantities of carbon into the atmosphere, but only in very recent decades have we come to realize that this could have a very serious long-term effect, and that there is no easy way of quickly undoing the damage we have already done.

Climate change has altered politics before. In the distant past, short-term changes to climate sometimes resulted in a few years of bad harvests. Very bad harvest years were often brought about by extremely large volcanic eruptions, as happened in 1883 with Krakatoa, or caused by some other very rare natural event such as an asteroid hitting the Earth, resulting in widespread forest fires. It has been argued that short-term climate change was an important trigger for political upheavals that transformed societies, most notably the French Revolution.[1] Could human-induced climate change have similar effects in the near future?

When the price of bread or rice rose, when the reliability of food supplies faltered, when the promise of future stability seemed to have been broken—that is when trust dissipated and allegiances changed. Current governments fear a rapidly warming world with more unpredictable weather in part because a threat to the status quo on this scale could derail their own futures. (And many politicians—but far from all—really do care about the issue.) However, because the changes are not concentrated in just a few years, they do not secure the attention of politicians in the same way that more immediate concerns do. Furthermore, most politicians are of a generation that was not taught at school about global warming. It is not something they've been aware of all their lives.

In the past when the rains did not come, we were told we had angered the gods. If the dry spell continued, we looked for new gods. In later bad times, we overturned the rule of kings and queens, of tsars and other dictators who told us that they ruled by some kind of divine right. More recently, we are beginning to question our elected leaders when they and their economists tell us that all will be fine, but the priests of the new gods, our scientists, say it is not so. The good news is that because almost everything else is slowing down, we should be better able to concentrate on climate change.

THE INVENTION OF TEMPERATURE

Temperature used to be thought of as subjective, like happiness. Then the thermometer was invented. We have actual temperature records only for the period since we first constructed accurate thermometers, although proxy methods can produce reasonable records for the past two thousand years. Carbon dioxide levels have been accurately related to global temperatures for much earlier periods only very recently.[2] The Intergovernmental Panel on Climate Change Fourth Assessment Report of 2007 concluded that "average Northern Hemisphere temperatures during the second half of the 20th century were *very likely* higher than during any other 50-year period in the last 500 years and *likely* the highest in at least the past 1,300 years" (emphasis added).[3] The science of paleoclimatology has now produced global temperature graphs extending back 500 million years. We now know how unusual our times are. But just a few generations ago we did not know what the temperature was!

Gabriel Fahrenheit died in 1736, Andres Celsius in 1744. We have known precisely about temperature for just a quarter of a millennium and have measured it reliably for hospital patients only since 1868. Temperature began to be measured at many points around the planet around the same time as it started to be measured within people. Figure 17 starts at around that point in time.[4] It shows the data series for global annual mean surface air temperature changes released by the U.S. National Aeronautics and Space Administration (NASA) and smoothed by averaging over a five-year period to reduce the effects of individual measurement errors and anomalies.[5]

There are various ways of estimating average global temperature. Unlike with CO_2 emissions, there is no single system by which you can obtain a definitive global temperature measurement. Perhaps satellite measurements combined with surface measures will produce something better in future, but current estimates of average global temperatures are still only estimates, weighted averages of thousands of thermometers' measurements. However, all the various measures available produce a very similar pattern. The lines appear more irregular on the graphs if not smoothed.[6]

We began to measure both our own temperatures (roughly 37 degrees Celsius) and the planet's (then roughly averaging 15 degrees Celsius) with thermometers around the same time that we first understood our bodies were just another species of animal bodies. We have had to take a great deal on board in a very short amount of time, including the recent understanding that globally our economies are inexorably intertwined, now part of one single indivisible economic web, with a global set of consequences. The extremities of our planet, like the extremities of our bodies, tend to be a little cooler and less well connected, but they are still interdependent.

Again and again over the course of human history there have been times when the speed of change itself increased, times when plants were domesticated, times when a new religion swept a subcontinent, times when the aftermath of an ancient plague brought about a fundamental reordering. But there has never been anything comparable to what we have recently experienced. The speed at which new understandings came and new markets opened up has been staggering most recently. This phenomenon was echoed in one very small way by the speed at which the thermometer proliferated all around the globe, and more and more regular temperature measurements were taken in our obsession to understand our surroundings and to try to predict, if not to control, change.

Around the world white slatted boxes were opened, often several times daily, and the temperature within them read and recorded. These so-called Stevenson screens were invented in the 1860s by Thomas Stevenson, the father of *Treasure Island* author Robert Louis Stevenson. At first we discovered that the temperatures did not change much over the years. But then something changed. An acceleration was quietly beginning.

THE PAST FIVE GENERATIONS

Only within the past five generations have global temperatures noticeably warmed. If we use U.K. birth records to define the length of a generation (the average age of mothers when giving birth), then it is convenient to define the first of these past five generations as comprising the people born in the years between 1901 and 1928.[7] They entered a world where on-land average temperatures were just four-thousandths of a degree Celsius lower than the average when the babies of the second generation were born, hardly a detectable difference. You could even imagine that the planet was cooling and an ice age was ever so slowly approaching. Many did come to believe that a generation later.

The second generation (born between 1929 and 1955) experienced average temperatures just five-thousandths of a degree lower than the third generation. We'll call the third group Generation X, since many others do: they are the generation born between 1956 and 1981.[8] I was born bang in the middle of X. For me, and everyone else in my generational cohort, the world was warmer than that of our parents, but only slightly.

It was during the birth years of Generation X that the ideas of successive ice ages and interglacial periods within ice ages began to gain currency. Calculations were then only just being made of how the orbit and slowly changing angle of the Earth had led to a succession of interglacials.[9] We were currently in an interglacial and, all other things being equal, the

Earth was on course to get colder. But then, just after this knowledge was being propagated around the planet, something changed: all other things were certainly *not* equal.

The fourth generation, Y, those born in the years 1982 to 2011, experienced temperature rises three times greater than any of the previous three: fifteen-thousandths of a degree (so hardly noticeable). Then the fifth generation, Z, saw another threefold rise in just its first five years of existence, thrice as large as that experienced by the fourth. By the time the last members of the fifth generation are born, around the year 2042, the rise is expected to be far higher. However, between the point when this book was proposed and when it was written, an additional data point was added to the graph in figure 17 below, and the acceleration increased again, albeit ever so slightly.

If we are to appreciate change, we have to step back and see time differently than how we normally view it. Figure 17 demonstrates how hard it was to spot the upward trend until fairly recently. But it is always the question of what is to come that causes the most worry, not what has happened to date. Worry is about the future. We don't tend to worry about the recent past other than in how we should interpret it today, and the distant past—well, that is just history. Yet we can still learn a great deal from how people in that distant past chose to live their lives, organize themselves, and how they treated each other.

Calls to reduce affluent nations' consumption of goods have proliferated in recent years, although pleas to adopt a simpler life and eschew material riches go back millennia. One interpretation of recent findings by U.K. economist and climate adviser Nicolas Stern is that in order to avert catastrophic climate change, there will need to be an annual 6 percent a year drop in both production and consumption in affluent countries from 2015 onward. Bans on advertising have been proposed to help achieve this.[10] But by how much do we need to adjust and how much change for the better has already been set in motion? We must face the fact that the impending global catastrophe is the fault—largely unwittingly—of previous recent generations. But how well do we really understand what is going on?

One metric gigaton of greenhouse gases (GHG) is 1 billion metric tonnes. It is the equivalent of the emissions released by 211 million cars in a year. A gigaton is what 100 million households in the United States release in total each year by heating and powering their homes. It is almost an unfathomably large amount of gas. According to the source from which these statistics were derived, the retail mega-corporation Walmart, it will oblige its suppliers to reduce GHG emissions by one gigaton by the year 2030, or by three times the annual emissions of the state of California.[11] According to the poster in which Walmart makes this promise, a gigaton of greenhouse gases is equal to the mass of 6 million blue whales, or 100 million male African elephants.

When considering just the carbon dioxide, the average American emits about 17 metric tonnes a year as a result of consumption and travel behavior. This is about 5.5 gigatons a year for the combined total of the 2017 population of the United States, about 323 million people. A little more math tells you that $5.5 \times 6 = 33$ million blue whales, or about a tenth of a blue whale a year per American human in terms of the carbon pollution they contribute by driving their cars, flying, overconsuming, air-conditioning their homes, and so on. Or almost two African elephants' worth per American per year. What Walmart neglected to tell us in its poster was how many gigatons the company itself, not just its suppliers, currently emits.

Table 5 shows the largest firms in the world as measured by the revenue they made in 2018, the most recent year for which data are available. They are all directly involved either in the production of oil and gas, in

Table 5. Ten largest companies in the world by revenue, 2018

Company	Industry	Revenue (millions U.S.$)	Country
Walmart	Retail	514,430	United States
State Grid	Electricity	363,125	China
Sinopec	Oil and gas	326,953	China
National Petroleum	Oil and gas	326,008	China
Royal Dutch Shell	Oil and gas	311,870	Netherlands/U.K.
Toyota	Automotive	265,172	Japan
Volkswagen	Automotive	260,028	Germany
BP (British Petroleum)	Oil and gas	244,582	United Kingdom
Exxon Mobil	Oil and gas	244,363	United States
Berkshire Hathaway	Financials	242,137	United States

Source: "List of Largest Companies by Revenue," *Wikipedia*, accessed 22 April 2019, https://en.wikipedia.org/wiki/List_of_largest_companies_by_revenue.

making the cars that run on the oil, in building and running the enormous supermarkets with gigantic car parks to which you drive in your car using that oil (in the case of Walmart), or—they are the "largest shareholder in United Airlines and Delta Air Lines and a top 3 shareholder in Southwest Airlines and American Airlines" (in the case of Berkshire Hathaway, run by Warren Buffet), among much else.[12]

ONE DEGREE ABOVE NORMAL BY 2018

The timeline in figure 17 shows what is widely believed to be the effect of the relentless rise in CO_2 pollution around the planet. That pollution is measured each June high up on a mountain on a Hawaiian island in the Pacific Ocean. The average temperature around the planet, and how it is changing, is much harder to estimate because it does not spread out evenly like a gas. Temperature varies greatly not just between day and night, but according to weather, over the course of seasons, and from place to place as well as by altitude on land and in the air. There are different ways to estimate how average temperature has changed, both in recent years and across many decades. All these different methods compare their estimates to a baseline average, but that baseline varies both between methods and over time. If you are already confused, you are not alone.

Figures 17–19 and one more conventional graph (figure 20) show three different estimates of global temperature change made by different groups of scientists. They all suggest the same thing: the Earth is now quickly warming. They differ in the amount each suggests it is warming and exactly when the temperatures rose and fell. A small part of the reason for this is that different smoothing techniques have been used in each case, either by the original creators of the data or by me to try to produce a clearer picture. They are also all very unusual in the context of this book, because all indicate recent acceleration.

In figure 17 almost everything after 1990 is on the right-hand side, always rising year after year. The increase itself is also increasing, accelerating, which is why the timeline is veering further and further to the right and why climate change is our current greatest fear. As mentioned before, these graphs need high-quality data. The data for figures 17 and 18 are of high quality, but they are derived only from isolated land-based thermometers, which tend to be clustered in more affluent countries.

There are relatively few weather stations positioned out at sea and even fewer in the coldest parts of the globe. Much of the jittery nature of figure 17 is likely to be attributable to local or short-term factors, where the measurements were taken, or to volcanic eruptions. The effects of El Niño on wind patterns in the Pacific, of economic depression, or of past global war can cause a temporary lull in how much pollution is produced. To make the most of available measurements, individual results have to be weighted to produce a best guess for the overall global average of temperature.

When a global average temperature is calculated, as shown in figure 17, then a possible correlation appears to emerge between the changing price of crude oil over time and the faster and slower rises in temperatures worldwide.[13] The data used to construct figure 17 are from the NASA Goddard Institute for Space Studies (GISS). The data used here are the LOWESS (locally weighted scatterplot smoothing) five-year smoothed estimate of the annual Land-Ocean Temperature Index that these organizations produce. If you look up the source, you will discover much more detail, and also see that this is an average that includes only the open ocean: those parts of the ocean that are free of ice at all times. What matters here is that this is the time series most often presented to the world; it has just been shown in a different way in this timeline than on a conventional graph.

It is worth reiterating—especially for anyone who has been impatient enough to jump into the middle—instead of starting with the first chapter of this book—that the graph in figure 17, which I here call a timeline, uses a very rare technique in the social sciences: it graphs the change and rate of change over time together and simultaneously. When the annual temperature rise is falling, the timeline swings to the left, and when it is rising it swings to the right; how far it swings depends on the rate of change. The height of any point in the timeline shows the average temperature at that time. The data are smoothed so as to show overall changes more clearly. Even given this, the time series data have to be of high quality for this technique to work; otherwise you get spurious swings. Extra smoothing is done by always using the average of the previous and subsequent points, rather than the actual data for each point in time. This gets rid of many quirks.

Figure 17 highlights how average global land and open-ocean temperatures are now approaching 1 degree above their 1950–80 average levels. In fact, they should have passed that point long before this book is printed. But the timeline also shows how two world wars, along with other major events, may have tempered human-induced climate change, including the dramatic rise in the price of petroleum in the 1970s that led to less oil being burned and fewer new emissions at that time (as noted above

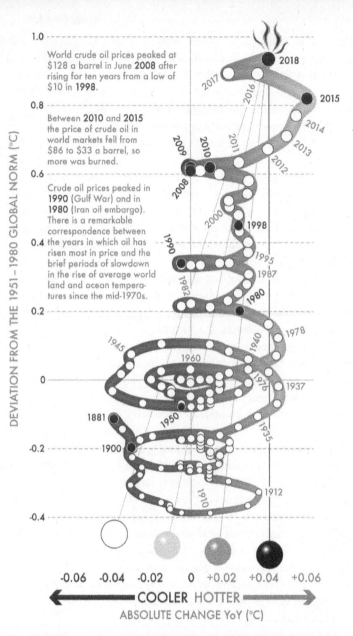

17. Average world annual land and ocean temperature, 1881–2018. (NASA Goddard Institute for Space Studies, GISTEMP v4 2019, "Global Mean Estimates Based on Land and Ocean Data," accessed 19 September 2019, https://data.giss.nasa.gov/gistemp/graphs/graph_data/Global_Mean_Estimates_based_on_Land_and_Ocean_Data/graph.csv.)

in relation to earlier graphs of emissions) and, for a time, to temperatures rising less quickly. Recession in the early 1990s and again in 2008 could be what caused temperatures not to rise around those years—perhaps. It is easy to speculate after you see one of these graphs, but look at the next two (figure 18 and figure 19) before you try to tell a particular story.

Given how slowly global temperatures were rising before the 1980s, it is remarkable that the rise was noticed at all. Given how fast they are rising now, it is remarkable that there is not more concern. Perhaps, a little like the proverbial frog being warmed up so slowly in the pot that it fails to notice and jump out before it is too late, we have become so used to being told that the world is warming slightly that when it really begins to dangerously heat up, we are no longer so surprised. As always with change, very shortly after it has happened we become used to it. According to the NASA data series, the last year that global temperatures dropped perceptibly was in 1969. They later fell, but only imperceptibly, in 1981 and 1990.

The years after 2011 require a special mention. These years have been truly remarkable. Not long into this period, the climate change deniers began to fall quiet. Following the 2008 financial crisis, the world was still sunk into the greatest economic depression since the 1930s—in fact, it was larger even than the famous Great Depression itself—and yet this event appeared to have no impact on the rise in temperature, apparently none at all. Had we reached a stage by 2008 in which the greenhouse gas levels in the atmosphere, with so much more CO_2 still being pumped into it, were such that the slight perturbations in emissions brought about by the recession no longer had much effect on the annual temperature rise?

By early 2016 it looked as if the global temperature might soon be completely out of control. Sea levels are currently about 130 meters higher than they were twenty thousand years ago. They have risen twenty-three centimeters since 1880 and are currently rising over three centimeters a decade. Increasing extreme weather events magnify the seriousness of any sea level rise. Melting of all the ice caps and glaciers could potentially raise it by many tens of meters. Just one meter would be devastating for much of humanity. Have we entered a period of very dangerous "positive feedback" as a result of changes that have already happened? At the very least, we should be scared.

And then, finally, there was a speck of hope. The temperature rise in 2016 was not quite as fast as the rise in 2015. Perhaps we were not yet entering our species' death spiral? However, much else affects global temperatures apart from human-induced emissions of CO_2 and overall greenhouse gas levels, including deforestation, the melting of the permafrost, and global livestock farming, which includes about a billion cattle and around another billion sheep. Then there is the absorption of gases by the oceans and the (not yet known) extent to which the deep ocean is a heat sink. Add in the effect of the shrinking overall size of the ice caps that reflect solar energy, in what is called the albedo effect, and you can begin to veer again toward despair. The relative future contributions of all these factors are still uncertain. This is despite the enormous numbers of books and scientific papers written, and the unprecedented (but no longer accelerating) quantity of scientific research being undertaken worldwide.

There is, of course, still much controversy. The next timeline, figure 18, uses a different data series. This one is constructed by Kevin Cowtan and Robert Way of the University of York in the United Kingdom. It is a particular correction to the HadCRUT4 U.K. Meteorological (Met) Office temperature record and runs from 1850 until 2017.[14] The Met Office temperature record was based on data that excluded the polar regions and covers only five-sixths of the planet. The data have been adjusted to cover the whole planet, and they show a record that is very similar to that in the timeline above—except that there is now no sign of any deceleration in 2016 and 2017. The speck of hope has gone.

The timeline in figure 18 starts a little earlier than that in figure 17. It suggests that in the period 1850 to 1922 there was little systematic change, and that whatever contribution the First World War or the greater temporary reduction in industrial production due to the 1918–19 influenza pandemic might have made, it really did not matter in the greater scheme of things. Instead, it was not until 1922 that something changed significantly. But you would not have concluded that if you looked only at the timeline in figure 17.

As the authors of figure 18 have pointed out: "Climate scientists have traditionally looked at climate over long periods—30 years or more. However, media and public interest in shorter term trends has focused attention on the past 15–16 years. Short term trends are much more complex because they can be affected by many factors which cancel out over longer periods. To interpret the 16-year trend, it is necessary to take into account all of these factors, including volcanoes, the solar cycle, particulate emissions

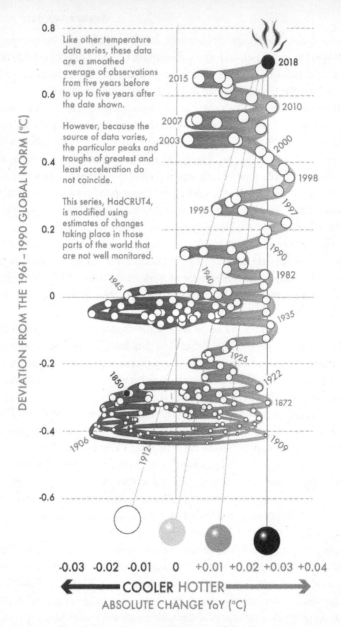

Like other temperature data series, these data are a smoothed average of observations from five years before to up to five years after the date shown.

However, because the source of data varies, the particular peaks and troughs of greatest and least acceleration do not coincide.

This series, HadCRUT4, is modified using estimates of changes taking place in those parts of the world that are not well monitored.

DEVIATION FROM THE 1961–1990 GLOBAL NORM (°C)

0.8
0.6
0.4
0.2
0
-0.2
-0.4
-0.6

2015
2018
2010
2007
2003
2000
1998
1997
1995
1990
1982
1940
1945
1935
1925
1922
1872
1850
1906
1912
1909

-0.03 -0.02 -0.01   0   +0.01 +0.02 +0.03 +0.04

⟵ COOLER HOTTER ⟶

ABSOLUTE CHANGE YoY (°C)

18. Average world annual land and ocean temperature, 1850–2018. (Data adapted from Kevin Cowtan and Robert Way, Version 2.0 temperature series, long reconstruction [1850–present], updated 21 June 2019, with corrections for bias from the HadCRUT4 data set, U.K. Met Office, http://www-users.york.ac.uk/~kdc3/papers/coverage2013/series.html.)

from the far East and changes in ocean circulation. The bias addressed by this paper is just one piece in that puzzle, although a largish one."[15]

The one question raised by both figure 17 and figure 18 is: What occurred after 1978? Why does the temperature appear to have truly escaped control from that point onward? If you look back at the record of emissions in figure 16, you can see a buildup prior to 1978 that was unusually large. Next, after a brief hiatus during the economic recession of the early 1980s, the temperatures simply rise and rise. There have been no unusually large volcanic eruptions in recent decades; the solar cycle (of sunspots) has not been especially unusual; there have at times been huge forest fires in Southeast Asia that may have had particular influences, but we do not know of any especially great changes in ocean circulation other than the periodic ones that we have now become used to.

The one thing we can be fairly sure of is that many people's behavior has altered considerably since the late 1970s. If you base a global society and economy on ever-increasing consumerism (the dream of almost every business) and on ever-rising debt (which many money lenders prefer to call investment), and if becoming wealthy as quickly as you can is seen as the most laudable thing a person can do, then what happens? The one surefire way to become wealthier is to use more energy from burning fossil fuels to make many more things, especially things such as cars, which themselves spew out yet more CO_2, and then you will increase the amount of greenhouse gases in the atmosphere almost as quickly as it is possible to do. We know that this leads to global warming, with a time lag that isn't very long at all.

At some point the two timelines above will cross back over the vertical axis. If you are young today, it might well be when you are still alive. What we must hope is that it does not rise too high before it does that. Because the rise in the timelines is largely up to us, it is also up to us to ensure that the last great acceleration ends as soon as possible.

CLIMATE CHANGE SKEPTICS

We are the first generation to know we are destroying our planet and the last one that can do anything about it.

—*Tanya Steele, chief executive, World Wildlife Fund*[16]

Some people are extremely skeptical of claims that we are destroying the ecosystems we rely on. They advocate the use of alternative data series that, they suggest, do not show such incontrovertible warming. The third and final temperature estimate data set used in this book is version 6.0 of the University of Alabama in Huntsville (UAH) Temperature Dataset, shown here in figure 19, which indicates far greater fluctuation than the two series above. It is based on estimates of monthly temperatures around the globe as sourced from satellite images. (Note that this data series begins only in 1978, when satellites first began to send back suitable data.)

This third data series looks very different from those above—and the source of the information used to construct this series is also very different. Information from successive NOAA (U.S. National Oceanic and Atmospheric Administration) satellites have been used, as these carry instruments that measure radiances: specifically, the natural microwave thermal emissions from oxygen in the atmosphere. After multiple revisions to their calculations, John Christy and Roy Spencer of the University of Alabama produced the current data series. Here the calculations shown are for average annual world lower troposphere temperature (note they are not smoothed over several years as figures 17 and 18 are). Corrections had to be made for the satellites slowly moving nearer to the Earth and thus monitoring slightly smaller areas of the planet, for the use of different instruments in newer satellites, and for much else besides those two complex issues. Because the satellite data, with their wide geographical sweep, were thought to be more accurate than data collected by thermometer, they were not smoothed over time.

Timelines produce a mess like the one shown in figure 19 if there are no long-term significant trends, if they have not been smoothed over several years, and if the quality of the data is poor. Figure 20 at the end of this chapter shows exactly the same data using a more conventional method, and you may conclude that this third data series does not actually differ greatly in what it implies is happening compared with figures 17 and 18. The data are just far more jittery, but they do not refute the now widespread conclusion that the world really is heating up and most of the heating has occurred recently and is showing—as yet—absolutely no signs of slowing down.

Note that the lower years in the tangled mess shown in figure 19 tend to be in the 1970s or 1980s, and the more recent years are highest up, in the warmest period of the timeline. Note also that the baseline we are comparing against has been changed to the very recent 1981–2010 period, as the baseline can include years only for which there are satellite data.

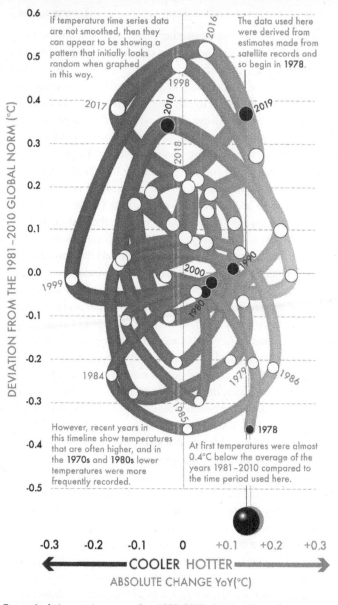

19. Tropospheric temperature anomalies, 1978–2019. (National Space Science and Technology Center, University of Alabama, Huntsville, UAH v6.0 satellite temperature data set, global temperature report, version 6, lower troposphere data, updated December 2018, https://www.nsstc.uah.edu/data/msu/v6.0/tlt/uahncdc_lt_6.0.txt.)

Consequently, the average temperature above the baseline between 1981 and 2010 is, by definition, zero. Note also the incredible rise and fall in global temperature estimated to have taken place from 1997 to 1999. Was this real or an error? Did the whole planet really rise in temperature by almost half a degree Celsius in just one year and fall again by as much in the next twelve months? Using the raw satellite data to postulate average atmospheric temperatures is a complex proxy process, and it is worth noting that a different research team (Remote Sensing Systems), using exactly the same data, calculated considerably higher temperature rises that were much more consistent with the surface temperature records used in the previous timelines in this book. However, here I have used the University of Alabama figures, not because I consider them more accurate, but because this is the set that climate change skeptics frequently used to cite.

The rise in temperatures within the past decade has now ended the debate. Most people in the world who know about these issues understood by early 2019 that we had at that point twelve years to reduce human-created emissions of carbon dioxide by 50 percent if we—the people with just one planet—were to probably avoid warming of 1.5 degrees Celsius. The Intergovernmental Panel on Climate Change at that time could have picked any other reduction target, and had it done that, people would then have become fixated on a different time period rather than twelve years, but the message would have been the same. The relationship between the amount of carbon we emit and the rise in temperatures has now been shown to be linear. Understanding this and its implications is what matters most.

The message is that if we do not start now, in 2019–20, then we will have to collectively curb our emissions far faster in future or even somehow achieve negative emissions. We would have to find ways of taking more CO_2 out of the atmosphere than we put in. This cannot easily be done just by planting trees; they take so long to grow and we generate so much carbon now. But all this does not mean we are doomed if we haven't reached the target of halving emissions by around 2030.

The world as we know it will not end if there is a rise in global average temperature above 1.5 degrees Celsius, but the harm to the planet and to us brought about by further increases in temperature almost certainly increases nonlinearly. We don't have to wait until the rise has reached that point to make such statements. There is already enough evidence of that. While the twelve-year target set in late 2018 fits neatly into a catchy slogan, it is arbitrary, and must not be seen as implying that there is a particular deadline after which all is lost, or before which we can worry less.

Given what we know now, and with things changing as they are, we should expect average global sea level rises of between one and two meters by 2100. That might not sound like much, but it would be devastating for many coastal cities. Because of how water expands when warmer, and because of the melting of polar ice, we now know that longer-term sea level rise can be confidently predicted by the temperature level reached at the point of the final rise in human-induced warming. It is now thought that it could possibly reach ten meters (on average worldwide) if we don't limit warming to 2 degrees Celsius and avoid most of the ice caps melting at higher temperatures than that.

Many weather extremes, including heat waves and droughts, have already become more frequent. Strong hurricanes and tornadoes are now expected to occur more often; weaker hurricanes might, in turn, happen less often. The jet stream might oscillate more widely, resulting in much more common and very much more severe winter storms, more heat waves, and more summer flooding. But the scientific analyses published in the next few years will better inform us. What we know for sure now is that between 1850 and 2020, the world will have warmed by approximately 1.1 degrees and—bar the odd volcanic contribution—all that extra warming has been caused by us.

We rightly associate acceleration with being out of control. The arrow or rock that accelerates toward us is a highly unpredictable danger. But faced with phenomena that are utterly new, we find that we have no inherent sense of danger other than the extent to which we can associate modern accelerations with our previous mental models of danger. A new type of disaster is very hard to imagine.

Even the data most favored by climate skeptics show clear evidence of global warming. Figure 20 uses data identical to those used to draw figure 19. Again, the zero line merely shows the 1981–2010 average. Sometimes conventional methods are better to show data that contain high variability, especially when what should be revealed has become so obvious. When you look at the conventional graph in figure 20 it is easier to dismiss the 1998 result as spurious. In fact, you can also see that the 1996–2000 average is only slightly higher than 1995 and slightly lower than 2001, but that might be just a coincidence. We have no idea why some of the annual

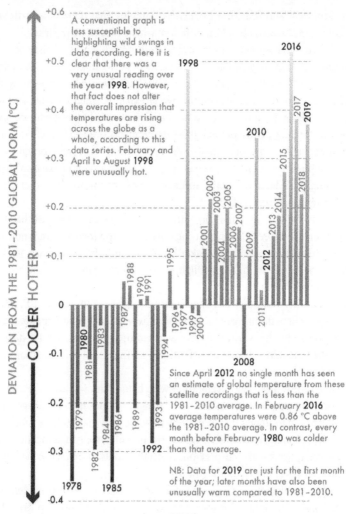

A conventional graph is less susceptible to highlighting wild swings in data recording. Here it is clear that there was a very unusual reading over the year **1998**. However, that fact does not alter the overall impression that temperatures are rising across the globe as a whole, according to this data series. February and April to August **1998** were unusually hot.

Since April **2012** no single month has seen an estimate of global temperature from these satellite recordings that is less than the 1981–2010 average. In February **2016** average temperatures were 0.86 °C above the 1981–2010 average. In contrast, every month before February **1980** was colder than that average.

NB: Data for **2019** are just for the first month of the year; later months have also been unusually warm compared to 1981–2010.

YEAR

20. Tropospheric temperature anomalies, 1978–2019. (This uses exactly the same data as figure 19, but shown on a conventional graph.)

data in figure 20 spike so abruptly. We do know that it does not alter the overall medium-term trend toward hotter and hotter weather.

So, halfway through the story of this book, let's next turn to how many people are likely to be affected in the near future by the temperature rises to come and how the population growth projected by the United Nations to occur in the next eighty years compares to how human numbers have been growing in the past 2,020 years, both worldwide and within particular parts of the planet. How many of us will there soon be, and to what extent might the slowdown in our future population growth help mitigate our failure, to date, to curtail the excessive behavior of the few that has now resulted in accelerating and very damaging climate change?

7

demographics

hitting the population brakes

A growing body of opinion believes the UN is wrong. We will not reach
11 billion by 2100. Instead, the human population will top out at somewhere between 8 and 9 billion around the middle of the century, and then
begin to decline.

—*Darrell Bricker and John Ibbitson, 27 January 2019*

In early 2019 awareness that human population growth was ending began
to spread more widely. To much acclaim, Darrell Bricker, the chief operating officer of the polling firm Ipsos Public Affairs, and his colleague John
Ibbitson published the book *Empty Planet: The Shock of Global Population
Decline*. As one journalist put it: "It is full of fascinating speculation and
written with an energy that degenerates only occasionally into jauntiness."[1]

Bricker and Ibbitson had amassed a wealth of evidence for their central claim that the United Nations had simply got its future projections very
wrong. In particular they quoted Jørgen Randers, a Norwegian academic
who had in 1972 predicted an unsustainable world population of 15 billion
people by 2030, but had now changed his assessment because fertility rates
had fallen so rapidly recently: "The world population will never reach nine
billion people. . . . It will peak at 8 billion in 2040, and then decline."

Randers, a professor of climate strategy based in Oslo, believes that
birth rates will decline faster than UN demographers currently project.
Randers is no utopian. Despite his belief that there will be around 3 billion fewer people than the UN demographers project in the next fourscore
years, "the world will [still] be well on its way towards a climate catastro-

phe in the second half of the 21st century," with CO_2 emissions peaking in 2040, resulting in temperatures passing 2 degrees above what was recently normal by 2050.[2] Suggestions that even more rapid population growth slowdown will occur in the very near future are not predictions that all will soon be well. This is because the pollution problem was never a population problem.

Bricker and Ibbitson concentrated on population growth decline, not the wider picture, and so are far more optimistic. They reported that Wolfgang Lutz, one of the world's most well-respected demographers, along with his colleagues at the International Institute for Applied Systems Analysis in Vienna, now believe that the global human population will stabilize by 2050 and then begin to fall because the human slowdown is now already accelerating. In 2018 Lutz and his colleagues stated that they would now forecast the world population peak to occur shortly after 2070. Their projection would mean between 2 billion and 3 billion fewer humans by 2100 than the UN estimate.[3]

It has been obvious for some time to a small group of demographers that the human population slowdown began many decades ago, but just how rapid that slowdown is has been apparent only more recently. This is true when people are counted across the globe as a whole, but the slowdown began even earlier in certain countries and, especially when it comes to very low birth rates, within a few cities in those countries. The global point of greatest change, the international pivot point, came around the year 1968. The evidence that slowdown is really upon us with a vengeance is now so strong that Bricker and Ibbitson were able to quote a recent Deutsche Bank report by Sanjeev Sanyal that suggests the peak in human numbers on Earth will be reached at just 8.7 billion in 2055, and decline to 8 billion by 2100.

There is currently much criticism of many of the more dramatic population slowdown scenarios.[4] The criticism is often aimed at the assumption that slowdowns will simply happen automatically, without further encouragement, such as the role and effect of expanding access to good-quality, free secondary education. I would add expanding free access to tertiary education, which appears to be the most effective contraception of all—not urbanization, as is often claimed. Perhaps the strongest criticism of these low projections of growth is that they assume no world war in the next few decades, no great famine, no pandemic, no new disaster that upsets our established social orders, which would all probably have, long term, the opposite effect. The idea that we will somehow avoid any such calamity in the 2020s, 2030s, 2040s, 2050s, and 2060s may be very wishful thinking indeed. I'll be dead by then. My children can find out. But if you have any faith in our ability to learn from past mistakes, in the power of a far better educated global population than we have ever had before, and in more and more women securing positions of power, then you can have some hope.

THE SLOWDOWN IN WORLD POPULATION

Because this fact is so very important, it is worth reiterating that the slowdown in global population was evident some time ago, and it has been well known among demographers for all of this current century. I was a little late to catch on: in 2013 I wrote a book titled *Population 10 Billion*. The publisher added the dramatic subtitle *The Coming Demographic Crisis and How to Survive It*, which did rather detract from the main point of the book—that there was no crisis, and that we could reasonably expect never to reach a global population of 10 billion. What I thought most likely at the time was that we would see a maximum of 9.3 billion around the year 2060, dipping perhaps to 7.4 billion by 2100. I made the mistake of putting that crucial information on page 350. No one reads as far as page 350 in a book like that. I should have put the news on the cover. To be honest, though, I was a little worried about sticking my neck out. I had previously published those estimates in 2011 in an obscure statistical magazine.[5] Statistical magazines are good places to hide things you are not sure of, just in case they turn out to be wrong. Almost no one reads them. So my estimate was that global human population would peak a little higher than the Deutsche Bank researcher Sanjeev Sanyal now estimates, but would also fall faster than many now think it may fall.

As events transpired, I was glad I had hidden my predictions. In the very week that *Population 10 Billion* was published, the United Nations upped its estimate of the future 2100 global human population total from 10 billion to 11 billion. I would have looked a little silly had I put the words *"7.4 billion—don't worry"* on the cover, but that would have been better than suggesting that the UN methodology was robust. In 2015 the UN published a revision that said the global population would reach 11.2 billion by 2100, and then in 2017 it suggested exactly the same number. It almost seemed as if the organization was getting better and better at this guessing game, but it turns out it wasn't. The UN's demographers were simply becoming surer of themselves. The same issue remained, one that I and many others had spotted years before: the UN's demographers had ignored a baby boom. Their models did not take into account the fact that birth rates between 2011 and 2019 were high because these were the great-grandchildren of so many people born worldwide shortly after the Second World War—the original peak was simply working its way through the generations. The UN also failed to recognize what had made fertility so high in African countries in recent years (on which more below) or that the world was still experiencing a huge cultural shift regarding the rights of, and respect for, women.

You might have thought that demographers would know all about baby booms (if not about cultural shifts), but that is not how their international models work. To be fair to the UN's demographers, the crucial baby boom was not well monitored in most of the world. At the time of the partition of India (1947) and the Chinese communist revolution (1949), there was enormous loss of life, but also many more babies were born than usual. When things appear to be going wrong, and when there is turmoil, we have more babies. When they go well, we have far fewer. When we feel really safe, we have even fewer than that. When you can trust that society will look after you, then you can more happily choose to have no babies, or just one. You do not need the insurance policy of having children to look after you in the future—or a great number of children, if their individual chances of survival are poor. And when women are able to make their own choices about whether to have a child and how many to have, then—everything changes.

It will soon become clear who was right and who was wrong. However, the slowdown that the UN's demographers have already reported, the slowdown to their current prediction of 11.2 billion by 2100, is clearly dramatic enough. The timelines in this chapter use the UN projections that lead to 11.2 billion eighty years from now, even though I believe they are overestimates. I use them because they still show rapid slowdown and because I think these are conservative estimates—the greatest that future growth will likely be. Population growth was enormous worldwide in the 1940s, 1950s, and at the start of the 1960s: the growth rate itself was growing! But then, quite suddenly, but also remarkably smoothly, the rate of growth began to slow, almost as if someone had pressed down on a giant brake pedal.

Between 1980 and today, global human population growth rates became stable at around 80 million more people being added per year. This stable growth is attributable to a combination of fewer births and, crucially, fewer deaths: there was now growth mainly because the people alive at that time were living longer. Next, because there are limits to the amount that life expectancy can increase, from 2020 onward that rate of worldwide population growth is itself projected to fall. The UN thinks that it will fall very steadily, to 70 million a year being added in 2030, 60 million in 2040, 50 million in 2050, 40 million in 2060, just over 30 million being added each year in 2070, and then a little slowdown itself in the rate of slowdown. Why? Because the UN demographers currently believe that the whole world will move toward a two-child norm. However, that key assumption has no historical or scientific basis. This, above all else, is why we should not necessarily expect to peak in our numbers as a species at the population maximum of 11.2 billion people in the near future. Everything has changed so much that choosing to have no children, or just one child, is for the majority of women worldwide now just as easy as—if not easier than—choosing to have two.

Sometimes insight can be found in the most unlikely places. Commenting on a February 2019 story in the British *Daily Mail* newspaper, sensationally headlined "Will the World RUN OUT of People?" "Paul" noted that there is no question that this is true, and that it has been obvious for a long time to anybody with a population chart and a basic understanding of mathematics. He said that the "negative second derivative of population (namely, a decline in growth) is as clear as day and must lead eventually to a negative first derivative (a decline in population itself)," concluding, "Why otherwise intelligent people (e.g., Stephen Hawking) can't/couldn't see this is astounding."[6]

Stephen Hawking's warning had been made a year before: "Humans must leave Earth in the next 200 years if we want to survive."[7] The human species is not, of course, neatly divided into two camps of remarkably clever and remarkably stupid people. We are mostly pretty average, and all of us are capable of being quite stupid from time to time. But occasionally someone, with time and space to think, is lucky enough to be in the right place at the right time to be the one to whom exceptional insight is later ascribed. Were we cleverer, we would not do this ascribing so frequently. We would not be so quick to put a few people—the brilliant—on pedestals and claim that the rest of humanity is largely incapable of insight.

The readers offering comments under this *Daily Mail* article will have been drawn from the most literate and highly educated tenth of the world's population. The observations that followed Paul's included: "The world will be a better place once all humans are gone"; "Over-population is becoming an issue, but Divine intervention will save the planet. God, in His infinite mercy and wisdom, will address this as always with famine, war and plague. Have faith!"; "Genghis Khan killed so many people it cooled the planet (so it's believed). Maybe he had the right idea?"; "I think Obama started this. We are doomed"; and (one of the nastiest) "Only partially true. The world will just run out of whites."

Don't despair. Just don't expect great demographic insights either from the people who spend their lives studying the Big Bang and black holes, or from the tiny minority of men (and very occasionally women) who splash their rapid-fire views, like graffiti, in the comment boxes underneath on-line newspaper articles. Neither group has put their minds to the matter of human population numbers for very long. Although occasionally a few, such as Paul above, have thought a little more carefully than others.

If you look carefully at figure 21, you'll see that all but the most recent 170 years of human demographic history squeezes into the bottom eleventh of the graph. Since that point, we have always had growth. The growth took off from around 1850, when the British Empire was beginning to approach its zenith. By this point Britain had already invaded some 171 of the present 193 members of the United Nations, although most were not yet actual countries.[8] The effects of these invasions were devastating. The British were not alone in this kind of endeavor, or the first to undertake these practices, but they were certainly the most effective.

If you invade a continent that had previously been largely or entirely left alone, such as Australia or the Americas, you fundamentally disrupt societies every bit as much as if they had been invaded by aliens landing from outer space with unbelievable weapons, incredibly lethal attitudes, and the deadliest of previously unencountered germs. At first there is rapid population decline in the territories that are invaded. The decline is so great that overall worldwide human population slowdown occurs. Look carefully at the decade prior to 1850 to see proof of this. The "scramble for Africa" took place long after the rise of the European slave trade, which was established to populate the Americas with free labor (free in terms of not wage-paid). The transatlantic slave trade devastated Africa. After the initial shock and destruction, the social structures and norms that had developed over centuries across the continent (and everywhere else in the world that was invaded and colonized), norms that had before produced relatively stable populations, broke down. Then acceleration set in. That acceleration

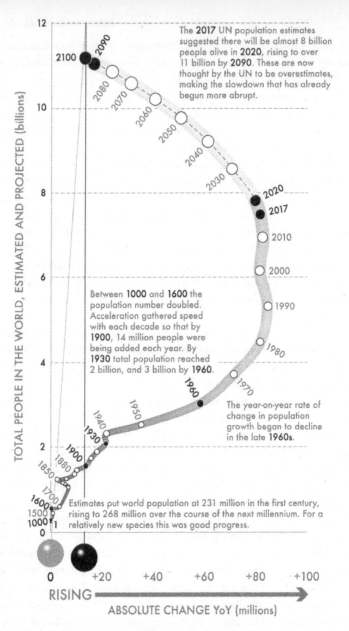

The **2017** UN population estimates suggested there will be almost 8 billion people alive in **2020**, rising to over 11 billion by **2090**. These are now thought by the UN to be overestimates, making the slowdown that has already begun more abrupt.

Between **1000** and **1600** the population number doubled. Acceleration gathered speed with each decade so that by **1900**, 14 million people were being added each year. By **1930** total population reached 2 billion, and 3 billion by **1960**.

The year-on-year rate of change in population growth began to decline in the late **1960s**.

Estimates put world population at 231 million in the first century, rising to 268 million over the course of the next millennium. For a relatively new species this was good progress.

TOTAL PEOPLE IN THE WORLD, ESTIMATED AND PROJECTED (billions)

RISING ➤

ABSOLUTE CHANGE YoY (millions)

21. World: total population, years 1–2100. (The data for figures 21–31 are from the Angus Maddison Project Database 2018, hosted by the University of Groningen, https://www.rug .nl/ggdc/historicaldevelopment/maddison/releases/maddison-project-database-2018, updated using data from UN Department of Economic and Social Affairs, *UN World Population Prospects: The 2017 Revision*, https://www.un.org/development/desa/publications/world -population-prospects-the-2017-revision.html.)

resulted in the huge human population growth, worldwide, from the 1850s to the 1930s.

In terms of total population, figure 21 shows that most of the slowdown is yet to come, but we know it has already begun because fertility has already fallen, and population continues to rise only because people are living longer. Figure 22 highlights the growth that comes after devastating events, including the invasion of the Americas and colonization of Africa.

World War II, which began in 1939, brought a temporary halt in the growing rate of population growth. Not only did many people die, many others avoided having children then, or were unable to have children because they were physically separated. Across Europe and North America fertility rates had fallen rapidly in the 1930s; then just a little later during the war, they plummeted. But once war was over, many couples that had delayed starting a family quickly began to have children. This baby boom extended across the postwar rich world, but also in China (following the turmoil of the revolution), and in India (following the terrible death toll in the time just after the partition of 1947). A second, smaller baby boom in the 1960s prolonged the acceleration, but in the late 1960s the rate of growth began to fall (shown by the circles in the graph beginning to bunch closer together), with the last spurt of acceleration petering out when the grandchildren of that first postwar baby boom generation were born in the 1980s and, finally, most recently, when their great-grandchildren appeared. It becomes clearer if you redraw figure 21 on a log scale, as the timeline in figure 22 shows.

Figure 22 actually employs a log-log scale. Not only is the total population number logged, but so too is the change. Three major interruptions in the growth of the global population become evident: the slowdowns from 1500 to 1600, 1820 to 1850, and 2020 onward. The first two ended in population explosions due partly to the great disruptions of those years.

If more frequent global estimates had been used, more interruptions would have been evident, such as those due to the Antonine plague of 165 CE; the plague of St. Justinian, which started in 541 (when around a sixth of the world's population died); and the Black Death, which reached Europe in 1347 and wiped out about half of the population. However, it is the impact of the diseases that Europeans brought to the Americas that show up most clearly. These resulted in the first sustained global slowdown in population growth, from 1500 to 1600, and are all too evident in figure 22. The second occurs with the colonization of the majority of the world by

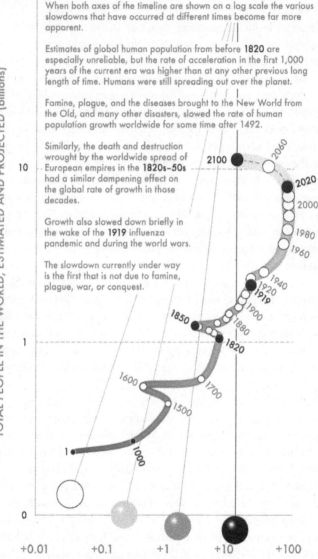

When both axes of the timeline are shown on a log scale the various slowdowns that have occurred at different times become far more apparent.

Estimates of global human population from before **1820** are especially unreliable, but the rate of acceleration in the first 1,000 years of the current era was higher than at any other previous long length of time. Humans were still spreading out over the planet.

Famine, plague, and the diseases brought to the New World from the Old, and many other disasters, slowed the rate of human population growth worldwide for some time after 1492.

Similarly, the death and destruction wrought by the worldwide spread of European empires in the **1820s–50s** had a similar dampening effect on the global rate of growth in those decades.

Growth also slowed down briefly in the wake of the **1919** influenza pandemic and during the world wars.

The slowdown currently under way is the first that is not due to famine, plague, war, or conquest.

TOTAL PEOPLE IN THE WORLD, ESTIMATED AND PROJECTED (billions)

RISING
ABSOLUTE CHANGE YoY (millions)

22. World: total population, years 1–2100 (log scale). (Data from the Angus Maddison Project and *UN World Population Prospects 2017*.)

Europeans at the start of the nineteenth century. The third great slowdown in the Earth's human population rise is taking place right now, arguably having begun with the faintest of signs in 1968, but with the greatest deceleration of all set to occur from 2020 onward.

You may look at figure 22 and conclude that history could repeat itself. The current global slowdown could rebound again after 2100. Stephen Hawking may turn out to be correct after all, and within the next two hundred years humans will leave the Earth and begin to expand rapidly in number again. However, this third great slowdown is a slowdown of our choosing, rather than one forced upon us or occurring without us realizing why, and the vast majority of people doing the choosing are women.

Space travel, in the main, is an archetypal modern boys' dream. Choosing to have no children, or just one or two children, is largely a female prerogative, although for women to be able to exercise that choice, the circumstances have to be right. The circumstances are now right, although they differ in different places. The rest of this chapter takes a tour around the planet and draws this same timeline graph for different countries and also the continents they lie in.

THE SLOWDOWN IN THE UNITED STATES AND CHINA

When it comes to money, the two most powerful states in the world today are the United States and China. When purchasing power parity is taken into account, China is estimated to be more productive than the United States. This is according to statistics produced by the World Bank, the International Monetary Fund, and the CIA. But, of course, that productivity, and the income it results in, is shared out among far more people in China, and (interestingly) roughly as unequally as it is shared out in the United States.[9]

The population estimates used here are a combination of two time series. The first was produced by Angus Maddison (1926–2010), one of the world's best-known economic historians. His series included only a limited number of years before 1950 and so, on these timelines, only those years are shown. He produced the most widely used estimates of past human populations according to contemporary geographical boundaries. Such was his tenacity and precision that a decade after his death they remain by far the best estimates available. Here Maddison's estimates have been adjusted slightly so they flow smoothly into the second data set, which is the

United Nations' 2017 revision of its world population prospects, running from 1950 through to 2100.

To produce the timelines shown in this chapter, Maddison's data are simply scaled by a constant factor in each geographical area so that his estimate for 1950 is adjusted to be equal to that which the UN today produces. The effect of doing this is minuscule, but it ensures that there is no sudden spurious change in that year. The UN data are the latest available at the time of writing and are now widely believed to underestimate the population changes we can expect to see in the next eighty years. In other words, what the timelines show here is very likely a less dramatic slowdown than the one that will actually occur.

The population of what is now the United States is estimated to have reached 2 million people by the year 1500. Those people were almost all the ancestors of the migrants who had arrived, possibly more than twenty millennia ago, most likely along a land bridge that is today submerged beneath the Bering Strait.[10] Others might well have arrived later from elsewhere, but they mixed and spread out. The earliest inhabitants of what is now the United States created origin stories that did not involve having come from somewhere else (very few such stories in the world do). The population of what is now the United States was almost always much lower than in the warmer lands to its south. But ever so slowly, the original Americans north of the Rio Grande grew in number to reach 2 million, or less than 0.5 percent of what was then the total size of the human species, at which point Columbus crossed the Atlantic and landed to the south of what is now the United States. Maddison and all other sources then report repeated decimation. Numbers fell to 1.5 million by 1600, and to just 1 million by 1700. The *Mayflower* made land in Cape Cod in 1620, but long before that date diseases had spread up from further south, from the first encounters. The diseases spread outward from the lands reached by the European invaders, including the conquistadors, and into regions they never invaded. All this is barely visible in the first few points in the timeline shown in figure 23.

From about 1700 onward, the population of the territory that would later be known as the United States of America grew and grew as more ships from the Old World arrived, bringing settlers from Europe and enslaved people from Africa, and the settlers and slaves started having children. The first U.S. census was conducted in 1790, and population estimates are much more reliable after that, although the indigenous population was not included in any census until 1870!

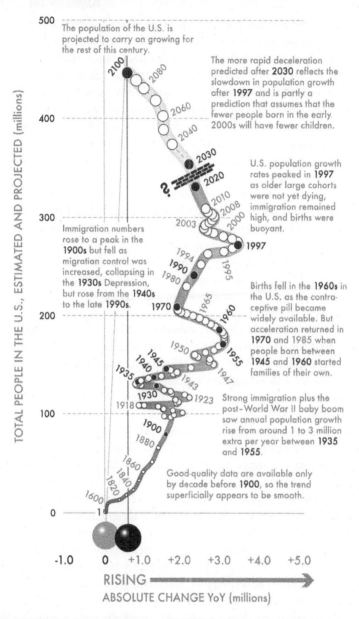

TOTAL PEOPLE IN THE U.S., ESTIMATED AND PROJECTED (millions)

The population of the U.S. is projected to carry on growing for the rest of this century.

The more rapid deceleration predicted after **2030** reflects the slowdown in population growth after **1997** and is partly a prediction that assumes that the fewer people born in the early 2000s will have fewer children.

U.S. population growth rates peaked in **1997** as older large cohorts were not yet dying, immigration remained high, and births were buoyant.

Immigration numbers rose to a peak in the **1900s** but fell as migration control was increased, collapsing in the **1930s** Depression, but rose from the **1940s** to the late **1990s**.

Births fell in the **1960s** in the U.S. as the contraceptive pill became widely available. But acceleration returned in **1970** and **1985** when people born between **1945** and **1960** started families of their own.

Strong immigration plus the post–World War II baby boom saw annual population growth rise from around 1 to 3 million extra per year between **1935** and **1955**.

Good-quality data are available only by decade before **1900**, so the trend superficially appears to be smooth.

RISING
ABSOLUTE CHANGE YoY (millions)

-1.0   0   +1.0   +2.0   +3.0   +4.0   +5.0

23. United States: total population, years 1–2100. (Data from the Angus Maddison Project and *UN World Population Prospects 2017*.)

Every decade from 1790 onward, despite the American Civil War, the U.S. population grew by more than the decade before, right through to 1902 when there was the first ever hint of a deceleration, then acceleration again through to 1905. Events far off in other continents were the main drivers of these fluctuations. Fewer migrants arrived in the United States during the First World War in Europe, when almost 3 million U.S. troops were sent abroad. The influenza pandemic increased the deceleration, but then the troops returned, along with yet more migrants, and population growth peaked in 1923. There was a brief hiatus in 1924, when racist quotas were brought in that favored immigrants from certain nations.

The 1930s brought slowdown, as a result of both the Great Depression and bigotry that not only affected who could come in, but led to the mass deportation of many people who had come to call the United States home (especially Mexicans). But immigration controls never regulate the total amount of immigration; they just alter (and even then only at first) the makeup of the migrant cohort by favoring certain countries of origin over others. The number of immigrants who stay depends on the availability of work and the viability of prospects elsewhere. In the United States, the Second World War created a lot of employment, and it was a less demographically debilitating event than the First World War. A baby boom began in 1946, accelerated into 1947, slowed slightly, and then rebounded upward. This, coupled with yet more immigration from 1950 to 1957, meant that the rate of growth once again grew: by this point, there was enormous acceleration—until there wasn't.

The demographic slowdown in the United States from 1957 to 1970 reflected the rebuilding of Europe and China. There were fewer people trying so very hard to escape those places and cross the Atlantic and Pacific to get into the Americas. Relative stability in Latin America also meant fewer of its people were migrating north, partly also because birth rates were falling in the south. The huge rise in economic equality in the United States in these years meant that there were far fewer jobs at the bottom of the income hierarchy intended for "people who did not count," such as migrants, to fill. High economic inequality and the creation of many low-paying jobs within a country almost always increases immigration into that country if it is technically rich (has a high GDP).

Inequality in the United States rose relentlessly from the mid-1970s onward. The pre-tax income share of the best-off 1 percent was as low as 10.4 percent in 1976, but by 2012 it had doubled to 20.8 percent. The wealth share of the country's wealthiest 1 percent grew similarly, from a low of 21.7 percent in 1978 to 40.1 percent in 2012 (after which wealth inequalities also fell).[11] Growing inequality drew in migrants, but all the time the birth rate was falling, which served to dampen the rate of U.S. population acceleration. More economically unequal countries have higher birth rates; as economic insecurity increases, people have more children, perhaps as an insurance policy to look after them in old age. But even the rampant inequality of the United States could not hold back the trend toward smaller families and slowdown. Furthermore, much of the migration from South America to the United States was from places that already had established lower fertility rates than the United States (see the notes within figure 46 in Chapter 8 to explain why that might have happened).

The final peak, before the most obvious U.S. slowdown, came in the 1990s. In 2006, when good-quality data on the movement of peoples around the world first became available, my colleagues and I started to draw hundreds of world maps of the differences between countries and changes over time as part of what became known as the Worldmapper project. At that time we noted that most of the migration into the United States that had taken place between 1990 and 2017 came from neighboring Mexico (12.7 million people). This resulted in Central America and the Caribbean accounting for just over 47 percent (22.4 million) of the total migration to the United States in that period. Mexico was followed by China, India, and the Philippines in importance, each contributing over 2 million people to the in-migration count. Six other countries contributed more than 1 million people to the United States' immigration numbers: Puerto Rico, Vietnam, El Salvador, Cuba, South Korea, and the Dominican Republic.[12] The great and growing economic inequality of the United States sucked in people from neighboring and nearby countries, especially Mexico.

U.S. politicians reacted to this acceleration with sanctions. The Illegal Immigration Reform and Immigrant Responsibility Act (IIRIRA) was signed into law in September 1996. "I don't think people fully appreciated what those laws had done," said New York University academic Nancy Morawetz, referring to both the IIRIRA and other 1996 laws that affected immigration. One effect was clear: after IIRIRA came into effect, deportation from the United States went from being a rare phenomenon to a relatively common one: "Before 1996, internal enforcement activities had not played a very significant role in immigration enforcement," noted sociologists Douglas Massey and Karen Pren. "Afterward, these activities rose to levels not seen since the deportation campaigns of the Great Depression." In 2016, describing this very recent history, journalist Dara Lind (who specializes in covering immigration) explained: "More immigration enforcement is one big reason why there are so many unauthorized immigrants in the US today."[13] People were actually more likely to remain in the United States because of the difficulty they encountered going back and forth to their country of origin, and obtaining legal status became much more problematic.

Population growth did turn from acceleration to deceleration in the United States upon the passing into law of IIRIRA, which really was an especially nasty piece of legislation, but that is coincidental. After all, there have been nasty pieces of immigration legislation passed in the United States before. What sustained the deceleration in the wake of the IIRIRA was fewer and fewer births.

Unlike the rest of the Americas, in 2100 the United States is still predicted to be growing in size. However, far from being the land of the free when its demographic record is examined, the United States may well become a less popular place for migrants to try to reach in the near future when the legacy of the Trump era strikes. I suspect the UN projections are especially overoptimistic as far as the United States is concerned and its population will actually fall at some point during this coming century.

China is very different from the United States, but the two countries are more connected than many people think, not least because there was so much migration from China to the United States over such a long time period. China grew due to births, at first, in the 1700s, far more slowly than the United States grew, until the British, in search of a "free-trade" market for their opium, sent gunboats to Hong Kong in 1839. But we need to take a step back from then. It will be a two-millennia step because, unlike the Americas, China was already very well populated two thousand years ago.

China's Han emperor Ping ordered a census to be taken in what we now call the second year of the current era.[14] In this same period, the Romans were taking censuses of all Roman citizens and subjects every twenty years. The total population of the Roman Empire was just under 57 million. China's population was 60 million at the start of the first millennium, but fell to around 50 million a century later. An estimate made in 606, during the Sui dynasty, put the Chinese population at 46 million; it had dropped to 37 million just a century later in a count taken in 705, a century into the

Tang dynasty (in the year of the death of the infamous Empress Wu Zetain, who—if you are being strict about these things—was really a member of the brief Zhou dynasty).[15]

By 1290, under Yuan rule, China's population was rising once again to 59 million, finally reaching 60 million in the year 1393 in the Ming era. The timeline in figure 24 shows the drop in population that occurred between 1600 and 1650 with the fall of the Ming dynasty. After that, growth set in again. There were 177 million people under Qing rule in 1749, rising to 304 million by 1791 and 359 million by 1811. The population fell between 1850 and 1864, a period that included the Taiping Rebellion following the First Opium War, in which as many as 100 million people may have died, with deaths spread out over many years.[16] Despite this huge setback, population growth returned, reaching 593 million by 1953 when the People's Republic of China was four years old. This total would be higher by just 2 million if Hong Kong had been included, although I have not done so here.

Unlike the series produced by Angus Maddison, which estimated that the population of mainland China fell from 667 million in 1960 to 660 million in 1961, the United Nations' estimates showed it rising by 10 million that year. For consistency across this chapter, the UN estimates are used here, but they hide a significant number of deaths that reflect the impact of the great Chinese famine years of 1958–61. That one very curious omission in the UN data is worth remarking on. According to data now available in China and in Angus Maddison's estimates, had the birth rate remained the same as in the 1953–57 period, then 92 million babies would have been born in the years 1958, 1959, 1960, and 1961. In the event, total births in the period 1958–61 numbered only 61 million. If the death rate had remained the same, then 29 million people would have died, not the 44 million who actually did perish during the famine. Births dropped by 30 million because so many women were too malnourished to be able to give birth, and deaths rose by 15 million; hence the population fell by 45 million from what might have been expected if the events of 1958–61 had not occurred.

The great Chinese famine was brought about by a combination of unusual weather and tragic human error. But in the UN data, it is as if this catastrophic event never happened. At the time, doctors in China were forbidden from listing starvation as a cause of death. It might be better, given that the numbers I have just cited are now widely known in China, if the UN were to update its figures.

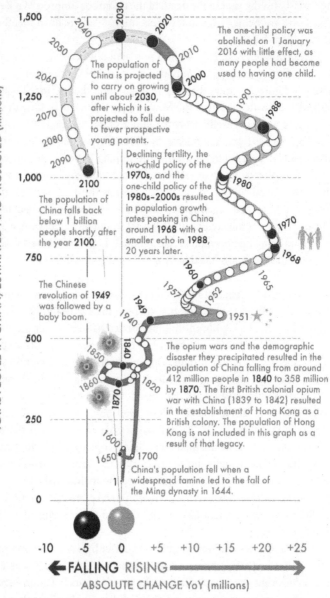

TOTAL PEOPLE IN CHINA, ESTIMATED AND PROJECTED (millions)

The one-child policy was abolished on 1 January 2016 with little effect, as many people had become used to having one child.

The population of China is projected to carry on growing until about **2030**, after which it is projected to fall due to fewer prospective young parents.

Declining fertility, the two-child policy of the **1970s**, and the one-child policy of the **1980s–2000s** resulted in population growth rates peaking in China around **1968** with a smaller echo in **1988**, 20 years later.

The population of China falls back below 1 billion people shortly after the year **2100**.

The Chinese revolution of **1949** was followed by a baby boom.

The opium wars and the demographic disaster they precipitated resulted in the population of China falling from around 412 million people in **1840** to 358 million by **1870**. The first British colonial opium war with China (1839 to 1842) resulted in the establishment of Hong Kong as a British colony. The population of Hong Kong is not included in this graph as a result of that legacy.

China's population fell when a widespread famine led to the fall of the Ming dynasty in 1644.

← FALLING RISING **——→**

ABSOLUTE CHANGE YoY (millions)

24. China: total population, years 1–2100. (Data from the Angus Maddison Project and *UN World Population Prospects 2017*.)

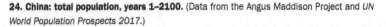

Following recovery from the famine, China's population reached 700 million in 1964, 800 million in 1969, 900 million in 1974, and 1 billion in 1981, after which the one-child policy helped accelerate the fertility slowdown that was already well under way. As a result, the 1.1 billion count was not reached until 1987; the 1.2 billion mark was reached in 1992, largely because of people living longer, rather than a rise in births; the 1.3 billion mark in 2003; and 1.4 billion in 2016. China's population is now expected to peak in 2030 at 1.44 billion and then drop to below 1.4 billion in 2044, dip below 1.3 billion by 2060, below 1.2 billion just after 2070, below 1.1 billion in 2086, and fall below 1 billion around the year 2104—but only if current projections turn out to be accurate. It could drop faster, since the relaxation of the one-child policy has not resulted in a substantial rise in births. Cultural attitudes to family size have changed in a way that would now be hard to reverse.

China's population growth has been slowing down since 1968, and the country will experience an absolute fall in just a decade from today. In contrast to the United States, China is still growing rapidly economically, although, as is touched on in later chapters, its economic growth is also, inevitably, slowing down. Furthermore, China's birth rate is currently dropping far more quickly than either the UN or official Chinese projections had envisaged.

In 2018 there were 15.2 million births in China, 2 million fewer than in 2017. This has resulted in the national population growth rate dropping from 0.53 percent to 0.38 percent in just one year. The slowdown is fastest in the cities to which people continue to migrate. Continued internal migration also brings more rapid slowdown to rural areas of China. In Qingdao in 2018, a small city (of "just" 9 million people) in Shandong province in the populous east of the country, the number of births recorded between January and November fell by 21 percent against the same period in 2017.[17] Qingdao, the most economically successful city in its province, is a key eastern node on the current government's planned "One Belt, One Road" economic route of prosperity. Progress means fewer babies.

THE SLOWDOWN IN AFRICA AND THE BRITISH ISLES

Next let's consider the continent of Africa and the islands of Britain, brought together here because the two areas have been so intimately connected in our recent past. The great contrast to China, in demographic terms, is the entire continent of Africa. By 2020 Africa's population will have grown to

1.35 billion people, which means it will still be less than that of China at 1.42 billion. However, very soon after 2020, as China slows down, and as most African countries are expected to continue to experience population acceleration, the continent as a whole is projected to far outstrip China in population. This will be the first time in many thousands of years that there will be more people living in Africa than in China. Because it was so very long ago, estimating when these two areas were last so similar in population levels relies on guesswork. The recent data in the timeline in figure 25 are low quality because UN data for many African countries are unreliable. This is one reason this timeline relates to an entire continent.

The projected future rise of the population of so many African states relies on a demographic model that is beginning to look very questionable. It is certainly true that Africa is home to many of the countries that currently have the highest fertility rates in the world. But the supposition that birth rates across Africa will in future slow down only at a pedestrian pace is dubious. It assumes that what is going on in the rest of the world will have little effect on the continent.

With much of the rest of the world approaching a population shortage, out-migration from Africa may well rise in future in response to the growing need for younger people around the rest of the planet. This would further dampen the rate of acceleration of population growth across Africa below that which is currently predicted by the UN. With higher adult out-migration from Africa, fewer children would be born within Africa. Furthermore, migrants who leave countries of high fertility tend to have fewer children over the course of their lives than those who remain. This, of course, also assumes that removal (by emigration) of some fraction of a peer group has no effect on the pace of fertility decline among those remaining. But what if conditions for those remaining also improve, access to secondary and tertiary education improves, and the reasons so many people had for leaving are reduced?

Changes in the choices that women across Africa make, and are able to make, about how many children to have will be made in a twenty-first century context. Just because past accelerations were similar in shape to what is shown in figure 25 does not mean that history will repeat itself, as that timeline (in this case based on 2017 UN estimates) suggests. If you look carefully at the timeline, you will see that the very recent years, 2000–2015, have seen unusually high population growth across Africa. It is the

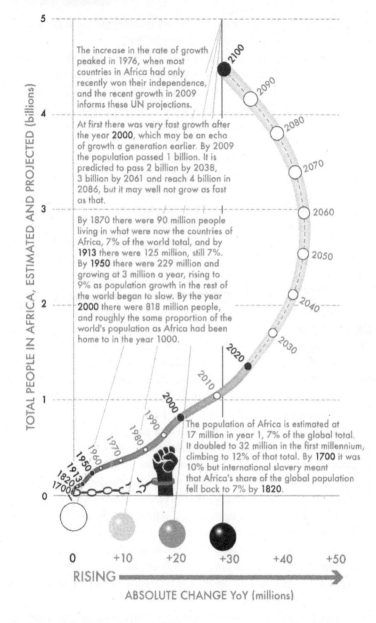

TOTAL PEOPLE IN AFRICA, ESTIMATED AND PROJECTED (billions)

The increase in the rate of growth peaked in 1976, when most countries in Africa had only recently won their independence, and the recent growth in 2009 informs these UN projections.

At first there was very fast growth after the year **2000**, which may be an echo of growth a generation earlier. By 2009 the population passed 1 billion. It is predicted to pass 2 billion by 2038, 3 billion by 2061 and reach 4 billion in 2086, but it may well not grow as fast as that.

By 1870 there were 90 million people living in what were now the countries of Africa, 7% of the world total, and by **1913** there were 125 million, still 7%. By **1950** there were 229 million and growing at 3 million a year, rising to 9% as population growth in the rest of the world began to slow. By the year **2000** there were 818 million people, and roughly the same proportion of the world's population as Africa had been home to in the year 1000.

The population of Africa is estimated at 17 million in year 1, 7% of the global total. It doubled to 32 million in the first millennium, climbing to 12% of that total. By **1700** it was 10% but international slavery meant that Africa's share of the global population fell back to 7% by **1820**.

0   +10   +20   +30   +40   +50

RISING ➡

ABSOLUTE CHANGE YoY (millions)

25. Africa: total population, years 1–2100. (Data from the Angus Maddison Project and *UN World Population Prospects 2017*.)

projection forward of that unusual and very recent high rate of growth that drove the UN projection model published in 2017.

There is growing evidence that the most recent years in Africa have been an aberration. In February 2019, research published in the *Proceedings of the National Academy of Sciences* was widely reported around the world. The researchers "began their research by noting that fertility rates ceased declining in several African countries in the early 2000s. To find out why, they obtained data from surveys conducted every few years in the countries under study. More specifically, they looked at data covering the years 1950 to 1995."[18] The researchers found that it was most likely a disruption in access to decent education in many African countries in the 1980s, especially for girls, that led to young women having more children, producing this recent (and very possibly temporary) aberration in what had previously been a faster rate of slowdown. That faster rate can be seen in the period from 1980 to 1995 in the timeline. Look carefully and you will see there was a break in what had been the beginnings of a fractionally faster slowdown, one that might have become even faster, but didn't.

In the past twenty years, access to education for girls across Africa has improved markedly. None of this is taken into account in the UN's models. The disruption to education in the 1980s was during the worst recorded period of economic decline that the countries of Africa had ever collectively suffered, a decline that occurred under the structural adjustment policies introduced by the International Monetary Fund and the World Bank. If you could curb the destructive behavior of international financial institutions, you could do quite a lot of good in the world. Failure to rein in the behavior of the most socially naive of economists—and some economists, it has to be said, can be very naive—and those who instituted policies based on their work would lead, just a few decades later, to accelerating population growth. Girls who couldn't attend school in the late 1980s and early 1990s due to structural adjustment became women who on average had children earlier and more children overall. Poverty, despair, and ignorance increase fertility. The damage wreaked on the continent by those structural adjustment programs was devastating. The total personal and government income across most countries in Africa fell between the early 1980s and late 1990s.[19]

Africa has a long history of harmful international intervention. Between 1500 and 1600, the entire population of the continent rose from 47 million people to 56 million. In the next century it climbed to 61 million, less than half that of China at that time. By 1870 the entire population of Africa was 91 million, just a quarter of that of China in the same year. It is useful to compare what was happening to Africa with the situation in China. China's population had been in decline following the forced importation of opium by the British over three decades earlier in a conflict described by William Gladstone, later British prime minister: "A war more unjust in its origin, a war more calculated in its progress to cover this country with permanent disgrace, I do not know and have not read of."[20] The landmass of Africa is over 30 million square kilometers, more than three times as large as China is today. Yet it is, in comparison to China, sparsely populated. Africa's population is currently projected by the UN to rise threefold in the sixty years from 2020 to 2080, to the same density as that of largely urban China today, but this is very unlikely to occur, not least because the amount of fertile land in Africa is similar to that in China.[21]

On the northern Mediterranean coast of Europe, a majority of the population of Spain, Greece, and Italy now believe that there should be emigration controls; in other words, such is the shortage of young people remaining at home that they would like limits on the number of younger citizens permitted to leave these three countries for protracted lengths of time. As yet, across all of Europe it is only in these three mainland European countries, the three closest to Africa, that such sentiments have majority support.[22] At some point soon, someone will point out that if it were easier for people from African countries to migrate across the Mediterranean, then the imbalance of too many young adults on the south Mediterranean coast and too few on its north coast would begin to correct itself.

But the southern countries of Europe are not the most averse to migration. To see the most migration-averse country in Europe you must look at England, and its dominance over migration policies affecting the entire British Isles, which at the time of writing all lie outside of the Schengen Area of free movement without border checks. Ireland and the United Kingdom are the only EU countries to have a permanent opt-out of the Schengen Agreement, despite the Schengen Area also including four non-EU (but still European Free Trade Area) countries.

Unlike the countries of Africa, the British Isles (mostly England, Ireland, Wales, and Scotland) experienced a population explosion between 1500 and 1600, with their total population growing by more than a third in that century. The total grew by more than a quarter in the next century to 1700, despite the 1665–66 Great Plague, which killed a quarter of the population of London. But then, between 1700 and 1800, the population rose by 85 percent, and Thomas Robert Malthus published the first version of his later much-revised essay that made dire predictions about unchecked population growth. Had Malthus lived in another place, or in a different era, or had he simply had a less puritanical nature, he would have seen things very differently. However, in the century that followed, the one that ended in 1900, the human population of the British Isles grew even faster, by 160 percent. Devastating famine in Ireland in the 1840s had appeared to confirm Malthus's warnings that population growth would lead to mass deaths.

The famine in Ireland was the single most momentous demographic event in the history of the British Isles since the Black Death in the fourteenth century. It claimed far more lives than the Black Death, because by 1845 there were many more people. The huge population fall resulting from the famine was exacerbated by so many people fleeing hunger: the rapid increase in Irish emigration to the United States pushed the population of the entire British Isles into decline for a year. If you want to see an area out of demographic control, turn to nineteenth-century Britain and Ireland, which experienced both unchecked expansion and great tragedy.

After the 1840s there was no further great famine within the British Isles. The famine began as a natural event, but it was the decision by a group of English politicians not to send food to the Irish that led to so many deaths and so much emigration. England's political class was marked by megalomania and a belief in its inherent moral superiority, a superiority whose impact was felt all the way across the globe, from justifying the shipping of opium to China as "free trade" to initially championing transatlantic slavery to, back at "home," allowing the Irish to die slowly and painfully as a form of "natural selection."

Another affliction might also have been in play, at the time known as "Dromomania"—"the uncontrollable urge to wander," or perhaps the uncontrollable urge to do anything possible to try to find a better life. Others were forced to migrate. Courts in England deported people to the American colonies prior to 1776, and to Australian penal colonies up to 1868. Emigration from all around the British Isles was growing exponentially, and yet, despite that, population growth was still slowly accelerating between 1852 and 1990; in the first part of this period, 150,000 people net were being added each year—the population size of contemporary Oxford.

At the time of Queen Victoria's death in 1901, this growth reached its peak at 380,000 net a year.

The year 1901 was a time of frenzy. The writer Emily Buchanan, in an article on E. M. Forster and the origins of humanism, offers a valuable insight into the impact, at the beginning of the twentieth century, of a world in which so much was changing so quickly for so many—at first in places like the British Isles, but soon everywhere.

> The turn of the century was a time of frenzied advance and rapid rural development. Queen Victoria had just died, kick-starting our modern propensity for progress, and machines had begun to dominate industry and culture. As Forster writes in *Howards End*, "month by month the roads smelt more strongly of petrol, and were more difficult to cross, and human beings heard each other speak with greater difficulty, breathed less of the air, and saw less of the sky." A state of "continual flux" gripped a society straddling the old and new, and this tension is captured with startling clarity in the social reportage films of Forster's contemporaries, Mitchell and Kenyon. In particular, a film of Bradford in 1902 shows electric trams sharing streets with horses and carts. If you look closely, ads for familiar brands display the first rumblings of 21st century capitalism and yet the people are timid and formal, every bit the Victorian. This is most clearly exhibited in their overt, often comical reactions to the camera. At the time, a hand-cranked camera would have been an impossibly advanced sight and this is why hordes of delighted children chase the filmmakers up the street and adults gawp at them with a frightened, almost ludditian curiosity. Their mesmerised discomfort is, in itself, mesmerising.[23]

Within just a few years of Mitchell and Kenyon capturing this mesmerized discomfort on film, mechanized war would arrive. But even before the First World War, there were two periods of slowdown: a modest one from 1880 to 1885 and a very significant one from 1910 to 1913. The condom had been popularized by the 1877 trial of social reformers and contraception campaigners Annie Besant and Charles Bradlaugh, leading to a fall in a birth rate that would never rise so high again. Furthermore, from 1910 to 1913 the population of Ireland fell a little more rapidly than before, as emigration to the United States increased to even higher rates right up until the start of the First World War. A corresponding 1910–13 influx can be seen in the U.S. timeline in figure 23 above.

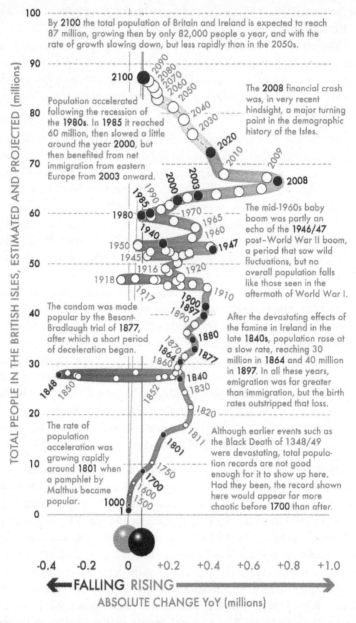

TOTAL PEOPLE IN THE BRITISH ISLES, ESTIMATED AND PROJECTED (millions)

By **2100** the total population of Britain and Ireland is expected to reach 87 million, growing then by only 82,000 people a year, and with the rate of growth slowing down, but less rapidly than in the 2050s.

Population accelerated following the recession of the **1980s**. In **1985** it reached 60 million, then slowed a little around the year **2000**, but then benefited from net immigration from eastern Europe from **2003** onward.

The **2008** financial crash was, in very recent hindsight, a major turning point in the demographic history of the Isles.

The mid-1960s baby boom was partly an echo of the **1946/47** post–World War II boom, a period that saw wild fluctuations, but no overall population falls like those seen in the aftermath of World War I.

The condom was made popular by the Besant-Bradlaugh trial of **1877**, after which a short period of deceleration began.

After the devastating effects of the famine in Ireland in the late 1840s, population rose at a slow rate, reaching 30 million in **1864** and 40 million in **1897**. In all these years, emigration was far greater than immigration, but the birth rates outstripped that loss.

The rate of population acceleration was growing rapidly around **1801** when a pamphlet by Malthus became popular.

Although earlier events such as the Black Death of 1348/49 were devastating, total population records are not good enough for it to show up here. Had they been, the record shown here would appear far more chaotic before **1700** than after.

-0.4   -0.2   0   +0.2   +0.4   +0.6   +0.8   +1.0

← **FALLING** RISING →

ABSOLUTE CHANGE YoY (millions)

26. British Isles: total population, years 1–2100. (Data from the Angus Maddison Project and *UN World Population Prospects 2017.*)

The more recent past is more obvious because we know it better. The Second World War was a little less devastating than the First for the British Isles, which was now separated into two states, the United Kingdom and the Republic of Ireland. A baby boom followed the end of the war in 1945, but as there were too few young adults in the 1960s due to too few births before 1945, migration from the Caribbean and the Indian subcontinent was positively encouraged by the U.K. government. But Britons (encouraged by self-serving politicians and newspapers) complained about the arrival of (former British Empire) immigrants from the former colonies, and an immigration control act was passed in 1965, to be followed by many more. Paradoxically, the 1965 act served to increase the immigrant population, as those already in the country dared not leave and many endeavored to bring over their elderly relatives while they still could.

Even though immigration actually increased despite attempts to control it, the underlying downward trend in total population increases prevailed nevertheless, and population growth slumped by the time of the early 1980s recession; in an odd echo of recent history and in one last great lurch forward, it then rose again as immigration was encouraged, most especially after 2003. Once again, the British invited migrants in, this time by allowing citizens of the EU accession states of eastern Europe to enter and live and work earlier than the rest of western Europe did.[24] Couple that with an economic boom in Ireland, and from 2003 to 2008 there would be the greatest population acceleration the islands had ever known—ending abruptly with the great economic crash of 2008. Quite why the future is projected by the UN demographers to be so steady is a mystery, given the turbulent past shown in figure 26.

THE SLOWDOWN IN INDIA AND JAPAN

The population trajectory of the Indian subcontinent, which comprises modern-day India, Pakistan, and Bangladesh, looks particularly smooth in comparison to that of the tiny British Isles. This is partly a chimera because early data are less reliable and hence not shown here, and partly simply what happens when far larger areas are averaged. The population of the subcontinent, by various estimates, numbered perhaps one hundred thousand people twelve thousand years ago, 1 million people six thousand years ago, and 6 million by four thousand years ago.

With the advent of cities, irrigation, and civilization in general, the population rose again, settling at approximately 75 million people around two thousand years ago and remaining at that number with only slight perturbations caused by the occasional plague and invasion until one thousand years ago, after which it gradually rose to 135 million by the year 1600, the year in which the British East India Company received its royal charter from Queen Elizabeth I. In the wake of the effects of that intervention—at first modest and then ferocious—the population grew and grew as the norms that had previously controlled growth were progressively undermined. By 1820, the population of the Indian subcontinent had reached just over 200 million people. Then acceleration really took off, as the timeline in figure 27 shows.

What the timeline in figure 27 does not reveal, because available accurate data on total population are too sparse, is the Great Bengal famine of 1769–70, in which 10 million people died, the Chalisa famine of 1783–84, in which as many as 11 million people died, and the Skull famine of 1791–92, in which as many millions again died in circumstances in which the bodies could not be cremated or buried. It does not show the 1 million who died in the Orissa famine of 1866, the 1.5 million who died in the Raj Punta famine in 1869, the 6 to 10 million who died in the Southern India famine of 1876–79, the 1 million who died in the 1896 famine that began in Bundelkhand, the 1 million who lost their lives in the 1899 West and Central Indian famine, or the 1.5 million who perished miserably in the Bengal famine of 1943–44. As with the famine in Ireland, British rule played a key part in ensuring that famine relief was inadequate—and in ensuring that the circumstances in which famine could be so deadly were so well established in the first place.

The population acceleration in India was slower before the First World War, growing by little more than 10 percent between the 1881 and 1891 censuses. However, after 1921, population growth in India became higher, right through to the present day and likely for some decades to come. When newborn babies began to be immunized and public sanitation was introduced while fertility remained high, acceleration could itself accelerate. A botched partition by the British in 1947 may have resulted in as many as 2 million deaths from the ensuing violence. However, as with wars, the disruption brought about by partition would also result in a baby boom.

Improved infant survival chances after Indian independence meant that the population of the new state of India grew by more than 20 percent every decade from 1951 onwards, right through until 2001–11, when growth slowed to just under 20 percent in the final ten years for which we

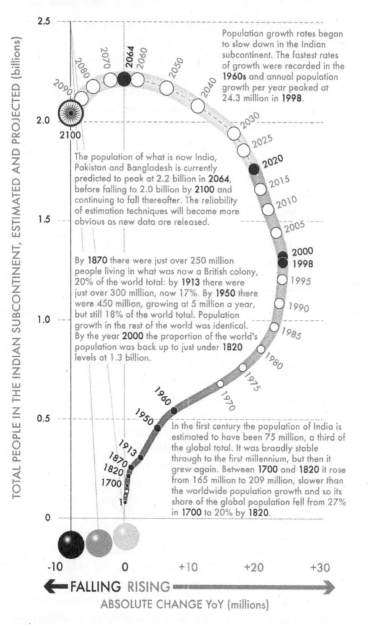

TOTAL PEOPLE IN THE INDIAN SUBCONTINENT, ESTIMATED AND PROJECTED (billions)

Population growth rates began to slow down in the Indian subcontinent. The fastest rates of growth were recorded in the **1960s** and annual population growth per year peaked at 24.3 million in **1998**.

The population of what is now India, Pakistan and Bangladesh is currently predicted to peak at 2.2 billion in **2064**, before falling to 2.0 billion by **2100** and continuing to fall thereafter. The reliability of estimation techniques will become more obvious as new data are released.

By **1870** there were just over 250 million people living in what was now a British colony, 20% of the world total: by **1913** there were just over 300 million, now 17%. By **1950** there were 450 million, growing at 5 million a year, but still 18% of the world total. Population growth in the rest of the world was identical. By the year **2000** the proportion of the world's population was back up to just under **1820** levels at 1.3 billion.

In the first century the population of India is estimated to have been 75 million, a third of the global total. It was broadly stable through to the first millennium, but then it grew again. Between **1700** and **1820** it rose from 165 million to 209 million, slower than the worldwide population growth and so its share of the global population fell from 27% in **1700** to 20% by **1820**.

← **FALLING** **RISING** ➡
ABSOLUTE CHANGE YoY (millions)

27. Indian subcontinent: total population, years 1–2100. (Data from the Angus Maddison Project and *UN World Population Prospects 2017*.)

have an accurate count. The population of Pakistan grew by just as much but slowed to 20.1 percent growth between 2001 and 2011, and it has been estimated to be decelerating throughout the most recent years. Most important, Bangladesh has slowed down the fastest, with its population growing by only 16.9 percent between 2001 and 2011, mostly due to people living longer, rather than more births, and with its rate of population growth also falling each year within that period due to the decline in births.

The period of acceleration of the population growth of the Indian subcontinent as a whole ended in 1995, when 24 million people were added in just one year. The slowdown has already begun. It started a quarter of a century ago in India, but it is currently projected to be a slow slowdown, with growth falling below the addition of 20 million people a year in 2020, below 10 million a year in 2043, and reaching zero growth—peak Indian subcontinent population—in 2063 (or 2059, according to the 2019 UN estimates). After that, the 2017 UN projections suggest the population will shrink by more than 7 million people a year for the first time in 2094, when the total is still above 2 billion people, 1 billion having been reached in 1987. However, there are very good reasons to believe that the slowdown could be quicker than that, with the very recent falls in fertility being the most obvious sign that the UN's projections, those made in both 2017 and 2019, overestimated future population in its "most probable" outcome. But the stories of other countries are telling, too. We can learn much from the recent past of other countries—as long as we look.

Japan, like India, suffered famines that are not part of the record shown here because the available data were not of good enough quality to include them in these timelines. The Great Kan'ei famine of 1640–43 killed up to one hundred thousand people. The Kyōhō famine of 1732 resulted in a death toll estimated at between twelve thousand and 1 million, depending on the source.

The Great Tenmei famine of 1782–88 reduced the population of Japan by almost 1 million, partly because the famine-weakened population was more susceptible to disease. The Tenpō famine of 1833–87 killed 3 to 4 percent of the population in some areas. But as the timeline in figure 28 shows, in the large majority of years in which there was no famine, the population of Japan grew steadily, and then accelerated, doubling between 1500 and 1700 to number at least 27 million people. After this, there was very slow growth, especially during the later Edo era of Shogun control,

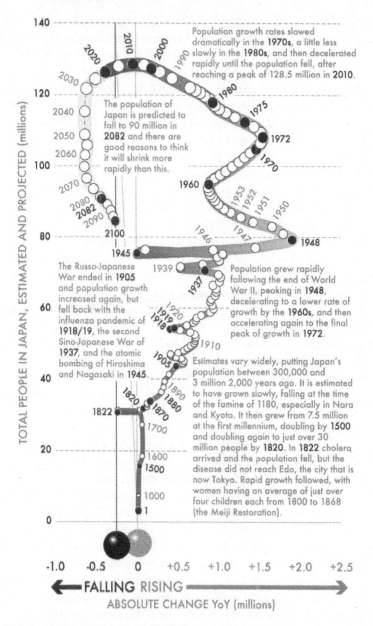

Population growth rates slowed dramatically in the **1970s**, a little less slowly in the **1980s**, and then decelerated rapidly until the population fell, after reaching a peak of 128.5 million in **2010**.

The population of Japan is predicted to fall to 90 million in **2082** and there are good reasons to think it will shrink more rapidly than this.

The Russo-Japanese War ended in **1905** and population growth increased again, but fell back with the influenza pandemic of **1918/19**, the second Sino-Japanese War of **1937**, and the atomic bombing of Hiroshima and Nagasaki in **1945**.

Population grew rapidly following the end of World War II, peaking in **1948**, decelerating to a lower rate of growth by the **1960s**, and then accelerating again to the final peak of growth in **1972**.

Estimates vary widely, putting Japan's population between 300,000 and 3 million 2,000 years ago. It is estimated to have grown slowly, falling at the time of the famine of 1180, especially in Nara and Kyoto. It then grew from 7.5 million at the first millennium, doubling by **1500** and doubling again to just over 30 million people by **1820**. In **1822** cholera arrived and the population fell, but the disease did not reach Edo, the city that is now Tokyo. Rapid growth followed, with women having an average of just over four children each from 1800 to 1868 (the Meiji Restoration).

TOTAL PEOPLE IN JAPAN, ESTIMATED AND PROJECTED (millions)

-1.0   -0.5   0   +0.5   +1.0   +1.5   +2.0   +2.5

← **FALLING RISING** →

ABSOLUTE CHANGE YoY (millions)

28. Japan: total population, years 1–2100. (Data from the Angus Maddison Project and *UN World Population Prospects 2017*.)

in which concerted attempts were made to prevent outside influence. An edict to repel "with cannon" any foreign vessels lacking proper trading permissions—in other words, any that were not owned by the Dutch East India Company—was passed in 1825, following the arrival of cholera in 1822, which may have caused population falls. This fall is apparent in the data used here, so it is shown, but it is hard to find any corroborative evidence that this cholera epidemic was quite so severe. We often forget how little we know for sure about our past as well as our future.

It was not until the Meiji Restoration of the emperor in 1868 that Japanese population acceleration renewed. There was a slowdown in 1891 when the Noubi (Mino-Owari) earthquake resulted in the spread of fire and many deaths.[25] During the First World War, Japanese armed forces helped spread influenza into Tokyo, and their mobilization prior to the war helped initiate a minor slowdown (due to fewer births). A similar slowdown was seen at the start of the Second World War, followed by the first fall in population since 1822, with the dropping of the two atomic bombs by the United States in 1945. This was followed by a baby boom which, at its peak in 1948, added 2 million people that year alone, although it is less apparent on this timeline due to smoothing. Fertility quickly reduced from that peak, to a low resulting in a net rise of only 890,000 people in 1960. Then the birth rate (the number of babies born in a year) but not the fertility rate (the average total number of children women were having) rose again, apart from the year 1966, climbing up briefly to 1.5 million by 1972 when the children of the Second World War baby boom began in greatest numbers to have children of their own.[26]

After 1972, Japan's birth rate fell and fell, at first quickly and then a little more slowly until 2009/2010, when the country reached its peak population. The average number of children born to each woman fell below 2 in 1975, below 1.5 in 1993, below 1.3 in 2003. Today it is 1.09 in Tokyo, and still falling. In December 2018, the *Japan Times* reported: "The data showed the pace of population decline is picking up amid the falling birth rate, suggesting it is increasingly difficult for the government to attain its goal of raising the total fertility rate to 1.8 by the end of fiscal 2025."[27] Setting a target to increase fertility by the end of a particular tax year is a nice illustration of policymakers' habit of seeing people as commodities. But without a change in policy in favor of more migration, the population of Japan is likely to drop precariously to below 100 million by 2065, and below 85 million in 2099.

Almost everything that was available to women in Japan after the early 1970s is available to women across the Indian subcontinent today: not just access to contraceptives and abortion, but also education, increased respect by men, and an awareness that your children will almost certainly now survive you into adulthood. There is no reason why what was seen in Japan around fifty years ago could not occur in many other parts of the world that currently have high fertility rates—and quickly. In 1970, children under fifteen made up one-quarter of the population of Japan. Today, one-quarter of India's population are children.

THE SLOWDOWN IN ALL OF EURASIA

What of the rest of Eurasia? The border between Asia and Europe is a meaningless line, as they are in no way two separate continents. So next let's consider that part of Eurasia that is not the British Isles, the Indian subcontinent, China, or Japan: in other words, the majority of the mega-continent we have not yet covered in this chapter. The timeline in figure 29 shows what will by now be a familiar picture, where at first there appears to be almost no significant population change, but this is only because the rate of population change was so low that dramatic changes would not be visible without using a log-log scale, even if we did have data good enough to plot.

After 1820, there was the start of a small acceleration in the population growth of the remainder of Eurasia. War and influenza brought this to an end, with negative growth in 1918. However, by 1920 the acceleration had resumed, only to be interrupted yet again by the Second World War, after which there was a baby boom, a fall in mortality rates, and an overall great rise, shifting the total from 1 billion people in 1965 to 2 billion by 2025. A peak will be reached in 2060, and by 2100 the population will have been falling for forty years and will be approaching 2 billion again. As always, the UN 2017 projection does not show the rapid slowdown that is currently being experienced in Japan, and it also predicts something smoother and slower than what is probably most likely and actually being experienced in very recent years. Past precedent suggests that when there is a slowdown that is not due to war, famine, or plague, it accelerates.

The dip in the timeline in figure 29 is the year 2000, which echoes an earlier baby slump around 1975, itself an echo of the end of the first great post–Second World War baby boom. But what is remarkable is how constant the relative population distribution within Eurasia has been over the course of the past twenty-one centuries. In the first year of the current era, the

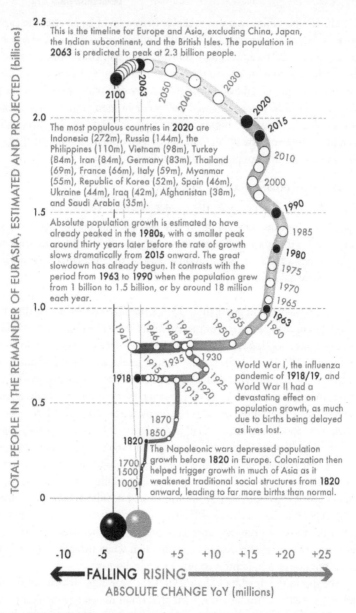

29. Remainder of Eurasia: total population, years 1–2100. (Data from the Angus Maddison Project and *UN World Population Prospects 2017*.)

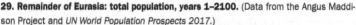

top ten most populous countries, calculated using modern-day boundaries, were Russia (7.5 million), Italy (7), Turkey (6.1), France (5), Spain (4.5), Iran (4), Germany (3), Indonesia (2.8), the Philippines (2.4), and Greece (2). By 1820 Poland and South Korea had just joined the top ten, and Iran and Greece had dropped out. By 2020 Indonesia will be first ranked (with 272 million people), and Iran will reenter the top ten, along with newcomers Vietnam, Thailand, and Myanmar, which will replace Spain, Poland, and South Korea. These are changes, but not the most dramatic of changes.

In short, people in Eurasia today generally live in the same locations, along the same river valleys, as they did two millennia ago. The great difference is not where people are found, but that there are thirty people alive today for every one human who was alive then. The overall projected change is dramatically less than past changes. By 2100 there are projected to be eleven people living in this "rest of Eurasia" area for every ten alive there today, a rise of only 10 percent over the course of the next eighty years. The projected ten most populous countries by then are shown in table 6.

Table 6. Most populous countries in Eurasia by 2100 (excluding India, Pakistan, Bangladesh, China, the British Isles, and Japan)

People (millions)	Country
306	Indonesia
173	Philippines
156	Iraq
124	Russian Federation
107	Vietnam
85	Turkey
74	France
72	Iran
71	Germany
70	Afghanistan

Source: UN Department of Economic and Social Affairs, *UN World Population Prospects: The 2017 Revision,* https://www.un.org/development/desa/publications/world-population-prospects-the-2017-revision.html.

Indonesia, by 2100, will have the population that the United States attained in 2009, the Philippines will be as populous as Brazil was in 1999, Iraq will have fewer people than Pakistan has today, and Russia will have returned to the population it had in 1963. So what, exactly, was it that you were worrying about—even if the population growth in the next eighty years occurs just as the UN projected it would in 2017?

What we worry about (when we worry about population growth) is not growth, but death. We worry about too many people resulting in famines—because we have yet to learn that famines were never caused by there being too many people, but by politics. We worry that population growth will lead to mass migration—because we lack the collective imagination to see that migrants will be in huge demand and we should be afraid of having too few migrants, not too many. We think "too many people" leads to war. But it is just a very small number of men who start wars, and sadly it takes many people and usually the loss of many lives to stop wars. We worry that such a large mass of human beings could lead to the spread of new diseases, completely forgetting how deadly diseases used to be when there were so very few of us.

We have a folk memory of fear. The Black Death is estimated to have killed between a third and 60 percent of Europe's total population in the years around 1350. This particular plague may have reduced the total population of the world from roughly 450 million to as little as 100 million. It took two centuries for the Earth's human population to recover to its previous level, and plague recurred again and again.

Table 6 will be wrong. It will be hugely wrong if there is a third world war or another pandemic. If events such as these do not occur, then it could still be very wrong. But most likely it will be wrong because Iraq and Afghanistan will not ever grow enough to join the top ten group again. It will be wrong because some of these countries will shrink faster, and some countries will no longer have the same borders or the borders will cease to exist in all but name. The boundaries between Germany and France, or other mainland European countries, could someday soon matter as little as the borders between Mercia and Wessex do in England today.

THE SLOWDOWN IN OCEANIA AND THE AMERICAS

The final two large areas of the planet we have not yet covered are Oceania and the Americas (excluding the United States, with which this chapter began).

The pre-conquest population of Oceania has been estimated at half a million people and was quite stable in its very slow growth from the year 1 until 1770, when Captain James Cook and his men landed at Botany Bay. After that terrible encounter, along with hundreds of similar encounters in so many small islands in the Pacific, about a fifth of the population died, shrinking Oceania's total to 539,000 by 1820, and it was still falling even then. If this story seems to be becoming repetitive, that is because it is.

Wherever they landed, the British caused havoc, and the germs they carried with them weakened the peoples they then defeated. The social order that they and other colonizers then imposed would destroy every stable social system on each of those thousands of small islands, as well as the few larger islands that make up Australia, New Guinea, and New Zealand, subsequently creating a great population acceleration.

By 1840, as both voluntary and forced migration by Europeans to Oceania began to accelerate, in-migration overtook the deaths caused by disease, hunger, and direct persecution. By 1852, Oceania's population had doubled to 1 million, accelerated further by the gold rush that began in 1851. By 1864 it was 2 million people. By 1877 it had hit 3 million, and the gold rushes became too frequent to list here. By 1885 4 million people were living in the area, mostly in Australia, and there were 5 million by 1893. Thus, between 1829 and 1885, in the space of just fifty-six years, the population increased tenfold. If you want to see out-of-control acceleration again, this is another example of what it looks like; and yet this period hardly features on the timeline in figure 30 because the total population was then still so small.

The First and Second World Wars were largely fought on the opposite side of the planet, but they took their tolls on Oceania's population all the same. Men fought—and many died—in far-off lands. In many cases enlistment was accomplished without the aid of conscription: in Australia, for example, conscription was enacted only in 1942. After the war, a baby boom was followed by yet more in-migration, mainly from Great Britain but also from China and a shattered Europe. After the baby booms faded away, the peak of acceleration was reached in 1989. Far away in Europe, the Berlin Wall was taken down and the Iron Curtain disappeared. In 2008, Kevin Rudd (the Australian prime minister) announced the closure of the controversial immigration detention facilities on Manus Island and in the tiny Pacific country of Nauru, as well as the processing of all future refugees on Christmas Island.[28] But that is not the reason the acceleration ended

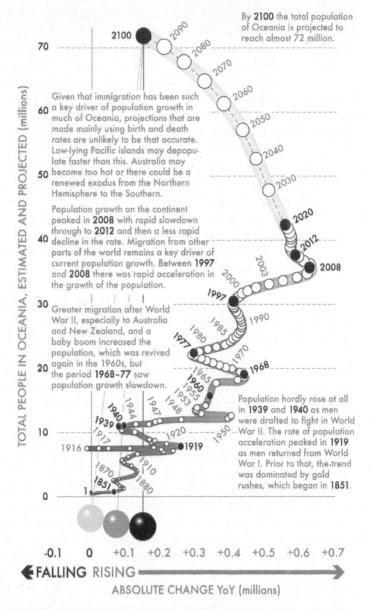

By **2100** the total population of Oceania is projected to reach almost 72 million.

Given that immigration has been such a key driver of population growth in much of Oceania, projections that are made mainly using birth and death rates are unlikely to be that accurate. Low-lying Pacific islands may depopulate faster than this. Australia may become too hot or there could be a renewed exodus from the Northern Hemisphere to the Southern.

Population growth on the continent peaked in **2008** with rapid slowdown through to **2012** and then a less rapid decline in the rate. Migration from other parts of the world remains a key driver of current population growth. Between **1997** and **2008** there was rapid acceleration in the growth of the population.

Greater migration after World War II, especially to Australia and New Zealand, and a baby boom increased the population, which was revived again in the 1960s, but the period **1968-77** saw population growth slowdown.

Population hardly rose at all in **1939** and **1940** as men were drafted to fight in World War II. The rate of population acceleration peaked in **1919** as men returned from World War I. Prior to that, the trend was dominated by gold rushes, which began in **1851**.

← FALLING **RISING →**

ABSOLUTE CHANGE YoY (millions)

TOTAL PEOPLE IN OCEANIA, ESTIMATED AND PROJECTED (millions)

-0.1 0 +0.1 +0.2 +0.3 +0.4 +0.5 +0.6 +0.7

30. Oceania: total population, years 1–2100. (Data from the Angus Maddison Project and *UN World Population Prospects 2017*.)

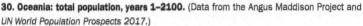

that year; the numbers of refugees were simply too small to have made an impact. The acceleration ended because the echo of the baby boom had come to an end.

By 2100, if the UN's projections are correct, Oceania will still be home to an extremely small proportion of the population of the world: some 72 million people, or just 1 person in every 155 people alive then on Earth. But the future could be so very different from that. The lowest-lying islands in Oceania are set to flood by 2100, yet the UN does not take that into account. It projects people still living in those areas—presumably underwater—while the vast, nearly empty spaces on the larger islands remain largely unfilled, just as though the UN expects the prejudices that fueled so many racist Australian and New Zealand immigration acts to continue, unchecked, forever; and also as if the UN officially expects that West Papua will never be granted its freedom, bringing stability and an end to the violence there.

Finally, what of the Americas? Remove the (still accelerating) United States from the total population and a very different picture emerges. It is a picture with which you are probably now quite familiar. The giant question mark shape of slowdown is again obvious in the timeline shown in figure 31. What we cannot clearly see from this timeline, however, is the earliest catastrophe that befell the Americas. A population of 5.7 million two millennia ago rose to 11.6 million by the year 1000 and 17.8 million by 1500, only to plummet by more than half, to 8.9 million, by the year 1600. Change on that scale required a 10 percent reduction in the population, seven times over, in just one hundred years. This all occurred not long after the year in which everything changed: 1492, when Columbus sailed the ocean blue. The Americas' population recovered only very slowly as the Spanish and Portuguese took control and began to bring enslaved people from Africa, contributing to a population rise to 12.3 million by 1700. But the British—other than in many of the islands of the Caribbean, in what is now Canada, and in what was formerly British Honduras and is now Belize—were, for once, largely absent from our story, because we have excluded from figure 31 the thirteen British colonies that would become the United States.

By 1800 the population of the remainder of the Americas had finally recovered, after three hundred years, to its pre-Columbian levels. It grew to 22.9 million in 1820, doubled to 52 million by 1880, and hit 121 million

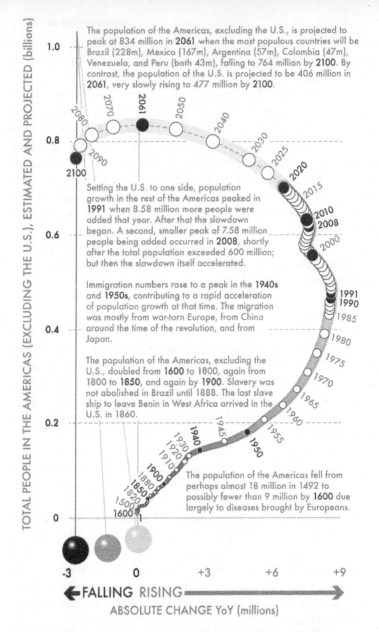

Y-axis label: TOTAL PEOPLE IN THE AMERICAS (EXCLUDING THE U.S.), ESTIMATED AND PROJECTED (billions)

The population of the Americas, excluding the U.S., is projected to peak at 834 million in **2061** when the most populous countries will be Brazil (228m), Mexico (167m), Argentina (57m), Colombia (47m), Venezuela, and Peru (both 43m), falling to 764 million by **2100**. By contrast, the population of the U.S. is projected to be 406 million in **2061**, very slowly rising to 477 million by **2100**.

Setting the U.S. to one side, population growth in the rest of the Americas peaked in **1991** when 8.58 million more people were added that year. After that the slowdown began. A second, smaller peak of 7.58 million people being added occurred in **2008**, shortly after the total population exceeded 600 million; but then the slowdown itself accelerated.

Immigration numbers rose to a peak in the **1940s** and **1950s**, contributing to a rapid acceleration of population growth at that time. The migration was mostly from war-torn Europe, from China around the time of the revolution, and from Japan.

The population of the Americas, excluding the U.S., doubled from **1600** to 1800, again from 1800 to **1850**, and again by **1900**. Slavery was not abolished in Brazil until 1888. The last slave ship to leave Benin in West Africa arrived in the U.S. in 1860.

The population of the Americas fell from perhaps almost 18 million in 1492 to possibly fewer than 9 million by **1600** due largely to diseases brought by Europeans.

X-axis label: ←FALLING RISING——→
ABSOLUTE CHANGE YoY (millions)

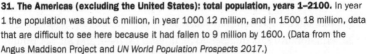

31. The Americas (excluding the United States): total population, years 1–2100. In year 1 the population was about 6 million, in year 1000 12 million, and in 1500 18 million, data that are difficult to see here because it had fallen to 9 million by 1600. (Data from the Angus Maddison Project and *UN World Population Prospects 2017*.)

by 1930, after which an even greater acceleration set in, with new waves of immigration spurred on by the economic depression that hit both the United States and Europe, as well as Japan and China. The concave curve in the timeline in figure 31 from 1940 to 1980 is an almost perfect example of decelerating acceleration, doubling population to 242 million by the year 1960 and, by 1991, 484 million. The latter was also the year of peak acceleration. The year of projected peak population is 2060, with 834 million people in the Americas excluding the United States, and then, as with everywhere else, it eventually falls. It may well fall both earlier and faster than predicted. We should expect it to, unless some great unforeseen disaster strikes, including one in which the folly and shortsightedness of people are largely to blame in one way or another. However, why, collectively, should we expect to be that stupid in future? More and more we are learning that war is evil, people have rights, famines can be entirely avoided, diseases must be both prevented and treated, and above all women have the right to choose if and when they have children.

Finally, there are four areas of the world we have yet to discuss: the population in the sky, which is still rising and reached over 1.3 million people, or two hundred thousand planes, in 2018; the population on ships, which has not been calculated; the population of Antarctica; and the population in space.[29] Antarctica is home to just under one thousand people in winter and just under four thousand in summer. The International Space Station peaked at a population of thirteen in 2009.[30] We are not going to escape the demographic time bomb by moving to outer space, not just because that is impossible, as there is not anywhere near enough to usefully get to, but because—there *is* no demographic time bomb. There never was a demographic time bomb. It is worth repeating that the projections given in this chapter are the UN's 2017 published "most probable" estimates and that they had almost all been reduced in size slightly already when the UN numbers were updated in June 2019. There are many reasons to suspect that the slowdown in world population will be much faster than that first official downward revision.

8

fertility
the greatest slowdown of all time

Time slips past, the people in the cohorts get older, the scientists embark on the next sweep of data collection, and discoveries about the cohorts flood out.

—*Helen Pearson, 2016*

Cohorts of thousands or even millions of people are increasingly used in medicine and epidemiology to establish the facts about generational changes. The British Doctors' Cohort (which began in the 1950s) led to the unexpected discovery of the multiple illnesses contributed to by tobacco. We are not making such staggering and important discoveries as quickly today. Contrary to how we feel about the state of the world and our global politics, things are not changing faster than they ever have before. Despite an ongoing flood of scientific papers, we are no longer learning vastly more about ourselves. We are learning more, a great deal more, but no longer vastly more. Those of us who work in universities often feel we have to say that we are making great discovery after great discovery. This is especially true in more economically unequal countries, where universities have to sell themselves as being special, as do individual researchers and scientific journals. To sell a book you need to be able to say its message is new. But the age of the most rapid discoveries has passed.

We are still living in an exceptionally interesting and unusual time precisely because so much is now *not* changing so quickly. Although slowdown is often presented as a curse, it need not be. It can be a time to reflect. It is a slowdown in wage growth, in innovation rates, in the no longer exponential expansion of consumption. It is a slowdown, above all, in people, especially in people having children. What we are seeing is almost precisely the kind of slowdown that is necessary if we are to survive in a way that will allow us to be happy. It appears that it is our good fortune to be living at the beginning of the end of capitalism, or at least the end of how it has been operating recently. We are at the end of perpetual growth. But we have yet to recognize the slowdown for what it is, let alone start to welcome it.

Worldwide, only the past five generations (see table 7 below for the past thirty-five generations) have lived lives fully immersed in the maelstrom that was rampant capitalism, where private profit became all-powerful, and where each generation's beliefs, chances of survival, and standards of living have experienced a tsunami of change. Before that point, most people around the world lived lives very like those of their parents, often doing the same or similar work, conducting similar lifestyles, having the same beliefs, and facing very similar risks. For most of human history, whole villages, cities, and countries were not suddenly transformed into something very different as profits dwindled and a place had to be abandoned, or when new ways of making vast amounts of money suddenly emerged and changed a village into a city.

We have become so used to change we think of it as normal. Think of the Oxfordshire village that in the 1950s had no electricity or gas supply, and whose inhabitants then were mostly farm laborers, but which now lies off the junction of a motorway that speeds you to London and where a single large house today costs more than the whole village did seven decades earlier. Think of the American city that was world-famous for making cars and music, now known for its abandoned lots and the lead in its water supply. Think of any country that just a century or so ago was not that country—such places comprise most of the world.

Settling back into the rhythm of living lives much like those of your parents may be about to happen again for our children and their children as the social tsunami subsides, as the speed of change reduces, as settlements settle, and fashions in clothing, ways of working, living, and learning become more fixed. Young and old may once again experience much more similar work and holidays, and have similar views and expectations. We are yet some way from this future, but it is where we appear to be heading.

There is already far less technical change in the lives of our youngest adult generation, Generation Y, than previous recent cohorts experienced. For them no new internet has been created, no new power source, no new form of transport, or (thankfully, and as far as we know) no new weapon of war. However, we are now so used to the inevitability of technological change that we find the simple fact of technological slowdown almost impossible to accept. But most *new* products released in the past decade have involved little more than tinkering around the edges. As societies across the world have become richer, each small incremental change to our quality of life has mattered less and less. There are now clearly diminishing returns to technological advancement, and soon this fact will be so commonplace that you will be bored when it is mentioned.[1]

What changed most abruptly, immediately before the slowdown, was a decline in extreme scarcity and acute hardship for our species. This is in marked contrast to what has occurred to the countless other species on Earth that we have driven to extinction, or to the brink of extinction. As our material life has become easier, as the slowdown progresses, and as we are less easily diverted by new technological toys, we have become increasingly cognizant of the harms we are causing. We see not only the collateral damage and the externalities, but also the inner harm to our psychological and emotional worlds. We have softened, and so have the class and social relations among us. Less is repressed. We are now less violent. We have become a little less hierarchical. We are much more aware of all that we harm or destroy.

Class and hierarchy are fundamentally about scarcity. One of the crucial benefits of the economic growth that accompanied the recent social tsunami has been a psychosocial softening.[2] Each recent generation for which we have measurements has become progressively more tolerant, more caring, less cruel, as compared with the previous generation—because it can.[3] Still, we have not become happier or less anxious. To live with less anxiety is part of a more fundamental happiness. Sadly, we are still a long way from that state, because we continue to face enormous insecurity and uncertainty, and we have not yet learned how to control the greedy. At least we now recognize their wealth as being the outcome of their greed, not of their ability or right, or of their talent or innate worth.

Above all else, what has helped us see each other differently than humankind used to is our transformation within the space of just a tiny number of generations from a species that expects to see many, if not most, of its offspring die in childhood to one that can now finally and happily contemplate stability, and decides to have just a few children each, or none. The timeline in figure 32 shows the enormous speed of the global deceleration in total fertility rates—in the number of children that women on average worldwide can expect to have, which is currently calculated yearly, but which in future may need to be measured in a different way as the slowdown brings changes that become far subtler.[4]

The total fertility is the average number of children a woman will have, assuming that current rates at specific ages continue. For example, in early 1960, Queen Elizabeth II, then thirty-four years old, was pregnant with her second son, Andrew. Her oldest son, Charles, was twelve; her daughter Anne was ten. She would go on to have a third son, Edward, in 1964 when she was thirty-eight. Her total fertility would be four, just a single child fewer than the 1960 global average of five children. The British royal family was not that different from everyone else, at least in terms of their fertility.

Figure 32 shows the cascading down of global total fertility rates that is the hallmark of slowdown. From initially slowly climbing in the early 1960s to its post–World War II peak of 5.07 in 1964 (the year Prince Edward was born), the global human total fertility rate plummeted down to 4 in 1976, 3 in 1992, 2.5 in 2010, and is currently rapidly heading to a worldwide average of below 2.4 children per woman. We often think of fertility rates as being very different in different parts of the world, but that is because the slowdown simply started a little earlier in some areas and later in others. It is now clearly a global slowdown.

As we will see, the story of slowdown is now largely the same everywhere, from China to the United States, from Guatemala to Korea, from Brazil to East Timor. We tend to overemphasize the difference between places, because it is the differences that are most interesting. However, the graphics in this chapter all show such a similar picture of decline that to differentiate them, Kirsten McClure (who drew them) has added a different bird carrying the babies to each place: a stork for the timelines of the world as a whole, a bald eagle for the United States, a red-crowned crane for China, an ostrich for Niger, a yellow-crested cockatoo for East Timor, a quetzal for Guatemala, a Hispaniolan trogon for Haiti, a cockerel for France, a robin for the United Kingdom, a Korean magpie for Korea, the Barcelos rooster for Portugal, and a toucan for Brazil. I mention them only so you don't miss them. However, not everyone likes birds.

Queen Elizabeth's mother, Elizabeth Angela Marguerite Bowes-Lyon, for instance, preferred horses. She was born in the year 1900. Over the course of her very long life—she died in 2002—she witnessed phenomenal changes. Cities transformed out all of all recognition. The Queen Mother

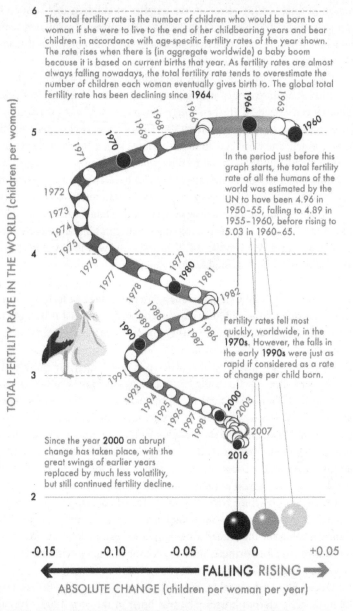

The total fertility rate is the number of children who would be born to a woman if she were to live to the end of her childbearing years and bear children in accordance with age-specific fertility rates of the year shown. The rate rises when there is (in aggregate worldwide) a baby boom because it is based on current births that year. As fertility rates are almost always falling nowadays, the total fertility rate tends to overestimate the number of children each woman eventually gives birth to. The global total fertility rate has been declining since **1964**.

In the period just before this graph starts, the total fertility rate of all the humans of the world was estimated by the UN to have been 4.96 in 1950–55, falling to 4.89 in 1955–1960, before rising to 5.03 in 1960–65.

Fertility rates fell most quickly, worldwide, in the **1970s**. However, the falls in the early **1990s** were just as rapid if considered as a rate of change per child born.

Since the year **2000** an abrupt change has taken place, with the great swings of earlier years replaced by much less volatility, but still continued fertility decline.

TOTAL FERTILITY RATE IN THE WORLD (children per woman)

FALLING RISING

ABSOLUTE CHANGE (children per woman per year)

32. World: total fertility rate, 1960–2016. (World Bank Open Data, fertility rate, estimates based on the 2017 *UN World Population Prospects* and other sources, https://data.world bank.org/indicator/sp.dyn.tfrt.in.)

was born in London, but exactly where is uncertain—because it may have been in a horse-drawn ambulance on the way to a hospital. London, the world's largest city in 1901, was characterized by extreme poverty. The city's wretched living conditions had only just been mapped and recognized a few years earlier, by a rich man, Charles Booth, who had actually set out to prove that poverty was not that widespread—he was shocked by what he found.[5] In 1901, most Londoners lived in conditions at least as bad as those their parents had faced. Many of that previous generation, if not most, were recent migrants from the countryside or abroad. In just one century, from 1800 to 1900, the population of London increased from 1 million to 6.5 million people. Overcrowding resulted in conditions worse than in almost any slum in any part of the world today: people lived alongside vermin and sewage. Infant mortality was reaching new peaks, recording its highest-ever numbers in the long hot summer of 1905. So many newborns died that constant immigration was required not just to grow the city, but simply to sustain its population of adults.

In the late eighteenth century, the philosopher Jean-Jacques Rousseau wrote that each woman in the world must produce four children for the human race to continue, such was the rate at which children then died of diseases. This was true even in France, where falls in fertility first began in earnest. Rousseau's comments may have been inspired by a sense of things changing.[6] Cities then were far more dangerous than the countryside, as disease spread so much more easily among concentrated populations. The necessity to give birth to four babies just to see two of your children go on to reproduce was the case right through to the start of the twentieth century, when infant mortality began to fall as sanitation was improved and germ theory was discovered and accepted. Today in China it is safer to be born in the city than the countryside. A baby born in urban China faces a lower risk of mortality in its first year of life than in many (if not most) areas of the United States.

Improved sanitation and health care made it possible to have fewer children. However, some women were encouraged to keep on having more. Writing during the 1930s, William Beveridge (who was subsequently influential in the establishment of the welfare state in the United Kingdom) suggested that middle-class British women—and, notably, *only* middle-class British women—needed to have four children for the good of the human race.[7] Beveridge was a social reformer who, like so many others of his day, was also a eugenicist when he was a young man. Thankfully we now understand that no identifiable elite gives birth to especially genetically able people destined to lead others. The idea of eugenics rose and fell as a symptom of the great transformation.

A century ago, the world was changing so rapidly that once it was no longer necessary for so many children to be born, people began a debate about *who* should be born. New York grew to become the world's largest city by the 1920s. It was not until that "decadent" decade that affluent New Yorkers countenanced regularly using the increasingly common elevators and the concept of the penthouse was created.[8] We so easily forget how *recently* our modern world was formed. We forget how, until a century ago, even in the most dynamic centers of what was only just becoming a world economy, the streets were full of horses and their manure. In both the city and the countryside, most people walked, often miles, to work, to shop, to do anything. We easily criticize the white (especially middle-class) people of the past for their abhorrent views on their supposed biological superiority, but we forget the maelstrom they were living though. No wonder they were confused. We have no such excuses today. We now know that eugenics is not just wrong, but evil.

Figure 33 shows an enlarged section of figure 32. This enlargement is needed because when the longer time period is considered, the most recent changes are not visible. The timeline in the more detailed figure appears, initially, to be showing acceleration returning, but please look at it in the broader context of figure 32: it is then far clearer that what we are looking at most recently is a stumbling turning point in the current global fertility trend. From 1998 to 2006 you could have believed that the rate of fertility was heading again toward growth, but in hindsight that was just a brief eight-year aberration and an echo of a past that has now ceased to reverberate.

Fertility rates were falling through the 1998–2016 period when viewed as a worldwide total, but between 2001 and 2003, and then 2004 and 2006, they appeared to be falling more and more slowly. However, after 2014, that hesitant trend was no longer evident; the fall in fertility was again accelerating. Once the statistics become available, we will know the extent to which the fall has continued to accelerate between 2017 and 2020, and how much fertility will continue to fall in the near future. This will be what determines the changes to come in the UN's total global population estimates, as well as any change in the thinking of UN demographers about what the underlying processes at play might be.

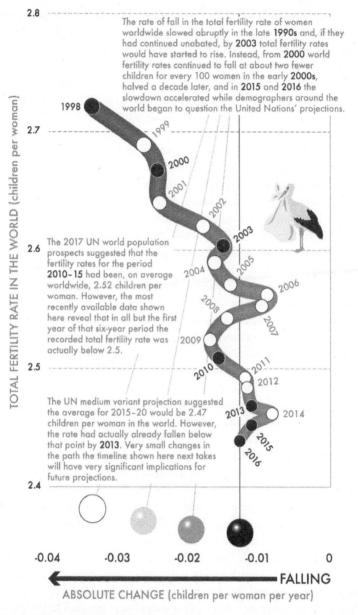

The rate of fall in the total fertility rate of women worldwide slowed abruptly in the late **1990s** and, if they had continued unabated, by **2003** total fertility rates would have started to rise. Instead, from **2000** world fertility rates continued to fall at about two fewer children for every 100 women in the early **2000s**, halved a decade later, and in **2015** and **2016** the slowdown accelerated while demographers around the world began to question the United Nations' projections.

The 2017 UN world population prospects suggested that the fertility rates for the period **2010–15** had been, on average worldwide, 2.52 children per woman. However, the most recently available data shown here reveal that in all but the first year of that six-year period the recorded total fertility rate was actually below 2.5.

The UN medium variant projection suggested the average for 2015–20 would be 2.47 children per woman in the world. However, the rate had actually already fallen below that point by **2013**. Very small changes in the path the timeline shown here next takes will have very significant implications for future projections.

TOTAL FERTILITY RATE IN THE WORLD (children per woman)

2.8
2.7
2.6
2.5
2.4

1998
1999
2000
2001
2002
2003
2004
2005
2006
2007
2008
2009
2010
2011
2012
2013
2014
2015
2016

ABSOLUTE CHANGE (children per woman per year)

-0.04   -0.03   -0.02   -0.01   0

FALLING

33. World: total fertility rate, 1998–2016. (World Bank Open Data, fertility rate, estimates based on the 2017 *UN World Population Prospects* and other sources, https://data.world bank.org/indicator/sp.dyn.tfrt.in.)

Once the timeline in figure 33 reaches 2, or in fact a little before that point, the human species will have stopped growing in number for the first time ever, and this will be the result of fewer births rather than more deaths. The length of both time and social change required to move from 2.4 to 2 could be roughly the same as that taken to get from just over 2.7 to just above 2.4 children per woman, which figure 33 shows was twenty years. Because not all children live through to the end of child-rearing age, or even into adulthood, the point at which stability is reached will be nearer 2.1 than 2. However, that may be irrelevant because the recent events described in this book, derived from the most recent reports available across the globe, suggest that the fall in fertility is not going to stop at 2 but continue on downward below that. What happens after that point is impossible to know. Remember, until recently we had no idea that fertility could fall this far and this quickly—worldwide. Given this unexpected and significant shift, we should not be too confident about what we believe might happen next.

Most people believe capitalism has a longer history than it actually does. The word *capitalism* was first used in the 1850s to describe unusual events in those few places associated with the full onslaught of the earliest industrialization and a new type of mercantile trade. England, and especially London, was one of the cradles of capitalism, alongside Amsterdam, Venice, and Lisbon.

However, in the 1850s, most people, even those living in those cradles of capitalism, did not work in industry, ports, factories, or mines. Most lives had not yet been much touched by the capitalists, those who had more and more money (in other words, more and more capital). But a few people were able to have more leisure time as a result of receiving an income from the new, and enormous, profits of industry, exploitation, and trade. They were the first group of any size to have the time to think, which is time that today millions (but not yet billions) of people have. They were some of the first to think about things that could only then begin to be imagined. In the 1850s, we did not even know we were a species.

The growth in trade that came with colonization and then industrialization resulted in much greater travel. It became possible to collect examples of animals and plants from around the globe and to piece together the connections between them. Many people were involved in this learning process, but today we remember one above all others: Charles Darwin. The most dramatic slowdown of all, the widespread slowdown in our fertility from the 1960s onward, occurred barely a century after Darwin was writing. So much has happened so very quickly that we are still in the process of taking stock. Old ideas, even when we can clearly see they were misguided, take time to die. New ones are still being formed, not least the ones that can explain slowdown and what humans are now aspiring to—and becoming.

THE SLOWDOWN OCCURS OVER GENERATIONS, NOT DECADES

Selection works by variation and inheritance, and only 240 human generations have elapsed since the first adoption of agriculture and perhaps no more than 160 generations since it became widespread.

—*James C. Scott, 2017*[9]

When anthropologist and political scientist James Scott wrote the words above, he was speculating that human beings had become domesticated. Had we become selectively bred, like the animals and grains we deliberately selected and bred? He conjectured that more docile, more communal, more servile humans were more likely to survive in settled communities. But he warned that 240 or 160 generations were too few to have had much of an evolutionary effect. In essence, most of us are still genetically very much like our hunter-gatherer forebears. So, if a few dozen generations are too few for us to have changed our inherent nature, think of just the seven generations of people that have been born since Darwin's *On the Origin of Species* was published, especially the last five, those born since 1901. The first of these last five generations, people born between 1901 and 1928 (inclusive), may well have been utterly bemused by what they saw unfold across the course of their lives. The Queen Mother famously liked her gin as well as her horses, so she may not have seen it all clearly. But her generation experienced the greatest social change of all, especially in what they witnessed happening in their own old age.

Figure 34 shows the fall in recent American fertility, from 1960 to 2016. From an average of nearly four children per woman before the 1960s, the number dropped to below three in 1965, to two and a half in 1969 (when momentarily it looked as if the total fertility rate might rise again), to two in 1972, and a low of 1.799 in 1983. The latest figure shown here, for 2016, has almost reached that point once again, and it is still falling. At least one year in the period 2017–20 will be the lowest ever recorded, if not each year in that period, with the year after each setting yet another new record.

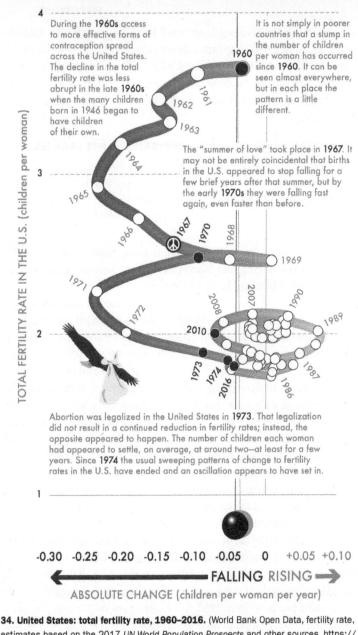

During the **1960s** access to more effective forms of contraception spread across the United States. The decline in the total fertility rate was less abrupt in the late **1960s** when the many children born in 1946 began to have children of their own.

It is not simply in poorer countries that a slump in the number of children per woman has occurred since **1960**. It can be seen almost everywhere, but in each place the pattern is a little different.

The "summer of love" took place in **1967**. It may not be entirely coincidental that births in the U.S. appeared to stop falling for a few brief years after that summer, but by the early **1970s** they were falling fast again, even faster than before.

Abortion was legalized in the United States in **1973**. That legalization did not result in a continued reduction in fertility rates; instead, the opposite appeared to happen. The number of children each woman had appeared to settle, on average, at around two—at least for a few years. Since **1974** the usual sweeping patterns of change to fertility rates in the U.S. have ended and an oscillation appears to have set in.

TOTAL FERTILITY RATE IN THE U.S. (children per woman)

-0.30 -0.25 -0.20 -0.15 -0.10 -0.05   0   +0.05 +0.10

← **FALLING** RISING →

ABSOLUTE CHANGE (children per woman per year)

34. United States: total fertility rate, 1960–2016. (World Bank Open Data, fertility rate, estimates based on the 2017 *UN World Population Prospects* and other sources, https://data.worldbank.org/indicator/sp.dyn.tfrt.in.)

"What has happened to the younger generations?" each older generation, in its turn, has asked. Charles Darwin was obsessed with generations. The word appears over two thousand times in his collected papers.[10] As explained in Chapter 1, long before the first of the five generations that the current chapter is most concerned with was born, Darwin described "the numerous recorded cases of the astonishingly rapid increase of various animals in a state of nature, when circumstances have been favourable to them during two or three following seasons." He was talking about other living organisms, but he could just as well have been talking about us. Furthermore, although to an outside observer the seasons may appear favorable as population numbers increase, the animals involved have little idea of why they suddenly appear to be part of a much bigger crowd.

Quite clearly the favorable seasons for humans are now over—but over in a very favorable way. The huge population expansion around the world occurred largely because of events that resulted in the irrevocable destruction of traditional fertility controls, but also because mortality rates subsequently began to fall. Eventually, when you know that your children will almost certainly survive you, that society will care for you in sickness and old age, and that you can begin to more easily control how many children you have, then (on average) you have far fewer.

Favorable seasons are what, in hindsight, were experienced by the first of the five generations born after 1901. We often think of these years as terrible times marked by worldwide warfare, but we forget what was quietly happening in the background. Those seasons were so favorable for us as a species that our numbers doubled and doubled again worldwide. But the effect on us was not to talk of this time with wonder, but to initially see the population growth as a bitter fruit. There was a sea change in our knowledge and experiences, accompanied by a growing sense of concern with what was to come—for us all collectively. When there had just been great change, and when we were still in the midst of acceleration, the future became especially uncertain.

Before 1901, for the majority of people in the world, it was obvious what was to come. The next generation would live much as the ones before it had. They would plow the fields with horses. (The first tractor was invented only as recently as 1901.)[11] The changes between generations, in comparison to what was to come, had all been slight. Land had been gradually enclosed. When enclosure happened locally, for the individual family that had been evicted the change would have felt sudden and catastrophic. But on the national, let alone the global scale, in the distant past change operated at a snail's pace. New agricultural techniques were adopted slowly. A concern about the future was then (in Western countries, at least) largely individualistic. Would you personally go to heaven or spend an eternity burning in hell? There was little general concern about the future of a country, let alone the world as a whole. Only princes carved up countries. The whole world was far too big to require our concern. That was God's domain.

The precursor to the transformation came when our numbers began to double, and then double again even more quickly worldwide, which occurred between 1820 and 1926. That doubling did not greatly affect the lives of most people in most places, even including most people in places then thought to be changing most rapidly, such as England and the United States. The vast majority of our very recent ancestors were living rural lives.

A global doubling of the population over 106 years resulted in rapid growth in only a minority of places and was experienced by only a minority of people worldwide because, on average, the doubling had been due to an increase of less than 0.7 percent each year. Globally, doubling the world population to 2 billion by 1926 happened without unprecedented effect in the majority of inhabited places. But double it again in just under half a century to 4 billion by 1974, and in another half century again to 8 billion by around 2024, and you change what it means to be part of humanity.

Figure 35 shows the timeline of total fertility rates for the United States in just the short period between 1973 and 2016. It is worth studying, trying to think why the rates repeatedly appear to settle at various points (the "knots" in the timeline), in the wake of various new norms being introduced, before being jolted out of position either upward or downward. Of course, the timeline is simply showing an aggregate demographic statistic, the total fertility rate. But it represents the individual decisions, collective chances, and outside influences that affected hundreds of millions of people and also what influenced the most important events in many of their lives, namely, the children they had.

The low of the 1970s that you can see in figure 35 was no longer caused by the influence of a baby boom, as we are not counting the total number of infants born, but the rate or frequency at which women were giving birth. The rate appears to stabilize around 1977 at under 1.8. It tries to settle again after 1980 at just over 1.8 children per woman. It rises in the 1980s to over 2 again during Ronald Reagan's fabled era of "morning in America," the

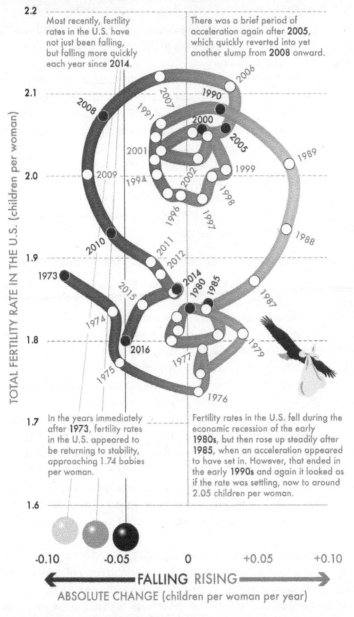

2.2

Most recently, fertility rates in the U.S. have not just been falling, but falling more quickly each year since **2014**.

There was a brief period of acceleration again after **2005**, which quickly reverted into yet another slump from **2008** onward.

2.1

2006
2008
2007
1990
1991
2000
2001
2005
1989
2.0
2009
1994
1999
2002
1996
2002
1998
1988
1997
2010
1.9
2011
2012
1973
2015
2014
1980
1985
1974
1987
1.8
2016
1977
1979
1975
1976

1.7

In the years immediately after **1973**, fertility rates in the U.S. appeared to be returning to stability, approaching 1.74 babies per woman.

Fertility rates in the U.S. fell during the economic recession of the early **1980s**, but then rose up steadily after **1985**, when an acceleration appeared to have set in. However, that ended in the early **1990s** and again it looked as if the rate was settling, now to around 2.05 children per woman.

1.6

-0.10   -0.05   0   +0.05   +0.10

← **FALLING** RISING →

ABSOLUTE CHANGE (children per woman per year)

TOTAL FERTILITY RATE IN THE U.S. (children per woman)

35. United States: total fertility rate, 1973–2016. (World Bank Open Data, fertility rate, estimates based on the 2017 *UN World Population Prospects* and other sources, https://data.worldbank.org/indicator/sp.dyn.tfrt.in.)

period in which poverty rates and economic insecurity exploded and economic inequality raced ahead owing to the political choices of those who put him in the White House.

From 1990 to 2005, the track of the timeline in figure 35 looked as if it had settled again, returning to 2.1 children per American woman—the rate last seen an entire generation earlier, back in the very early 1970s. But then something dragged it rapidly down. That something was global; it was the result of what was happening at this time outside of the United States. Immigrants to the United States were coming from places where it was now usual to have fewer children, and they had even fewer when they arrived. Hardly anywhere on Earth now appears able to buck the global slowdown trend. Since 2007, total fertility in the United States has fallen every year, heading faster and faster downward.

THE SLOWDOWN IS A RETURN TO MORE STABLE GENERATIONS

It was only in the last quarter-century of 1820–1926, that long slow period of the first global population doubling, that improvements in child health became a significant part of the reason for the overall population growth. Before then, it was social dislocation associated with rising trade and urbanization that led people to have more children, although not necessarily healthier children. Around 1901, all that changed very quickly, not least because of the discovery of germ theory in the preceding decades, for which Robert Koch was awarded a Nobel Prize in 1905.

The first Nobel Prize (of all) had been awarded four years earlier, in 1901, partly because people had begun to see themselves differently. Achievements are almost always a collective effort, but we were entering an era in which a few individuals would annually be celebrated as being extraordinarily special (remember, eugenics was then still popular). That is something else that might soon alter as we slow down. You should in future expect to see prizes more often awarded to larger groups than to single individuals.

Generations are often thought of as being around twenty-five years in length. However, because menarche (the first occurrence of menstruation) occurs at around age thirteen, and menopause (the ceasing of menstruation) occurs at around age fifty-one, on average, then thirty-two years (midway between the two) might be a better estimate prior to modern birth-control methods. Table 7, using that estimate alongside other data, shows one possible description of the past thirty-five generations in the world. A

Table 7. Thirty-five generations (based on English monarchs and the English life tables)

Token monarch	Birth–Death	Generation	Starts	Ends	Length (years)
Edmund I	921–946	1	900	934	34
Ethelred	968–1016	2	935	969	34
Edgar	1003–66	3	970	1004	34
William I	1028–87	4	1005	1036	31
William II	1056–1100	5	1037	1067	30
Henry I	1068–1135	6	1068	1101	33
Henry II	1133–89	7	1102	1135	33
Richard I	1157–99	8	1136	1166	30
John	1166–1216	9	1167	1200	33
Henry III	1207–72	A	1201	1234	33
Edward I	1239–1307	B	1235	1270	35
Edward II	1284–1327	C	1271	1305	34
Edward III	1312–77	D	1306	1341	35
Henry IV	1367–1413	E	1342	1376	34
Henry V	1386–1422	F	1377	1411	34
Richard III	1452–85	G	1412	1446	34
Henry VII	1457–1509	H	1447	1480	33
Henry VIII	1491–1547	I	1481	1514	33
Elizabeth I	1533–1603	J	1515	1548	33
James VI	1566–1625	K	1549	1582	33
Charles I	1600–49	L	1583	1616	33
Charles II	1630–85	M	1617	1650	33
George I	1660–1727	N	1651	1682	31
George II	1683–1760	O	1683	1718	35
George III	1738–1820	P	1719	1754	35
George IV	1762–1830	Q	1755	1787	32
Victoria	1819–1901	R	1788	1819	31
Edward VII	1841–1910	S	1820	1845	25
George V	1865–1936	T	1846	1875	29
George VI	1895–1952	U	1876	1900	24
Elizabeth II	**1926–**	**V**	**1901**	**1928**	**27**
Charles	*1948–*	*W*	*1929*	*1955*	*26*
Diana	*1961–97*	*X*	*1956*	*1981*	*25*
William	*1982–*	*Y*	*1982*	*2011*	*29*
George	*2013–*	*Z*	*2012*	*2042*	*30*

Source: Calculated by the author using English life tables and historical records.

monarch (or monarch-in-waiting) who was born within each generation is included to give some context for people who know British history. Note that the lengths of some earlier generations, which involve some guesswork, have been adjusted slightly to make the monarchs fit more neatly. From 1707 these were British, not only English, monarchs, and from 1876 to 1948 also empress or emperor of India. From 1901 onward, the generations are based on better-quality data on births and the actual average ages of mothers when they give birth (which includes all their children, not just their first child). Choosing 1901 as the start of a new generation fixes the dates for subsequent generations when using those data.

Although the list of generations given in table 7 is arbitrary—and very British-centric—it can easily be applied to other parts of the world. Figure 36 shows the recent timeline of total fertility rates in China. Generation V, women born in China between 1901 and 1928, would have had their children between 1914 and 1979, with most giving birth in the 1940s and 1950s. They were the mothers, on average, of more than six children each, which was one more at that time than the global average, and two more than Britain's Queen Elizabeth II gave birth to. Their high fertility rates contributed to the beginning of the timeline shown in figure 36. However, it was the women of China's Generation W, born between 1929 and 1955, who had their children mostly in the 1970s, who were the first to slow down dramatically compared with their mothers and grandmothers; they had four (and only a little later just three) children each, on average. Their daughters, Generation X, born between 1956 and 1981, were mostly 1960s and 1970s children. On average, they have far fewer children than their counterparts in the United States: mostly just one each, with as many having none as had two. Incidentally, Generation X here begins a little earlier than is usually thought to be the case, which has the generation beginning in the 1960s, and it ends a little later. That is because the generations in this book reflect the actual demographic length of generations based on the birth records of the time; they are not based on cultural ideas of particular generations, which are usually more narrowly defined in time as compared to the actual generations.

When you are planning to have just one child, you are very unlikely to have that one child early, but you are also unlikely to wait until the last possible few years. There is no rush, and you can plan. In the past, generations were spaced around thirty-two years apart because many women continued to have children as late as they could (or as late as they had to,

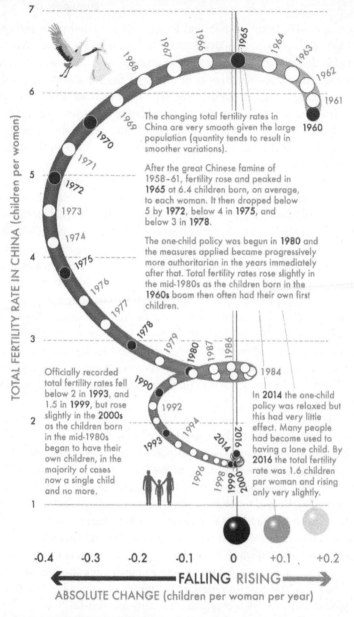

The changing total fertility rates in China are very smooth given the large population (quantity tends to result in smoother variations).

After the great Chinese famine of 1958–61, fertility rose and peaked in 1965 at 6.4 children born, on average, to each woman. It then dropped below 5 by 1972, below 4 in 1975, and below 3 in 1978.

The one-child policy was begun in 1980 and the measures applied became progressively more authoritarian in the years immediately after that. Total fertility rates rose slightly in the mid-1980s as the children born in the 1960s boom then often had their own first children.

Officially recorded total fertility rates fell below 2 in 1993, and 1.5 in 1999, but rose slightly in the 2000s as the children born in the mid-1980s began to have their own children, in the majority of cases now a single child and no more.

In 2014 the one-child policy was relaxed but this had very little effect. Many people had become used to having a lone child. By 2016 the total fertility rate was 1.6 children per woman and rising only very slightly.

TOTAL FERTILITY RATE IN CHINA (children per woman)

FALLING RISING

ABSOLUTE CHANGE (children per woman per year)

36. China: total fertility rate, 1960–2016. (World Bank Open Data, fertility rate, estimates based on the 2017 *UN World Population Prospects* and other sources, https://data.world bank.org/indicator/sp.dyn.tfrt.in.)

lacking reliable birth control), and because religious and other precepts discouraged very young women from having children. The generations defined in this chapter are used simply to illustrate how much has changed. They should not be thought of as in any way definitive, and there is nothing special about British royalty. Had there been space in table 7, I would also have listed the Chinese emperors who were in power at the time of each generation, but there are no longer any Chinese emperors, so Britain's royals can at least make themselves useful by adding faces to the figures through to the present day.

The five recent generations are the best known. Generation V is anyone born between 1901 and 1928, which includes both Queen Elizabeth II and Pu Yi, the last emperor of China, who was forced to abdicate at the end of the revolution of 1912 that established the Chinese republic. Elizabeth's firstborn son, Charles, was born in 1948 as part of the baby boom generation here called W, the generation that includes all those children born in China at the time of the later communist revolution. No British monarch was born during Generation X's whole period, so we have listed the late Diana Spencer—Charles's first wife—instead. The "millennials" are Generation Y, and Diana's firstborn son, William, who turned eighteen on the millennium, is one of the oldest of that generation. Generation Z has only just begun. Initially, these past five generations were less and less like their immediate predecessors, but now the youngest are becoming more similar to each other.

To return to an apt analogy that has been used again and again in this book: imagine you had spent the whole of your life on a train that had never slowed down, and so had your parents and their parents. The most recent five generations of humans always lived on a runaway train, from the very start, constantly expecting unimaginable change. The train has been moving so fast, for so long, that the passengers do not know what a stable life might be like. If this can be seen to be true for somewhere as stable as England, which has not been invaded (bar the Glorious Revolution) since 1066, and which has had much the same royal family in power for centuries, then it is not hard to see how much more this has been the case in places that have experienced the turmoil of multiple revolutions, invasions, and a complete overhaul of fundamental beliefs.

Before 1901, and as has been said before in this book but must here be emphasized, for most people in the world little changed from year to year. Each generation lived much as its forebears had. For example, most people living in England in 1066 would not have been affected by William the Conqueror becoming king. Twenty years later, they might have noticed someone coming to count the oxen for a census of their lord's lands, but that census did not count them: the "great survey" of England and Wales whose written record we know as the Domesday Book was not a census of people. At the same time in China, when the emperor was Daozong of the Liao dynasty, despite the turmoil then among the aristocracy of China, for most people life was much the same as their parents and their children experienced. Today, a similar stability is just around the corner, but now most people count—they matter—and we no longer see kings or emperors as supreme, but simply as useful markers of past eras and time.

Today the train is slowing down. Naturally, this is frightening. Constant change is our "normal." We have never known the speed of change to slow to walking pace, wages and salaries (on average) to stop rising, population numbers to stagnate, fashion to change far more slowly and less dramatically than it has for decades. It was not uncommon for nineteenth- and early twentieth-century novels to mention prices, such as the couple of pennies a protagonist might spend on a loaf of bread. But prices are rarely mentioned in today's fiction, because although inflation is low, it was until very recently historically high, and so any novel mentioning prices would date very quickly. Even the idea of something becoming quickly dated is very new, a product of our expectation of continued great change. Housing, teaching methods, one's kitchen, cars, gadgets, type of holiday—everything can be dated and becomes dated.

Nowadays we keep on expecting the next generation to differ greatly from the one before it, and we call that progress. But when did the use of *nowadays* become most popular? The word is ancient English, but became most commonly written down in the 1920s, by when its use had increased fourteenfold since 1860.[12] When the train slows down we see the slowdown as stasis—failure to progress. But why do we view stasis as bad? It is simply a period of relative equilibrium, a time when things change far less quickly, if at all. For the vast majority of human history stasis has been the norm. It is becoming the norm again.

You have to zoom in to see what stasis looks like. Figure 37 zooms in on the most recent period shown in figure 36, in which the trend is not at all clear because so little appears to be changing within that period of time—even though of course there was still change, and very structured (even if very slight) change. China's fertility rate began to creep up again, but then slowed down after 2002, and has just started to slow down again, marginally, since 2015. China is now, for all practical purposes, stable.

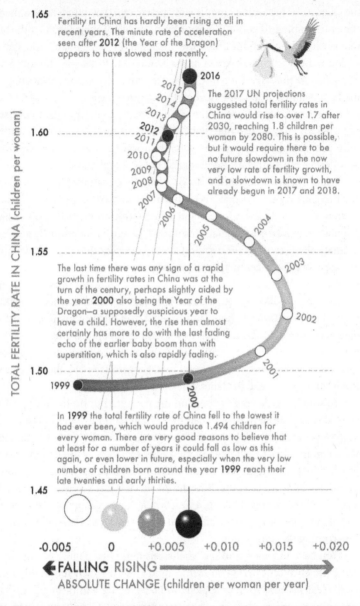

Fertility in China has hardly been rising at all in recent years. The minute rate of acceleration seen after **2012** (the Year of the Dragon) appears to have slowed most recently.

2016

2015
2014
2013
2012
2011
2010
2009
2008
2007
2006
2005
2004
2003
2002
2001
2000
1999

The 2017 UN projections suggested total fertility rates in China would rise to over 1.7 after 2030, reaching 1.8 children per woman by 2080. This is possible, but it would require there to be no future slowdown in the now very low rate of fertility growth, and a slowdown is known to have already begun in 2017 and 2018.

The last time there was any sign of a rapid growth in fertility rates in China was at the turn of the century, perhaps slightly aided by the year **2000** also being the Year of the Dragon—a supposedly auspicious year to have a child. However, the rise then almost certainly has more to do with the last fading echo of the earlier baby boom than with superstition, which is also rapidly fading.

In **1999** the total fertility rate of China fell to the lowest it had ever been, which would produce 1.494 children for every woman. There are very good reasons to believe that at least for a number of years it could fall as low as this again, or even lower in future, especially when the very low number of children born around the year **1999** reach their late twenties and early thirties.

TOTAL FERTILITY RATE IN CHINA (children per woman)

1.65
1.60
1.55
1.50
1.45

-0.005   0   +0.005   +0.010   +0.015   +0.020

◄ FALLING RISING ➤
ABSOLUTE CHANGE (children per woman per year)

37. China: total fertility rate, 1999–2016. (World Bank Open Data, fertility rate, estimates based on the 2017 *UN World Population Prospects* and other sources, https://data.world bank.org/indicator/sp.dyn.tfrt.in.)

THE SLOWDOWN IS NOW OCCURRING EVERYWHERE

It is not just in China, in the United States, and in the United Kingdom that each recent generation has seen its demographic world turned upside down; the social tsunami has swept the whole planet. For some generations the greatest changes have been the most recent ones, with the changes for their granddaughters' younger years the most dramatic. For others, it was during their own earlier lifetimes that the rate of slowdown was greatest. The babies of Generation V (born 1901–28) were born in the period that started the year that the British queen (and Indian empress) Victoria died, and ended the year before the Wall Street crash. This generation saw the most turbulent change of all, including two world wars and the fastest—truly phenomenal—population growth. In 1926 the first person to be born into a world containing 2 billion other humans arrived.

Just a few years before that, in 1922, in the heart of Northwest Africa, long after the French had invaded much of the rest of the continent that was not in British hands, a French colony was carved out of ancient kingdoms (including part of the former Kanem-Bornu Empire) through which flowed the Niger River that would give the country its name. In 2010, the seventh and most recent Republic of Niger was formed, following decades of military interventions designed to curtail dissent. Niger is included here because it might be the very last place you would expect to see slowdown, given that it currently has the highest total fertility rate recorded for any country in the world.

In both Niger and in England in 1901, as everywhere else in the world, the most common occupation was agricultural laborer, or farmer. Four-wheeled tractors would not be invented until 1908, three-wheeled industrial tractors only in 1901, and neither variety would arrive in Niger for many decades. In 2018 the government of Niger announced that it had secured 130 tractors and was working with Chinese firms to increase the amount of land being irrigated.[13] In 1901, women, children, and men in what would become Niger picked crops by hand, just as their parents and grandparents had done. Many were nomads; some were hunter-gatherers. Niger's Generation V would see the most changes of all: in childhood, in times of war, and in the technological advances that came during their later years. It was this generation that in 1960 gained independence from France, which was followed by a series of republics interrupted by military regimes. Although living, like farming, changed slowly at first in Niger, it would nevertheless change beyond all recognition.

Today we often characterize the era of Generation V, from Edwardian England to Jazz Age America, as lethargic. But for most ordinary people, it was anything but. Each year from 1901 to 1928, more than a million men in England and Wales would spend almost all of their days below ground in coal mines. Never before and never again would we experience a rate of change like that, and then see the absolute number of miners drop away in such huge numbers. Many people worked in the most appalling conditions. Women and children were forbidden to work in mines in Britain from before the transition began, but it would be wrong to call this progress. It would be better to call it turmoil. The births of Generation V ended in a general strike in the United Kingdom and the formation of a colony in Niger. Older British children still worked in factories during these years. Domestic servant was the most common job for an English woman. Children in Niger continued to work on the land, but coal and uranium mines were coming.

Worldwide, when the first of Generation V were born, roughly one in one thousand people died in war. That figure rose to nearer two in one thousand during adulthood for this generation, and also for their children. But for their grandchildren in Generation X, the war death toll was nearer one in ten thousand; and (so far) for their great-grandchildren (Generation Y), it is only two in one hundred thousand—although it is still much higher in Niger. Hopefully it will shrink yet again for Generation Z as the trend continues rapidly downward.[14] If these data are valid, then there has been a hundredfold reduction in deaths from legalized violence worldwide over the course of the lives of five generations.

Violence remains more common in some places than others. Rich states, such as the United States, France, and the United Kingdom, continue to wage international war that they often simply label "interventions," and use bombs and drones to avoid casualties among their own soldiers. In Niger the wars have been largely internal, including many attempted coups in the 1960s, when the initial slowdown in fertility that the country had enjoyed in the early 1960s then reversed. Following a military coup in 1974, in the wake of drought and famine, total fertility rose above 7.8 children per woman as the already weak social stability evaporated. Niger has the dubious honor of being the country in the world with the highest fertility rate because social progress in its past was so poor. Outside interference to gain control of mineral resources, including uranium, played more than a small part in this story. But as the timeline in figure 38 shows, even in

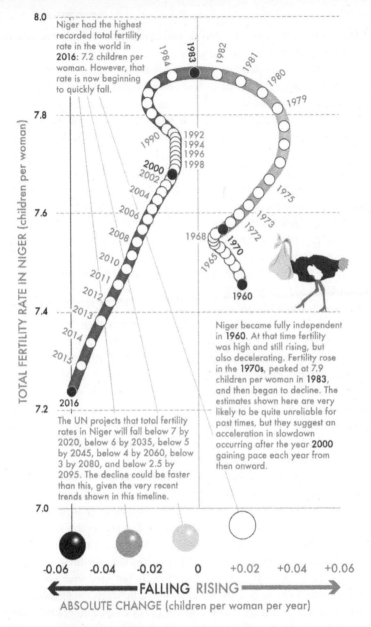

TOTAL FERTILITY RATE IN NIGER (children per woman)

Niger had the highest recorded total fertility rate in the world in **2016**: 7.2 children per woman. However, that rate is now beginning to quickly fall.

1984
1983
1982
1981
1980
1979

1990
1992
1994
1996
1998

2000
2002
2004
2006
2008
2010
2011
2012
2013
2014
2015
2016

1975
1973
1972
1970
1968
1965
1960

Niger became fully independent in **1960**. At that time fertility was high and still rising, but also decelerating. Fertility rose in the **1970s**, peaked at 7.9 children per woman in **1983**, and then began to decline. The estimates shown here are very likely to be quite unreliable for past times, but they suggest an acceleration in slowdown occurring after the year **2000** gaining pace each year from then onward.

The UN projects that total fertility rates in Niger will fall below 7 by 2020, below 6 by 2035, below 5 by 2045, below 4 by 2060, below 3 by 2080, and below 2.5 by 2095. The decline could be faster than this, given the very recent trends shown in this timeline.

-0.06   -0.04   -0.02   0   +0.02   +0.04   +0.06

⬅ **FALLING** RISING ➡

ABSOLUTE CHANGE (children per woman per year)

38. Niger: total fertility rate, 1960–2016. (World Bank Open Data, fertility rate, estimates based on the 2017 *UN World Population Prospects* and other sources. https://data.world bank.org/indicator/sp.dyn.tfrt.in.)

Niger fertility rates are now slowing, and that slowdown has been becoming more marked in very recent years.

Members of the past five generations have lived through some of the longest periods of relative peace humans have ever experienced. In most rich states of the world, only the first of the past five generations personally experienced war in adulthood, although in some cases their governments waged and supported war abroad. In great contrast, most children in Niger have seen war around their own homes, as have their parents: there was a Tuareg rebellion in the 1990s, a second Tuareg rebellion more recently, a Maghreb insurgency that began just after the start of the current century and, in recent years, a Boko Haram insurgency. For total fertility rates in Niger to continue to decelerate at a faster and faster pace, there will need to be peace—not just limited prosperity, another 130 tractors, and more Chinese-built irrigation.

To see the pace of change speeding up, we must turn to Generation W (born 1929–55). This was the generation that included the great 1946–50 baby boom. The birth rate rose around the world; in Britain it did not decline, and then only briefly, until 1955 in what was then "austerity Britain." In many other countries, the drop in births came later. In East Timor (notable because of its very high fertility rates) the birth rate did not stop declining in the 1960s and 1970s, which were times of slowdown almost everywhere. But then with war came a rise in fertility; the story is told within figure 39. Today, however, the slowdown is occurring everywhere, even in East Timor, following the end of the Indonesian occupation and over one hundred thousand conflict-related deaths. It still, however, has the highest total fertility rates in all of Asia.

Generation W was the generation whose members were born and survived to procreate in unprecedented numbers across Europe, in North America, and in Japan, and who had the greatest number of surviving siblings, nephews, and nieces. The final year of this generation saw a dip in births not just in the United Kingdom but also in the United States.[15] If it is at all possible to delimit a generation neatly, then for these two countries the Generation W dates work quite well, but they were not chosen because they work well. They are determined by when people born after 1901 themselves most often had children, and by when their grandchildren were born. They also tell you when your parents and grandparents were most likely to have been born.

Niger is on the same longitude as the United Kingdom, but further south by more than thirty degrees of latitude. East Timor is about as far away as it is possible to get from the center of the United States—it is literally on the opposite side of the planet—and yet it was also a place where fertility was falling, just as in the United Kingdom and the United States, until the great disruption of war came. Generation W in East Timor should have enjoyed peace and growing prosperity, but instead its members were, for a time—quite a long time—fated to live worse lives than their parents.

In affluent countries, the lives of Generation W differed so greatly from those of their parents that it is a great testament to human adaptability that the two generations were able to understand each other at all. Generation W was the generation that included hippies at one extreme and mass industrialized workers of the world at the other. It was the first generation to be chained in their millions to production lines as adults, making everything from cars to processed food.

When it came to high tech, Generation W was the nuclear generation. Most were born before the first—and mercifully so far only—time that nuclear bombs were used on people and cities, when the United States dropped "Fat Boy" and "Little Man" on Hiroshima and Nagasaki. But by the time people of that generation were adults, tens of thousands of nuclear bombs had been manufactured. When disarmament came, stockpiles fell worldwide at least sixfold. As the oldest members of Generation W contemplated retirement, the universal test ban treaty meant that almost no nuclear weapons were being tested or developed. If current trends continue, by the time the youngest and longest-lived of this generation die, the world could be largely free of nuclear weapons. It is not impossible. Since the 1980s there has been a rapid drop in the number of countries experimenting with nuclear weapons.[16]

Avoiding war is crucial for population stability. War brings about and sustains baby booms. East Timor is one of the world's most telling examples of this process, and yet even there, starting in 2002 when peace came at last, fertility rates began to plummet. But it is not just freedom from the threat of violence that people need to be able to slow down; they also need economic stability, a steady supply of affordable food, security of housing, better education, health care, and the confidence that their children have a very good chance of survival. All this has improved in East Timor, but only very recently, resulting in the particular timeline revealed in figure 39.

East Timor is now moving toward a state that became common much earlier elsewhere. Many people of Generation W saw the price of food

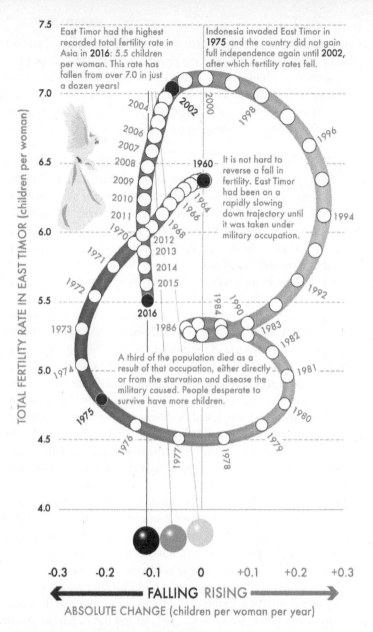

TOTAL FERTILITY RATE IN EAST TIMOR (children per woman)

East Timor had the highest recorded total fertility rate in Asia in **2016**: 5.5 children per woman. This rate has fallen from over 7.0 in just a dozen years!

Indonesia invaded East Timor in **1975** and the country did not gain full independence again until **2002**, after which fertility rates fell.

It is not hard to reverse a fall in fertility. East Timor had been on a rapidly slowing down trajectory until it was taken under military occupation.

A third of the population died as a result of that occupation, either directly or from the starvation and disease the military caused. People desperate to survive have more children.

7.5

7.0

6.5

6.0

5.5

5.0

4.5

4.0

2004 2002 2000 1998 1996
2006
2007
2008 1960
2009
2010
2011 1964
1970 1966
1971 1968
1972 2012
2013 1994
2014
2015 1992
1973 2016
1974 1986 1984 1990 1983
1975 1982
1976 1981
1977 1978 1979 1980

-0.3   -0.2   -0.1   0   +0.1   +0.2   +0.3

← **FALLING** RISING ➡
ABSOLUTE CHANGE (children per woman per year)

39. East Timor: total fertility rate, 1960–2016. (World Bank Open Data, fertility rate, estimates based on the 2017 *UN World Population Prospects* and other sources, https://data .worldbank.org/indicator/sp.dyn.tfrt.in.)

halve over the period from when the oldest of them were born through to the birth of the youngest. For instance, a loaf of bread in New Zealand cost nearly 8 pence shortly after 1929.[17] In real terms it cost less than half that a couple of years before 1955. Food had become much cheaper. In New Zealand the price of bread did not ever fall as fast again; in fact, it rose recently as international grain prices rose. But it should never again fall or rise by as much as it fell back then.

Food falling in price as its abundance rose occurred worldwide during the childhood of Generation W (born 1929–55). The rationing that came with war, which did not end in countries such as England until the 1950s, has left the impression of want. However, even that rationing included a greater allowance for children than the average amount of food they had eaten before rationing. Children were seen as the future in a way that they had not been before, partly because people were so certain that the future would be different.

Science fiction—popular-culture attempts to imagine the future—rose and rose in popularity through the years of Generation W's childhood because, with such enormous change, suddenly anything seemed possible. H. G. Wells wrote *The War of the Worlds* in 1898, at the start of the era of silent films and shortly before the first of our five generations was born. It is worth remembering that "the talkies" became a global phenomenon only in the early 1930s. *The War of the Worlds* would be adapted into a famous (and infamous) radio play broadcast in 1938, and first came to film screens in 1953, in Technicolor, just as the last of the second generation of these favorable seasons were arriving.

Diseases were being eradicated. Computers were being created. Universities were being established. Schooling years were being extended. Life expectancy was rising. Old age was becoming achievable and saving for a pension more commonplace, including universal provision by government for those in old age. Yet these were helter-skelter years.[18] East Timor declared independence from Portugal in November 1975 but was invaded by Indonesia (with Australian, U.K., and U.S. support) in December 1975. Never take progress for granted.

THE SLOWDOWN BEGAN WITH GENERATION X

The third of the five generations of great social transformation begins with those born in 1956, the year of the Suez Crisis and the final realization (in Europe at least) that the United States was the dominant world power.

If you are American or Canadian you may need to look up the Suez Crisis, because for your countries it was a relatively unimportant event! For the purposes of this book Generation X was born between 1956 and 1981. Other sources often use shorter periods and slightly different starting and end dates; but no other generation definition fits well into the longtime series of generations defined in table 7, set according to the actual length of time between generations.

Generation X differed most obviously from all previous generations, which partly explains why it was nicknamed before other generations were given alphabetic monikers. The Canadian writer Douglas Coupland is credited with christening this generation around the year 1987, shortly after its last members were born, almost all (by definition) to members of the previous and very different Generation W. A few were lucky enough to have "enlightened" parents, but most saw the older generation as old-fashioned. This generation all came of age long after the year sex began, which, according to Philip Larkin in his poem "Annus Mirabilis," was 1963. This generation was different.

Members of Generation X, who typically had very young Generation W parents, and their Generation V grandparents were also quite young (since that time, the average age at which people have their first child has got older). In Britain, as their grandparents were trying to come to terms with imperial demotion and their parents were mostly enjoying full employment (for men) and very rapidly improving attitudes about women, Generation X itself was watching the cathode ray tube TV. Their children would watch flat screens, their grandchildren may well use Google glasses or an electronic contact lens, but after that, the room for further technical advancement will start to diminish. Bypassing the eye to put images directly in the brain may turn out to be really useful only for blind people, and hopefully there will be fewer blind people in future.

Sometimes everything appears to change, but everything cannot change forever. Sex, drugs, rock 'n' roll, schools, jobs, homes, health, beliefs, views, experiences, and travel—they cannot always be more different for the next generation than the last. We now say the music is not as good as it was. In fact, it has probably simply stopped changing as quickly as it did during Generation X's youth. Their youthful years were especially politically active; including their growing concern for other parts of the world that they increasingly became aware of. Vietnam was the most obvious such place for Americans, but much nearer to home for them was Guatemala.

Guatemala is shown in the next timeline in this chapter (figure 40) because it is the country in the Americas that currently has the highest total fertility rate in that region; once again, this phenomenon is the result of outside intervention. Never blame a high-fertility country for its fertility rate, especially if you happen to live in one of the places that intervened. However, it makes little difference where we focus: the stories around the world in these years tend to be much more similar than we thought at the time.

Just before the first children of Generation X were born, the United States instigated a coup in Guatemala organized by the Central Intelligence Agency (CIA). The United States was dominant worldwide and believed it was in a fight to the death, via the nuclear annihilation of the planet, with the USSR. Ironically, Americans did not take too much notice of the rise of communist China. President Nixon's famous 1972 visit to China and the misunderstandings over "it being too early to tell" were mentioned earlier in this book. The United States was too busy interfering all across the Americas in what it thought were strategic enclaves, as well as in much of the rest of the world, to notice the start of China rising in a very different way from how states had become resurgent in the past.

Guatemala's American-instigated civil war began in 1960 and continued for almost four decades. All the countries of the world that currently have some of the highest fertility rates are in that position now because of events such as this. Had it not been the United States, it would probably have been some other world power wreaking havoc around the world, especially on countries with mineral resources or oil. Guatemala has uranium, nickel, oil, and other minerals. However, even despite a war (that lasted throughout the 1960s, 1970s, 1980s, and early 1990s) and especially after peace began to be established in the late 1990s, total fertility rates in Guatemala fell rapidly almost always after 1970. With rates of fewer than three children per woman today, what was once the most highly fertile place in the Americas has changed markedly. The human population of the entire continental mass of the Americas is now well set to slow down.

Let's zoom ahead to the children of Generation X. Generation Y began in 1982, and the year 2011 is most likely to be seen as its end point (once all the statistics are in). Its total duration will be a little longer if many older women have children very late in life in the next few years. Generation Y's oldest members, who include Britain's Prince William, were born in the year in which China's population first exceeded 1 billion, the first country

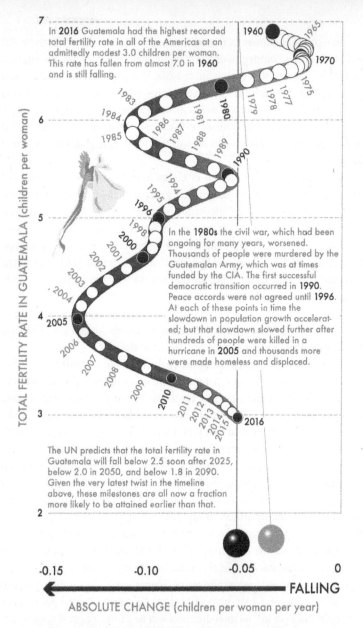

TOTAL FERTILITY RATE IN GUATEMALA (children per woman)

In **2016** Guatemala had the highest recorded total fertility rate in all of the Americas at an admittedly modest 3.0 children per woman. This rate has fallen from almost 7.0 in **1960** and is still falling.

In the **1980s** the civil war, which had been ongoing for many years, worsened. Thousands of people were murdered by the Guatemalan Army, which was at times funded by the CIA. The first successful democratic transition occurred in **1990**. Peace accords were not agreed until **1996**. At each of these points in time the slowdown in population growth accelerated; but that slowdown slowed further after hundreds of people were killed in a hurricane in **2005** and thousands more were made homeless and displaced.

The UN predicts that the total fertility rate in Guatemala will fall below 2.5 soon after 2025, below 2.0 in 2050, and below 1.8 in 2090. Given the very latest twist in the timeline above, these milestones are all now a fraction more likely to be attained earlier than that.

-0.15   -0.10   -0.05   0

FALLING

ABSOLUTE CHANGE (children per woman per year)

40. Guatemala: total fertility rate, 1960–2016. (World Bank Open Data, fertility rate, estimates based on the 2017 *UN World Population Prospects* and other sources, https://data .worldbank.org/indicator/sp.dyn.tfrt.in.)

to reach that mark. This generation was the first to see the slowdown begin in earnest, and so these young people are not as different from their parents' generation as they may think they are. Often, they are better behaved than their parents' generation: they drink less, they take fewer drugs, they rarely riot. When asked, a majority often say they would not go to war for their country. Only a minority of their parents were hippies. Their grandparents accepted conscription and did go to war; but Generation Y is different, even if not quite so different from the previous generation. Because the slowdown was now well under way, those in Generation Y were the first to behave and be a little more like their parents, at least so far as we can tell by the year 2020. They might be very different in their old age; we shall have to wait and see.

Thirty years ago, in 1990, the World Wide Web was spinning its first threads. Just nine years later, James Gleick published the book *Faster: The Acceleration of Just about Everything,* in which he said that everything, from finance to our relationships, was speeding up. Our money would move around faster, we would have more sexual partners, and all this would most affect Generation Y, the generation that came to be called the millennials.

Gleick, and so many others who predicted an impending acceleration, got it wrong. In the event we actually had fewer relationships, especially in those places that adapted to new technologies first. In 1970 just one in sixty men in Japan was unmarried at age fifty. By 2015 one in four Japanese men, and one in seven Japanese women, did not have a spouse.[19] In 2016 some 42 percent of Japanese men and 44 percent of Japanese women under the age of thirty-five "admitted they were virgins."[20] There is no reason Gleick should have known in 1990 that the slowdown was beginning in technology and lifestyle as it had begun earlier in population, but in hindsight, it is clear it had. In many ways Gleick was, as everyone is and doubtless as I am, reflecting the past when he thought he was writing about the future.[21]

For Generation Y there was less change to computers, phones, vehicles, airplanes, and technology in general. As I am typing these words I am watching a report about a foldable smartphone with a screen that bends, but doesn't really work very well. What we think of as new is now so often not fundamentally different from what came before: not as new as new used to be, or even that usefully new. Ordering from a catalog on a screen is not that different from using a printed one, and seeing the person you are talking to on a video screen is not as big a jump as being able to talk on the phone in the first place. This is also the generation who wait longer to have children. On average their first children are born at the same age that their great-grandparents had their middle children.

Of course, in a few places in the world Generation Y may have arrived a little later than the years given here. Some places, like Japan, are ahead of their time, while others appear to be behind the times. One place in the latter situation is Haiti, the country with the second-highest total fertility rate in the Americas today. From 1960 through 1986 Haiti's birth rate was, as far as we can tell, oscillating. The circles in figure 41 are so neatly aligned in these years that their precise positions are almost certainly the product of the mathematical models used to estimate them.

If you want to claim that there are still places in the world untouched by progress, then you have to explain the sudden change in Haiti from 1986, when it was usual for each woman to have six children on average, some of those six being the youngest of Generation Y, to 2016, just a generation later, when the majority of the first of Haiti's Generation Z had only two siblings each, not five.

The final generation in this short story-within-a-story is Generation Z, whose first members were born in 2012 and the last of whom may be born as late as 2042. Here, we are in the realm of almost pure speculation—necessarily—but nevertheless based on projections made by others and well worth considering. The possible future king of England—Prince George Alexander Louis of Cambridge, born in 2013—was born into this generation. George has the same number of siblings as a child born in Haiti today will probably have. His sibling count is two (Louis and Charlotte). His best-known great-grandmother (everyone has at least four) is Queen Elizabeth, who was one of the younger members of Generation V (born in 1926). One of his grandfathers, Charles, was born in 1948, plumb in the middle of Generation W; one of his grandmothers, Diana, was born in 1961 and was a member of Generation X; and his parents were both born in 1982, at the start of Generation Y. Generation Z will have the lowest average family size. There will be more only children in this generation than there have ever been before in the history of our species. Less common will be children such as George, with two or more siblings.

Generation Z could also be the first generation in this series to live a life not very different at all from their parents—not to earn higher incomes, to have much more wealth, a larger home, a faster and flashier vehicle, more exotic holidays, a life filled with increased activity every waking minute. It is conventional wisdom to say that we now do more and more in the time

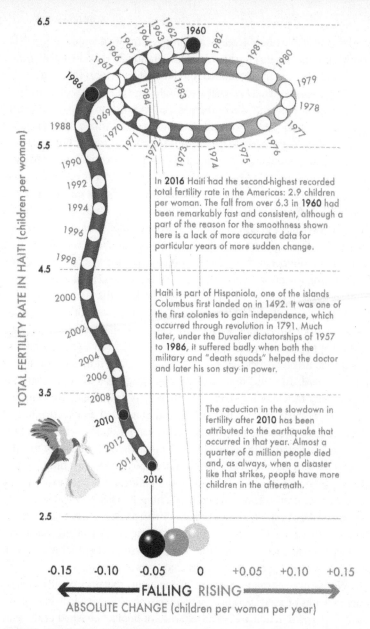

TOTAL FERTILITY RATE IN HAITI (children per woman)

6.5

5.5

4.5

3.5

2.5

In **2016** Haiti had the second-highest recorded total fertility rate in the Americas: 2.9 children per woman. The fall from over 6.3 in **1960** had been remarkably fast and consistent, although a part of the reason for the smoothness shown here is a lack of more accurate data for particular years of more sudden change.

Haiti is part of Hispaniola, one of the islands Columbus first landed on in 1492. It was one of the first colonies to gain independence, which occurred through revolution in 1791. Much later, under the Duvalier dictatorships of 1957 to **1986**, it suffered badly when both the military and "death squads" helped the doctor and later his son stay in power.

The reduction in the slowdown in fertility after **2010** has been attributed to the earthquake that occurred in that year. Almost a quarter of a million people died and, as always, when a disaster like that strikes, people have more children in the aftermath.

-0.15   -0.10   -0.05   0   +0.05   +0.10   +0.15

← **FALLING** RISING ➡

ABSOLUTE CHANGE (children per woman per year)

41. Haiti: total fertility rate, 1960–2016. (World Bank Open Data, fertility rate, estimates based on the 2017 *UN World Population Prospects* and other sources, https://data.world bank.org/indicator/sp.dyn.tfrt.in.)

we have available since "acceleration" implies that we do more things in less time.[22] But that needn't be the case of Generation Z. They do not all need to work and play and live life harder and faster than before. They can't.

It is in places like Haiti that we should expect the lives of Generation Z to be most different, where there is still so much to change, where the provision of basic services is still not universal and where life expectancy, literacy, health, and welfare can all still improve so much. But elsewhere, although we often hanker after great changes, we are much more likely to see small ones instead. America will not become "great again," but its people may soon come to realize that its recent past was not that great, just as slowdown helps the British begin to realize that the empire they were at the heart of was a place of destabilization, the opposite of stability.[23] Generation Z is the first-ever generation whose members will live to see human total population numbers fall naturally. By then, with just a little more technological progress on the very old technology of the census, we may with some accuracy even be able to name the month in which it occurs.

When thinking about Generation Z, we can talk only of what we think we know from projections: what trends are now well established, and what could happen to throw all this off course—climate change, war, famine, pestilence, disease, the usual suspects from the four horses of the apocalypse onward. The 1982 film *Blade Runner* imagines a dystopian, socially divided city in which the dominant imagery is East Asian. This imagery was used because at that time the United States had a collective fear of the economic rise of Japan. It would have been far more prescient had the imagery suggested an imagined future China. The 2017 sequel of the film was released to great acclaim, but it was a trope that was beginning to tire. Korea was now used as the slightly more politically correct exotica. The original film itself was an adaption of Philip K. Dick's 1968 science fiction novel, *Do Androids Dream of Electric Sheep?* There were many similar books at that time. Chapter 12, the concluding chapter of this book, begins with a reference to yet another work of dystopic 1968 sci-fi, *Stand on Zanzibar,* and a suggestion as to why it too was written then.

We live in an era when the growing inequality that once could be found only in works of 1960s fiction is now often seen as inevitable, when "new" ideas in science fiction are often rehashes of books published at the end of the acceleration. This was at the very moment of change in the second derivative, namely, change in the growth rate from increasing to decreasing or, visually on the timelines shown here, the point in time that the pendulum begins swinging in the opposite direction.

We find impending disaster captivating because it fits our current favorite (but probably incorrect) theory that the near future will be very different to the recent past. It fits our learned experience that great change is what happens to each generation, but we need to recognize that such change is slowing; there is no inevitability to the fear that because change is still happening, disaster must be on the way. It could be, but it need not be, and change is not happening at anything like the pace it was. Stability tends not to provoke disasters. Disasters—war deaths, flu epidemics, mass starvation, and the last of the great famines—all peaked during the peak years of the capitalist transition, during the lives of the past five generations (with the great Chinese famine of 1958–61 being worse than any of the earlier terrible huge Indian famines, or the East Africa famine of the 1980s). Only global temperature rises are still accelerating, and their peak could well lag behind other changes by many decades.

In France, modern fertility peaked in 1963, the year in which "sex began" in England.[24] Figure 42 shows the rapid deceleration from 2.9 children per woman then, to less than 1.9 when *Blade Runner* first hit cinema screens (2.1 would be needed at that time for stability). Numerous attempts by the French authorities to boost fertility only managed to nudge the total fertility rate over 2 for a very few years. In the past couple of years, it has hung in the balance, at 1.96, and it will soon almost certainly settle a little lower than that, given the current trends in so much of the rest of the world. Young adults with fewer children of their own make demonstrating easier, as you don't have to take a baby to the protest. Modern mass protesting began in France in 1968. It is not easy to demonstrate when at any moment you may have to change a diaper. The precursors of today's climate change protests were the protests that took place in 1968 about everything being wrong—and especially the protests in France.

A time is coming when rampant consumption will wane; when it is recognized that wealth does not engender happiness, and that much advertising is designed to create jealousy; when the lives of most people will be improved by better organization and cooperation, not by more competition; and when we understand that much that is enjoyable is free or virtually free—dramatically more so with the rise of the World Wide Web. Love, friendship, and caring preceded capitalism and will outlive it. Capitalism is a transition, not a steady state. The protesters of 1968 were simply ahead of their time.

Unaware of the dramatic slowdown under way, in 2018 people were still writing books with titles such as *Save the Earth . . . Don't Give Birth.*[25]

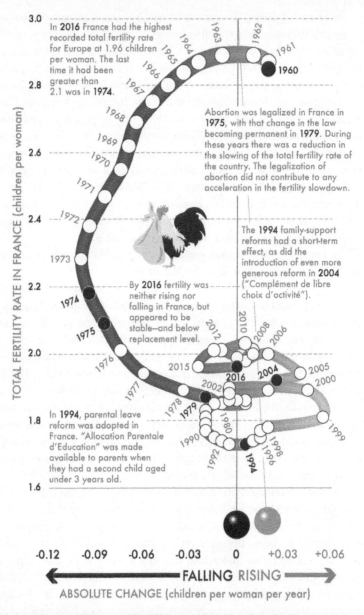

In **2016** France had the highest recorded total fertility rate for Europe at 1.96 children per woman. The last time it had been greater than 2.1 was in **1974**.

Abortion was legalized in France in **1975**, with that change in the law becoming permanent in **1979**. During these years there was a reduction in the slowing of the total fertility rate of the country. The legalization of abortion did not contribute to any acceleration in the fertility slowdown.

The **1994** family-support reforms had a short-term effect, as did the introduction of even more generous reform in **2004** ("Complément de libre choix d'activité").

By **2016** fertility was neither rising nor falling in France, but appeared to be stable—and below replacement level.

In **1994**, parental leave reform was adopted in France. "Allocation Parentale d'Education" was made available to parents when they had a second child aged under 3 years old.

TOTAL FERTILITY RATE IN FRANCE (children per woman)

FALLING   RISING

ABSOLUTE CHANGE (children per woman per year)

42. France: total fertility rate, 1960–2016. (World Bank Open Data, fertility rate, estimates based on the 2017 *UN World Population Prospects* and other sources, https://data.worldbank.org/indicator/sp.dyn.tfrt.in.)

Others were complaining about what they called "the negative attitudes to the population issue by the influential 'green' writer and columnist George Monbiot which 'had done great damage to the public's understanding of population issues.'"[26] But the slowdown is not always easily seen. Monbiot was one of the first environmentalists to recognize it in human population numbers. The slowdown occurs unhurriedly, in some cases over the course of several generations. We are tuned to look for what is new, exciting, and different, to expect continued rapid social progress and change.

The favorable seasons for human expansion, rapid technological change, and a rapid geographical reordering of where we live are all coming to an end. This is nothing to be scared about in regard to our demography. Assuredly, climate breakdown is something to be very scared about. But other than that emergency, which has to be addressed urgently, there will still be more and slower change, a less dramatic change compared with what has just occurred. The favorable seasons could not last for long and they were not all universally beneficial—far from it. However, by their very definition, the vast majority of us would not be alive today had they not taken place.

In the case of humans, the great population increase was also associated with a transformation of what it meant to be human. We migrated to cities, included some women in our upper echelons, became a lot taller, a little less racist, cleaner, and more educated, but perhaps also greedier—and any persistent admiration of that greed has to rapidly change if we are to survive well in our new numbers. We cannot have more and more property and possessions, even though there will soon be fewer of us in total. Greed was defended in the past by eugenicist ideas that some humans were worth more than others and so should be more rewarded. Eugenics is now rightly seen for the evil it is. Greed cannot be good.

THE SLOWDOWN IS UNIVERSAL

It was a geographical event, the connecting of the Old and New Worlds in 1492, that began the changes that eventually led to the capitalist transition, but for the vast majority of people in the world it was not until 1901 that the most important implications began to be felt. Rulers came and went, wars were fought, but for most people in most of the world life carried on much as it had before. Even in England, which was industrialized earlier than anywhere else, it was not until the turn of that century that there was great change for the majority of people in what mattered most in their lives: that their children survive them. Once you are sure that your children will survive, why have more than two? And once you realize that your genes are not that special, nor that different from your siblings' or cousins', why feel pressure to have any? You can care for other humans very well without having to be a biological parent. Figure 43 shows the recent fertility timeline for the United Kingdom. The trend should by now be familiar.

One of the many trends that could be chosen to justify selecting 1901 as the year in which the transition toward faster acceleration began, the year in which members of the first generation of the greater transition start to be born, is infant mortality. In the United States that year, for every 100,000 babies born, 2,000 *fewer* infants died than in 1900, the year immediately before. This was possibly a faster fall in infant mortality than ever happened before or afterward.[27] In 1900 in the United Kingdom, 13,000 babies died for every 100,000 born, dropping to 2,000 by 1960, 790 by 1990, 560 by 2000, 430 by 2010, 390 by 2014, and 370 in 2015, only to rise again to 380 in 2016 and 390 in 2017.[28] But it should fall again soon once the current cuts to health services, especially maternity services in the United Kingdom, and the country's devastating but short-term current rise in poverty rates are ended (when the government elected in 2017, and the regime in power since 2010, falls).[29]

A different infant mortality data set for a much poorer country would show the key infant mortality change beginning later. In the United Kingdom, that improvement began a littler earlier, around 1870, although infant mortality rates stopped dropping a few decades after that, then rose slightly, and then shot downward only after 1905. From that year onward, everywhere in the world, once the improvement in infant mortality began to set in, it almost always continued to improve. Everywhere in the world infant and child mortality has plummeted, and the plummeting began in the richest countries around the year 1901. The reasons are now well known, including dramatically improved sanitation and hygiene, as well as changing attitudes to women and the poor.[30]

In 1890, half of all the women aged twenty to twenty-four in England and Wales were married. A century later that proportion was below a fifth, and the most common age to marry was over thirty. That is one of the multiple facets of the great change.[31] But it is nothing compared to seeing the risk of your newborn children dying by age five fall in just a few years from one in four to one in five, then to one in ten by the time their children become parents, to one in fifty for their grandchildren and then to even much less than that, to a risk so small that it is not a serious worry now for the vast majority of people worldwide.

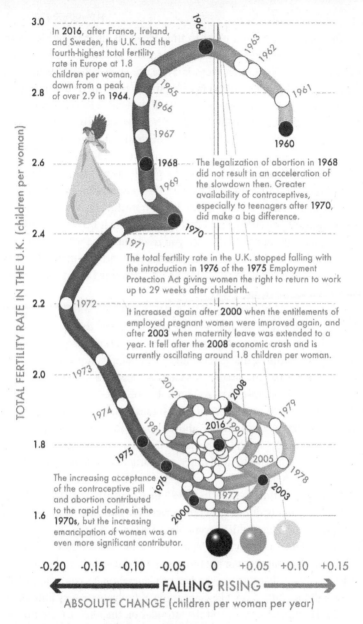

In **2016**, after France, Ireland, and Sweden, the U.K. had the fourth-highest total fertility rate in Europe at 1.8 children per woman, down from a peak of over 2.9 in **1964**.

The legalization of abortion in **1968** did not result in an acceleration of the slowdown then. Greater availability of contraceptives, especially to teenagers after **1970**, did make a big difference.

The total fertility rate in the U.K. stopped falling with the introduction in **1976** of the **1975** Employment Protection Act giving women the right to return to work up to 29 weeks after childbirth.

It increased again after **2000** when the entitlements of employed pregnant women were improved again, and after **2003** when maternity leave was extended to a year. It fell after the **2008** economic crash and is currently oscillating around 1.8 children per woman.

The increasing acceptance of the contraceptive pill and abortion contributed to the rapid decline in the **1970s**, but the increasing emancipation of women was an even more significant contributor.

TOTAL FERTILITY RATE IN THE U.K. (children per woman)

-0.20   -0.15   -0.10   -0.05   0   +0.05   +0.10   +0.15

← FALLING RISING →

ABSOLUTE CHANGE (children per woman per year)

43. United Kingdom: total fertility rate, 1960–2016. (World Bank Open Data, fertility rate, estimates based on the 2017 *UN World Population Prospects* and other sources, https://data.worldbank.org/indicator/sp.dyn.tfrt.in.)

The identification of a point in time when "it all changed" is always arbitrary. In the United Kingdom, January 1901 is known as "the end of an era" with the death of Queen Victoria. Here, the choice of 1901 as the great turning point is partly justified because it was the date of that first great drop in infant mortality across the whole of the United States. Before then, generation after generation had lived with worse (sometimes worsening) life chances—much worse in the newly industrialized cities, and somewhat better in the countryside. After 1901, the transition was truly in motion. It first resulted in accelerating numbers of people, as so many more infants made it through to become adults, and then deceleration as adults realized that their babies would survive. It is a transition that has to come to an end, most obviously for child mortality, because it becomes *impossible* to see significant improvement once you reach the point where almost no children die under age five anymore. We are now close to that in the very best-off countries of the world, although not yet in the United States, especially if you are black and poor.

Why use generations, rather than decades? Generations are the traditional way in which we interpret the kind of change that transition implies. A decade is both too short and too arbitrary a timescale. We compare our lives with those of our parents and grandparents, not with people in the 1990s or 1940s. The reason this chapter considers five generations is very simple. It is because that is the number of generations we have seen since 1901, since the experience of what it means to be human changed so abruptly for the majority. Table 7 above showed the period during which each generation was or will be born, for the most recent five generations, in the context of a hypothesized thirty-one earlier more stable and less unusual set of generations.

Although the time periods in table 7 may look arbitrary, the vast majority of the parents of one generation were the children of the previous generation, and their children were or will almost all be born within the next generation. To estimate the dates, I used the average ages of women having children, but they are not too precise. If you were born in 1981 you need not lament that you are the last of Generation X; you could easily behave and be a little more like Generation Y, but you are very unlikely to have similar experiences to, and the attitudes of, the older Generation W or the younger generation Z. This is true of any place in the world today.

Figure 44 shows the fertility rate trend in the Republic of Korea since 1960. Marvel at how it tumbles down. The fastest fertility falls of all have

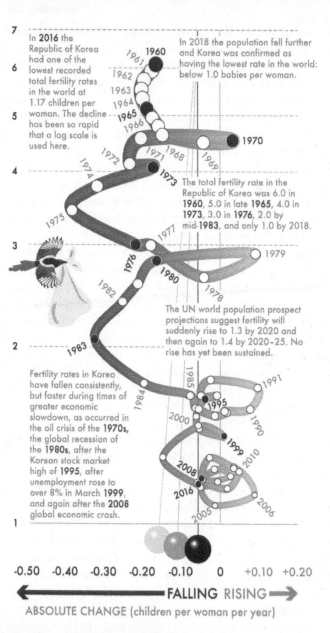

In **2016** the Republic of Korea had one of the lowest recorded total fertility rates in the world at 1.17 children per woman. The decline has been so rapid that a log scale is used here.

In 2018 the population fell further and Korea was confirmed as having the lowest rate in the world: below 1.0 babies per woman.

The total fertility rate in the Republic of Korea was 6.0 in **1960**, 5.0 in late **1965**, 4.0 in **1973**, 3.0 in **1976**, 2.0 by mid-**1983**, and only 1.0 by 2018.

The UN world population prospect projections suggest fertility will suddenly rise to 1.3 by 2020 and then again to 1.4 by 2020–25. No rise has yet been sustained.

Fertility rates in Korea have fallen consistently, but faster during times of greater economic slowdown, as occurred in the oil crisis of the **1970s**, the global recession of the **1980s**, after the Korean stock market high of **1995**, after unemployment rose to over 8% in March **1999**, and again after the **2008** global economic crash.

TOTAL FERTILITY RATE IN REPUBLIC OF KOREA (children per woman) LOG SCALE

-0.50   -0.40   -0.30   -0.20   -0.10   0   +0.10   +0.20

⬅ **FALLING** RISING ➡

ABSOLUTE CHANGE (children per woman per year)

44. Republic of Korea: total fertility rate, 1960–2016. (World Bank Open Data, fertility rate, estimates based on the 2017 *UN World Population Prospects* and other sources, https://data.worldbank.org/indicator/sp.dyn.tfrt.in.)

not been in what we once mistakenly called "the advanced economies" or "developed countries." There are not many separate transition models operating at different times in different places, just one model worldwide that exhibits quite a lot of variation. The outside intervention in Korea occurred earlier, in the war of 1950–54. Since then, there has been social stability and ever-rising economic prosperity in the Republic of Korea.

Table 7 above allows you to determine your own generation. A woman born in Korea in Generation W (1929–55) was most likely as an adult to have five or six children, all of whom were of Generation X. If they were one of the youngest of their generation, then they might have given birth to only three or four children. Even within a generation, average fertility experience varied greatly by birth year, such was the speed of change in Korea during the 1960s and 1970s.

The children born in Generation X (1956–81) in the Republic of Korea, when they became adults, were unlikely to have more than three children, and the later they were born the more likely they were to have two, one, or none. The South Korean children of Generation Y (1982–2011) will most commonly have a single child; more will have no children than two children. In 2019 it was reported that rural areas in the Republic of Korea were now enrolling illiterate grandmothers around age seventy into elementary schools, because they were running out of children to fill the classrooms.[32]

The younger the group you are in, the more recently you were born, the less likely you are to think that there has been a great change within the space of your lifetime. That is not just because you have fewer years to compare; it is also because great change didn't happen to you, and much of what is most important in life is *not* changing as fast today as it was for earlier generations.

The generations used in this chapter vary a little in length because initially, people had children earlier and earlier as the transition progressed during the first three of the last five generations, with the earliest childbearing ages being in the early 1970s. But then women worldwide became more and more likely to have their first child later and later in their lives, although not as late as many women in previous generations had the last of their children. These generations are useful because they conveniently partition people into groups who have had, or are expected to have, similar experiences, and they allow us to concentrate on just how different those experiences have been. Most recently, what is normal has stopped changing very quickly at all. Once fertility drops toward the large majority of women having zero, one, or two children, there is little scope for further change save for a small upward rise—which is what will eventually be needed to ensure stability sometime in the distant future.

Consider the recent story of fertility decline in Portugal, as shown in figure 45. The timeline here is not that very different from that of Korea. A small shift occurs between 1960 and 1975, a much greater shift from then until 1999, and then a smaller shift again until 2016. At each point—1960, 1975, 1999, and 2016—for a brief year or couple of years, the total fertility rate is not falling, and then it cascades down again.

In the medium term, Portugal will either depopulate, replace its losses with in-migration, or at some point see fertility rise a little again. Most likely it will be a combination of all three. Fertility rose in this period only in the aftermath of, or during, great social disturbance, as highlighted in the text within figure 45.

One way to consider trends is to subdivide the world into regions. In 1960, 9 percent of people in the world lived in Africa, 14 percent in the Americas, 22 percent in China, 15 percent in India, 26 percent in the rest of West Eurasia (west and north of India and China), and 14 percent in the East Asia/Pacific region, if it is defined as including Asia to the east and the south of India and China (of which the most populous countries in the 1960s were Japan, Indonesia, Bangladesh, Vietnam, Thailand, the Philippines, and the Republic of Korea).

In contrast, by 2017, 17 percent of people in the world lived in Africa, 13 percent in the Americas, only 18 percent in China, 18 percent in India, just 19 percent in the rest of West Eurasia (west and north of India and China), and 15 percent in the East Asia/Pacific region. These six regions are each home to a roughly equal share of today's global population.

Table 8 shows how the average number of children women gave birth to changed during each decade, both worldwide and by the roughly equal-sized six world regions defined above, from 1960 to 2017. Note that the final decade is not quite complete, and the first members of the final generation have only just been born. The table lists decades by the generation responsible for the majority of births in that decade. Individual years are shown for the most recent decade, and the absolute changes below that.

The exceptional continent is Africa, where more has changed for women when it comes to fertility falls than anywhere else in the world. If we were to single out a second place as exceptional, it would be West Eurasia. Fertility declines there were greater in the 1980s and 1990s than

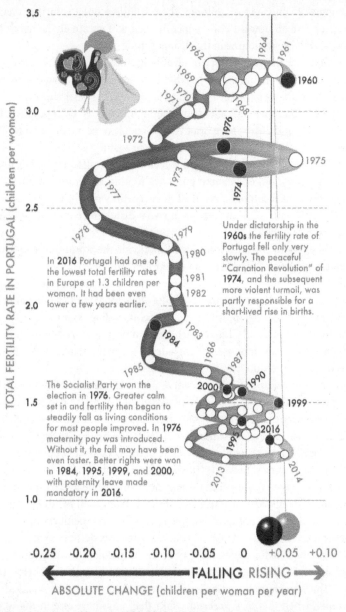

3.5

3.0

1962 *1964* *1961*
● **1960**
1969
1970
1971 *1968*
1972 ● **1976**
1973 ○ **1975**
● **1974**

TOTAL FERTILITY RATE IN PORTUGAL (children per woman)

2.5

1977
1978 *1979*
1980

Under dictatorship in the **1960s** the fertility rate of Portugal fell only very slowly. The peaceful "Carnation Revolution" of **1974**, and the subsequent more violent turmoil, was partly responsible for a short-lived rise in births.

In **2016** Portugal had one of the lowest total fertility rates in Europe at 1.3 children per woman. It had been even lower a few years earlier.

2.0
1981
1982
1983
● **1984**
1986
1985 *1987* *1990*
2000 ● **1999**

1.5
The Socialist Party won the election in **1976**. Greater calm set in and fertility then began to steadily fall as living conditions for most people improved. In **1976** maternity pay was introduced. Without it, the fall may have been even faster. Better rights were won in **1984**, **1995**, **1999**, and **2000**, with paternity leave made mandatory in **2016**.
1995 **2016**
2013 *2014*

1.0

-0.25   -0.20   -0.15   -0.10   -0.05   0   +0.05   +0.10

◄──── **FALLING RISING** ──►

ABSOLUTE CHANGE (children per woman per year)

45. Portugal: total fertility rate, 1960–2016. (World Bank Open Data, fertility rate, estimates based on the 2017 *UN World Population Prospects* and other sources, https://data.worldbank.org/indicator/sp.dyn.tfrt.in.)

the 1960s and 1970s. However, the rate had already fallen to only just over three children per woman by the early 1960s.

In contrast, in the Americas the fastest fall was a drop of almost one child per woman between the 1960s and 1970s. In China at the same time, that drop was of more than two children per woman. In India the 1980s saw the fastest change, and in the East Asia/Pacific region fertility fell fastest all through the 1970s and into the 1980s. Worldwide, fertility fell faster in the 1960s than the 1970s, faster in the 1970s than the 1980s, and so on and on. The fastest and most dramatic change has come and gone.

Mapping whole regions produces dull timelines, because rapid and interesting changes get averaged out—things happen at different times in different countries. However, the tables here show that the general trend to lower fertility rates is widespread. The data for individual years in the most recent decade also show that there has been absolutely no letdown in the rate of fertility slowdown. If anything, that rate has accelerated across Africa since 2012, across the Americas since 2014, and it was fastest in Western Eurasia and East Asia/Pacific most recently. In India it is not accelerating, but total fertility rates are now only 2.3 children per woman, and in China it is rising, but only by one hundredth of a child a year, and currently stands at 1.6 children per woman. Worldwide the global fertility rate has just dropped to 2.4 children per woman and that drop is—overall—accelerating. We are now truly living in slowdown.

Let's end with the most populous state in the Americas, Brazil. The timeline shown in figure 46 looks at first sight almost as if someone is trying to tie a knot at the end. The world has changed, Brazil has changed, the Americas have changed. We are now living through something new.

THE END OF POPULATION GROWTH

If you take the long view, then recent falls in fertility worldwide are not just short-term signs of hope; they should lead to a long-term realization that everything has utterly changed. The last children born when fertility rates were still accelerating worldwide were among the first of the older adults who now expect to live longer than ever before. There are limits to how long a human can live happily and healthily, and our obsession with pushing this on further and further is itself, thankfully, abating. A small group of rich-world demographers used to be obsessed with how long people in the future might live. Today the variation between the great continental regions of the world is diminishing. The six regions described above are each

Table 8a. Average number of children per woman by region and worldwide, 1960–2017, according to maternal generation affected, by decade of new births

Generation	Africa	Americas	China	West Eurasia	India	East Asia/ Pacific	World
W: 1960s	6.8	4.5	6.2	3.4	5.8	5.1	5.1
W: 1970s	6.7	3.6	4.0	3.1	5.2	4.6	4.3
X: 1980s	6.4	3.0	2.6	3.0	4.5	3.6	3.6
X: 1990s	5.6	2.6	1.8	2.5	3.7	2.8	3.0
X/Y 2000s	5.1	2.3	1.5	2.2	3.0	2.3	2.7
Y: 2010s	4.7	2.0	1.6	2.2	2.4	2.1	2.5
Annual breakdown of the numbers during the 2010s							
2010	4.9	2.1	1.6	2.3	2.6	2.2	2.6
2011	4.9	2.1	1.6	2.2	2.5	2.2	2.5
2012	4.8	2.0	1.6	2.3	2.5	2.2	2.5
2013	4.8	2.0	1.6	2.2	2.4	2.1	2.5
2014	4.7	2.0	1.6	2.2	2.4	2.1	2.5
2015	4.7	2.0	1.6	2.2	2.4	2.1	2.5
2016	4.6	2.0	1.6	2.2	2.3	2.1	2.5
2017	4.5	1.9	1.6	2.2	2.3	2.1	2.4

home to a roughly equal share of today's global population. What matters most (in the long view) is not how long you live, but how much time you get to spend with those you love.

We are currently living through a time of what researchers in the *Lancet* recently called "a remarkable transition." They reported in late 2018 that the most recent data showed that the acceleration in fertility rate falls meant nearly half of countries were now facing a "baby bust"—meaning there are insufficient children to maintain their population size. The researchers said the findings were a "huge surprise." And there would be profound consequences for societies with "more grandparents than grandchildren."[33]

What are the key ways in which we are slowing down? First of all, we are having fewer children. This is occurring almost everywhere worldwide, and this chapter has hopefully made clear just how profound that change has been. It has been touched on before in this book, but it has required an

Table 8b. Change in average number of children from previous decade

Generation	Africa	Americas	China	West Eurasia	India	East Asia/ Pacific	World
1960s–70s	−0.04	−0.92	−2.12	−0.25	−0.59	−0.52	−0.78
1970s–80s	−0.34	−0.60	−1.43	−0.12	−0.73	−0.97	−0.67
1980s–90s	−0.75	−0.43	−0.82	−0.47	−0.81	−0.84	−0.63
1990s–2000s	−0.52	−0.33	−0.23	−0.27	−0.70	−0.45	−0.34
2000s–10s	−0.38	−0.24	+0.06	−0.01	−0.57	−0.20	−0.15
Annual breakdown of change during the 2010s							
2010–11	−0.04	−0.03	+0.00	−0.02	−0.07	−0.02	−0.02
2011–12	−0.04	−0.02	+0.01	+0.01	−0.06	−0.01	−0.01
2012–13	−0.05	−0.02	+0.00	−0.02	−0.05	−0.02	−0.02
2013–14	−0.06	−0.01	+0.01	+0.00	−0.04	−0.02	−0.01
2014–15	−0.06	−0.02	+0.01	−0.01	−0.03	−0.01	−0.01
2015–16	−0.06	−0.02	+0.01	−0.01	−0.03	−0.02	−0.02
2016–17	−0.06	−0.03	+0.01	−0.02	−0.02	−0.02	−0.02

Source: World Bank, "World Development Indicators, Fertility Rate, Total (Births per Woman)," accessed 24 April 2019, https://data.worldbank.org/indicator/SP.DYN.TFRT.IN.

entire chapter to fully explain the magnitude and universal nature of the fertility fall, not least because the most recent changes in the rates at which we are having children are the most fascinating of all. In the most recent years, the slowdown has been accelerating. It is because of this that we can talk about slowdown with such confidence today. In many very populous places, such as China and Brazil, the norm has now settled at well under two children per woman in her lifetime.

The transition from acceleration to deceleration occurred around 1968, but then a generation later, around the year 2000, there was a second birth deceleration worldwide. Clearly the two are linked, but the second is not just the consequence of the first. The slowdown is itself slowing down faster than we thought it would—and even faster than we thought possible. Increasingly, in more and more regions, governments are now trying (and almost always failing) to boost fertility rates.

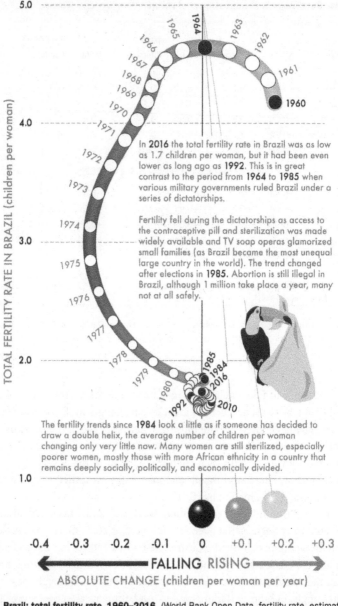

TOTAL FERTILITY RATE IN BRAZIL (children per woman)

5.0

1964
1965
1966
1967
1968
1969
1970
1971
1963
1962
1961
1960

4.0

1972
1973
1974
1975
1976
1977
1978
1979
1980

In **2016** the total fertility rate in Brazil was as low as 1.7 children per woman, but it had been even lower as long ago as **1992**. This is in great contrast to the period from **1964** to **1985** when various military governments ruled Brazil under a series of dictatorships.

Fertility fell during the dictatorships as access to the contraceptive pill and sterilization was made widely available and TV soap operas glamorized small families (as Brazil became the most unequal large country in the world). The trend changed after elections in **1985**. Abortion is still illegal in Brazil, although 1 million take place a year, many not at all safely.

3.0

2.0

1985
1984
2016
1992
2010

The fertility trends since **1984** look a little as if someone has decided to draw a double helix, the average number of children per woman changing only very little now. Many women are still sterilized, especially poorer women, mostly those with more African ethnicity in a country that remains deeply socially, politically, and economically divided.

1.0

-0.4   -0.3   -0.2   -0.1   0   +0.1   +0.2   +0.3

← **FALLING** RISING →

ABSOLUTE CHANGE (children per woman per year)

46. Brazil: total fertility rate, 1960–2016. (World Bank Open Data, fertility rate, estimates based on the 2017 *UN World Population Prospects* and other sources, https://data.world bank.org/indicator/sp.dyn.tfrt.in.)

Fertility rates began slowing in the 1970s in most countries in Africa. They had already begun slowing much earlier everywhere else in the world. By the first decade of the current century, in half of the world, rates had reached 2.3 children per couple or below, and even lower in the sixth of humanity that is China or the thirty-sixth that is Brazil. Then they fell again around 2010.

What matters most is that our fertility will soon reach two children per couple worldwide: it is already a reality for most people, and the rate is falling even faster and further in the world's major cities. It may well, for a time, fall below two per couple worldwide for a generation or two or three. After that, we do not know.

economics

stabilizing standards of living

Amazingly, prior to 2009, the Bank of England never lent to banks at a
short-term rate below 2 per cent. That had been low enough to cope with
the Napoleonic wars, two world wars and the Depression. Yet, for a decade
its rate has been close to zero. The bank has been in good company. The US
Federal Reserve has managed to raise its federal funds rate to 2.5 per cent,
but only with difficulty. The European Central Bank's rate is still near zero,
as is the Bank of Japan's. The latter's rate has been close to zero since 1995.
                                                      —*Martin Wolf, 7 May 2019*

England, the epicenter of the Industrial Revolution, would be pivotal in the
transition that took place during the favorable seasons of human population expansion. By 2005, more carbon had been placed in the atmosphere,
per person, due to the current and historical activities of people living in
the United Kingdom than anywhere else on the planet.[1] That record has
since been overtaken by other states. England repatriated profit from all
around the world, and without its empire it would not have had the large
and apparently ever-expanding captive markets needed to sell its carbon-
fueled manufactured goods. England is the first place that capitalism was
recognized to have solidly settled, and to be unstoppable—or at least unstoppable without great turmoil. Now more people can imagine the end of
the world than the end of capitalism.

In 1867 Karl Marx wrote, "Up to the present time, [the capitalists']
classic ground is England."[2] England is not where capitalism first began.
Perhaps that was Amsterdam, Venice, or Lisbon—but England is where
capitalist behavior was first most obviously transformative to the lives

of so many millions, and eventually billions, of people living elsewhere in the world.

The great transformation quickly found its safest home in London, only much later skipping over the Atlantic where a twin was born: New York. London and New York have since been seen as a pair working together—binary stars, orbiting around each other at the heart of the twentieth-century world economy.[3] However, the energy in their economic orbit has now waned.

We are living in an ongoing transformation. It may not at any future point stop abruptly, but it is certainly slowing, a fact that only recently has become increasingly apparent. Despite the impending shift in the global center toward the other side of the Pacific, we should not now expect Beijing, or any single city or pair of cities, to be its next center. All transitions eventually come to an end. We should expect finance, manufacturing, and political power to spread and disperse around the globe for some time to come now, from here on in.

Capitalism is a transition. It is not a mode of production. A mode implies a degree of stability. There has been no stability under capitalism (or the communist reactions to it)—neither demographic, economic, nor social. Capitalism is a period of change from social systems that were stable, in which lives were led in very similar ways generation after generation, to something else that we have not yet reached, which will probably also be stable. It is the very speed of the change, the very instability of capitalism, that reveals it to be a transition. It is so clear now, given so much change, that it is not a steady way in which the economy operates in a particular repeated manner.

Capitalism depends on the relentless creation of ever more new products and the social engineering of new markets, engendering new demands and needs. In the course of the past century this has been done most effectively through the explosion of advertising. To survive, capitalism requires ever-greater demand and perpetual change—progress for progress's sake. To keep buying and selling the next best thing, you have to keep creating new things and markets interested in acquiring them. By its very nature, capitalism is not sustainable. Why should it be?

Think of your recent ancestors' consumption patterns, their religious beliefs, how they dressed, where the material they wore came from, how and how often they traveled, what entertainment they enjoyed, what they ate. It is when you step back and consider the speed of change that you realize how wrong it is to think of capitalism as a settled era.

To understand why capitalism is a change, a turmoil, not an epoch, just look at how fast life under capitalism has, until recently, been continually transformed. To do so in England and Wales, you could count coal miners, using data from past decadal censuses. You would find that there were 1.24 million men working underground as miners in 1921, in the first of the five recent generations highlighted in the previous chapter. That number more than halved, to 0.59 million, by the end years of the second generation (by 1951), then halved again by the third generation to 0.23 million (by 1971), and then more than halved in the next generation and will almost certainly be negligible by the fifth.[4]

In May 2019, people in Britain managed to carry on living, playing, and working without using coal to generate electricity for 114 hours, the longest continuous time period since 1882, when the Edison Electric Light Station, the first coal-fired public power station, opened in London. By 7 May 2019, Britain had survived a total of one thousand hours without coal power.[5] Ireland then recorded a six-hundred-hour period without producing electricity from burning coal. This was around 10 May 2019, the longest period since the creation of an all-Ireland grid.[6] Many other countries are already coal-free, or always have been.

Recent decades have not been typified by a stable system of production, but by a radical, all-encompassing transformation of humanity. Within living memory, we have fundamentally changed and changed again our major sources of industrial power, the jobs that most people do, even how we simply heat our homes and talk to each other. Such rapid change is a historical aberration, a transformation that can happen only very rarely in the history of a species.

The fact that newspapers and magazines now celebrate the length of coal-free spells is an illustration of how much we are coming to appreciate changing to a more stable situation. The fact that it was made possible as much by unusually warm weather as by the switch to other sources of power generation is less encouraging.

PEAK GROWTH

Gross domestic product (GDP) is a weird concept. It has been measured only since the Second World War, and its definition is constantly being tinkered with. However, recently it has been made more and more comparable and consistent over time by international agreement. Its most simple definition is the total value of all the finished goods made and services provided during a specific period of time in a particular place. Angus Maddison, whose historical world population figures were used earlier in this book, is best known for having constructed a series of estimates of GDP and having then projected them back in time and across the globe. Since his death in 2010, updates of his estimates have been made by his former colleagues carrying on his work, and they are what is used here.[7]

The timeline in figure 47 shows the absolute growth in GDP per capita worldwide from as far back as we have measured or estimated it through to the latest year for which data were available at the time of writing. Drawn as it is, 2006 looks like the year of fastest growth, followed by subsiding peaks in 2010 and then 2017. However, in relative terms, the fastest-ever single year of growth was 1964, when GDP per capita rose by 4.15 percent worldwide. In the timeline this is shown as an increase of $230 per person on average, worldwide, and it doesn't look that large—but if you were to draw a line diagonally from the origin of the figure through to the 1964 point (all points represent the same relative rise) you would see that no other point is further to the right of this line.

In 1972, worldwide, GDP grew by $262 per person, but this represented only a 3.75 percent rise; in 2006 it grew by a massive $470 per person, but this was only 3.38 percent. Since 1964, global GDP has never again grown as quickly as it did in that year. It fell in 2008 and then exceeded 2 percent growth a year only in three of the subsequent ten years. The 2006 to 2018 trend is for global slowdown. Figure 60 in Chapter 11 in this book makes this all even clearer by using a log scale; but you can also see it here in figure 47 because the trend is now so obvious that it is even apparent without that transformation to log space being necessary.

We now know that we cannot continue to use more and more resources—especially fossil fuels for energy production. Just one generation ago, we did not know this fact. We will not see the number of people mining coal fall by very much in future because so few people are doing so today. Today giant machines mine coal. Today the highest production is in China, followed by India and then the United States. The fourth most "productive" country is Australia: 23 percent of its coal is exported to Japan and 18 percent to China, all of it going to power electricity-generating stations.

Currently China extracts 45 percent of annual world coal, but (unlike in America) the Chinese people and their government know very well that they have limited time to change over to other power sources. All mining industry employment will also soon be even lower worldwide as we begin

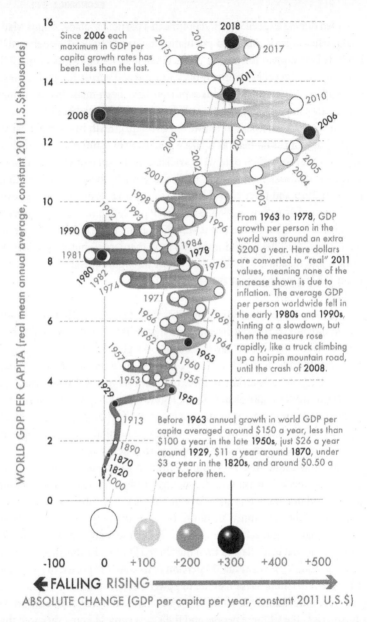

Since **2006** each maximum in GDP per capita growth rates has been less than the last.

From **1963** to **1978**, GDP growth per person in the world was around an extra $200 a year. Here dollars are converted to "real" 2011 values, meaning none of the increase shown is due to inflation. The average GDP per person worldwide fell in the early 1980s and 1990s, hinting at a slowdown, but then the measure rose rapidly, like a truck climbing up a hairpin mountain road, until the crash of **2008**.

Before **1963** annual growth in world GDP per capita averaged around $150 a year, less than $100 a year in the late **1950s**, just $26 a year around 1929, $11 a year around 1870, under $3 a year in the 1820s, and around $0.50 a year before then.

WORLD GDP PER CAPITA (real mean annual average, constant 2011 U.S.$thousands)

← FALLING RISING →

ABSOLUTE CHANGE (GDP per capita per year, constant 2011 U.S.$)

47. World GDP per capita, 1–2018. (Data adapted from Maddison Project Database 2018, hosted by the University of Groningen, updated using World Bank and IMF data, https://www.rug.nl/ggdc/historicaldevelopment/maddison/releases/maddison-project-database-2018.)

to learn to extract less. Currently, globally, coal extraction is falling even as population is still rising.[8] Most mining jobs were terrible jobs, despite the sense of solidarity created, and losing them is a good thing for us all, but nevertheless, this change does not mean that all is well. Today the lives of the vast majority of people around the world, even (and especially) in the wealthiest of countries, are still bedeviled by insecurity and uncertainty, just as mining was before workers unionized.

Much has improved, but we still live surrounded by poverty, greed, and ignorance—and all of these are the hallmarks of a transition. Mass poverty, greed, and ignorance were not ubiquitous in most previous periods of stability. People had enough to get by—their daily bread. The greedy were constrained by customs, rules, and religions that kept a lid on avarice. Ignorance was *low* because the vast majority knew what they *needed to know* for the jobs that they would do and the lives that they lived (just as most of us do now). We often think of people in the past as misguided, believing in gods and superstitions that we sneer at today. In the future people will look back at the confused plethora of religious, business, and evolving scientific beliefs that we have lived with, including their rapid mutations over the last five generations, and ask how on Earth we could not see that our age of acceleration and transition could not last. How did we not grasp the urgency of the climate emergency more quickly? We are the most ignorant ones.

It can be argued that in the distant past, before the transition began, before capitalism, there was less uncertainty. Most people were not ignorant of what they needed to know. Their occupations were usually the same as those of their parents, and training happened as a matter of course. Most people were well informed by religious authorities about how they should behave. Most were fed well enough not to get too fat or too thin. Most societies appear to have been more relaxed; individuals were often more autonomous. Members of hunter-gatherer societies, in particular, enjoyed a great deal of leisure time. Those who were greedy were brought to book, in the long run, through the rulings of religious authorities or even via the creation of new religions, which often started and became popular enough to eventually become a world religion because greed had grown too great at the time and place of their origin.[9]

We are so used to growth that when growth slows slightly, as is happening now worldwide, newspaper headline writers are swift to sound the alarm. In April 2019, the *Financial Times* reported that the global economy was entering a synchronized slowdown, and that the "findings follow generally disappointing economic indicators over the past six months that have shown a similar picture in the US, China and in Europe."[10] Of course, whether or not a slowdown is disappointing depends on what you think might be possible. If you think that economic growth can and should rise year after year, bar the few odd years in which there are recessions, then you will find the synchronized slowdown of today as frightening as the screak of the sharp slamming on of the brakes of a train.

Capitalism may well come to an end with a whimper, not a bang. Feudalism came to an end almost everywhere when traders began to arrive and settle, using their capital to invest and their armies to impose. So, too, it is possible that capitalism is already being pushed out from certain parts of the world by governments that use money raised from taxation to invest and employ the rule of law to better the behavior of the rich. At first, we will not see the change as that much different than what we had before. We may just tell ourselves that certain places have a more protective welfare state and are less entrepreneurial, although invention tends to be higher where there is more cooperation; we may say that these places have more of a tradition of supporting the rights of women, although this is a tradition that was hard won. We might argue that these trends have grown a little more strongly in particular cultures, but then we might also notice that, in general, the areas where these changes are happening are spreading.

The clues may well come from looking at where the slowdown in our fertility is greatest, or at where emissions of carbon per capita are falling fastest, or where there has genuinely been the greatest expansion of education—rather than a marketized bonanza in the selling of what are, in effect, fake university degrees. A university degree that is purchased, rather like the absolving of a sin by paying indulgence money in the past, is more likely to be a fake degree. Attending a profit-driven university is not really learning, just as those sinners paying for absolution were not really recanting. Once money is directly involved, education moves toward fooling young people and their parents into believing that they are learning something useful and then awarding them with very high marks to confirm to them just how well they have done.

In August 2018, Jeremy Grantham, the co-founder of a $1 billion-plus U.S. asset management firm, put some of his thoughts about the future on paper in a report entitled "Dealing with Climate Change: The Race of Our Lives." It is interesting to look at his views because he is especially well informed, not least by all the research into global warming that he funds. Nevertheless, he is prone to making claims such as this: "Our main disadvantage is that our species has developed over the last few hundred thousand years not to address this kind of long-term, slow-burning issue, but to stay alive and well-fed today and perhaps tomorrow."[11]

Grantham could not be more wrong about what the human species has developed to achieve. Over the course of the last sixty thousand years we have established a huge number of sustainable societies. Some in Australia may have been very stable for as long as fifty thousand years.[12] Humans learned to address slow-burning issues a long time ago. It is only recently, in our fast-burning times, that we began to so easily fail to recognize the sustainability of the past and blame our current woes on some imagined inbuilt deficit of people as individuals, rather than on what we collectively and unwittingly let loose upon ourselves—fueled by the intense greed of a few. We live in an age in which people who appear to make a huge amount of money buying and selling assets can easily come to believe that their amassed wealth means they will automatically be good at governing or otherwise directing policy. In the era of the divine right of kings, there were men who had similar opinions of themselves.

In "The Race of Our Lives Revisited," Grantham makes grand claims about the fallibility of individuals versus the wonders of the work of a few. "We should never underestimate technology but also never underestimate the ability of us humans to really mess it up." He goes on to suggest: "It is calculated that there are only 30 to 70 good harvest years left, depending on your location." But he does recognize the inherent and usual problems of a few countries where the interests of oil barons have held the most sway. Talking of "merchants of doubt" and someone he particularly disapproved of, Grantham suggests that "one of those merchants, MIT professor Richard Lindzen, actually went seamlessly from defending tobacco—where he famously puffed cigarettes through his TV interviews—to denying most of the problems of climate change. . . . This does not happen in China, India, Germany, or Argentina. This is unique to the English-speaking, oily countries—the US, the UK, and Australia—where the power of the fossil fuel interests is used to influence both politics and public opinion."[13] He might be heartened to see the slowdown shape of the current trend in GDP growth in the United States in figure 48.

Look carefully at figure 48 and ask yourself in which year the relative rise was actually greatest. Absolute change was greatest in 1998 and 1999, and so that period stands out the most, given the way change is calculated

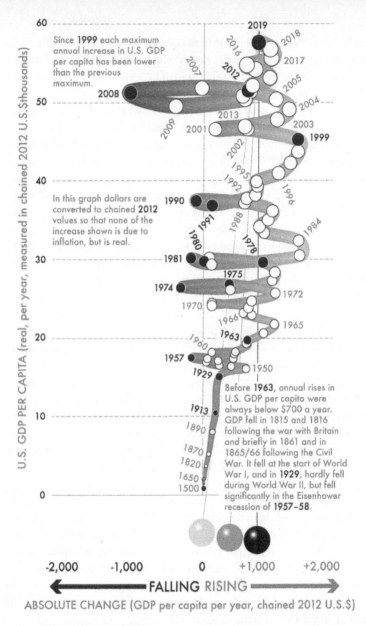

48. U.S. GDP per capita, 1500–2019. (Data adapted from Maddison Project Database 2018, updated using U.S. Bureau of Economic Analysis Gross Domestic Product estimates for 1950–2019, retrieved from FRED, Federal Reserve Bank of St. Louis, accessed 15 May 2019, https://fred.stlouisfed.org/series/A939RX0Q048SBEA.)

here, from the year before to the year after. However, if you were to consider relative increases, then the answer is 1965, when U.S. GDP grew by 5.15 percent, with the second-largest peak coming nearly two decades later, in 1984 (4.59 percent). The last time GDP grew by more than 2 percent in the United States was 2005, when it grew by only 2.19 percent. Human beings are learning to consume and produce less, despite their access to ever "higher technology." We should never *overestimate* the importance of technology, nor *underestimate* the ability of human beings to begin to sort themselves out into living in a steady state. For almost all of our existence as a species, the vast majority of us have lived in stable communities, which is how we survived. Today is a temporary aberration.

What about the second-biggest economy in the world, you may wonder—what about China? China is the largest country in the world by population, and the one in which people have sorted themselves out most dramatically of all over the course of the past seventy years without recourse to seeing the market as a god, but with great suffering (see figure 24). Many people in the richest parts of the world still find it hard to believe that China can now be so successful in so many different ways. For a long time there was skepticism in the United States about China's GDP figures. That skepticism has now evaporated.[14] In fact, a leading U.S. company is now using China as the excuse for its financial difficulties. The long quote below from its CEO, Tim Cook, is well worth reading carefully. The goods being discussed are the most high-tech that many consumers have ever owned, but what they do is not so essential that you must always have the latest version:

> While we anticipated some challenges in key emerging markets, we did not foresee the magnitude of the economic deceleration, particularly in Greater China. In fact, most of our revenue shortfall to our guidance [of estimated future earnings], and over 100 percent of our year-over-year worldwide revenue decline, occurred in Greater China across iPhone, Mac and iPad.
>
> China's economy began to slow in the second half of 2018. The government-reported GDP growth during the September quarter was the second lowest in the last 25 years. We believe the economic environment in China has been further impacted by rising trade tensions with the United States. As the climate of mounting uncertainty weighed on financial markets, the effects appeared to reach consumers

as well, with traffic to our retail stores and our channel partners in China declining as the quarter progressed. And market data has shown that the contraction in Greater China's smartphone market has been particularly sharp.[15]

Slowdown is shocking at first. The repercussions of slowdown shock us. What is happening, we ask? Why are trade wars beginning again? What is really being argued over? And what happens when our politicians and business leaders can no longer promise "their people" that the next generation will be better off than the last? Do you quickly look for people in another country to blame? Do that and then it becomes hard to maintain a common front. Some businesspeople will turn on their own politicians— turning on Donald Trump, in the case referred to above—to try to explain why their government's approach is not helping. Although to see that in Tim Cook's message, you need to read between the lines.

That the chief executive officer of Apple, the eleventh-largest company in the world by revenue in 2019 and the fourth largest in America, should be so concerned about U.S. relations with China is telling. His predecessors were worried about whether it was best to manufacture in China and what the risks might be. Cook is now increasingly worried about the country as a place where he will be able to continue to sell his products, about the competing products the Chinese may make, and especially about China's slowing GDP growth.

The timeline in figure 49 shows that China has rebounded from two very recent and almost identical growth per capita maxima, in 2010 and 2017 (both as measured in absolute terms). The relative rate of GDP per capita growth in China had three earlier recent maxima: 13.4 percent in 1984, 13.0 percent in 1992, and 14.8 percent in 2006. It has been below 10 percent every year since 2010, and typically well below. The acceleration of the very recent falls in fertility in China have been linked to the most recent economic slowdown. We now know very well how the population in China will soon fall, but we cannot know with anything like as much certainty where GDP per head in China is heading. It may well jolt up a few times yet before it begins to revert again toward heading more steadily toward the left-hand axis that represents zero growth. What we now do know for sure, because it began long ago, is that the number of people, especially young people who will soon be contributing to the creation of most of that GDP in China, is already falling.

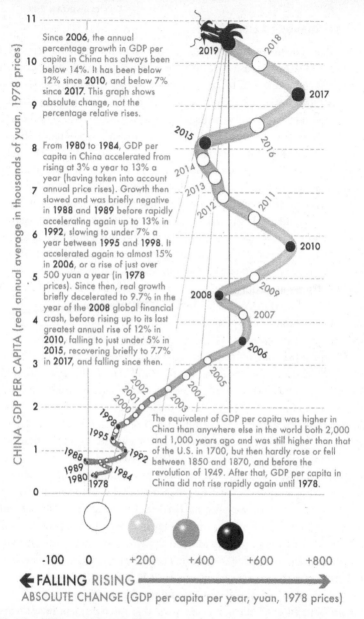

CHINA GDP PER CAPITA (real annual average in thousands of yuan, 1978 prices)

Since **2006**, the annual percentage growth in GDP per capita in China has always been below 14%. It has been below 12% since **2010**, and below 7% since **2017**. This graph shows absolute change, not the percentage relative rises.

From **1980** to **1984**, GDP per capita in China accelerated from rising at 3% a year to 13% a year (having taken into account annual price rises). Growth then slowed and was briefly negative in **1988** and **1989** before rapidly accelerating again up to 13% in **1992**, slowing to under 7% a year between **1995** and **1998**. It accelerated again to almost 15% in **2006**, or a rise of just over 500 yuan a year (in **1978** prices). Since then, real growth briefly decelerated to 9.7% in the year of the **2008** global financial crash, before rising up to its last greatest annual rise of 12% in **2010**, falling to just under 5% in **2015**, recovering briefly to 7.7% in **2017**, and falling since then.

The equivalent of GDP per capita was higher in China than anywhere else in the world both 2,000 and 1,000 years ago and was still higher than that of the U.S. in 1700, but then hardly rose or fell between 1850 and 1870, and before the revolution of 1949. After that, GDP per capita in China did not rise rapidly again until **1978**.

←FALLING RISING ➡
ABSOLUTE CHANGE (GDP per capita per year, yuan, 1978 prices)

-100   0   +200   +400   +600   +800

49. China GDP per capita, 1978–2019. (Data adapted from National Bureau of Statistics of China, China Statistical Yearbook 2018, with adjustments for inflation, http://www.stats.gov.cn/tjsj/ndsj/2018/indexeh.htm.)

STANDARDS OF LIVING

GDP does not measure happiness or how clean the drinking water is. It does not measure a sense of security or people's quality of life or even the typical income range of the vast majority of people. The more weapons you manufacture and sell, the greater will be the GDP of your country. The better the health care you provide, the lower the GDP may be, because those health-care workers could have been making weapons to sell at a great profit instead. You can refine GDP to include providing health care as productive, as British prime minister Gordon Brown once tried to do; but it is better to think in terms of median living standards and not abstract measures of productivity if you really want to know what matters most.

Living standards began to deteriorate long before GDP growth slowed down, and this was seen first in places such as the United Kingdom. In short, for most people in the United Kingdom, the period 1974–76 was better than today. In 2004 Tim Jackson wrote a report for the New Economics Foundation titled *Chasing Progress: Beyond Measuring Economic Growth*. He found that as we became better at measuring quality of life, it became clear that social progress in Britain had become increasingly decoupled from economic growth over the previous fifty years (since 1954) and had stalled completely in the preceding three decades (since 1974). In 1974 there was full male employment and remarkably low economic inequality, and the vast majority of people could begin a family at a young age, secure a home to live in without paying huge rents to a private landlord, and go on holiday. Today almost half of all children in the United Kingdom have no annual holiday, while the children of the richest fifth have, on average, several overseas holidays a year.

Jackson was building on earlier work by economists that had already been moving away from the crude measure of GDP. He advocated creating a measure of domestic progress (MDP), calculated like GDP, but with a number of key adjustments. The money that must be spent on mitigating the social costs of production and the environmental costs of pollution is no longer included in Jackson's measures as productive. The arms industry, known as defensive expenditure, is removed, while the costs of longer-term environmental damage and the depreciation of natural capital are factored in. Adjustments are made that value prudent investments more highly, and positive trade balances are included as laudable. The value of household work, cooking and cleaning at home, is included, and "changes in the distribution of income are accounted for, reflecting the fact that an additional pound in the pocket means more to the poor than to the rich."[16]

According to Jackson's estimate, the U.K.'s MDP peaked in 1976 and hit its lowest points during the 1980s economic recession. It has never yet returned to its 1976 maximum. In 2004 the ecologist George Monbiot responded to the creation of the MDP with this observation: "Our quality of life peaked in 1976. . . . We live in the happiest, healthiest and most peaceful era in human history. And it will not last long."[17] So far his pessimism has not been entirely borne out. The peace that the world was enjoying in 2004 has lasted, even though it has been interrupted frequently by imperialist wars when the world's richest nations fly their billion-dollar warplanes over the skies of Iraq, Syria, and Yemen to showcase their defense industries' most expensive products.[18]

Health is improving worldwide, and George Monbiot may be too pessimistic in warning that this will soon cease to be the case. But happiness is not currently improving and neither is overall well-being. Environmental degradation is certainly continuing. However, as Tim Jackson commented over a decade after his first report, in the wake of many similar reports to his, and in the run-up to the June 2017 U.K. general election: "Something strange is happening in British politics. I'm not talking about the divisive quagmire of Brexit or the frightening rise of xenophobia. I'm talking about a broad cross-party agreement that the economic model of the last half a century has failed. I'm referring to an (almost) ubiquitous call across the multi-coloured manifestos of the 2017 election to start building 'an economy that works'—for everyone."[19] What had been a minority view in 2004 had become mainstream by 2017.

In April 2019 Andrew Oswald and his many colleagues circulated a preprint of a paper that tried to explain why there is so much distress among middle-aged people in affluent countries. They found that, in affluent countries, what they termed midlife (around age fifty) has become a time when people are disproportionately more likely than those older or younger to take their own lives. Many more people around that age are also finding that they have trouble sleeping. Age fifty is when people in the affluent world are now most likely to become dependent on alcohol, to spend time thinking about suicide, to begin to feel that life is not worth living, to "find it hard to concentrate, forget things, feel overwhelmed in their workplace, and suffer from disabling headaches."[20] It's quite a collection of ailments, traversing down from the most serious of all to what you might consider almost trivial (unless you have ever had a lot of trouble getting to sleep).[21]

Oswald and his colleagues could not ascertain why this trend had developed, but they did note: "It remains possible that it is a by-product of some special aspect of modern living. Or it might be driven . . . by some deeply subtle and currently unknown kinds of cohort effects or period effects." One such possible cohort and period effect is having had a childhood in the best of times, in the 1970s, when hopes were high, but then having had to live through the years of subsequent great disappointment, especially in the United States and the United Kingdom, although Oswald and his colleagues also note that "the midlife pattern is not caused merely by having young children; nor is it found just in one or two special countries." However, given where most of their data come from, it is worth turning now to one special country, the United States, and looking at recent patterns in the measure of how people are valued in that place.

Wages are how society tells you how much you are worth in the modern world. The median wage is the wage level when the number of people earning more than that amount is equal to the number who earn less. Figure 50 shows the timeline of median weekly earnings for a privileged group that is currently shrinking in number in the United States—full-time workers. Although full-time workers are rarely described as privileged, full-time work tends to be far better rewarded and less precarious than part-time work. Having any paid work at all automatically puts you above the most disadvantaged in any society, at least for as long as we continue to reward some people so much more than others, rather than allocating to people what they need, and encouraging them to choose to do what is most useful rather than what will make the most money for the man or woman who employs them.

The early 1970s were the best of times for American workers. Inequality was at its lowest (ever) and real weekly wages were at their highest. However, when measured in constant dollars, so that a dollar is of the same value in terms of what it can buy over time, U.S. median wages plummeted at the end of the 1970s, as figure 50 makes clear. The average U.S. worker did worse and worse. For the median full-time employee, there were falls in real income of over 4 percent and then over 3 percent a year in 1979 and 1980. Ronald Reagan proclaimed the start of his time in office "morning in America"—it turned out to be a cold and dismal morning for the majority.

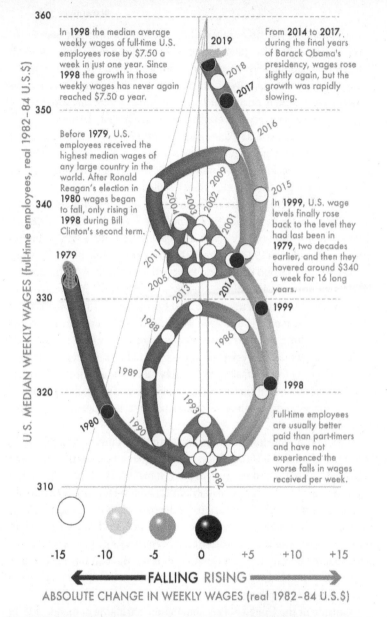

360

In **1998** the median average weekly wages of full-time U.S. employees rose by $7.50 a week in just one year. Since **1998** the growth in those weekly wages has never again reached $7.50 a year.

2019

2018

2017

From **2014** to **2017**, during the final years of Barack Obama's presidency, wages rose slightly again, but the growth was rapidly slowing.

350

2016

Before **1979**, U.S. employees received the highest median wages of any large country in the world. After Ronald Reagan's election in **1980** wages began to fall, only rising in **1998** during Bill Clinton's second term.

2009

2003 **2002**

2004 **2001**

2015

In **1999**, U.S. wage levels finally rose back to the level they had last been in **1979**, two decades earlier, and then they hovered around $340 a week for 16 long years.

340

1979

2011

2005

2013 **2014**

330

1988

1986

1999

1989

320

1993

1998

1980

1990

Full-time employees are usually better paid than part-timers and have not experienced the worse falls in wages received per week.

1982

310

-15   -10   -5   0   +5   +10   +15

⟵ **FALLING** RISING ⟶

ABSOLUTE CHANGE IN WEEKLY WAGES (real 1982–84 U.S.$)

U.S. MEDIAN WEEKLY WAGES (full-time employees, real 1982–84 U.S.$)

50. U.S. median full-time employee weekly real earnings, 1979–2019. (Data adapted from U.S. Bureau of Labor Statistics, "Employed Full Time: Median Usual Weekly Real Earnings; Wage and Salary Workers; 16 Years and Over" [in 1982–84 CPI-adjusted dollars], retrieved from FRED, Federal Reserve Bank of St. Louis, accessed 19 May 2019, https://fred .stlouisfed.org/series/LEU0252881600A.)

U.S. median full-time wages plummeted to a low of just over $310 a week in 1981. The subsequent recovery was trivial: a real-terms rise by the late 1980s to not quite $330 a week, about $3 a day more. Half of all full-time workers and a majority of Americans were taking home less than $47 a day to live on. Then, during the late 1980s, most of that tiny gain was lost. The early 1990s recovery was even more trivial. The late 1990s recovery finally secured that extra $3 a day again. Twenty years of technological gains had led to mass unemployment, constant layoffs, insecurity, the breaking of unions, the breaking of communities, the breaking of families, and the breaking of people. U.S. life expectancy stalled.

Today U.S. median wages are again ever so slightly on the rise. Another $3-a-day increase in standards of living was secured between 1999 and 2019—but that took twenty years, or a gain of 15 cents a year. What can you buy with three (1983) dollars? The most recent full-time U.S. workers are now the second generation to have lived their lives in this particular déjà vu universe. But all has not remained the same. Inequalities have widened greatly during these years. That half of U.S. full-time workers living beneath the median fared even worse, as do almost all of the growing army of part-time and zero-hours workers. Only a few very far above the median have actually experienced any substantial rises in their compensation/remittances/reward/salary (it is rarely called a wage for the rich). The number who have seen significant income growth is so small that it would be insignificant, save for the enormous share of U.S. national income they now consume.[22]

People fear slowdown because they think the current situation is the way it has to be. In the United States, people believe, because they are told it is so, that without economic growth the vast majority will suffer. Stability is equated with poverty. But there is absolutely no need for this to be the case. It is not just that there were periods in the past when the United States as a whole had far less, but more people were far better off. You can also look today at places where the slowdown has been most abrupt, but where they have adapted best to it. If you think Japan is too difficult for most Americans to use as a point of comparison, then look to Europe and at what is currently happening there.

Outside of the United States, automation, shrinking demand, and the new deal for the sharing of resources are often dealt with very differently. In Finland they employ "tripartite labour market cooperation" to ensure that middle-aged median workers do not fall behind the rest, but instead actually enjoy the fruits of their labor.[23] Tripartite cooperation is common in Denmark, even though it is blamed for being too slow at times.[24] In Germany and Sweden, "social partners . . . had participated in at least eight large tripartite commissions on digitalization and labor market issues by 2016." If you don't know what a tripartite commission is, you probably live in the United Kingdom or the United States. It is the agreement of contracts between employers' organizations, trade unions, and the government of a country.

Outside of the rich world, conditions are sometimes much worse than those found today in the United States. In February 2019 the Malaysian newspaper *New Straits Times* reported that hundreds of millions of people remained very poor despite holding down one or more jobs. It cited a global report that concluded that "a majority of the 3.3 billion people employed around the globe last year suffered a 'lack of material well-being, economic security, equal opportunities or scope for human development' [and that] . . . a full 700 million people are living in extreme or moderate poverty despite having employment."[25] The *Straits Times* told its readers that 61 percent of all workers worldwide, some 2 billion people, were in informal employment, with few or no social and/or contractual protections. The countries where these people live and work have very often adopted the practices of the United States, and so alongside that country they may be among the last to take part in the transition to greater stability; but they might well make the turn required more quickly in future. The United States is currently the least progressive rich country in the world in terms of improving the living standards of its people. In some other parts of the world, in contrast, the great acceleration occurred a very long time ago, and the transition towards stability is now well under way. Consider Amsterdam.

THE MONEY ILLUSION

So much is slowing down that it is hard to know what to include in any list. Today, the greatest expense for many people in the rich world is housing. In the poor world it is food. In between the two, and for a time in rich countries, the most expensive items in people's budgets not very long ago were cars. We often think of housing as an asset that, bar a few setbacks, will always increase in value. But this is not the case universally, around the world and across the ages—it has simply been the experience of a few of us in just the most recent few generations.

Figure 51 shows the timeline of the world's most famous house-price index: a record of the average real value of homes on an especially affluent street in Amsterdam that begins in 1628 and does not end until 1973. If it were updated to the present day, it would not look very different from what is shown here. In real terms, when compared to wages and salaries, house prices in the long run are generally stable. Their worth can be as little as 4.8 times below their maximum value: in the case of the Herengracht Canal houses, that low was achieved in 1814, against a peak of 1724. For over a quarter of a millennium, housing prices in Amsterdam have been below their peak, but most of the time they will hover around a stable value. To see this, however, we have to look back over the course of generations, not just back a few decades.

Thanks to U.K. data gathered since 1952 by the Nationwide Building Society, it is not hard to find out that an average home in Britain in the year that the first people of Generation X were born was priced and sold (at non-inflation-adjusted prices) for just under £2,000.[26] That year was 1956. By 1982, the birth year of the very first of Generation Y (the millennials), that price had risen to £24,000, and by the first year of Generation Z (2012) it reached £164,000.

The absolute jumps appear huge, but the relative rate of rise had slowed over this period—by almost half. For the parents of the first of Generation Z, house prices were *only* six times higher than those faced by newborn Generation Y's parents—compared to twelve times higher for the previous generation. To the people living through these times, it did not feel that the price rise had slowed, especially because incomes had not risen as fast. Nevertheless, the rise in the price of homes was indeed slowing down. The key short-term factors were two housing market crashes, one in 1989 and the other in 2008. If I had space here to include the U.K. timeline, then you would see both crashes as loops into negative territory. (I have put those timelines in the spreadsheet for figure 51 on the website of this book, which includes many more timelines than can be printed in these pages—see www.dannydorling.org.)

We tend to be obsessed by the most recent changes in housing prices, or at least that is the case for those of us who are old enough to have a mortgage on a home, or are rich enough to own several. The U.K. value of new homes has fallen from a peak (calculated by the Nationwide Building Society's statisticians, with startling precision, to the nearest pound) of £219,881 in the third quarter of 2016, dropping to £216,824 by the start

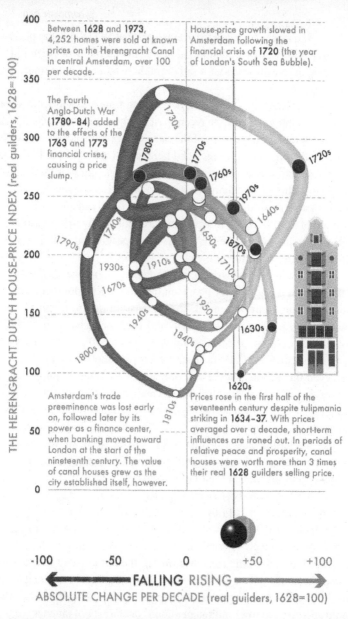

THE HERENGRACHT DUTCH HOUSE-PRICE INDEX (real guilders, 1628=100)

Between **1628** and **1973**, 4,252 homes were sold at known prices on the Herengracht Canal in central Amsterdam, over 100 per decade.

House-price growth slowed in Amsterdam following the financial crisis of **1720** (the year of London's South Sea Bubble).

The Fourth Anglo-Dutch War (**1780–84**) added to the effects of the **1763** and **1773** financial crises, causing a price slump.

1730s
1780s
1770s
1760s
1720s
1740s
1970s
1640s
1790s
1650s
1870s
1710s
1930s
1910s
1670s
1940s
1950s
1830s
1800s
1840s
1630s
1810s
1620s

Amsterdam's trade preeminence was lost early on, followed later by its power as a finance center, when banking moved toward London at the start of the nineteenth century. The value of canal houses grew as the city established itself, however.

Prices rose in the first half of the seventeenth century despite tulipmania striking in **1634–37**. With prices averaged over a decade, short-term influences are ironed out. In periods of relative peace and prosperity, canal houses were worth more than 3 times their real **1628** guilders selling price.

-100   -50   0   +50   +100

◄ **FALLING** RISING ►

ABSOLUTE CHANGE PER DECADE (real guilders, 1628=100)

51. The Herengracht Dutch house-price index, 1628–1973. Shown is the cost as a percentage of average 1628 house prices adjusted for inflation, referred to as "real guilders" as opposed to the unadjusted nominal index. (Adapted from Piet Eichholtz, "A Long Run House Price Index: The Herengracht Index, 1628–1973," *Real Estate Economics* 25, no. 2 [1997]: 175–92, https://papers.ssrn.com/sol3/papers.cfm?abstract_id=598.)

of 2017. The seasonally adjusted average price of all U.K. houses peaked at £217,010 in July 2018, and stood at just £214,920 by April 2019. But let's step back, ignore the spurious accuracy of these numbers, and consider the long term.

Look at the United Kingdom over a long time and suddenly a completely different picture of the recent past emerges. Now the 1989 housing price crash looks much larger, of the same order of magnitude as the 2008 crash. If this timeline were included here, you would see that both loops are of a similar size, but by now you have seen enough of these graphs to be able to picture it. Suddenly, the peaks of price rises become more clearly visible as a series of diminishing heights over time. Inflation was not just a feature of the 1970s. It has been with us continuously in the ensuing decades, but with each successive house-price peak diminishing in size as general inflation also slows down.

In 2014, a journalist writing for the *Financial Times* attempted to explain what all this meant for people in the United Kingdom and what the money illusion means in general. The explanation was inevitably tortuous: "Between 1975, when the data starts, and 1983 for instance there was no overall gain for house prices, even though they rose 50 per cent in nominal terms between 1978 and 1980. Homeowners probably felt a lot richer, however, even though their house was only worth the same amount of goods and services as before. That feeling, when applied to income in periods of rising inflation is known as money illusion. It can feel good (for a while at least) to have a rising wage even if inflation is at the same time destroying the purchasing power of that wage. But for someone who owned a house, they did get richer in the sense that their mortgage payment quickly shrinks as a proportion of their fast growing pay packet."[27]

In 1972 U.K. house prices rose by 11 percent, in 1979 by 8 percent, in 1988 by 6 percent, in 2014 by 3 percent, and in July 2018 by 2.5 percent. But by April 2019, the peak was a rise of just 0.9 percent a year. Most peaks of rises were relatively lower than the previous peak, and the overall rate of change is also becoming less over time. If the earlier trend were to carry on, with a small, brief upward rebound at some point to the long erratic slowdown in house-price rises over time, then U.K. average housing prices would end up close to £1 million per home, or at least not much more than that. And they could peak at a far lower value if the U.K. economy were to slow down more quickly. The price of houses will not keep rising forever. Nothing can.

A graph that uses absolute values suggests runaway prices and greater and greater crashes to come. In contrast, a graph that shows relative changes and uses a log scale suggests much more regularity and points to price falls in the past being of at least the same order of magnitude as the two most recent periods of actual housing price falls. The deceleration in price rise from 1972 to 1974 was greater than that from 1979 to 1981. The early 1980s price slowdown was, in turn, comparable to the falls from 1988 to 1990. Then those housing price falls in Britain from 2007 to 2009 were greater than the most recent falls (the most recent seen so far since 2016), but smaller falls as compared to before when measured on a rela-tive—log—scale. A similar pattern has occurred in the United States.

So what is going to happen? We simply do not know. But we can estab-lish some general limits on what is likely to happen. For instance, a sudden housing price acceleration such as the one that occurred in the early 1970s is now extremely unlikely. All prices were rising rapidly then: not just housing, but wages as well. In contrast, housing price falls in the near fu-ture would not be remarkable given the general direction of the long-term trends and the falls in both the 1990s and the last decade. The long-term trend is toward price stability, back toward negligible quarterly change.

How on earth is it possible, given how much housing prices have risen in recent decades, to say that the rise is slowing? Well, there are at least two ways to look at this. First, in 2017, 2018, and 2019, the U.K. housing market clearly slowed down, however it is graphed. More important, any rise was very slow as compared to the long term. Almost every decade since the 1970s has seen a *smaller* proportionate rise in U.K. and U.S. housing prices compared with the decade before it. The capital appreciation of housing, just as an investment, is falling. Soon we might even start thinking of a house as a home—not as a retirement investment for the wealthy.

Before we return to the subject of house prices, consider something a little different—gold. In figure 52 the gold price timeline has not been adjusted for inflation, and so the price appears to rise and rise. But each period of increase is always abruptly brought to a halt by a crash, followed normally by a period of price stability for a few years when the price ap-pears to oscillate around a fixed point, before it again begins to climb up-ward. Today that oscillatory point in the global price of gold is around $1,250 an ounce.

The price of gold is interesting because gold is seen as a safe haven, a little like property. When times are uncertain money floods into gold,

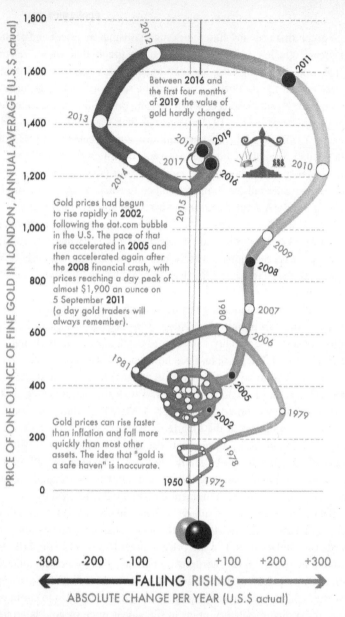

PRICE OF ONE OUNCE OF FINE GOLD IN LONDON, ANNUAL AVERAGE (U.S.$ actual)

1,800

2012

Between **2016** and
the first four months
of **2019** the value of
gold hardly changed.

2011

1,600

2013

1,400

2018
2019
2017
2016
2010

1,200

2014

2015

Gold prices had begun
to rise rapidly in **2002**,
following the dot.com bubble
in the U.S. The pace of that
rise accelerated in **2005** and
then accelerated again after
the **2008** financial crash, with
prices reaching a day peak of
almost $1,900 an ounce on
5 September **2011**
(a day gold traders will
always remember).

1,000

2009

2008

800

2007

1980

600

2006

1981

2005

400

2002

1979

Gold prices can rise faster
than inflation and fall more
quickly than most other
assets. The idea that "gold is
a safe haven" is inaccurate.

200

1978

1950   1972

0

-300   -200   -100   0   +100   +200   +300

◀— **FALLING** RISING —▶

ABSOLUTE CHANGE PER YEAR (U.S.$ actual)

52. The price of gold in U.S.$, 1950–2019. (Data adapted from *Financial Times* [April
1968–March 1974]; Samuel Montagu & Co. Ltd. [April 1974–December 1980]; *Financial
Times* [January 1981–December 1998]; the London Bullion Market Association [January
1999–present]. See "Historical Gold Prices—1833 to Present," accessed 9 September 2019, https://nma.org/wp-content/uploads/2016/09/historic_gold_prices_1833
_pres.pdf.)

because gold, it is assumed, will keep its value (and you can try to hide your gold from the tax authorities). However, its value, other than for use in jewelry and a few electrical components, lies mainly in the belief that other people will continue to favor gold as a hedge against speculating in other assets. Once the reality of slowdown becomes more widely accepted, it will become necessary to ask ourselves: why risk having so much wealth held in the form of gold, an asset whose intrinsic value (essentially as a status symbol) is no longer what it once was?

Between 1956 and 1982, gold rose in value 10.7-fold, a fraction less than the twelvefold nominal rise in the value of U.K. housing over the same period. Between 1982 and 2012 gold rose by 4.4 times, some way below the 6.8-fold increase in the price of U.K. housing. According to yet another data source, in this case the Bank of England's composite house-price index, house prices during the years when members of Generation V were born—from 1901 to 1928—rose by 67 percent. From 1929 to 1955, during the years of Generation W, they rose by 169 percent, more than doubling. But then they rose by 1,152 percent, or around twelvefold, from the first to last birth year of Generation X (1956 to 1981). Since then, in real terms, they have been stable, or rising ever so slowly and falling occasionally. Can a rise as fast as that ever happen again? As housing price growth and general inflation peaked during the birth years of Generation X, we should be very surprised if it ever does.

Why should housing prices in the United Kingdom have risen so fast, along with the worldwide price of gold, between 1956 and 1981? First, it has nothing to do with supply and demand. The supply of housing during this period rose far faster than the demand for housing. By the time of the 1981 census, even the worst-housed tenth of the population enjoyed, on average, a house with as many rooms as people. The greatest improvement in that and many other measures had occurred between the censuses of 1951 and 1981, during the postwar housing boom.[28] Similarly, more and more gold was being mined around the world. By 2010, well over two thousand metric tonnes a year was being mined; by 2018 that figure had risen to well over three thousand metric tonnes a year.[29]

Consumers suspect that the prices of neither gold nor homes are determined or altered by supply and demand. In 1988, economists Karl Case and Robert J. Shiller sent 2,030 questionnaires to recent home buyers in four U.S. cities asking them what they thought had determined recent changes in housing prices where they lived. "Not a single person from among the

886 respondents cited any quantitative evidence about future trends in supply or demand, or professional forecasts of future supply or demand."[30] At the time, the economists concluded, "There is a peculiar lack of interest in objective evidence about fundamentals." They would have been more insightful if they had recognized that buyers knew that supply and demand is not a fundamental determinant of price—how could it be, when housing supply in the United States had also been growing so quickly throughout the childhoods of Generation X?

Robert J. Shiller was awarded the Nobel Memorial Prize for economics twenty-five years after sending out those questionnaires with his colleague Karl Case. So if it is not supply and demand that determines housing prices, what could it be? What consumers thought did matter were speculative considerations. Housing economists don't have the answer. They assumed that the rationing of mortgages in the past would deflate prices, but in hindsight we see that prices actually rose faster during those years. To make their models appear to work, they have to include "frenzy" measures, arguing that "at these times of heightened activity or 'frenzy,' sharply increased demand feeds back into higher prices and, as in 1971–3, 1978–9 and 1986–9, substantial increases in house prices then occur."[31] In other words, they are saying that something strange and unpredictable happened each time that prices rose. Buyers and sellers suddenly began to speculate that the prices would rise and rise, and so for a time they did. But the economists' models could not predict such frenzy rises, nor when the periods of frenzy would begin to abate.

What, in hindsight, might explain each of the rises in prices? Whatever it is, it has to have occurred before the price began to increase, in the years 1970, 1977, 1982, 1986, 1996, and 2010, when increases were low but about to become much greater. By 1977, a young man who would later become the governor of the Bank of England pointed out that rental prices were as regulated as they had ever been, including even furnished, privately rented properties.[32] So why would people be prepared to pay more to buy housing around that time?

The consumers surveyed in 1988 were correct: a key answer is speculation. In 1970, the U.K. general election was won by the right-wing Conservative Party. Conservatives tend to look after homeowners, older home buyers, and landlords, the groups that initially appear to benefit when house prices rise. In 1977 it was thought that the government headed by Labour (the left-wing party that had won the 1974 election) would decide to go to the polls again, but it waited until 1979. Similarly, 1982 and 1986 were years before Conservative election victories, and 1996 was the year before the first election victory of "New Labour" (a one-nation-Conservative version of Old Labour). Then 2010 saw prices recover a little following an election that ushered in a coalition government of Conservatives and Liberal Democrats.

Economists who have looked at house-price trends in the United States often attribute the surge in the 1970s to falling real interest rates and the surge in the 1980s to tax changes, but both of these were in turn the result of shifts in the political policies of governments, in the choices made by Democratic and Republican politicians and the officials they appointed. Furthermore, neither of the standard explanations noted above accounts for local surges in prices in the United States that can only be put down to speculation: "Investors in owner-occupied homes do not have rational expectations, but extrapolate the past in estimating the prospective capital gains on housing."[33]

Economists looking at the longest housing prices series of all, the 355-year records for central Amsterdam shown in figure 51, find that if there is a "correction back to equilibrium" following a price surge or fall, it is one that can often take decades and the equilibrium settled on can be very different than the last, which has to prompt questions about what, if anything, equilibrium might really mean.[34]

STOCKS AND SHARES SPECULATION

Mainstream economists have come under great pressure in recent years. They cannot foresee, or even model after the fact, the movement of values as basic as housing prices. It may well be impossible to do this, but those economists are also a stubborn bunch. For instance, as scholar Matthew Drennan points out, "Mainstream economists have adhered to a theory of consumption that assigns no role to the distribution of income, and therefore is inadequate for fully understanding the Great Recession."[35]

There were many recessions before the most recent one that began in 2008 and arguably continues today in its long-run effect of very sluggish growth. At various points in this book so far, mention has been made of the dot.com bubble. To see how such a bubble might grow, imagine yourself sitting in an office in New York in the week before Christmas 1996. You have clients' money to invest—your exceedingly rich clients care a great deal about money. You want to keep your job over the course of the year to come, and perhaps also secure yourself a bonus. It is your job to advise your clients on where to place their money, and you do so, skimming off a small percentage for your trouble. On your top-of-the-range beige, curved, color, multisync, Video Graphics Array (VGA) cathode ray tube monitor, you have a version of the timeline in figure 53 that shows the evolution of the NASDAQ Composite stock market index, which includes many information technology companies.[36] So what would you do?

You now know, in your old age today, that understanding speculation becomes harder and harder as an increasing amount of speculative money moves across national borders, out of and into housing and many other investments. The money is chasing profit, the highest profit it can possibly secure. The people with the most money want more profit than anyone else: in their eyes, 2 percent or 4 percent growth a year is unacceptable. They want to see their fortune grow by at least 10 percent a year, in real terms. And they can afford "the best advice," which is supposed to be you. In 2018, as the futility of the ever-more-desperate search for ever-greater profits became more obvious in an era of slowdown, some economists were calling for the judicious application of capital controls, limiting the money to enter or leave the country.[37] Capital controls are a heresy for those who worship Profit. But knowing any of this would have been of little use to you in 1996.

So there you are, sitting at your desk in America almost a quarter of a century ago. To imagine this you have to forget what we have learned most recently. You are working before the first serious calls to curb speculation were made, long before China was considered a potential economic rival to the United States.

Well before 2018, there had been repeated calls for more state control over speculation, especially in the case of China, where house-price crashes in a number of major cities were predicted for 2017 and 2018.[38] In 2017, a list of cities was published in which the government was encouraged to intervene to prevent local bubbles bursting: Beijing, Shenyang, Chengdu, Wuhan, Xi'an, Shenzhen, and Chongqing.[39] The Chinese government did intervene, explaining that "houses are for living in, not for speculating on," but investors around the world were still encouraging the Chinese government in 2019 not to let the housing bubble grow too large.[40] That is one small part of the story now, but let's go back in time again.

In December 1996, sitting in your well-appointed New York office, you know none of this. You have Christmas presents to buy, a boss to keep

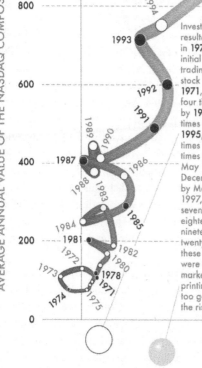

The NASDAQ was founded in February **1971** by the National Association of Securities Dealers to produce automated quotations—from whence the acronym is derived. It is an American stock exchange that was also the world's first electronic stock market and the first to trade online. As a result it attracted a disproportionate number of new high-tech companies on its listings, initially including Microsoft, Apple, and Oracle. Its main index is called the Composite Index and is a weighted average of the value of the stock listed on its (electronic) books.

Investing in the NASDAQ initially resulted in poor returns. Its worth fell in **1974** to just three-quarters of its initial value, but by **1978** it was trading at 17.5% above, by **1981** stock was worth twice as much as in **1971**, by **1985** three times as much, four times as much by **1987**, five times by **1991**, six times by **1992**, seven times by **1993**, eight times by March **1995**, nine times by June **1995**, ten times by July of that year, eleven times by March **1996**, twelve times by May **1996**, thirteen times by December of that year, fourteen times by May 1997, fifteen times by July 1997, sixteen times by August, seventeen times by October, eighteenfold by March 1998, nineteen times by April 1998, and twentyfold by July 1998. In between these peaks there were falls, but they were always very short-lived. The market appeared to be akin to printing money. And, of course, it was too good to be true. Just the start of the rise is shown here.

AVERAGE ANNUAL VALUE OF THE NASDAQ COMPOSITE INDEX (1971=100)

◄FALLING RISING ➡

ABSOLUTE CHANGE PER YEAR
(NASDAQ Composite Index [1971=100])

53. The NASDAQ Composite Index, February 1971–December 1996, shown as a percentage of 1971 prices. (Data adapted from NASDAQ OMX Group, "NASDAQ Composite Index [NASDAQCOM]," retrieved from FRED, Federal Reserve Bank of St. Louis, accessed 12 May 2019, https://fred.stlouisfed.org/series/NASDAQCOM.)

happy, a family holiday to look forward to, you are still young. You have no crystal ball that will allow you to see into the future. You cannot imagine a future in which a UN body would have to explain: "Global wage growth in 2017 was not only lower than in 2016, but fell to its lowest growth rate since 2008, remaining far below the levels obtaining before the global financial crisis. Global wage growth in real terms (that is, adjusted for price inflation) has declined from 2.4 per cent in 2016 to just 1.8 per cent in 2017. If China, whose large population and rapid wage growth significantly influence the global average, is excluded, global wage growth in real terms fell from 1.8 per cent in 2016 to 1.1 per cent in 2017."[41]

For all of your life, you have only ever known growth, and usually accelerating growth, punctuated by the occasional fall in prices to take out the odd sucker and short-term investor. You were born at the start of the 1960s as part of a secondary baby boom. You do not know that "peak baby" will be repeated in subdued form in 1990, because the statistics have yet to be released, let alone studied. It is 1996 and you believe that computers can do amazing things and that if your clients invest in the latest technology, they will stand to make huge gains. And you tell yourself that this is only right and proper, because their investments are what drive innovation and progress forward. What's more, you believe that your high salary is merely a fair market reward for your long hours at your desk, and for what you imagine to be your immense talent. You have heard that next year, in 1997, liquid crystal displays will be the next big thing; and you believe that there will always be a next big thing.

You also know that stock prices can, in the short term, take what's called a random walk. No one without insider knowledge (which is illegal to use) can know what is about to happen. However, you have access to over $1 billion of your clients' money. And you have a very simple strategy: "construct a large, suitably leveraged, market-neutral equity portfolio and then systematically expand it in the morning and contract it in the afternoon, day after day."[42] Although your index is based largely on the NASDAQ, you tweak a few components to reflect your talent. But not too many tweaks, because in your heart of hearts you don't really rate your talent that highly, except when you need to excuse the fact that you are paid so much more than your parents ever were. And, as prices are in general rising, you do well.

In fact, with an average daily drift upward of a mere 0.04 percent— which, as you know, is well within the typical morning spread of most publicly traded stocks—when this rise is then compounded over twenty-five years, there will be an elevenfold increase in the value of your investments between 1996 and 2019, which is above the normal gains that the market at its most successful itself makes.[43] Your clients will eventually receive most of this, as long as the sums you invest are sufficiently large that the fees for the transactions are small enough not to wipe out your own special extra profit—which is just a little greater than the profits of all the other traders who have a little less each to invest each day.

You are feeling lucky; you put a little more into the NASDAQ investments than before. You'll have a Christmas drink at lunchtime. And it turns out that you are lucky. Christmas 1996 was the perfect time to buy those high-tech shares. As the timeline in figure 54 shows, prices really took off after that. The fastest acceleration of the price of shares the world had ever known occurred over the next thirty-six months. You purchased, in effect, multiple billions at a unit price of around $1,287.63 each on Christmas Eve 1996.

By the end of December 1999, just three years later, your clients' assets were worth $4,069.31 per unit. Your own take had increased more than threefold in three years. You have become immensely rich. Other people, all of them unknown to you, had simultaneously become much poorer. You had no idea that they became poorer as a direct result of your trading actions. Of course the money you made had to actually come at the expense of others, you were not doing anything of such great actual value; but you believed the market was efficient and that the "trickle-down effect" would sort out the poor.[44]

Later, of course, disaster will strike. But you have long since diversified. You purchased some properties with your winnings, a few in 1997 and more in both 1998 and 1999. The rental income was good, the capital appreciation even better. You survived the dot.com crash of 2000 and 2001, although your salary and bonuses would never rise as fast again. You were prudent during the mini-boom of 2003–7, and so were made a partner of your trading firm.

Your signature trick of buying in bulk in the morning on trading around the world and selling just before the markets closed each day (in each place) appeared to be working. However, once you had survived the crash of 2008, all that seemed to matter a little less. Younger traders were better able to take the pressure. The market, even very shortly after 2008, began climbing and climbing again. There was a scare in 2015, but it was

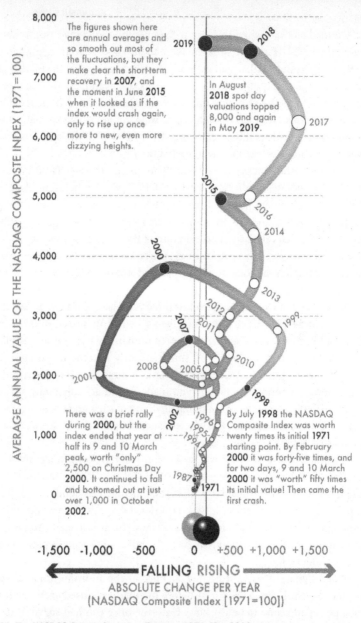

The figures shown here are annual averages and so smooth out most of the fluctuations, but they make clear the short-term recovery in **2007**, and the moment in June **2015** when it looked as if the index would crash again, only to rise up once more to new, even more dizzying heights.

In August **2018** spot day valuations topped 8,000 and again in May **2019**.

There was a brief rally during **2000**, but the index ended that year at half its 9 and 10 March peak, worth "only" 2,500 on Christmas Day **2000**. It continued to fall and bottomed out at just over 1,000 in October **2002**.

By July **1998** the NASDAQ Composite Index was worth twenty times its initial **1971** starting point. By February **2000** it was forty-five times, and for two days, 9 and 10 March **2000** it was "worth" fifty times its initial value! Then came the first crash.

AVERAGE ANNUAL VALUE OF THE NASDAQ COMPOSITE INDEX (1971=100)

-1,500 -1,000 -500 0 +500 +1,000 +1,500

◄—— **FALLING** RISING ——►

ABSOLUTE CHANGE PER YEAR
(NASDAQ Composite Index [1971=100])

54. The NASDAQ Composite Index, February 1971–May 2019, shown as a percentage of 1971 prices. (Data adapted from NASDAQ OMX Group, "NASDAQ Composite Index [NASDAQCOM]," retrieved from FRED, Federal Reserve Bank of St. Louis, accessed 12 May 2019, https://fred.stlouisfed.org/series/NASDAQCOM.)

short-lived, and another in summer 2019. But the unbelievably rich still had money burning a hole in their pockets, and they still came to you for advice, and so too did the now-adult children of your original clients who had inherited so much. You made them even richer and, what's more, you were now becoming one of them. And then one day, the scam stopped working.

Sometime in the 2020s confidence in the market begins to fall—not short-term confidence, but long-term confidence. Something fundamentally different is happening, something that you do not recognize the size or shape of. You have not seen this before. This time really is different. Clients are increasingly demanding more and wanting to risk less. Your attempts to hire "the brightest and the best" are beginning to fall short. Few young adults with much self-respect still worship the god of Profit or believe in his little sister, the goddess Trickle Down. The states where your personal rental properties are located are threatening to bring in rent controls, and President Trump had changed the tax code back in 2019 so that you can no longer offset all those higher taxes being paid in New York against your federal tax liabilities. You contemplate moving to Florida—but life is too short and the risk of skin cancer too high.

You look at the timeline, the one you had so successfully and with such excitement followed just over a quarter of a century ago, back on Christmas Eve 1996. And suddenly you realize that there is almost nothing of value being held in those shares, just the intellectual property within a series of companies that had not invented anything fundamentally new for many decades. It has all been a fantasy over high-tech companies that were for a brief time fetishized. Companies had become rich relying on the young being naive and ignorant, and the old being cunning and greedy. Companies that had been able to survive as they were only by continually paying very little corporate tax. Companies that had not even existed when you were born.

Suddenly it dawns on you that for you and the few others who are so rich in the world, with slowdown upon us nothing is safe, nothing for your small group is stable. What would happen, you wonder, if politics also change alongside the slowdown? You retire early, sell up, and move to Florida. You write the odd comment under newspaper articles online. As you enter your final age, you begin to realize just how much of what you always believed to be right was so very wrong.

10

geopolitics

in an age of slowdown

You know that we have lost the sense of space. We say "space is annihilated,"
but we have annihilated not space, but the sense thereof.

—*E. M. Forster, 1909*

It is only in your latter years that you can begin to realize the errors in
many of your beliefs, because only once you are more mature can you
question them properly. However, many, if not most, people never do this;
they go through their whole life believing much the same story. I am one
of that majority. A few people do fundamentally change their opinions,
and if what they come to think spreads to the young—those who are just
forming their first views of the world—then the long-term political effect
can be enormous.

Ideas tend to spread geographically. However, with the advent of the
telegraph in 1837 and the telephone in E. M. Forster's day, then the internet
in 1974, space was being shrunk so rapidly that some thought it might be
annihilated.[1] Instead, ideas began to jump across space more quickly as our
connecting machines spread. However, despite this, the huge geographical
variation between the politics of different social climates should give us
great hope that we can be discerning and robust thinkers. Another world
is possible because that other world is already here, somewhere on Earth.
It is found in particular places: countries that are "ahead" in the slowdown.
And it is found in particular minds.

People in particular places are coming to realize that they can act collectively, and that the era of selfishness lionized in the work of philosopher
and novelist Ayn Rand, which flourished in the years of maximum accel-

eration, is over. Rand (1905–82), a terrible novelist, was the high priestess of a movement she termed *Objectivism*—the cult of selfishness. She believed that working for the common good was senseless. There are always a few selfish individuals like Rand, and a successful geopolitics of the age of slowdown will have to overcome her followers. The fact that you may not have heard of her, even though she was a heroine to many far-right politicians and libertarian business elites, is a sign of hope and a testament to our collective victory over the selfish among us.[2]

The rise of modern selfishness was first observed in seventeenth-century Amsterdam, on the docksides where housing was approaching its highest-ever value (see figure 51), where "everyone but myself is engaged in trade, and thus is so focused on his own profit that I could live here all my life without ever being noticed by anyone," as René Descartes noted in 1631.[3] Descartes actually sounded pretty cheerful in the letter to Jean-Louis Guez de Balzac that contained those words. Although not being noticed suited Descartes, it does not suit most people most of the time. Most of us require a little recognition. Politically, the way we tell people that they don't matter is to ignore them, and we do that most effectively when we pay them very little, or nothing at all (slavery).

The geopolitics of slowdown will be a politics of the previously ignored, of the humble, because without great acceleration it is so much harder for a few to trample over the many. In the eighteenth century it was Paris that appeared to be the most remarkably sped-up place, and the next locus for the moving center of selfishness after Amsterdam. In Paris in 1721, the French were always in a hurry "because [it was said] they have important business to do."[4] In Paris they would only rest when dead. Many did die in the revolution that started in Haiti in 1791 with an uprising of enslaved people and ended in Paris in 1793.

Many fled from France across the English Channel. Subsequently it was London that would build the most extensive dockside in the world, a site that by the 1830s was inspiring shock and awe. New York City next took on the mantle, with Times Square christened in 1904, although it was named after a newspaper rather than time itself. Today it is Beijing that is growing most quickly in both population and riches, but not in quite the same selfish way as its predecessors, although many Western scholars have yet to fully recognize this particular change.[5]

As of summer 2017, the world's top financial centers in rank order were London, New York, Singapore, Hong Kong, and Tokyo.[6] The last three of these are now clustered around China—around Beijing. Whether the ranking is sophisticated or crude matters little. It is the image that is everything. Almost no one checks to see how a ranking is made. Almost everyone simply accepts the ordering given. Less than two years later, in 2019, the rank order—produced by the same organization—was a little different: New York, London, Hong Kong, Singapore, and Shanghai.[7] This is not at all a stable world order, but one that is settling into a particular shape as it slows down. London is falling. The fastest-ever drop was when London went from first to second place in just two years. China is rising (but also slowing), New York teeters, Tokyo has been replaced by Shanghai. Overall, power is spreading out, not simply reconcentrating.

DEMOCRACY AND PROGRESS

Geopolitics is about time as much as space. We are currently learning more about our distant past than we have ever known. What is it possible for humans to be? Very recently a team of U.S.-based archaeologists working near Lake Turkana in Kenya discovered graves that led them to conclude that five thousand years ago, large groups of people once shared their workload without significant social hierarchy—successfully, generation after generation, for centuries.[8]

Four thousand years ago, the people of what later came to be known as the Indus Valley Civilization built cities without significant social hierarchies. One was Harappa, which had well-planned, wide public streets, both public and private wells, drains, and bathing places, and communal reservoirs. Until the 1920s nothing was known of this history at all.[9] At school I was taught that it had been the Romans who first created these things, but they were simply some of the first to do so in Europe, reproducing what had already been achieved elsewhere in the world two millennia earlier.

Assembly-based democracies have recently been dated back to societies contemporaneous with the Indus Valley civilizations, in what are now modern-day Syria, Iraq, and Iran. In India they are thought to have emerged in the early Vedic period, when "republics governed by assemblies became common."[10] Such ideas were adopted by the young, those who traveled the most, and the ideas traveled with them to Phoenician cities, including Byblos and Sidon, and then slowly on to Athens. We tend to remember and reconstruct only the histories of those civilizations closest to Europe, such as Athens.

Once upon a time Wikipedia reported, "The oldest known existence of a democratic kingdom (Ganarajya) where the king was chosen by people's votes can be traced way back in 599 BC at Vajji, Vaishali in ancient India. It was the birthplace of 24th and last Tirthankara in Jainism, named Maha- vira," but that statement has now been edited out and a longer, more convo- luted description has replaced it. Presumably this is because academics and other pundits, hidden behind Wikipedia editor pseudonyms, argue over the past so much more today as much else slows down, each keen to paint it differently in an attempt to help shape a different future.[11]

The idea that all people were equal did not "begin" in one place. It was obvious from the outset. Early democracies in Australia may be the longest uninterrupted examples, across generations that stretched far back into dreamtime. But even in the United Kingdom, two thousand years after the socialists of Lake Turkana were thriving in what is now Kenya, the pattern of Devon's ancient stone dwellings suggest that there was little in the way of social hierarchy and that war was rare three thousand years ago because, without elites, who is there to order you to fight each other?[12]

In the northern plains of China, over one hundred generations are thought to have lived much the same life, stable and sustainable, at a high population density, and that kind of society is only possible when the elites are controlled. Out-of-control elites lead to war.[13] There are always a few people who seemingly can't help sucking up to elites and who suggest that all will be well if we just allow a few people "who know what is best for us" to be in control. In 2018 Steven Pinker wrote a book, *Enlightenment Now: The Case for Reason, Science, Humanism, and Progress*, in which he sug- gested that the human race has never had it so good as it does today. Bill Gates promptly declared it his "new favorite book of all time."[14]

It is not hard to see how Pinker's story is wrong. Today many people other than Pinker know that we are consuming too much. They know that only the rich will benefit from Pinker's ideas, such as pretending (or even actually believing) that trickle-down economics works. Pinker has a par- ticular liking for the old-fashioned economic measurement of GDP, but as Jeremy Lent made clear in his critique of Pinker's suggestions, various measures of the world's genuine progress rate (GPR) peaked around the year 1976 and "they have been steadily falling ever since." Lent explained: "By painting this black and white, Manichean landscape of capitalist good versus communist evil, Pinker obliterates from view the complex, sophisti- cated models of a hopeful future that have been diligently constructed over decades by a wide range of progressive thinkers. These fresh perspectives eschew the Pinker-style false dichotomy of traditional left versus right.

Instead, they explore the possibilities of replacing a destructive global economic system with one that offers potential for greater fairness, sustainability, and human flourishing. In short, a model for continued progress for the twenty-first century."[15]

TALLER, CLEANER, SMARTER

Of course, there is evidence of many things getting better, from infant mortality to literacy, but often things are getting better only because they first became worse, or were not essential (as being able to read is not when there is little to read). A good example is the height of human beings, which was greatest when we hunted and gathered (but mostly gathered, if we are being honest about it) and then reduced when we had to farm. We farmed when there was too little to gather, and then our heights were reduced even further once people were made to work on plantations, called *fazenda* in Portuguese. The Portuguese were also quick off the mark in establishing *feitorias*, trading posts that were later known (when the Dutch and British built them in the sixteenth century) as "factories."[16] These then developed into factories of a different kind in England, where factory life resulted in the lowest human heights of all.[17]

Later, as conditions in factories in the United States and western Europe improved from the 1870s to the 1970s, the average height of people began to revert back to what their forefathers and mothers had known. Heights over this period rose by eleven centimeters (four inches) on average, or more than one centimeter per decade. The northern European and central European countries recorded the greatest gains in height between 1911 and 1955. Advances in public health and hygiene outweighed the damage done by war and economic depression but, more important than that, people were gaining more rights and building democracies. The researchers who discovered this concluded that many other factors mattered as well. For instance, "smaller family size was a key factor that made possible such improvements in child nurturing practices. Thus the fertility transition, which saw a dramatic fall in birth rates from the late 19th century, may have been important. For the countries studied here the downward trend was particularly strong between the 1900s and the 1930s."[18] That was the period when women won the vote in these countries. Given how fast fertility is now falling worldwide, we could well anticipate a future planet of generally taller people, but that growth too will slow down—because it is already slowing down and because there are biological limits to our height.

For people in what are now affluent nations, the greatest gains in height were all in the very recent past. The slowest recent gain has been in northern Europe, in Denmark, Finland, the Netherlands, Norway, and Sweden, where from 1955 to 1980, just 0.99 of a centimeter was gained per decade, as the greatest gains had already been made there.[19] The global height graph (figure 55) shows that average adult heights are now falling, because the mix of people is changing so rapidly. In short (with apologies for the awful pun), people in the taller countries of the world have been having fewer babies for longer, and people in countries with lower average heights have been having more babies. All the babies have been becoming, on average, taller than their parents, but the average heights of people worldwide have dropped as the mix has changed. As the mix stabilizes, we should expect to see an acceleration again in the global average heights—but only for a brief time. We will not become giants.

It is not only in the sudden speeding up and then slowing down of average heights that we can see that everything has been changing for us as a species. The signs of the current transformation coming toward an end are now so many. They can be seen in everyday objects beginning to change less and less. Sinks, washing machines, showers, and bathtubs all changed dramatically over the past five generations, but they are now becoming much more fixed in appearance. Although new versions may be a little more energy-efficient, we are no longer seeing transformations similar in importance to the arrival of running cold water and then hot water on demand, or moving from mangles to upright tubs to do laundry, or from no bath to tin baths to electric showers. The everyday reality of something as simple as cleaning ourselves is beginning to become fixed again, just as fixed as drawing water from a well used to be, for generation after generation—before the most rapid period of acceleration, which began around 1901.

No one today suggests inventing a new kind of shower without running water, or some sort of completely new toilet bowl (although a few people do suggest a return to squatting while defecating because it might be healthier). In fact, technological progress is now so slow that a minor adaptation to a common household appliance can be heralded as a great advance, as happened in 2007 when James Dyson was knighted for inventing a bagless vacuum cleaner. Back in 1901, several people in the United States and the United Kingdom invented slightly different versions of the original vacuum cleaner, but none was knighted for it, or otherwise lauded,

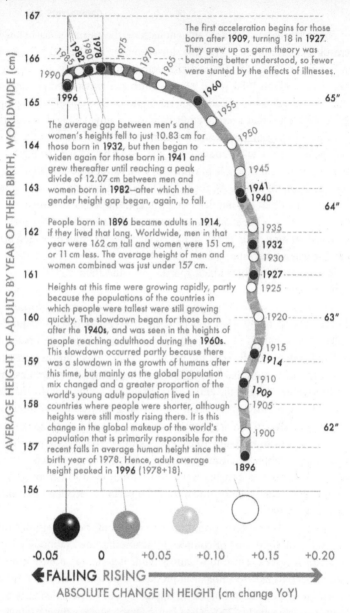

The first acceleration begins for those born after **1909**, turning 18 in **1927**. They grew up as germ theory was becoming better understood, so fewer were stunted by the effects of illnesses.

The average gap between men's and women's heights fell to just 10.83 cm for those born in **1932**, but then began to widen again for those born in **1941** and grew thereafter until reaching a peak divide of 12.07 cm between men and women born in **1982**—after which the gender height gap began, again, to fall.

People born in **1896** became adults in **1914**, if they lived that long. Worldwide, men in that year were 162 cm tall and women were 151 cm, or 11 cm less. The average height of men and women combined was just under 157 cm.

Heights at this time were growing rapidly, partly because the populations of the countries in which people were tallest were still growing quickly. The slowdown began for those born after the **1940s**, and was seen in the heights of people reaching adulthood during the **1960s**. This slowdown occurred partly because there was a slowdown in the growth of humans after this time, but mainly as the global population mix changed and a greater proportion of the world's young adult population lived in countries where people were shorter, although heights were still mostly rising there. It is this change in the global makeup of the world's population that is primarily responsible for the recent falls in average human height since the birth year of **1978**. Hence, adult average height peaked in **1996** (1978+18).

-0.05   0   +0.05   +0.10   +0.15   +0.20

← FALLING RISING **⟶**

ABSOLUTE CHANGE IN HEIGHT (cm change YoY)

55. Average height of adults worldwide, born 1896–1996. The timeline shows people's year of birth and their average height at 18 years, in centimeters on the left and inches on the right. (Data adapted from Majid Ezzati et al., "A Century of Trends in Adult Human Height," *NCD-RisC*, 26 July 2016, http://www.ncdrisc.org/data-downloads-height.html.)

because back then such progress was so rapid that before you knew it, there was another invention.[20] Today we have to search very hard to find examples of innovation. This is not because we are less innovative, but because the easy wins have all happened. And they were mostly won within the past five generations.

The easy wins freed huge numbers of us from laboring in factories, and allowed us to much more easily clean our homes, our clothes, and ourselves. The easy wins make it possible for the next and subsequent generations to grow tall again—until that too slows down within every country (and not just on average worldwide).

If you doubt the situation I am describing of so little technological progress very recently, consider the process we currently use in sewage plants around the world to extract clean water from waste, which was not invented until 1913. The following year, 1914, William Lockett and Edward Ardern published details of the "active sludge" method in the *Journal of the Society of Industrial Chemistry*. It first became operational in Manchester's Davyhulme wastewater treatment plant during the childhoods of Generation V.[21] Good sanitation for very large numbers of people is a very recent development, beginning only within the lives of the first of the past five generations. True progress now will not be so much through new inventions, but in spreading the benefits of what are now old inventions to many more people and more countries.

Globally, the phenomenon of each generation becoming much taller than the one before it began shortly before 1900, but when the world as a whole is considered, it appeared to end abruptly for those born shortly after the 1960s. In some of the best-off places in the world, our heights were rising by about two centimeters per decade when progress first spread.[22] The speed of the transformation could be seen in our bodies in ways other than our height. Not long after our heights began to shoot up, we also appeared to become cleverer.

The same increase that has been seen in height also appears in measurements of intelligence, although, unlike height, as yet there has been no leveling off. During the acceleration, IQ has risen by about three points per decade.[23] Note that IQ is simply the ability to perform well on an IQ test, and increases in IQ do not necessarily mean we are becoming more emotionally and intellectually able. It just means that we are becoming better trained at dealing with things like paper-based mathematical ability, analytical thinking, spatial recognition, and short-term memory, but quite possibly less able to do many of the practical tasks that our great-grandparents were very good at.

The rises are not at first evenly spread out. Average heights and average IQ rise first, and rise more quickly, in more affluent countries and especially for more affluent social groups within those countries. There appears to be a cascading effect down the social hierarchies and across space. We can find similar patterns in everything from the use of heroin (first "enjoyed" by the upper classes) to the size and comfort of houses. It is at first the rich who benefit, including often being the first to start abstaining from harmful practices, such as smoking cigarettes, eating too much food, or consuming too many drugs, and the first to acquire things that are beneficial, such as glass windows, piped water, toilets, better ventilated and better heated homes. The rich were also the first to have the opportunity to go to university, once the universities became more than just places to learn how to become a cleric (figure 56).

In general, the rise in tertiary education worldwide has been funded in a very similar way to the rise in secondary education that preceded it. However, in some of the places experiencing more severe economic slowdown, such as the United States, the most recent rise in university graduates has been accompanied by a huge rise in debt. As Ariane de Gayardon and her colleagues recently noted: "The total amount borrowed per year from all federal loan sources tripled between 1995 and 2010, then began to slow in 2010, reflecting a change in policy regarding eligibility for federal subsidized loans. . . . As of 2014–15, the average undergraduate borrower attending a baccalaureate degree-granting institution took out approximately $7,500 in loans each year of her undergraduate enrolment."[24] In the United States, the total number of university student borrowers and the average debt increased (see figure 6 in Chapter 3). However, as the number of loans has increased and the number of university students has also risen we have seen increasing paranoia in some of the richest countries on Earth about what will happen in the next generation, because education is seen as an arms race: "Couples undergoing IVF treatment could be given the option to pick the 'smartest' embryo within the next 10 years, a leading US scientist has predicted."[25]

The idea of "accurate IQ predictors" for fetuses ever being available, let alone "in the next 10 years," is laughable. You will likely get a much better prediction of an unborn child's future measured IQ by finding out his or her parents' income than by looking at his or her genes. You could,

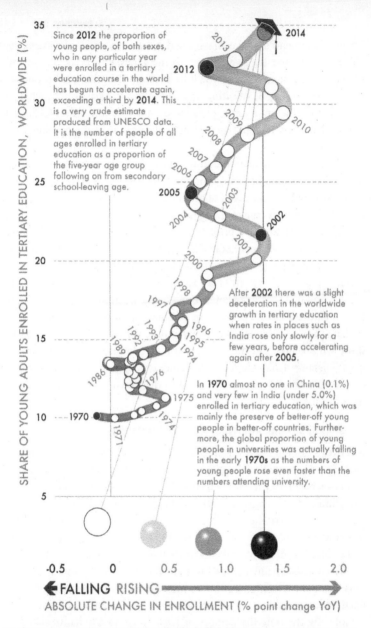

SHARE OF YOUNG ADULTS ENROLLED IN TERTIARY EDUCATION, WORLDWIDE (%)

Since **2012** the proportion of young people, of both sexes, who in any particular year were enrolled in a tertiary education course in the world has begun to accelerate again, exceeding a third by **2014**. This is a very crude estimate produced from UNESCO data. It is the number of people of all ages enrolled in tertiary education as a proportion of the five-year age group following on from secondary school-leaving age.

After **2002** there was a slight deceleration in the worldwide growth in tertiary education when rates in places such as India rose only slowly for a few years, before accelerating again after **2005**.

In **1970** almost no one in China (0.1%) and very few in India (under 5.0%) enrolled in tertiary education, which was mainly the preserve of better-off young people in better-off countries. Further-more, the global proportion of young people in universities was actually falling in the early **1970s** as the numbers of young people rose even faster than the numbers attending university.

← FALLING RISING ➡

ABSOLUTE CHANGE IN ENROLLMENT (% point change YoY)

56. Enrollment in tertiary education worldwide, 1970–2014. (Data adapted from World Bank, UNESCO Institute for Statistics, "World Bank EdStats," accessed 15 June 2019, https://data.worldbank.org/data-catalog/ed-stats.)

I suppose, pretend to make an educated guess as to which of two embryos will have a higher IQ given access to the genome of each, but you will be wrong almost as often as you'll be correct. The additional problem is that while you may be selecting on IQ, you would have no idea what else you are selecting on. Human genetics are not well enough understood to know what else you could be playing with other than the particular trait of interest.

Returning to the matter of how tall we are or could become, although height has a strong genetic component, changes in average height over time have not been the result of genetic changes, but of cultural and social factors. The same is true of changes in average IQ over time. It is therefore not surprising to find that prior educational attainment (as well as parents' socioeconomic position or education) is as good a predictor of future educational achievement for individuals as all their genetic data (summarized through polygenic scores).[26] For example, looking at much the same data, we also find that whether a child enjoys being at school is at least as important as all these factors in terms of whether she or he does comparatively well at school.[27] To most people, this finding would be obvious, but not to those who believe that the determinants of educational outcome are primarily genetic. Coincidentally, those same people also often believe that their own "success" can be attributed to their own superior genes, not to their privilege.

SPEED, SEXUAL POLITICS, AND THE ZEITGEIST

Just over a decade ago it was not unusual to read books with titles such as *High-Speed Society: Social Acceleration, Power, and Modernity*. This particular book began by presenting its first evidence of acceleration (on page 2) from film and TV, suggesting, "The shot lengths in movies, advertisements, and even documentaries have [decreased] by a factor of at least 50."[28] More recent analysis of those data concluded that average shot lengths in films had reduced from twelve seconds in 1930 to about two and a half seconds in 2010, but older films tended to pack more characters into a shot and thus filmmakers had to allow more time for viewers to register the scene. Each additional character added one and a half seconds to the length of a shot.[29] By the time the authors of *High-Speed Society* had reached the seventh page of their text they were talking about a period in the more distant past, claiming that "most authors agree that a significant period of acceleration took place between 1880 and 1920." In fact, that may well have been the most significant period, and that book, which is supposed to be about speeding up, actually helps confirm that we are now in slowdown.[30]

Much of the change in the time we spend doing things can be put down to changes to procedures. Athletic record breaking was the result of more people being sponsored, giving them the time to train, the development of new training techniques and sports equipment, and the introduction of performance-enhancing drugs that led to some spectacular new records by athletes from particular countries in past Olympics. The last factor is something we have certainly now slowed down at in an age of more wide-spread drug tests.

Humans have always had to be fast thinkers, and arguably more so in the distant past in a dangerous natural world; and more recently thinking fast was essential in dangerous industrial settings. However, there is no evolutionary reason (or evidence) that we have become faster and faster thinkers.

Surely, you might say, I am missing the point, and forgetting that we are now packing more into our lives than ever before. The only way to achieve that is to live life at a faster pace. It is, you might say, possible to travel so much faster today than in the era of the horse and carriage. However, we probably spend as much time traveling between A and B as we have ever done; it is just that the distances between A and B have increased. Only in a limited sense are we traveling more: over further distances, yes, but not traveling for a higher proportion of our lives—so that although we do travel further and faster today, it's not *ever* faster and *ever* further.

When a few things do fundamentally change, that change is often not gradual but comes in a sudden generational leap. Consider sexual politics. If we are really speeding up, why aren't we having more and more sexual partners, more marriages, more affairs?[31] Let's look at England and Wales since the Second World War. In 1947, about 400,000 couples a year were getting married. That total fell a little in subsequent years as those who had been forced to delay marriage due to the war got to tie the knot. And then, for about fifteen years, the annual number oscillated around 350,000 a year until the first of the babies of those first marriages, conceived in 1947 and born in 1948, turned sixteen and were able to marry in 1964. Add to them the huge number of babies born to parents in 1945, 1946, and 1947, who were aged nineteen, eighteen, and seventeen in 1964, and you have the beginnings of a rise in the supply of young brides and bridegrooms.

In the heady days of the mid-1960s, the numbers of marriages accelerated. At first this rise was the result of the growth in the number of people of marriageable age, but that rise soon slowed down. Once abortion was legalized by the very end of the 1960s, coupled with the widespread use of the contraceptive pill, the growth in marriages began to decelerate rapidly. The greatest jump down was from 1972 to 1973, and by the time teenagers were listening to the Sex Pistols in 1976 (singing "Anarchy in the UK"), we were back down to 350,000 marriages a year, but now drawn from a much larger population of both younger couples and the newly divorced. The number fell again in 1977 coincident with the Pistols' release of "God Save the Queen" ("the fascist regime"). Fewer and fewer people were getting married as a proportion of the population each year, but roughly the same number were getting married each year. And then something else happened in 1990. Something the timeline in figure 57 reveals to be very significant. By 1994 we were down to just 300,000 marriages a year, but in 2001 that total fell to just 250,000. So what changed?

We may never quite know. Those who delayed getting married in the earlier 1970s had fewer babies; hence, about two decades later, there were fewer people to get married. There was a small economic recession at the start of the 1990s. But above all else, marriage suddenly became an option rather than an expectation. Gay people no longer had to pretend they were not—or at least not as often, for as long, and to pretend to as many people. At the same time, being an unmarried couple with children became more acceptable. The average age of first marriage for women rose from around twenty-three in 1971 to thirty-one by 2015, and for men from twenty-five to thirty-three (the average for all marriages became thirty-six and thirty-eight years old, respectively). The point is, something changed in 1990, and something else sped up—the decline of marriage. That speeding up, too, has now settled down.

PLACES OF THE FUTURE

Some places tend to be a little culturally ahead of others. The place in the United Kingdom where marriage declined first was London. This was clearly first seen across all of London after the 1991 census was released. In the United States, the television drama *Sex and the City*, set in New York City, was first broadcast in 1998. Some places are just ahead of the trend: whole large places. *Les liaisons dangereuses* (1782) may have been far racier; Weimar Berlin had 1930s cabaret; and Jazz Age New York was more daring; but all were only for the minority.[32] In London by 1991 the 1985 film *My Beautiful Launderette* had become old school. At first, the

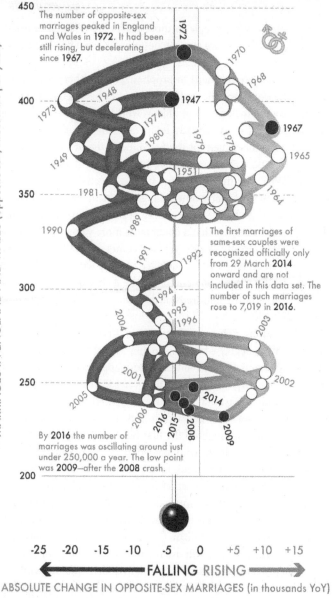

The number of opposite-sex marriages peaked in England and Wales in **1972**. It had been still rising, but decelerating since **1967**.

The first marriages of same-sex couples were recognized officially only from 29 March **2014** onward and are not included in this data set. The number of such marriages rose to 7,019 in **2016**.

By **2016** the number of marriages was oscillating around just under 250,000 a year. The low point was **2009**—after the **2008** crash.

MARRIAGES IN ENGLAND AND WALES (opposite-sex, thousands per year)

-25   -20   -15   -10   -5   0   +5   +10   +15

← FALLING RISING →

ABSOLUTE CHANGE IN OPPOSITE-SEX MARRIAGES (in thousands YoY)

57. Opposite-sex marriages in England and Wales, 1947–2016. (Data adapted from U.K. Office for National Statistics, "Marriages in England and Wales: 2016," 28 March 2019, and previous releases, https://www.ons.gov.uk/peoplepopulationandcommunity/births deathsandmarriages/marriagecohabitationandcivilpartnerships/bulletins/marriagesin englandandwalesprovisional/2016.)

trend is unclear—what people in those places are doing is unusual—and then, suddenly, everywhere else catches up with what has just become the new normal.

Some trends are not hard to prophesize. Soon there will be 4 billion women in the world, and they will, on average, be better educated than most men. Already the majority of graduates worldwide are women. Soon—so soon that perhaps it has already happened—the number of women on Earth will outnumber men for the first time in the history of our species. More men are born, but women live longer, more than six years longer in Japan.[33] What will tip the balance into us becoming a majority-female planet will be when fewer women die giving birth. We are so very close. What may seal this change is the ending of sex-selective abortion that will come with the realization that a daughter is more valuable than a son (especially in a low-fertility world). When it comes to a transformation of our politics, and an acceptance that violence really is wrong, the next Gandhi will likely not be a man. She could well be a sixteen-year-old girl called Greta or another of the hundreds of thousands of young people now protesting worldwide.

We don't know. Some say that putting flowers into gun barrels only works to a certain degree—but how do they know?[34] Is the speed of politics itself slowing down? Why do human beings appear not to have identified or invented a new significant "ism" for over 130 years? Socialism and anarchism are both at least that old. The word *feminism* was first used in the 1880s. There were so many new words in that decade. *Unemployment* was fairly new in 1888, although on the first Bloody Sunday, on 13 November 1887, it was the unemployed who massed in Trafalgar Square.

Given that it is hard to think of any substantive new "ism" since the 1880s, it makes you wonder whether people are now circling around a few ideas that are mutating slowly into a combined ism that might work better. We don't have a new set of ideas. Socialism has, for instance, softened, or at least become less clear. Capitalism, too, is less brutal than it once was. Imperialism, colonialism—we still use the words, but now to describe things that are much weaker echoes of their original forms; so too with fascism. Still evil, but so far not so effectively deadly. And what new ism is there? Thatcherism? Trumpism? Xi(Jinping)ism?

Scholars keep a close eye on whether we are going backward. In 2019 Anna Lührmann and Staffan Lindberg looked at the history of "autocratization," in which states become autocracies again, ruled by a single individual who often has nearly absolute power. Creating a time series for the period 1900–2017, they found 217 cases of autocratization in 109 countries. Only a minority of the world, some 69 states, had been unaffected during this period, and Lührmann and Lindberg concluded that 33 countries could still be classified as autocracies in 2017. But they also found no evidence of a worrying rise in autocratization. Instead, the rate was slowly falling, and the pace of change was also slowing. As the authors conclude: "A third wave of autocratization is indeed unfolding. It mainly affects democracies with gradual setbacks under a legal façade. While this is a cause for concern, the historical perspective presented in this article shows that panic is not warranted: the current declines are relatively mild and the global share of democratic countries remains close to its all-time high. As it was premature to announce the 'end of history' in 1992, it is premature to proclaim the 'end of democracy' now."[35]

In some ways, politics in Europe today is farcical. It is as if people are trying to prove that Karl Marx was correct when he said that history repeated itself, "the first as tragedy, then as farce," referring respectively to Napoleon I and to his nephew Louis Napoleon (Napoleon III). In May 2019 the Danish far-right political party Stram Kurs, which was demanding the deportation of all Muslims from Denmark, presented some of the most farcical candidates ever put before a voting public. One was a literal "piss-artist."[36] Stram Kurs won only 1.8 percent of the vote, and thus did not get any seats in the Folketing. As the South African political scientist Sithembile Mbete has observed, populism is a kind of theater.[37]

It is not just South Africa, Brazil, Turkey, and Russia that are today so often put forward as examples of populism rising around the world. With the advent of Donald Trump, the United States usually gets first mention (and of course Trump likes being mentioned). However, as Lührmann and Lindberg point out, populism is generally on the wane. As we try to work out what it is that we, collectively, really believe in, some places tend to be ahead of others in helping individualism, selfishness, bigotry, and populism wane. Two such places today are London and New York.

Figure 58 considers the voting in presidential elections in the state of New York from 1932 to 2016. The measure shown is the advantage the Democratic Party had at each election over the Republican Party. In 1932, of all Americans who voted in the presidential election, some 57.4 percent voted for the Democratic candidate, Franklin D. Roosevelt, but only 54.1 percent in New York State did so. The majority of New York State's

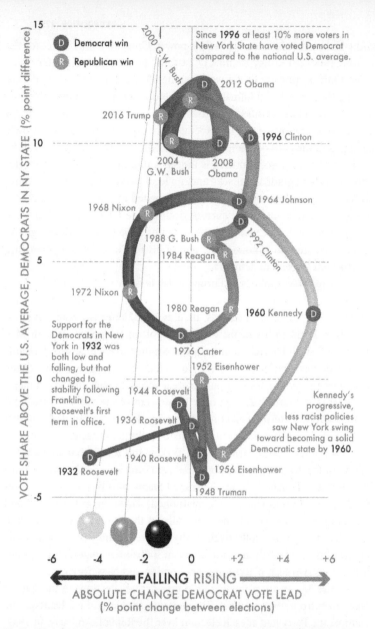

15 — 2000 G.W. Bush

D Democrat win
R Republican win

Since **1996** at least 10% more voters in New York State have voted Democrat compared to the national U.S. average.

D 2012 Obama

2016 Trump R — R

R

1996 Clinton D

2004 G.W. Bush   2008 Obama

10 —

VOTE SHARE ABOVE THE U.S. AVERAGE, DEMOCRATS IN NY STATE (% point difference)

1968 Nixon R

D **1964** Johnson

D

1988 G. Bush R   1992 Clinton

1984 Reagan R

5 —

1972 Nixon R

1980 Reagan R

1960 Kennedy   D

1976 Carter D

1952 Eisenhower

Support for the Democrats in New York in **1932** was both low and falling, but that changed to stability following Franklin D. Roosevelt's first term in office.

R

0 —

1944 Roosevelt D

Kennedy's progressive, less racist policies saw New York swing toward becoming a solid Democratic state by **1960**.

1936 Roosevelt D

D

D **1932** Roosevelt   1940 Roosevelt   R

1956 Eisenhower

D

-5 —   1948 Truman

-6   -4   -2   0   +2   +4   +6

← FALLING RISING **→**

ABSOLUTE CHANGE DEMOCRAT VOTE LEAD
(% point change between elections)

58. New York State Democrats' advantage in presidential elections, 1932–2016. (Data adapted from Dean Lacy and Zachary D. Markovich, "Why Don't States Switch Sides Anymore? The Rise and Fall of American Electoral Volatility" [working paper, 2016], https://cpb-us-e1.wpmucdn.com/sites.dartmouth.edu/dist/9/280/files/2016/10/Volatility.Simple.v8.pdf; and personal correspondence.)

voters are in New York City. However, change was in the air. By 1936 New Yorkers were voting Democratic nearly in the same proportion as the United States as a whole. They were slowly coming to see the Democrats as their party, but it was not until John F. Kennedy was elected in 1960 that New York first recorded a solid Democratic advantage.

The Democrats began as the political party of the southern states, originally opposed the creation of the federal government, and supported slavery. However, under Franklin D. Roosevelt the party shifted its stance toward progressivism, supporting unions and civil rights and becoming more anti-racist. It was at this point that New Yorkers, on average, began to warm to the Democrats and the opponents of the Democrats began to call themselves conservatives—those who wished to conserve what they suggested were the good old ways. New York was then all about the new.

Since the Great Depression, New York has supported a Republican president only six times—in 1948, 1952, 1956, 1972, 1980, and 1984. Support for the Democrats has spiraled upward, always rising more than it fell. It fell a little when Richard Nixon gained power; but rose again after Jimmy Carter gained office in 1976. Ronald Reagan's eight years in power were eight years in which New Yorkers as a whole became more and more sure that the Democratic Party was for them. Support fell back slightly under George W. Bush, but then rose to a new height with the second election of Barack Obama, when 63.4 percent of New Yorkers voted Democratic, against 50.9 percent of the national electorate who chose (or were able) to vote.

Both long-term and recent Democratic ascendancy in New York is mirrored by the rise of anti-conservative forces in London (figure 59). It will be interesting to see how New Yorkers react in future when the United States begins to realize that it is no longer as great as it was, and that U.S. hegemony is ending. After all, the British are still harking back today to when their country was top dog! In 2018 Paul Beaumont put it thus: "When Brits learn they once 'ruled the world,' the European Union's practices of compromise compare poorly: Cooperation is easily presented as subordination. Brexit can thus be understood as a radical attempt to arrest Britain's decline by setting sail for a future based on a nostalgic vision of the past."[38] Brits learned at school that they once ruled the world, and the older they are, the more likely they were taught that this was a great thing. One of the most compelling explanations of why it was mostly older British people, and especially older middle-class English people, who voted to leave the European Union in the 2016 referendum was what they were taught in school as children.[39]

Perceived status on the rank order of states, compared with how they actually perform in terms of standards of living, differs between countries and over time. The United States is often ranked as the world's greatest power, although by many measures, such as in economic innovation and educational achievement, it no longer is, and by even more measures (especially related to population health) it is now rapidly falling down the ranks. In contrast, Russia has recently been characterized as an "overperforming status-dissatisfied power"—a place where the elite feel they are not being taken seriously enough by the outside world.[40] Great Britain, too, is a place where those in charge think they should be shown more respect. But Britain, unlike Russia, has very little oil left, and thus has little to bargain with.

As Eli Zaretsky recently explained: "In England—the propulsive force behind Brexit—we are dealing with the psychology of a favoured, even chosen people. When 'God is decreeing to begin some new and great period.' . . . The mechanism underlying the cult of heroic failure is regression to narcissism."[41] However, at the heart of England is London, and London is becoming more and more politically different—in a very similar way to how New York City is now moving politically so much further ahead of the rest of the United States. Its mayor, Bill de Blasio, has made the police wear body cameras, instructed them to prosecute fewer people for smoking cannabis, attempted to tax millionaires more, and decried inequality.

When political change is studied over years, decades, and centuries, we can begin to see a slowdown. Slowdown is not a new utopia—and stability does not mean no change. There is always change, but there need not always, and cannot often, be explosive change. Take poverty as an example. Think about the fairly grinding poverty of medieval times, and the lack of education then. Stability produces a reduced sense of relative poverty and less uncertainty—stable societies can find ways to better cope with the conditions they have. They can thus provide more security. But the United States and especially the United Kingdom were both very far from stable in 2019.

Londoners are very aware of what is happening to the country as a whole. The majority of the poorest areas of the United Kingdom are in London, including half of the dozen top-ranked local authority areas with the greatest proportion of children living in poverty.[42] Children in the United Kingdom are becoming more and more segregated between schools and areas, not in terms of their religion or ethnicity, but in terms of being rich, poor, or in a shrinking middle group. The number of schools in Northern Ireland whose pupils are either almost all Catholic or almost all Protestant fell from 827 to 493 between 1997 and 2012.[43] But even as we see long-standing divides such as these narrow, social and economic divisions in the United Kingdom are widening.

When it comes to politics, we tend to be preoccupied with short-term events rather than long-term trends. In early May 2019, the *Observer* suggested that according to its poll data, "the Brexit party, launched only last month, is now on course for a thumping victory that Farage [leader of the Brexit Party] will, MPs fear, use to back his argument that the UK must leave the EU immediately without a deal."[44] In the event, the Brexit Party, which had first been created as a private commercial company by Katherine Blaiklock in 2018, did well in the European Parliament elections that month. However, if it is considered along with its Brexit-supporting allies (the Conservative Party, UKIP [UK Independence Party], and the Unionist Parties in Northern Ireland, all of which are to the right of mainstream European conservatives), then the Brexit cause had a combined loss of eleven seats in the European Parliament, or a massive 15 percent of total representation out of the seventy-three U.K. seats.[45] The twenty-nine new MEPs (members of the European Parliament) of the U.K. Brexit Party found themselves in limbo, unable to find any allies in the European Parliament with whom to work: first they were a tragedy, and now they are a farce.

Immediate commentary on political events quickly dates. By the time you read this, Jeremy Corbyn will certainly no longer be U.K. Labour Party leader. And if you live outside of the United Kingdom you may not have heard of him. If so, imagine that Bernie Sanders had become the U.S. Democratic Party presidential nominee. In the United Kingdom in 2017 this was said by political progressive outriders who supported Corbyn, whose unexpected electoral success denied the Conservatives a working majority: "Let's face it, we've all been on a high but looking at the shifting Overton window shows that we've been hallucinating new possibilities into existence. This suggests that the excitement generated by the prospect of political power can be used to conjure up the social power required for radical change. If not then we're in trouble. Acid Corbynism must act as a gateway drug else it will disappear altogether."[46] That commentary is indicative of change. There is a longer evolution of voting and public opinion. If opinion

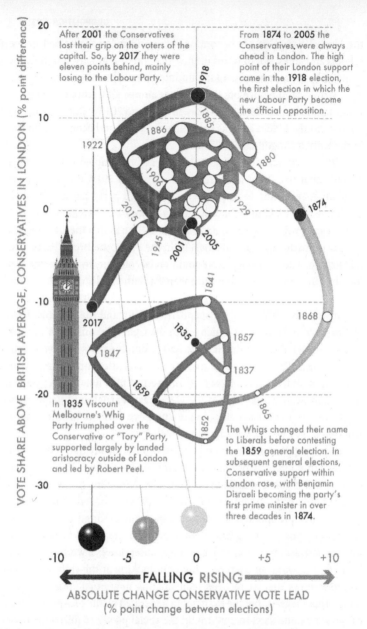

VOTE SHARE ABOVE BRITISH AVERAGE, CONSERVATIVES IN LONDON (% point difference)

After **2001** the Conservatives lost their grip on the voters of the capital. So, by **2017** they were eleven points behind, mainly losing to the Labour Party.

From **1874** to **2005** the Conservatives were always ahead in London. The high point of their London support came in the **1918** election, the first election in which the new Labour Party became the official opposition.

In **1835** Viscount Melbourne's Whig Party triumphed over the Conservative or "Tory" Party, supported largely by landed aristocracy outside of London and led by Robert Peel.

The Whigs changed their name to Liberals before contesting the **1859** general election. In subsequent general elections, Conservative support within London rose, with Benjamin Disraeli becoming the party's first prime minister in over three decades in **1874**.

FALLING RISING

ABSOLUTE CHANGE CONSERVATIVE VOTE LEAD
(% point change between elections)

59. London Conservatives' advantage in general elections, 1835–2017. (Data from a data set constructed by the author from many records, most recently of the Electoral Commission. See https://beta.ukdataservice.ac.uk/datacatalogue/studies/study?id=3061.)

polls are studied using timelines, it becomes clear that voters can be manipulated in the short term to suddenly support the far right in large numbers, but such support quickly fades away when it is no longer stoked up.

How did London, or at least a substantial number of Londoners, react to the recent rise of radicalism in the British Labour Party and the message of its leader Jeremy Corbyn in particular? We are lucky in the United Kingdom—we can go back to at least 1835 to consider voting trends, in this case in general elections. London in 1835 was anti-Conservative. The Whigs (who later became Liberals) secured proportionately more votes in London than they did in the country as a whole. After 1865, when Lord Palmerston won for the Liberals nationally, London began to swing toward the landed interest of the Tories. Palmerston was a warmonger, among much else. London then remained relatively pro-Tory, as shown in figure 59, until at least 2015, when Jeremy Corbyn became leader of the Labour Party. It was clear then that Londoners had become radical again. The radicalization began a little earlier when, against the wishes of the then Labour leadership, Ken Livingstone became the first radical London mayor in the year 2000.

THE TRANSFORMATION OF A SPECIES

The Anthropocene is not the end of our world. It's just the beginning. Collectively, we have the potential to create a much better planet than the one we are creating now. So let's start talking about the better future we want, and less about the future we don't. It's about articulating values, and about sharing, fairly, the only planet we have with one another and the rest of life on earth. The planet we make will reflect the people we are.

—*Erle Ellis, 2018*[47]

Not everything slows with slowdown. Evidence is mounting that our capitalist transition is coming to its end. The trends in politics can be seen to fit that theory—depending on your perspective. You have to step back and take a wider view, rather than being blinded by everyday trivia. As a species, we have fundamentally changed. We have changed in how we organize ourselves, in how we communicate, in what we believe, in how we relate to each other, and in what we know. We have also changed physically. If you were to transport young adults from today back to the time of their great-grandparents, they would most likely tower over their ancestors. This is now true almost no matter where they were born. However, despite knowing that there is more change to come, and although we do not yet know what our settled state will be, we can know that in many fundamental aspects of human life the fastest change is over. We will, for instance, never again see infant mortality fall as fast worldwide as has been falling recently—because infant mortality rates cannot become negative.

People in each generation have also become more intellectually able than their parents were, as education spread; each succeeding generation has many more material goods and has traveled much further, although recently we have often been doing this increasingly unequally. But all that is ending because we can grow only so tall, individually learn only so much, do only so much traveling around our one (now quite small) planet, and tolerate rising inequality only for a few decades. Income inequality is now falling in more countries than it is rising. We are heading toward a more just and stable future.[48]

The pace and nature of the five-generation transition, this progress toward the unknown, have varied across the world. The slowdown is misinterpreted as an economic decline in the West, or as the result of the rise of China. China has, in fact, seen the greatest slowdown of all in fertility and, in the most recent years, a rapid deceleration in its economic growth rates. Recent economic change is neither a decline of the West, nor the replacement of the United States by China at the top of the pile. It is the ending of the capitalist transition that has rippled out around the globe. It is the beginning of a new stability. This is not dystopia or utopia—just very different from the stability that was the norm before these five generations. And it is a state that will differ fundamentally from capitalism because capitalism is a process of change; it is not stability.

Capitalism demands change, ever-expanding markets, and increasing consumption: grow or go bust. In many ways, we are now heading toward zero growth, back to very low global interest rates. We are very unprepared for stability and so we try to avoid it at all costs as we burden young people with debt and young countries with dictators. The new politics in Britain is becoming more aware of all this. The old politics in the United States has yet to catch up.

None of this became at all clear until recently and much is still uncertain, still shrouded in fog. Because it is not yet clear, it would be so easy to be wrong, but it is worth recognizing now that the favorable seasons are almost over. We are still living through the time of transition, but slowing. There is at least one more generation of turmoil, but subsiding turmoil, to go, if the current rates of change do not suddenly all reverse what the most recent decades have experienced. The change already in play for the next generation is slow change.

Global human population is scheduled to rise, we are told, fivefold: from 2 billion in 1901 to 10 billion by the mid-twenty-first century. This was according to the central UN projection of 2017. On the morning of 17 June 2019 I wrote the following words: "I am awaiting the release later today of the next set of worldwide UN statistics. Whatever they show, we know they will only confirm the precise pace of the most recent slow-down."[49] It was true. They did. Such a huge change last happened (much more slowly) during the many separate Neolithic revolutions. Those revolutions took place over dozens, if not hundreds, of generations. This revolution, the one we are living through now, is just half a dozen generations long and is now slamming to a halt.

There is nothing normal about instability and constant change. There is nothing normal about what we have been used to. We of the five generations, mostly of just two or three, have been living through an anomaly. One way to appreciate this is to compare the speed of change in different places. Some places speed up before others, but now everywhere is beginning to slow down—to settle down—at roughly the same time, and very quickly.

The transition between the experiences of one generation and the next has been different in different places. Not everywhere will end up the same and not everywhere is following an identical trajectory. A geographical understanding is key to seeing the transition in its true light, or at least to seeing it as well as we can see something that is still taking shape. It is the geographical coming together of so many different trends that suggests stability ahead, from the sizes of families moving almost everywhere toward a one- or two-child norm, to child survival rates almost all converging on a state where very high chances of survival are normal.

If you find it hard to conceive of the change having come, consider what Charles Darwin, the man with whose words this book began, believed. In *The Descent of Man*, Darwin suggested that the supposedly more civilized Caucasian races would exterminate the "savage" human races based on a belief, earlier outlined by the philosopher G. W. F. Hegel, in a nonsensical hierarchy of what Hegel thought of as distinct human races.[50] We are slowing down in our degree of prejudice. In the most progressive cities of two of the least economically and socially progressive countries of the rich world,

London and New York, views are becoming less conventional and more radical a little more quickly again now.

Let's end with the words of a fifteen-year-old girl who spoke in London's Parliament Square on 31 October 2018. Why, she asked, does "no one ever speak about the aspect of equality, or climate justice[?] . . . Rich countries need to get down to zero emissions, within six to twelve years, so that people in poorer countries can heighten their standard of living by building some of the infrastructure that we have already built. Such as roads, hospitals, electricity, schools and clean drinking water. Because how can we expect countries like India or Nigeria to care about the climate crisis if we, who already have everything, don't care even a second about it or our actual commitments to the Paris Agreement?"[51] Compare her insight with Darwin's blundering over "savages." She wanted to know why people did not connect economic inequality and climate change. They do now. Slowdown is happening; we have no choice.

life

after the great acceleration

I do feel that the government is just not in touch with us.
—*Carol, Liverpool, 2017*

Agnosia is the inability to recognize certain things, despite not having any specific hearing, visual, or memory loss. One variant, social-emotional agnosia, is the inability to interpret facial expressions, body language, and voice intonation. Agnosia is a defined medical condition, typically caused by a neurological condition or by brain damage. Why do so many people in government act in ways that look strikingly like agnosia's political equivalent, as though they have gradually lost the ability to see the signs that all is not well among those they were elected to represent? They *cannot* see the whole, the "us," the group of everyone else that Carol (quoted above) talks about. This is especially true when it comes to the impacts of slowdown, particularly economic impacts. They promise growth as the cure, but the old conventional growth is over. Some places have slowed down earlier than others. Liverpool in England, where Carol lives, is one of those places.

In the 1980s in the United Kingdom, the BBC broadcast a sitcom called *Bread*. It was set in Liverpool. "Bread" has a double meaning: the usual one, and a slang term for money (think "breadwinner" or "make some dough"). For many decades economic historians have used the changing price of bread and wheat as a proxy for the general price of food and have compared that to wages. One of the spurs to the French Revolution was the rising price of bread. Bread in 1980s England became more expensive, and it is doing so again today. When we say that real wages have fallen, we mean that the relative price of bread (and other essentials) has risen.

The Lord's Prayer came into being under the Roman occupation of Judea. It was a prayer not just for individuals, but also for the group that they were part of, for "us," for simple subsistence for all—"Give us this day our daily bread." When there are signs of scarcity, when there is no growth or only slight growth in what is available for all, we begin again to ask for what is sufficient, and how we can better share that out, rather than always thinking that we should all have more, and that trickle down will reach the hindmost. However, when government is out of touch and refuses to see the slowdown, all it can offer is fantasy.

You may well question my conclusions. Are we entering a new age in which each person who has more will have a little less at some point very soon, much less if they currently have much more? Or are the slowdowns shown in this book mostly just short-term economic cycles? Is all that we have considered here just a matter of changes in the sectors, industries, demographic measurements, and social indicators that always tend to have the same pattern of rapid growth followed by slowdown? If it is not, what are the implications for life after the great acceleration?

On seeing the timelines in this book, some people have suggested that, rather than each being a symptom of the signs of a general slowdown, we are seeing how one social norm, or one technology, is simply being superseded by the next. I do not agree, but I can understand this argument. Such critics maintain that what is taking place are life-cycle alterations in quantitative change, albeit driven by qualitative change as each new form supersedes the old. They give examples: canals, railways, motorways, airports, spaceports, each with its heyday, and each superseded by the next thing. But in reality, each of these was a less fundamental change than the preceding one. Although we may be planning to build spaceports—the U.K. government committed £2 million in 2018 toward their development—we know in our heart of hearts that these are not going to be the next great leap forward.[1] The U.S. space shuttle program was supposed to be an even greater leap forward, but it actually produced a craft that never left low Earth orbit. If we thought there were possibilities for exploration, we would be spending much more public money in preparation. We subconsciously know we are slowing down.

For another example of why the slowdown is real, think of 1880s sound-recording wax cylinders replaced by 78 rpm shellac-based records, which in turn were replaced by vinyl records, then superseded by tape, then by compact discs, which were soon replaced by sound files, and then by sound stored on the cloud (server farms housed in the middle of nowhere, preferably a cold nowhere). People who are skeptical that we are in an era of slowdown say that if you were to draw the timeline of any of these developments, you would see a rapid rise, a slowdown, and then a rapid fall as each new technology eclipses the last. I would respond that each development has been less impressive than the one before. We will then probably find ourselves in disagreement, but I would predict that the next few generations will listen to music much as we, in rich countries, do now. So, in this chapter on the impacts of slowdown, to try to break this impasse, let's turn to a few of the aggregate measures that are not ephemeral to support the conclusion that less change is coming. These are the total world gross domestic product, the total number of species worldwide, total air travel, and the total of all human babies who have been born or are soon expected to be born in the last few years of peak human.[2]

If the process of qualitative change from old things to new things is itself becoming slower, then we would expect the rise in total overall energy use per person, total population growth, and total GDP per capita to be slowing down too. The American anthropologist Leslie White saw energy use as the great driver of cultural evolution—starting with human muscle power, then the use of draft animals, then local wind and water power, then fossil fuels, and finally nuclear energy.[3] No doubt he would have added renewables had he not died in 1975 and thus not had the opportunity to see their rise. White noted that it has been those societies (which he called cultures) that diverted the most energy to human needs to whom the power and the glory flowed most.

In 1973 in the book *Poverty and Progress,* social epidemiologist Richard Wilkinson pondered "the essential preconditions for the stability of cultural systems . . . a society which has settled into a known and proven way of life which allows it to deal with all eventualities without innovation . . . the development of a balanced relationship with the environment."[4] On page 144 of that short, pithy book, Wilkinson showed how the efficiency of the steam engine had improved by almost 40 percent between the early Newcomen engine (to be precise, the model of 1718) and the engines of the late 1750s, with the efficiency almost doubling again by the 1760s and again by the late 1780s as the amount of nonwasted energy that could be extracted from the same quantity of coal rose and rose. It doubled again by the 1830s and, with the invention of steam turbines, again by 1910. Note that the length of time between each of these technological jumps lengthens after 1750 from ten years to twenty to forty to eighty. However, we should not expect a doubling again from 1910 to the year 2070, because as yet there is no sign of it. Efficiency gains in the production of electricity from turbines have also been slowing down. The next few generations are likely to use the technology we have today for longer; they will not experience the acceleration of technological innovation facilitated by steam engines in the late 1700s or silicon chips in the late 1900s.

Steam engines were initially niche. The growth in our use of energy has been enormous since we moved from the horse- or oxen-drawn plow to the tractor around a century ago, but the current growth in the rate of energy use per person is now declining worldwide. Overall use is still growing, but not by anything like the rate at which it was accelerating in the eighteenth and nineteenth centuries, and for almost all of the twentieth century. Our total energy use is now growing relatively more slowly per capita than ever before. Today, the greater the efficiency of energy conversion achieved (as, say, solar panels are improved), the more we will enter a pattern of diminishing returns to further increases in efficiency, just as we did with those first coal-powered steam engines. Fortunately, the great slowdown in human population growth means that this is no longer an apparently insurmountable problem.

We will know when we have reached stability: not just when the human population of the planet no longer rises, which is now expected to occur well within the lifetimes of most babies born today, but when our total energy consumption falls as a stable human population modernizes to use less energy per person in future. We could speculate on what might happen then to our many measures of well-being, both economic well-being and the many genuine progress indicators such as happiness statistics, life satisfaction, and healthy human life expectancy itself. To date, all of these measures have either ceased to rise in some places, or are rising much more slowly than they were before.

In future, technical change is likely to become slower because much of it no longer promotes well-being. Consider, again, the example of recorded sound. The development of each of the early technologies represented great progress. Those flat spinning discs called 78s, because they rotated some seventy-eight times per minute, were a revelation to the few people in 1898 who were rich enough to listen to them first. But they were primitive in comparison to the 45s and 33s that came later, to the cassette tape and compact disc, and to the sound file in all its many formats. We see diminishing returns in terms of the real improvement to sound quality and human benefit (or no sound-quality improvement at all, when comparing an MP3 to a CD). We appear to be approaching a steady state economy similar to what ecologists call a steady state climatic climax community (think of a mature rain forest). Eventually, whatever happens to human beings has to be sustainable. The key questions are then: what kind of sustainability, for how many humans, and living what kind of lives?

GLOBAL ECONOMIC SLOWDOWN

Any attempt to make sense of the human condition at the start of the new century must begin with the analysis of the social experience of speed.
—*William Scheuerman, 2004*[5]

Economically almost everywhere is now slowing, especially in those places with the most people. Three centuries ago, Thomas Newcomen's steam engine was one of the precursors to acceleration. Two centuries ago a newly independent United States was quietly expanding and innovating without monarchs, which itself was innovative. One century ago, the rich world was at war and innovation abounded. Today the most economically successful social climber of our times, the most amazing place, the place we least expected, is China. However, unlike those earlier centers of industrial or political innovation, which each grew for far longer, China is already slowing down.[6]

China is now slowing much more quickly than Britain or the United States ever did at the height of capitalism, because capitalism was (and still is) a process, a transition, not an arrival point to be continually repeated until overthrown by revolution. The years of most rapid economic progress have been something of an aberration, and we are heading back to stasis. We now find it very hard to remember that it has almost always been stasis, an equilibrium, that humanity has lived under. Stasis can be good: the opposite of upheaval. It does not mean inactivity, just far less rapid change. And a transition toward what philosophers often write convoluted sentences about: "an egalitarian symbolization that will guide, code, and form the peaceful subjective basis for the collectivization of resources, the effective elimination of inequalities, the recognition of differences, with equal subjective rights, and, ultimately, the withering away of separate, state-type entities."[7] They write these sentences today because they can now see the signs that this is possible; it is not simply a theoretical dream.

We have become too used to desperately seeking new developments and ever-greater change. Take global GDP per head. In some years during the 1950s it was rising by $100 to $150 a year, $260 a year in the inflation-heady year of 1972, then $470 a year by 2006, and nowadays it sits at a global average of just over $15,000. However, the absolute rise that got us there has not only been slowing down very rapidly since the global crash of 2008, the rate of rise was slowing down much earlier than that. In absolute terms (as shown earlier in figure 47) the slowdown began in 2006. In relative terms (see figure 60 here), GDP growth per person has been falling since 1964 and possibly even since 1950, which was shortly after GDP was first formally defined.

Look at the trend in figure 60 and ask yourself whether the veering to the left, from 1950 to 2018, appears to be a steady shift in state as compared to the rapid deceleration from 1890 to 1929. It is, of course, always "too early to say" until you know, and then it is obvious. It is safe to say that we have been on an economic roller coaster, and that the roller coaster has only very recently swung through its greatest-ever ups and downs—booms and busts. We live in dread that there is more to come, but it may well be over. There are probably only smaller perturbations to come. The ride we have been on is coming to an end. Not the end of history, just the end of the roller coaster.

One way of viewing the current global economy is to think of it as something that has its origins in what happened in 1492. Since then, although more and more people have been drawn into it, we have not known what globalization really is. At times, especially after World War II, we attempted to manage it. In some ways the economy and our resources are like what happens to the soil when you first farm. The soil is quickly exhausted and your crops fail. You get diminishing returns. Capitalism appears to have been such a learning process, rather than the end state. So what is next? We don't know; we can't tell. But it will have to be sustainable. That is not a plea, but simply an observation. We are now slowing down toward it, and understanding that is enough of a leap of thinking for one book. It is a leap that has many implications, from the trivial—our grandchildren may be wearing jeans all their lives, just as we have—to the profound: the richer economies have slowed first so we are heading toward a more equitable future.

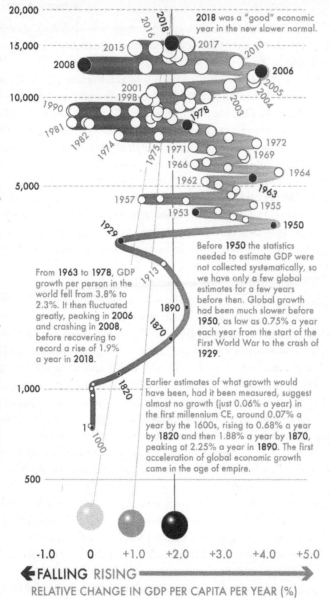

WORLD GDP PER CAPITA (real mean annual average, constant 2011 U.S.$—log scale)

2018 was a "good" economic year in the new slower normal.

From **1963** to **1978**, GDP growth per person in the world fell from 3.8% to 2.3%. It then fluctuated greatly, peaking in **2006** and crashing in **2008**, before recovering to record a rise of 1.9% a year in **2018**.

Before **1950** the statistics needed to estimate GDP were not collected systematically, so we have only a few global estimates for a few years before then. Global growth had been much slower before **1950**, as low as 0.75% a year each year from the start of the First World War to the crash of **1929**.

Earlier estimates of what growth would have been, had it been measured, suggest almost no growth (just 0.06% a year) in the first millennium CE, around 0.07% a year by the 1600s, rising to 0.68% a year by **1820** and then 1.88% a year by **1870**, peaking at 2.25% a year in **1890**. The first acceleration of global economic growth came in the age of empire.

← FALLING RISING **⟶**

RELATIVE CHANGE IN GDP PER CAPITA PER YEAR (%)

60. World GDP per capita, log scale, 1–2018. (Data adapted from Maddison Project Database 2018, University of Groningen, https://www.rug.nl/ggdc/historicaldevelopment/maddison/releases/maddison-project-database-2018, updated using World Bank and IMF data.)

There is much that still needs to change, but achieving greater economic stability, rather than simply accepting the roller coaster as usual, could help us bring about some of that change more quickly and more carefully. Worldwide in 2017, some 1.4 billion workers were estimated to be in vulnerable employment, without secure contracts, and the International Labour Organisation (ILO) forecasts that by 2019 an additional 35 million will have joined them. The ILO estimates that in the poorest of countries, vulnerable employment still affects three out of four workers, and in richer countries "the number of workers living in extreme poverty is expected to remain stubbornly above 114 million for the coming years, affecting 40 per cent of all employed people in 2018."[8] In 2019 on the occasion of the ILO's centenary, the organization called for "a universal labour guarantee that protects fundamental workers' rights, an adequate living wage, limits on hours of work and safe and healthy workplaces."[9] Clearly such a change is possible.

Between 2018 and 2019 the annual ILO report went from despair to optimism, from focusing on what was worst about the world of work globally to a practical goal worth striving for. And then in July 2019 the news was dire again: "the lowest 20 per cent of income earners—around 650 million workers—earn less than 1 per cent of global labour income" (although the small print explained that "overall global labour income inequality has fallen since 2004").[10] It may be that the ILO reports' key messages veer widely from one extreme to the other each year in a desperate attempt to get newspaper and television programs around the world to report the organization's findings. The details in the annual findings themselves are rather more dull: things are getting better, slowly, but not always linearly. This has been, and will be, a very long process, but the overall arc is bending toward rising equality.

In 1883 the phrase *labour-giver*, meaning one who provides work, was derided in the preface to the third edition of Karl Marx's *Das Kapital*.[11] Today we are still having to explain how stupid the term *wealth creator* is to describe those who simply happen to be so rich that they can invest. Every large profitable investment ultimately derives from the debts or poverty of the many, and increasingly brings about diminishing returns for the investors compared to the returns they used to reap when population and markets were growing so fast. As growth slows, redistribution becomes an imperative, not simply an aspiration. Predicting the headlines in the United States in 2020, the Brookings Institute suggested that the Democratic Party nominee for president will argue for a wealth tax of 1 percent of the wealth of the richest 1 percent of U.S. households, amounting to $2.5 trillion over ten years, which would be used to give all American families a $1,400 annual tax break.[12] This is because future technological innovation will not make the poor better off. Only redistribution and social innovation can do that now. Americans would each be far better off with better health care, funded by that $1,400 per family per year, to be used by any individual who fell ill. If you become seriously ill, then the amount spent on you will far exceed $1,400 a year, and if you don't, you are very lucky. A lot can and must change with slowdown.

THE TECHNOLOGICAL MIRAGE

We now lament that the technological innovations that will make the greatest changes to our lives have already been made. As Robert Gordon made clear in 2012: "The frontier established by the US for output per capita, and the UK before it, gradually began to grow more rapidly after 1750, reached its fastest growth rate in the middle of the 20th century, and has slowed down since. It is in the process of slowing down further."[13] He did not notice or mention it, but innovation is also not speeding up elsewhere. Everywhere, innovation is now slowing. Gordon went on to explain that many of the improvements that have happened could happen only once. Within just one century we went from the horse being the fastest mode of transport to the jet plane. We cannot do such a leap ever again. A century from now, we will not be teleporting. It's time to get used to what we have and use it better than we currently do.

Gordon gave the example of how the interior temperatures of many buildings alternated in the 1870s, and all the years before then, from freezing cold in the winter to stifling heat in the summer. Today, in the very many places that have air-conditioning, they are a stable 72 degrees Fahrenheit (22 degrees Celsius) all year round. That aids productivity. But the change has come; the deed is done. It cannot be done again. He noted the shift in the United Sates from being an almost entirely rural nation to one that is almost entirely urban—that, too, cannot happen again. There is no super-urban lifestyle we can next shift to. He gives many other examples in which no further substantial shift can be made. And he concludes that for those who live in the United States, what will be "most important quantitatively in holding down the growth of our future income is rising inequality."

Today many of the most equitable countries of the word, such as Japan and the Scandinavian states, are the most equitable urban societies the world has ever known. People in those societies are more innovative than in the United States or the United Kingdom, but even there rates of innovation are falling.[14] There is no society on Earth that could not become more equal than it currently is, but the most equitable ones today will not see as great a growth again in equality as they have already experienced over the course of the past century. That is because during that century, the most significant economic inequality in such places was eliminated.

Gordon ended his message to Americans by advocating greater unskilled immigration. However, as Darrell Bricker and John Ibbitson recently observed, "Immigrants in the not-too-distant future may be hard to come by."[15] Economists find it hard to accept that productivity is not just slowing, but is set to slow further. As one group of economists recently explained: "The slowdown is real, and . . . while many factors matter, it can be largely explained by a slowdown of investment, an increasing gap between frontier and laggard firms, a slowdown in trade, and technological change. An apparent paradox, which contrasts the slowdown in productivity growth with accelerating technological change, may be explained by mismeasurement, implementation lags for technologies, and creative destruction processes."[16] What they did not say is that they don't really know why things are slowing. As conventional economists, they still think there should be acceleration and that acceleration is good, so they try to explain away the slowdown as the result of recent "creative destruction," the lull before yet another new capitalist dawn and a return to acceleration.

Creative destruction, an idea that was devised very recently by an economist, is itself also now dying away. There is nothing creative about destruction, and nothing stable in pinning your hopes on slowdown being a mirage. This is because there are so many signs now that it is real. Since around the year 2000, there has been negligible growth in the development of new classes of invention in the United States, despite the tendency there to patent almost any new idea, despite that country's still growing population, and despite the even more rapid growth of its universities and research and development establishments. Even patenting, after building up a head of steam, appears to have flatlined. A continual steady increase in innovation now requires ever-greater investment to produce any substantial results.[17]

Much of the current slowdown is still being described as creative destruction, and as the process of "market clearing," wherein the obsolete is perpetually replaced by the new, as if the capitalist transition were some end-of-history process that we will always be stuck in. Financial analysts make arrogant claims based on the 1980s and 1990s economics they learned at school, failing to spot the new reality. They repeat a particular mantra in the hope that they will be taken seriously as great soothsayers. Here is just one example from one analyst among a million possible examples of attempts to explain the current slowing down. This one is about the decline of shopping centers in Australia: "We, therefore, expect shopping centre values will continue to fall, as pricing adjusts to help clear the market."[18] The implication is that once the market has "cleared," prices will rise ever higher yet again, and new shopping centers will emerge selling new and ever more expensive goods. It need not, they need not—we may instead be learning to be happy with what most of us have and not think that we always need to consume more.

In Britain, reports are regularly published bearing titles such as "UK Rich Increase Their Wealth by £274 Billion over Five Years," in this case reporting on the £724 billion the wealthiest one thousand families in the country are said to have held in 2018 and how that rose from £450 billion in 2013.[19] A year later, when the wealth of the latest one thousand richest U.K. families was assessed, slower growth was revealed for the same group, excluding any who had fallen out of the top cohort over that one year, and including their replacements.

In 2019, when the total amount of the thousand richest groups' wealth was found to have increased by only £48 billion, the title of the next report was "A Nation of Ferraris and Foodbanks—UK Rich Increase Wealth by £253 Billion over Five Years."[20] It could have easily read: "Rich List Wealth Growth Peaked in 2017 When It Rose by £82 Billion That Year, Then Declined to a Rise of £66 Billion in 2018 and Fell to a Rise of Just £48 Billion in 2019." That rate of U.K. wealth growth and inequality may possibly change direction and climb again, but for the moment the rise in the wealth of even the most wealthy of all is slowing down. And so the people who were very recently in the top one thousand wealthiest in Britain have, as a group (and most important because of those who have fallen out of the top thousand), actually seen their total wealth drop most recently.

The global economic slowdown is so great that the rich cannot carry on getting ever richer. In 1950 the worldwide average GDP per person rose by about $156 in today's money, or by about 4.3 percent. By 2015 it rose by $158, or nearer to 1.6 percent a year—almost three times slower.[21] And these snapshots are taken from the economists' high points! However, just because there are more and more signs that we might finally be slowing down economically, that we may possibly even be beginning to become more united socially, it does not necessarily follow that we are learning quickly enough how to live sustainable lives in order to be able to slow down without a series of crises. At least we have been worrying more and more about our sustainability for longer than I have been alive. In our heart of hearts, more and more of us now know we must slow down.

LETTING DOWN THE WORLD

You maniacs! You blew it up! Damn you! Goddamn you all to hell!
—*Final lines of the movie Planet of the Apes, 1968*[22]

In the very first chapter of this book, I asked you to try to imagine the future, or in effect what your great-great-great-great-great-grandchildren (assuming you have children and they have children, and so on) might worry about in 2222. This is when the population has not been rising for three or four generations, when economic inequality has been low for several generations, and the planet is no longer warming up. It will hopefully be a time when sea levels, after rising for many decades, have stabilized, and when power sources have become so secure that they are barely ever commented upon. In that future time, long after the pattern-recognition powers of AI, as also suggested earlier on, turn out to be very useful, but not to be very intelligent, we could all be well fed and few of us will be too fat. What then would your great-great-great-great-great-grandchildren worry about?

With continued slowdown, you may have 100 such descendants; with population stability, you would have had (on average) 128. If you don't have children, think of the children of your siblings, cousins, second cousins—it makes little difference. Watered down, your genes will survive, if only from descending elsewhere from above your own self. We all have descendants, even if we don't ourselves have children, and whatever they worry about, it will definitely be a great worry. We will never *not* worry—we will always have concerns. To be human, as was suggested at the very beginning of this book, is to worry imaginatively. Could our greatest future worries concern the realized repercussions of living alongside so few other species?

In 2019 the United Nations reported: "Nature's Dangerous Decline 'Unprecedented'; Species Extinction Rates 'Accelerating.'"[23] In fact, a glance at figure 61 shows that the extinction rate has not been accelerating since the 1980s. It shows the worst case of three scenarios produced as components of the Living Planet Index (LPI), the authors of which reported in 2018: "The global LPI . . . shows a 60% decline between 1970 and 2014. . . . This means that, on average, animal populations are well over half the size they were in 1970."[24] Although the rate of decline in the LPI is no longer accelerating, the implications of continued rapid extinctions remain an as yet unquantified but potentially enormous threat and a catastrophic loss. If the current rate were to accelerate at all, then within a few decades almost all life on Earth would become extinct, most certainly all human life. Furthermore, every time more species are assessed, the news gets worse: "The IUCN [International Union for Conservation of Nature] Red List grows larger with each update as newly described species and species from the less well-known groups are assessed for the first time."[25]

We were once so full of hope and now so many of us are full of dread. At least we can truly say that for the most part, we did not know what we were doing. We were not maniacs; we were just ignorant apes. After all, we discovered that there were interrelated species that included us only remarkably recently; when our great-great-great-grandparents were children or young adults. Our great-great-grandparents were some of the very first in their families to go to school. Our great-grandparents began to learn about extinction. Our grandparents (for those readers who are young) were the first to be taught that our planet was made up of plates of rock that floated on the mantle. Our parents were some of the first people ever to hear that the world was heating up. We are the very first generation to know that we have created one of the largest, and fastest, great extinction events that Earth has ever faced. It is, to say the least, mind-blowing. And all in just five generations.

Figure 61 shows that, according to the worst of three scenarios, the majority of biodiversity that existed in the world in 1970 had been lost by 1994. When it comes to mammals and other larger animals, during the first half of my life we killed off a majority of the rarest species on Earth. We did not plan to. We had no idea that so many were on the edge of extinction already, driven there by us, our cattle and our grain, our pigs, sheep, goats, and chickens, our land clearance, our wheat and rice, our ocean acidification, and everything else that we did to destroy habitats, poison the rivers, pollute the seas, and change the entire climate. Forgive us, we ask, because we knew not what we did.

We were so optimistic at the start of the great acceleration. In 1914, Bradford town councilor Fred Liles made a banner for the East Bradford

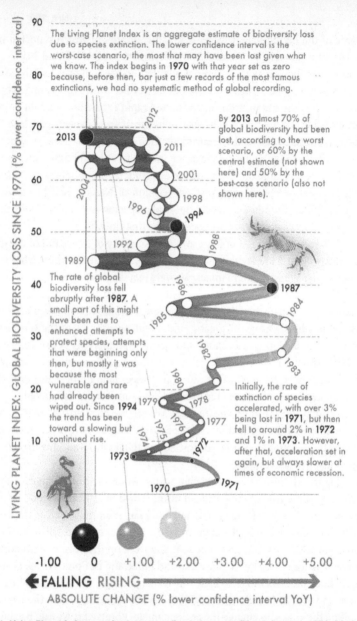

LIVING PLANET INDEX: GLOBAL BIODIVERSITY LOSS SINCE 1970 (% lower confidence interval)

The Living Planet Index is an aggregate estimate of biodiversity loss due to species extinction. The lower confidence interval is the worst-case scenario, the most that may have been lost given what we know. The index begins in **1970** with that year set as zero because, before then, bar just a few records of the most famous extinctions, we had no systematic method of global recording.

By **2013** almost 70% of global biodiversity had been lost, according to the worst scenario, or 60% by the central estimate (not shown here) and 50% by the best-case scenario (also not shown here).

The rate of global biodiversity loss fell abruptly after **1987**. A small part of this might have been due to enhanced attempts to protect species, attempts that were beginning only then, but mostly it was because the most vulnerable and rare had already been wiped out. Since **1994** the trend has been toward a slowing but continued rise.

Initially, the rate of extinction of species accelerated, with over 3% being lost in **1971**, but then fell to around 2% in **1972** and 1% in **1973**. However, after that, acceleration set in again, but always slower at times of economic recession.

-1.00   0   +1.00   +2.00   +3.00   +4.00   +5.00

← FALLING RISING ➡

ABSOLUTE CHANGE (% lower confidence interval YoY)

61. Living Planet Index: species loss according to lower confidence interval, 1970–2013. (Data adapted from Living Planet Index 2018, worse scenario; and personal communication, Richard Grenyer [Oxford University], Monika Bohm, and Louise McRae [Institute of Zoology, London].)

Socialist Sunday School that is one of the happiest and most uplifting, in its hope and simplicity, that you will ever see.[26] There are two fruit trees in its center, representing knowledge and truth. Behind them is a field of wheat symbolizing a world of plenty (of our daily bread). In the grass beneath the trees poppies are growing, because (or so one description of the banner explains) the Sunday school children were learning about the beauty that can emerge from disturbed earth. (Just a few years later, poppies would suddenly appear across Flanders Field and all the First World War battlefields, and would later be adopted as a symbol of remembrance.) The rising sun in the background of the banner represents a brave new dawn. The words "peace," "happiness," and "plenty" adorn the bases of the trees.[27]

We need to be optimistic again, even in the face of all that we now know. The children of that Socialist Sunday School in Bradford did not yet know that there were two world wars, the crash of 1929, and a Great Depression to come. Those who survived would also live to see, in their middle age, the arrival of the new dawn that they had been promised, a welfare state, free health service, full employment, high and still growing equality, and rapidly rising living standards. That is why this banner has survived: they won, despite all the adversity of their times. We need to plan to win again.

Exactly a century after that banner was made, a research fellow at the Future of Humanity Institute at the University of Oxford published an article in which he detailed what he believed remain the five biggest threats to human existence: nuclear war, a bioengineered pandemic, superintelligence, nanotechnology, and unknown unknowns. A century before, none of these five had been threats. Of the five, the threat of nuclear war is high but diminishing: since 1984, there has been not just a slowdown, but a huge global decommissioning of nuclear weapons. A bioengineered pandemic is entirely in our own hands to create or prevent. On superintelligence, the author of the report himself admits that it is not necessarily a worry, as "the unusual thing about superintelligence is that we do not know if rapid and powerful intelligence explosions are possible."[28] Nanotechnology is also entirely in our own hands. And there are always unknown unknowns. Interestingly, the author did not mention climate change or species extinction.

Five years later the same author announced, after doing "a lot of work on Artificial Intelligence," "As with biotechnology, the risk right now is pretty minimal, but it might grow in time as AI become better and smarter."[29] The implication was that in those five years, not much had happened to cause any new worry. This time he did mention climate change, although once again he did not discuss species extinction. That was odd, as his article was published five weeks after more than one thousand young people had been arrested just fifty miles away in London as part of the Extinction Rebellion protest during Easter 2019. We do not know how long the Future of Humanity Institute will survive, but the fact that even it omits to mention species extinction as a possible great threat to humanity suggests that we are going to have to learn a great deal more about where we live, and how we should live—and quickly. Fortunately there are now a great many of us to share the load, and we do not have to rely on a few great thinkers ensconced in a few great ivory towers. So please look again at figure 61 and then turn to figure 62, and then worry (most of us humans are very good at worrying).

Since life began on Earth, there have been five major mass extinction events. Some six out of seven of all the planet's species died around 450 million years ago due to global cooling; then 380 to 360 million years ago three-quarters were wiped out, probably due to multiple causes, including falling CO_2 levels and climate cooling. About 250 million years ago there was again very rapid climate change, a five-degree warming, and only one species in every twenty-five survived. Some 200 million years ago the climate changed again and only one in five species on Earth survived, and then the last of the great five mass extinctions occurred around 65 million years ago when an asteroid, six to nine miles wide, hit Earth, and three out of four of all species (including almost all of the dinosaurs) became extinct. Today we are just a few decades into the sixth and most rapid of all mass extinctions. Humanity has had a worse effect on the biodiversity of the planet than a huge asteroid.[30] However, at the very same time, we have shipped more surviving species around the planet than have ever traveled between the islands of the Earth so quickly before, and we may well be doing other things that will accelerate the appearance of new species. We have almost no idea of the repercussions of any of this.

This may be a good point to pause for a moment and consider one of the phenomena that certainly is not slowing down at all—the number of passengers flying around the world each year in airplanes. It has been 65 million years since close relatives of the dinosaurs were flying in the sky with wingspans of up to sixteen meters. The largest of the known pterosaurs, Quetzalcoatlus, very probably died out with most of the dinosaurs. The largest known raptor, Haast's eagle, had a comparatively modest

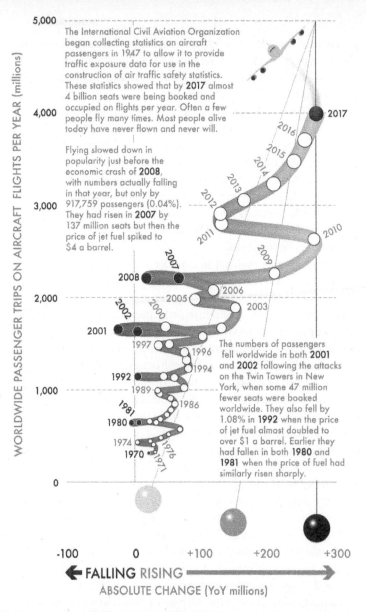

The International Civil Aviation Organization began collecting statistics on aircraft passengers in 1947 to allow it to provide traffic exposure data for use in the construction of air traffic safety statistics. These statistics showed that by **2017** almost 4 billion seats were being booked and occupied on flights per year. Often a few people fly many times. Most people alive today have never flown and never will.

Flying slowed down in popularity just before the economic crash of **2008**, with numbers actually falling in that year, but only by 917,759 passengers (0.04%). They had risen in **2007** by 137 million seats but then the price of jet fuel spiked to $4 a barrel.

The numbers of passengers fell worldwide in both **2001** and **2002** following the attacks on the Twin Towers in New York, when some 47 million fewer seats were booked worldwide. They also fell by 1.08% in **1992** when the price of jet fuel almost doubled to over $1 a barrel. Earlier they had fallen in both **1980** and **1981** when the price of fuel had similarly risen sharply.

WORLDWIDE PASSENGER TRIPS ON AIRCRAFT FLIGHTS PER YEAR (millions)

← **FALLING** RISING →
ABSOLUTE CHANGE (YoY millions)

62. Passengers on air flights worldwide, 1970–2017. (Data adapted from International Civil Aviation Organization, Civil Aviation Statistics of the World, and ICAO staff estimates, collated by the World Bank, accessed 8 September 2019, https://data.worldbank.org/indicator/IS.AIR.PSGR.)

wingspan of about three meters, not much more than an albatross. The last Haast's eagle died out about six hundred years ago after its major prey, a flightless bird called the moa that could weigh over five hundred pounds, was hunted to extinction in New Zealand.

In 1903, in Kitty Hawk, North Carolina, the first powered airplane took to the skies with a wingspan of twelve meters. Today the sky is full of monster planes, the largest objects that have ever flown—and inside them is us. They now transport 4 billion passengers every year, and thus far we show no signs of slowing down in our keenness for air travel, unless we become forced to do so by the introduction of new carbon taxes on flying. These taxes have already been instituted in Sweden and are now proposed for France. I suspect there will be many more in place in other countries before this book is printed.

Having taken a moment to consider the dismal news on flying, let's return to the sixth-largest mass extinction event ever. The good news is that if you take extinction as the disappearance (in sexual species, at least) of the very last breeding pair, then extinction is quite hard to achieve, although by no means impossible. The bad news is that this is not really the kind of extinction that matters for wider environmentalism. It's the extinction of function, of a species no longer having the numbers to fully play its part in the web of connections, that matters most.[31] However, the loss of anatomic, biochemical, and genetic variation that has high human utility value is actually lost only with the death of the last few individuals, so there is arguably some comfort in knowing this. We also suffer a less tangible loss of meaning when a species is gone, remembered now only in tales; but there is still a great deal, most of a planet, in fact, that can be saved—if we care enough to do so.[32]

On 8 May 2019 Amanda Goodall of Cass Business School in London and Andrew Oswald, an economist based at the University of Warwick, published a letter in the *Financial Times* in which they explained: "Environmental degradation is predominantly the result of economic and business forces."[33] They pointed out that within the top fifty journals the *Financial Times* recommended for research conducted in university business schools, only eleven of the forty-seven thousand papers most recently published concerned biodiversity and species decline. Business was not interested. The authors went on to suggest that "business and economic researchers have, for status and incentive reasons, become obsessed with getting on to your FT [*Financial Times*] Journals list, largely by imitating work done in the past, rather than tackling today's problems. Yet natural scientists have done their job and now social scientists must do theirs." They concluded that the academic journals recommended by the *Financial Times* were "letting down the world."

Obsession with status leads to anxiety and much misdirected effort. Furthermore, typically, the more status someone has, the more essential it becomes that other people should be aware of it. For some academics status has become almost all-consuming, and for my part, I am as yet unable to ignore completely whether people think my academic work is any good (although that gets easier as you get older). Fortunately, researchers who are more committed than I are now explaining why we have to stop writing mostly useless articles in journals that are hardly ever read, and instead start to do something more useful.[34] Although much current academic work is useful, of course, much can be simply wrong or almost utterly misdirected. More important, much of the fascinating work scientists produce today could possibly also be vital to our survival, if only we could learn to be bothered about a group far bigger than our family, tribe, city, and country—and better work out how to sift the wheat from the chaff.

Complex modeling carried out a decade ago suggests that abrupt but not almost instantaneous climate change (that not caused by asteroids or humans, but by slower processes) tended to be preceded by a period of remarkable system slowdown.[35] We have the knowledge now to determine what trajectory we were on before we caused all the additional heating up because although "predicting such critical points before they are reached is extremely difficult, work in different scientific fields is now suggesting the existence of generic early-warning signals that may indicate for a wide class of systems if a critical threshold is approaching."[36] We can work out what would most likely have happened without our massively polluting intervention. The future would not have been some balance of nature; but we can see what it most probably would have been, and hence what we should be aiming for.

Erle Ellis, professor of geography and environmental systems at the University of Maryland, Baltimore County, studies the ecology of human landscapes. He explains that we cannot rely on either our leaders or our experts to solve our complex issues: "The problem is, what works for me will very likely not work for you. So by focusing on environmental limits instead of on the social strategies that enable better environmental and social outcomes, we fail to engage the only force of nature that can help us: human aspirations for a better future. . . . If we truly intend to make this work, we need to leave behind treasured but outmoded beliefs in a stable balance of nature, unlimited human ingenuity and nonnegotiable environmental limits defined only by experts."[37] The question, then, is how we can achieve an aspiration for slowdown. How can we get to the point of caring enough?

The turbulent change that has taken place over the course of the last five generations includes the realization that how we live has repercussions, and they, in their turn, are now expected to be turbulent. Chief among these is even more rapid climate change. Those predictions may be expressed the way they are partly because we have become used to framing everything we can as a "dramatic" change, but the truth remains that a great deal of the climate change to come (including the turbulence) is very predictable, as is the future rate of species extinction. We, and only we, have the power to alter what transpires in the future: it depends on what we choose to do. In a slowing world we have more choice.

The climate change that has occurred to date has been almost entirely unintended. It is an outcome of the unthought-through expansion of mechanized farming, industrialization, international flying, and heedless resource extraction. It is the global equivalent of overfarming a fertile area because you have no idea that overfarming is even possible. But then you have to learn to live with the consequences and change your ways.

If we are to survive as a populous species, the human-made component of climate change must abruptly slow down, and do so at least as quickly as we decommissioned most nuclear weapons over the course of the last few decades. The situation is analogous to it not being possible to drain aquifers for irrigation and then continue to water as many crops as you used to on the edge of the desert. With the current extremely high rate of extraction of ancient fossil fuels worldwide, there will never again be as great a potential to do so much damage, to draw out too much too quickly without thinking of the consequences, or even not having a clue that there might be consequences. Just as when wells were originally bored into those aquifers of old, all appeared fine until the water first began to taste of salt.

All of the slowdowns described in this book are a mixture of active informed choices and inevitability. In every slowdown human agency has been involved, but so has human ignorance. Ultimately, and regardless of what people do, there will at one point be a slowdown in human-induced climate change. This will either be when our civilizations collapse and our numbers tumble, or when we reduce our levels of pollution and avoid both of those fates. One way to save ourselves may in fact be to thoughtfully accelerate the current economic slowdown, coupling that with greater (accelerating) redistribution. The alternative is a continuation of the 2 percent growth in total carbon emissions announced at the 24th Conference of the Parties to the United Nations Framework Convention on Climate Change (UNFCCC, known as COP24), which is as unsustainable as continuous global population growth of 2 percent was in 1968, exactly fifty years earlier.[38]

It is possible to be hopeful. Those who called for nuclear disarmament in the past were hopeful. Had they not been, they would not have bothered. Regarding the precursors of climate change, there is now massive slowdown already afoot not only in population growth, but also in the consumption of goods by weight and a current huge acceleration in our aspiration to be greener in the future. We (who are affluent) are likely to each have fewer possessions in future (imagine–if you can). Many will say that this action has not been enough. However, we are still adapting and learning. Slowing down does not happen that quickly, although this much-needed extra slowdown, like the rise in CO_2 emissions before it, will mostly take place over just a couple of decades. Geologically what has occurred in the last two decades is little different, and no less dangerous, than a series of huge volcanic explosions (which probably contributed to some of the previous five mass extinctions). However, unlike volcanoes, we have a choice over our future emissions. A simple choice.

CHANGES IN OUR UNDERSTANDING

On Monday, 17 June 2019, the United Nations revealed its latest "World Population Prospects."[39] The headline read: "9.7 billion on Earth by 2050, but Growth Rate Slowing." A day earlier the UN projection for the year 2050 had been nearer 9.8 billion people, and the projection for 2100 had been 11.2 billion, which was now suddenly reduced to 10.9 billion. We are slowing in our rising numbers even faster than we thought.

The UN report focused first on where there will still be the greatest population growth. It did not highlight the fact that most of that growth is due to people living longer, rather than to more births. This is what was highlighted: "India is expected to show the highest population increase between now and 2050, overtaking China as the world's most populous country, by around 2027. India, along with eight other countries, will make up over half of the estimated population growth between now and 2050. The nine countries expected to show the biggest increase are India, Nigeria and Pakistan, followed by the Democratic Republic of the Congo, Ethiopia, Tanzania, Indonesia, Egypt and the United States of America."

Yes, the United States is in the list of most populous problematic countries. However, the UN report continued, "The population size of more and more countries is actually falling. Since 2010, 27 countries or areas have seen a drop of at least one per cent, because of persistently low fertility rates. Between now and 2050, that is expected to expand to 55 countries which will see a population decrease of one per cent or more, and almost half of these will experience a drop of at least 10 per cent." The report did not highlight the fact that the UN's new 2100 prediction was below 11 billion. The UN did release new data that accompanied the main report for revised past estimates and new figures for projected babies under one year old. That is shown in figure 63.

In case you have skipped parts of this book and did not read about how these graphs work, here is a recap using figure 63 as an example. In 1950 just under 80 million children were born worldwide. That can be seen from the black dot just to the left of the text "1950" in the timeline. On the vertical axis, that black dot lies just under the horizontal dashed gray line that is labeled 80 million. On the horizontal axis, it lies directly above the number 4, telling you that the number of babies being born a year worldwide was rising by 4 million babies a year back then. It rose by just a little less in 1951, and as early as 1956 the rate of change was actually falling (the timeline moved to the left of the vertical axis). The timeline shows that fewer babies were born in 1958 than in 1955. Not every dot is labeled, as the timeline would then be a mess of labels, but you can work out which is which by counting backward or forward. The pendulum at the bottom of the timeline shows the overall trend as a swing from acceleration to predicted stability—a slowdown from the white circle with black outline (beneath the label for 1950) to the solid black circle pendulum weight lying directly beneath the 2100 point.

Step back and look at the timeline in figure 63 as a whole. It shows a series of loops and then a great loop, rising up to almost 135 million babies being born in 1989 (that year is not labeled on the timeline as it is too cluttered there). That looping ends around 1998 and after that, suddenly, a different trajectory is embarked upon. This has something, but not everything, to do with China (see Chapters 7 and 8). At the time of writing the

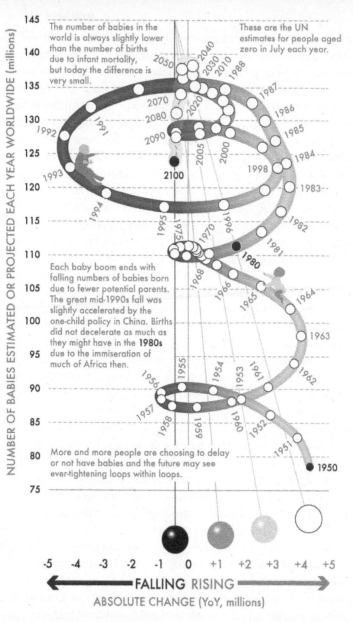

NUMBER OF BABIES ESTIMATED OR PROJECTED EACH YEAR WORLDWIDE (millions)

The number of babies in the world is always slightly lower than the number of births due to infant mortality, but today the difference is very small.

These are the UN estimates for people aged zero in July each year.

Each baby boom ends with falling numbers of babies born due to fewer potential parents. The great mid-1990s fall was slightly accelerated by the one-child policy in China. Births did not decelerate as much as they might have in the **1980s** due to the immiseration of much of Africa then.

More and more people are choosing to delay or not have babies and the future may see ever-tightening loops within loops.

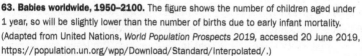

-5 -4 -3 -2 -1 0 +1 +2 +3 +4 +5

⟵ **FALLING RISING** ⟶

ABSOLUTE CHANGE (YoY, millions)

63. Babies worldwide, 1950–2100. The figure shows the number of children aged under 1 year, so will be slightly lower than the number of births due to early infant mortality. (Adapted from United Nations, *World Population Prospects 2019*, accessed 20 June 2019, https://population.un.org/wpp/Download/Standard/Interpolated/.)

trend is heading a little faster toward the vertical axis than it was a few months ago—toward another fall in the numbers of babies being born, but now with no visual promise of any future upswing to come. You can easily imagine a future even lower loop in the timeline when the UN revises its estimates in 2021 and again in 2023, but then it will be further to the left, depicting great slowdown in the very near future. However, no such loop is as yet prophesied by the demographers providing these data. Instead the United Nations demographers are assuming that things are about to suddenly stabilize and everyone almost everywhere will move toward having, on average, two children each—even in places having far fewer than that now. Could they be doing this because donors who supply free condoms around the world might cease to do so if they thought the slowdown had so thoroughly set in? I suspect we will see far faster future fertility decline than the UN predicts, and I am far from alone in saying so.

In their 17 June 2019 "World Population Prospects" report, UN demographers suggested that 136 million babies will most probably be born and still be alive, also aged under one year, during the month of July 2025. Then, by 2030, there will be 137 million; by 2040, 138 million; by 2050, still 138 million; by 2060, 137 million; by 2070, 135 million. However, the future will not be as steady as that: for many reasons, births are very likely to be much lower, but at least the officials' projections are now falling. Again, remember just how much changed so quickly in our recent past and so how much still could change. In 1844 Charles Goodyear (of Goodyear tire fame) patented his vulcanization process. In 1855 the first rubber condoms were produced. It took a little time for the news to spread and for the invention to aid the great 1870–1930 European fertility decline. As the decline set in, many attempts were made to encourage more pregnancies in order to reverse local population declines and to provide manpower for armies. They all failed, and this is good news, as were the social and political benefits that came from those attempts.

In the very near future, partly as a reaction to slowdown, we can expect more maternity and paternity support to try to encourage people to have more children. The Organisation for Economic Co-operation and Development (OECD) has helpfully collected as much data as it can on direct maternity support, which was often introduced to try to encourage more mothers to give birth, especially in Europe, and it is no coincidence that this all began as the numbers of births began to fall.[40] In 1877 the first federal law on maternity leave was passed in Switzerland. The leave was unpaid, but the mother's job was protected for eight weeks. In 1878, Germany mandated that pregnant women could not work for three weeks before birth. In 1885, Austria introduced working restrictions for pregnant women. None of these measures abated the decline in fertility, and neither did the introduction of paid, job-protected maternity leave in Austria in 1957.

In 1889, Belgium and the Netherlands legislated for four weeks of unpaid leave for women giving birth; it became paid leave in Belgium from 1954, and in the Netherlands from 1966. The Czech Republic (at the time still part of Czechoslovakia) had already done so in 1948, but starting in 1956 paid leave went up to eighteen weeks. However, Iceland was earlier still, offering financial support from 1938. Denmark introduced its first mandatory unpaid maternity leave in 1892; Spain in 1900; Sweden in 1902; and, by 1902, Italy had forbidden women from working four weeks after birth, all unpaid.

In France maternity leave—four unpaid weeks—was introduced in 1909. In Greece pregnant women were banned from working in 1910. Finland first introduced unpaid maternity leave in 1917, the same year that Mexico introduced a month of paid maternity care. Poland offered twelve weeks of fully paid maternity leave from 1924. In 1930 Turkey insisted on six weeks of unpaid leave. Japan brought in maternity leave during 1947 (when the abortion rate was almost unbelievably high in the aftermath of war and defeat); the United Kingdom in 1948 introduced it for thirteen weeks, although women workers would not have their jobs protected during their leave for many more decades. Korea introduced maternity leave in 1953, Luxembourg in 1962, and Portugal in 1963. Canada introduced maternity leave in 1971. Australia was quite late, introducing the Maternity Leave Act only in 1973, with twelve weeks of paid leave and up to forty weeks unpaid. Latest of all was the United States, which did not introduce any significant policy on maternity rights until 1978, and even that was risible, giving few more rights than already existed with any illness or disability. Today the United States is the only industrialized democracy in the world that does not provide comprehensive job-protected paid parental leave to working women and men. It is very likely the United States was so slow because concerns over shrinking populations began much later there than elsewhere.

In many countries across Europe, there was support (usually financial) for those who married, those who had children, and for families. However, the simultaneous introduction of family-planning clinics resulted in a net fall in births. Where this did not happen, it was usually due to re-cent immigrants having children, although the number was almost always lower than for people back in their homelands. The more migration there is in the world, the faster birth rates in future will fall. So what did all this achieve if it was not the intended aim of more babies? It achieved more freedom for women. Freedom to choose. It was women, not men, who led the great deceleration, and who will very likely be its greatest future pro-ponents. It is no coincidence that so many Green politicians are women, or that the Swedish schoolchild who began the climate change school strikes was a girl. We should expect to see even greater participation of women in our politics in the very near future, as women hold more and more senior political offices. That may be something that does not slow down for some time to come.

In December 2019 the most unequal countries of the affluent world were ruled by very right-wing men: Donald Trump in the United States, Vladimir Putin in Russia, Recep Tayyip Erdoğan in Turkey, Sebastián Piñera in Chile, and Boris Johnson in the United Kingdom. In contrast, women were increasingly winning power in countries where greater equal-ity was also being won. This was most notable that month in Finland with the appointment of the new prime minister, Sanna Marin of the Social Democratic Party, who then governed in coalition with Li Anderson (Left Alliance), Katri Kulmuni (Centre Party), Maria Ohisalo (Green League), and Anna-Maja Henriksson (Swedish People's Party of Finland).[41]

Pause to think of how much has changed in such a short space of time, and it is easy to become more optimistic. Not long ago, women were not allowed even a basic education. A few male physicists and mathematicians developed the phase space diagrams used in this book not long before the very first universal maternity provision was introduced in the 1870s to try to halt the start of the most human aspect of slowdown—fewer humans. They did so at a time when so much of human life was actually accelerating.

One twenty-first-century study of the pace of social change that chose fertility as the change to measure noted, "Commentators frequently ob-serve that the pace of social change accelerated during the 20th century."[42] Another study begins, "If stability, facilitating a degree of control and plan-ning in life, is seemingly being undermined, thereby giving rise to feelings of social acceleration it seems appropriate and is likely essential, that before I go about questioning the cause of its loss, I first enquire into its nature and how it arises in the first place where it does."[43] But we are not accelerat-ing. If we feel we are, it is time to change that feeling.

Why do we not yet see what should be so obvious? In the countries where fertility began to decline first, most of them in western Europe just prior to 1900, the rate of decline was slowest. In the countries where it began to decline most recently, after 1972, the rate has been fastest. Most of these countries are in Africa. Thus a "crescendo effect" has been present after 1972, as the whole orchestra comes together and everywhere we are now hurtling more rapidly toward fertility stability than ever before.

Before 1972 there was probably no way of knowing that the crescendo was about to come about. In 1968 a book was published with the title *Indicators of Social Change: Concepts and Measurements*.[44] The book was almost entirely concerned with the United States. Perhaps what is most interesting about it is how similar its measures of change are to those used today, although rates of change are now usually far less than then. Other things also do not change that much. The book's authors suggested: "One of the most important problems that will be faced is the increasing demand of the lower social strata in the United States for political expression, and the contemporary and increasing loss of credence given to the dominant social strata." Almost everything changes less quickly as we slow down. The year 1968 was far more similar to 2018 than to 1918. The year 2018 will likely be much more similar to 2068 than to 1968. This is one of the many implications of slowdown.

Jamie Ducharme, a *Time* magazine journalist, observed in a recent article titled "It May Not Be a Bad Thing Fewer U.S. Babies Were Born in 2018 Than in Any Year since 1986" that part of the reason for the fall is a decline in births to teenage mothers. She concluded by quoting Hans-Peter Kohler, a sociology professor at the University at Pennsylvania, in a thinly veiled rebuke to President Trump and a thank-you to President Obama: "That's good, of course, because most teenage pregnancies are 'mistimed' or 'unwanted,'" Kohler says. He notes that the downturn in birth rates for teenagers likely reflects more widespread use of effective and long-lasting forms of contraception, perhaps due to expanded access under the Affordable Care Act."[45] By 2016 the number of uninsured Americans had halved in comparison to 2014 because of the introduction of this act. We understand more as we slow down: we progress. Part of that progression is our increased worry and despair over bad decisions being made by bad people (usually wealthy men). It was only so very recently that we used to just accept what they told us to do—not anymore.

people

cognition and catfish

> Fears over recession are once again stalking markets, but many investors
> and analysts are more worried about a deeper, more structural shift: that the
> world economy is succumbing to a phenomenon dubbed "Japanification."
> —*Robin Wigglesworth, 27 August 2019*

Published in 1968, the science-fiction novel *Stand on Zanzibar* imagined
an overpopulated world that turned to eugenics to decide who would be allowed to have children. Its British author, John Brunner (1934–95), wrote,
often with eerie prescience, about subjects such as "artificial intelligence,
racism, drugs, the environment, space travel, and hi-tech warfare"[1] He predicted that the human population of our planet would reach 7 billion in
2010. He was close: that milestone was attained during late spring 2011.

Brunner was already well known, having penned the lyrics to a famous anti–nuclear war song, "The H-bomb's Thunder," which was used by
the Campaign for Nuclear Disarmament (CND) on it first Aldermaston
marches from London to the United Kingdom's main atomic weapons research establishment. In 1968, people like Brunner thought it very likely
that we were all, very soon, going to die. He and CND had been almost
completely ignored for a decade. However, he had hope.

The years 1901–68 had seen the most sudden changes in the history
of humanity, from the end of horsepower to the invention of the hydrogen
bomb in less than a single human lifetime. Before 1901, any improvements
in standards of living filtered down only ever so slowly to the bulk of the
human population, both within affluent countries and around the world.

After 1901, however, change came thick and fast. In the United Kingdom, 1901 was a census year, and marked the start of a decade that would bring the fastest-ever population growth in the British Isles.[2] Worldwide, 1901 was the first time that annual global human population increases of over 1 percent were ever recorded.

Outside brief periods of wartime and pandemic, the global rates of population growth have exceeded 1 percent every year since 1901. However, according to the latest UN estimates published in June 2019, they will now almost certainly fall below that level by 2023, then quickly drop to below 0.9 percent annual growth around the year 2027, and then fall not quite as rapidly. However, the UN demographers have brought forward the date for below 0.9 percent growth, although their estimates do still become more conservative as they stretch into the future. The UN now predicts that annual total global population growth will fall below 0.5 percent only in 2051, and below 0 percent (marking the peak) shortly after 2100. In recent years the UN reports have repeatedly revised estimates of population growth downward, and so we should probably expect the peak to come well before the end of this century. It was only very recently that we discovered that in 2015 the annual population growth rate fell to 1.15 percent.[3]

If you still doubt that slowdown is upon us, remember how much else is slowing—and not just our numbers. Educational divisions are on the decline too. For British men such as John Brunner, born between the two world wars, attending a prestigious (expensive and private) school made it almost inevitable that they would succeed economically. For Brunner's female contemporaries, the great majority of whom did not attend university, being privately schooled had little effect on their futures other than in influencing whom they might later marry.[4] Prior to 1870 almost half of the children in the United Kingdom had no formal education whatsoever, but soon after that, almost all children aged five to twelve had access to free public education. In the Britain of 1920, hardly anyone went to university: just over three thousand men and one thousand women a year, 1920 being the year when women were first permitted to graduate from the University of Oxford. Today 42 percent of people aged twenty-one to sixty-four in the U.K. workforce are graduates, and a majority of those in the youngest age groups are, even though English university tuition fees are the highest in the rich world—in 2019 almost all £9,250 (U.S.$13,050) a year.[5]

Everything changed so quickly during the past five generations, but that is no longer the case. There is still some way to go in our slowdown.

One day—in a slower future—whether one has graduated from university will make little difference for either men or women. It already makes much less difference than it did fifty years ago. Neither will being a man or a woman matter so much. We will all become more equal. In that future, people may learn bizarre facts about our esoteric and quaint past. They will have to be taught what a British private school was, and told of the time (today) when 65 percent of senior British judges attended such a school, but only one in six leaders of British universities (quaintly called vice-chancellors in the United Kingdom). You may think that this future is centuries away, but currently both those measures of past elite nepotism are falling, down from 71 percent for the senior U.K. judges and one-fifth for the university leaders in just five years.[6] British snobbery is yet another aspect of our lives that is slowing down. Hopefully, hubris in the United States is also now in decline (it is hard to measure well). An unequal human economic world is unsustainable and so it will end; but some possible ends are much better than others.

We worry about acceleration even as we decelerate. As recently as 2018, a charity was still telling us that "Africa is sitting on a demographic time bomb. Without massive investment in their health and education, the growing child and youth population could become a huge burden, and create a serious human development crisis."[7] They were wrong about the demographic time bomb, as has been repeated throughout this book, but they're right about much else. This particular organization highlighted the terrible reality that the growth of just under a third of children on the continent has been stunted by malnutrition, and that "while African children may attend school in large numbers, they are not learning. Two in every five children leave primary school without learning how to read, write or do simple arithmetic." However, that situation is also rapidly changing. At the very same time the elite of Britain are finally being taught to be a little less arrogant about the fact that they can read and write and carry out simple arithmetic earlier than their compatriots (often due to rote learning), so more and more children across the African continent are now being given access to the most basic of educational tools, including a decent secondary education.

The 2018 report on children in Africa that began by warning of a demographic time bomb also pointed out that Africa's children are now healthier, on average live longer, and are better schooled (even if almost all of the schools they attend remain poorly resourced). Almost all of them can now aspire to a better life than could previously have been dreamed of. It also noted that governments across Africa have gradually become more child-friendly, and are spending more money on services for children than ever before. The report might have gone further and suggested that African societies could avoid what John Brunner's generation feared and what Rwanda experienced—a genocidal war. Moreover, in the future, follies such as a woman's university study having little effect on her later employment will end. We are only just departing from the time when what most mattered for a woman's life chances was whom she married. We are slowing down from that extreme snobbishness and inequality too; and we are now doing so everywhere.

THE CHANGING CENTER OF THE WORLD

> Life itself is change—we are always giving up something for something else.
> —*Stephen Grosz, 2013*[8]

If the numbers we collect about ourselves could speak, perhaps they would say: "We have given you all the information we have and given you all the options; if you humans don't slow down, you are finished." It is perhaps inevitable that we feel slowdown means something is being lost. What we are losing, however, is our sense of uncertainty. For many people worldwide, life had been like an extreme sport, full of risk, danger, and uncertainty. Most will be glad to not have such "excitement" forced upon them in future. We now mostly know what we have to do and what resources we have to do it with. There is no sudden ship of technological marvels about to appear over the horizon to save us. The big economic wheel keeps on turning; and its central axis is moving, but a slower set of gears is engaging, and soon it will slow to stop, even reverse. Disaster capitalists—the people who came to believe in the cult of creative destruction—hate not having a choice to continue as we are. Although we don't know for sure what will happen between now and peak human (the day after which the total number alive begins to slowly fall), we can now work out what can't happen.

When the capitalist transition began, we believed that the world was at the center of the universe. As the transition accelerated, we learned that there might not be a god or gods. Each generation had so much new to learn. So what happens when, for the first time in many years, there are two generations, perhaps Generations X and Y, surely Generations Y and Z, who largely agree on most things? We are not quite yet there. We now know that when the transition started there was no single key economic center to the world and that there will very likely be no single key center when the transition ends. We should not concern ourselves with what country will be hegemonic in future. We don't have to worry about whether Beijing will take over from London and New York. Such questions are questions of the past; questions that mattered greatly at the height of the age of transition.

Today the most minor of changes are still being presented as great changes. For instance, there was once a time when American and European cities were growing rapidly; now, if they grow at all, it is only slowly. And yet the addition of any suburb, the building of any new set of apartments, is often described as if it were a great change. People in England talk of immigration adding the equivalent of a town like Coventry, Swindon, or Sunderland to the national population every year. In the United States, Santa Ana in California or Baltimore in Maryland are particular favorites to try to scare the population over immigrant numbers.[9] Other than the few Machiavellian politicians who want to stoke up fear, most don't realize how little these increases are. Three or four hundred thousand people represents a U.K.-wide population increase of only 0.4 percent to 0.6 percent.

Today the shock is not change. The shock is when the change stops. When the cranes are taken down, and we are building mostly to repair and renew what we first built a long time ago. The shock is that we are no longer expanding, and no longer seeing a geographical shift to a single new center of dominance. However, as we adapt to slowdown, we may not sense that our pace of change is slowing. Everything is relative. Even the feeling of time passing is relative. When you are young, your summer holidays feel like they go on forever. When you are old, you wonder where all the time went and why birthdays come around so quickly. No wonder we cannot easily see that slowdown is occurring. And just as we find it hard to understand change, so too will we find it hard to understand a state of very little change—until it becomes normal, until the stories we tell fit the times we experience.

We should not expect humans to be great soothsayers. As sociologist Steven Shapin observed when reviewing Yuval Noah Harari's book *Homo Deus: A Brief History of Tomorrow,* before DNA was discovered no one, not even the most imaginative writers of science fiction, envisioned polymerase chain reactions or their use in the biotech industry.[10] Similarly, no one foresaw the actual, full multidirectional nature of the World Wide

Web, even during those years when the personal computer was being first used. The future has never been accurately foretold. It cannot be. Only a set of plausible guesses is possible, and occasionally one or two of those guesses come close. A true prediction would appear too otherworldly to be feasible and very probably too optimistic. Optimism tends to be viewed as naive, so we prefer to postulate dystopia.

Of course, there is so much that is still so very wrong with our world. Management expert Umair Haque very recently attempted to rank our problems, concluding that our recent overdoses of capitalism, supremacy (rule by wealthy countries), and patriarchy (rule by wealthy families in turn ruled by men) are what has "led us to a dead end in human progress— a dystopian hellscape made of inequality, stagnation, fascism, and climate change. America exemplifies it. . . . To make progress this century, we are going to have to transcend those old ways, those old ideologies, those tired, weary, and failed mindsets."[11] Haque details how adherence to beliefs in the supposed destructive-creative powers of capitalism, of the supremacy of a few, and of patriarchy as natural, leads to predatory exploitative collapse. He includes the collapse of ecologies, at times of whole economies, occasionally of smaller democracies, and (with man-made demons such as nuclear weapons) possibly the destruction of entire societies.

The H-bomb was born of the West's fear of communism and the desire to preserve global inequalities. Its gestation was the supreme achievement of the 1950s period of U.S. military dominance, a world of mothers concentrating on motherhood and apple pie and fathers standing tall. Now all those apparent certainties and the global inequality that the bomb was supposed to preserve are evaporating into the ether or, at the very least, narrowing.

INEQUALITY, SLOWDOWN, AND BOREDOM

Some gaps are narrowing faster than others, some remain very wide, and a few, although not many, are still widening. However, when it comes to the most important gaps of all, such as child mortality, the absolute gaps in life chances between and within countries are almost all now falling, while the relative gaps can be more stubborn and often narrow more slowly.[12]

In just a few unusually dysfunctional places currently experiencing very odd periods in their history, like the United Kingdom and the United States, infant mortality is for a short period rising as I write these words (but hopefully no longer doing so as you read them).[13] Such widening gaps are now easily avoidable where there is the will, as is most of the very wide gap between men and women's mortality.

Only one year's difference, or about 20 percent of the male/female mortality gap, appears to be due to any inherent biological difference.[14] The far greater part of the gap is due to our genders, to the roles men and women are expected to play, and those roles are now changing quickly as we slow down. So next we turn to the combined life expectancy of all men and women on the planet and how the rise in that has been slowing down.

Figure 64 shows the combined life expectancy of all people worldwide. It is measured from all actual deaths recorded before 2019 and those projected to occur thereafter. Various possible reasons for why the trajectory of ever-rising global life expectancy wiggles back and forth are given in the text surrounding the timeline within that figure. Future study will determine the extent to which these observations, which are often merely informed guesses, turn out to be true. However, when you consider the pattern before 2020 with that suggested for after it, the trend afterward looks a little too optimistic. Why is there such a break in slope immediately after 2019? These are the most recent United Nations projections, part of its current projections for total human population.

Just how legitimate is it to combine male and female life expectancies as figure 64 does? As fewer women die each year in childbirth and fewer men die in wars—most years, at least—some of the obvious causes for the difference between the sexes are diminishing in importance. Men and women may become more similar than many of us currently think possible, and this could be yet another aspect of human life waiting to be fully revealed with the continued slowdown.

If you don't believe that men and women are becoming more similar, and that this could have an impact on how long each sex will live, then consider monks and nuns. Marc Luy's work on cloistered populations is a comparison of the differences in life expectancy between these groups of men and women who live in single-sex, faith-based communities—and whose environments and behaviors are very similar to each other—and those of men and women in society as a whole.[15] Luy's research leads him to estimate that around 80 percent of the sex difference in life expectancy outcome is really a gender difference, with the earlier mortality of men appearing to be closely related to how maleness is performed in the majority of societies. Compared to the general population, monks and nuns have longer life expectancy, with significantly less of a gap between the sexes.

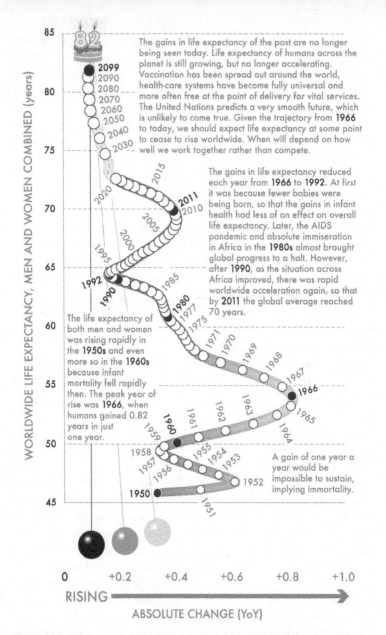

The gains in life expectancy of the past are no longer being seen today. Life expectancy of humans across the planet is still growing, but no longer accelerating. Vaccination has been spread out around the world, health-care systems have become fully universal and more often free at the point of delivery for vital services. The United Nations predicts a very smooth future, which is unlikely to come true. Given the trajectory from **1966** to today, we should expect life expectancy at some point to cease to rise worldwide. When will depend on how well we work together rather than compete.

The gains in life expectancy reduced each year from **1966** to **1992**. At first it was because fewer babies were being born, so that the gains in infant health had less of an effect on overall life expectancy. Later, the AIDS pandemic and absolute immiseration in Africa in the **1980s** almost brought global progress to a halt. However, after **1990**, as the situation across Africa improved, there was rapid worldwide acceleration again, so that by **2011** the global average reached 70 years.

The life expectancy of both men and women was rising rapidly in the **1950s** and even more so in the **1960s** because infant mortality fell rapidly then. The peak year of rise was **1966**, when humans gained 0.82 years in just one year.

A gain of one year a year would be impossible to sustain, implying immortality.

RISING

ABSOLUTE CHANGE (YoY)

64. Worldwide life expectancy, men and women combined, 1950–2099. (Data adapted from United Nations, *World Population Prospects 2019*, accessed 20 June 2019, https://population.un.org/wpp/Download/Standard/Interpolated/.)

There is also less difference in how often monks and nuns are ill. With so much current focus in the social sciences on performing masculinities (playing the man) and the social construction of so much that we recently considered to be biological, it is surprising Luy's work isn't better known and discussed.

As we slow down we finally have time to begin to question so many previously established constraints. One such constraint is boredom. For instance, there is absolutely no reason why a more slowly changing world should be more boring. Humans detest boredom. Animals in zoos suffer from boredom, and similarly, boredom for us might well go back at least to the Neolithic revolution, when we enclosed ourselves into villages and tedious tasks became widespread. We have developed many ways to counter boredom. It is easy to imagine that people have sung while they work for many, many centuries, whether in fields or building pyramids.[16] This chapter began making reference to a peace protester's song, "The H Bomb's Thunder."[17] It was originally set to the tune known to Americans as "Miner's Lifeguard," based on a rousing anti-materialistic Welsh hymn, "Calon Lan," which is still sung at Welsh rugby matches. It starts (in translation): "I don't ask for a luxurious life, the world's gold or its fine pearls."

Both sport and entertainment in general are a response to boredom. There was a dramatic increase in boredom with the Industrial Revolution. Workers had to carry out repetitive and tedious tasks, and over time each step in the process became more simplified (and thus more boring) in order for production lines to move faster. Singing at work was not an option because factories were extraordinarily noisy.

As time progressed, the factory became rather quieter. In industrial countries during the first half of the twentieth century, much work became less noisy, and on 23 June 1940, the British Broadcasting Corporation (BBC) first transmitted a radio program that would run for twenty-seven years: *Music While You Work*. It was a twice-daily, half-hour program of music "meant specially for factory workers." It was also during this period that working hours most quickly reduced and leisure time became a feature of many men's lives, if less so of women's. More entertainment was needed to prevent boredom arising during leisure time.

There were three big changes in entertainment during the twentieth century. The first was that it no longer needed to be live, as exemplified by the cinema. For many people, this brought much more excitement than had previously been available locally. The second was that entertainment could be beamed directly into your own home. The wireless radio was the dramatic breakthrough that changed people's way of life, with television a relatively minor improvement that swapped one box for another. The third was portable entertainment. The portable radio-cassette player was the breakthrough (the 1979 Walkman); the smartphone was just an upgrade. As each generation grew up, it had fewer and fewer really significant technological changes to contend with.

For five generations, the old have lamented the passing of a very different era. Today, the passing of the era of acceleration is something to be very thankful for. The alternative to slowing down—an ever-growing total human population, ever more divided societies, ever-greater consumption per head—would be a catastrophe. Without material economic growth, capitalism as we know it is transforming into something else, something far more stable.

The rapid pace of change is no longer so rapid. It is less and less the case that we are being hurled into an unknown future; we are only now emerging from the unnerving dense fog of our roller-coaster past and can just begin to see the clouds parting. There are good seasons, albeit not Darwin's favorable seasons, to come.

SETTLING DOWN

Think of the three largest cities in the United States: New York, with its 8 million people; Los Angeles with 4 million; and Chicago ever so slowly growing toward 3 million. These are minnows in world city rankings. They stopped expanding quickly a long time ago. Think of the three largest cities in or on the edge of Europe: Istanbul is home to almost 13 million people, Moscow to just over 13 million, and London almost 9 million—with millions more living under its dominant influence in southeast England. What do these cities have in common? London and its wider region is the richest and largest city of Europe, but London is also a relic. It is outsized because it is the former heart of the greatest empire the world has ever known. Moscow is oversized because it was once the capital of the USSR, and Istanbul is so large today only because it was once the nerve center of the Ottoman Empire, and before that of the Holy Roman and Byzantine Empires.

The three largest U.S. cities are also largely relics of bygone, if more recent, eras when each was in its prime. The fourth-largest city, Houston (Texas), with just over 2 million inhabitants, is a relic of the time when oil was king. Europe's fourth-largest city is Madrid, with 3 million residents. Paris is home to just over 2 million people, although the city is within an urban agglomeration that contains, if defined very widely, over 10 million people. But the important point is that no cities in the world today are growing at the rates that London, Istanbul, and Moscow once grew, let alone at the rates that Los Angeles, New York, Chicago, Houston, or—perhaps more appropriately—Mumbai, São Paulo, or Shanghai once grew, all at the height of the great transition.

It is true that the populations of the largest cities of the world, almost now all in Asia, are still swelling by millions, but the rate, the proportionate growth year on year, has been slowing for a long time. Urbanization continues apace, but with every decade that passes the pace slows further, leaving fossil relics of bygone eras still standing proud in the statistical league tables of the largest global cities.

The usual story begins by saying how amazing it is that cities around the world are growing so big so quickly. However, they are no longer growing quickly, not at the rate that cities grew every year when John Brunner was writing *Stand on Zanzibar*. Istanbul was home to under 1 million people in 1950.[18] No large city on Earth can now experience the rate of population growth that occurred there over the past seventy years. There are just not enough migrants, and there is not enough space. Everywhere now has to slow down, because the previous rate of increase became unsustainable.

Slowdown is not seen as news worth reporting, and that is why you so rarely hear about it. Many academics who pontificate before they measure seem to think that we are still living through an age of rapid social transformation, even though so much appears to be solidifying and changing so much more slowly than before. While class, war, poverty, and precarity are firmly with us, to continue to suggest that social change is amazingly rapid is in many ways naive. We are going slower partly because of the recoil from an earlier acceleration, but there is so much more to it than that.

As women gain emancipation, as population numbers settle, as we learn so much more, we are stabilizing, but we are also conditioned not to accept this story. We assume any slowdown is temporary. We assume that things can stop only with a bang, not that they can simply slow with a whimper. We are becoming so used to there always being something new that we do not notice that new things are emerging less and less frequently.

It can be hard to make the case for something that is not happening, but here are some examples. There has been no sudden resurgence in fertility worldwide, nor have there been reports of it for fifty years now. The echoes of each baby boom are smaller than the ones before. Peak population growth came and went around 1968–71. In the past five years we have seen even faster worldwide population deceleration than ever before, without calamity. Furthermore, other than the 1942 realization of nuclear power (long after the physics had been proven), since the late 1930s there has been no new great invention on the order of the computer, flight, or nylon clothing.

A century ago there were many great inventions; there are very few now. In the United States people are offered innovations such as Mark Zuckerberg's "Facebook credits," invented in 2009 and defunct by 2013, and Elon Musk's SpaceX's promise of an inaugural private passenger trip around the moon and back on a "Big Falcon Rocket" in 2023. The responses of many are "Why?" and "Really?" In the United Kingdom, we are forced to celebrate Sir James Dyson's hand dryer and Sir Richard Branson's tilting trains, even though he and his Virgin company did not invent them: businesses invent brands now, not completely new machines.

For the foreseeable future, no great new economic step forward is being taken—China is very slowly catching up on a declining United States, but it will be many decades before the two countries' per capita GDP is similar. In contrast, GDP per capita in the United States overtook Britain much more quickly, back (coincidentally) in 1901. No one even ventures to suggest a new superpower after China, with India destined to be average in a future world where we'll see a lot more that is "average." As for a new politics, the most recent is environmentalism, and the first Green parties were formed in Tasmania, New Zealand, and Switzerland way back in 1972.

We are not at an "end of history," just at the start of a new era of history—but this is still surprising to us, as our grandparents went through an era akin to a social, political, and economic tsunami. We should expect slower changes in future, although we may well describe them as big. So much points toward a settling now, rather than any quickening. Most important, there is no sign of a significant change in us as human beings: suddenly becoming much taller as we did until recent decades, or our life expectancy accelerating; even in India, which has seen some of the greatest recent improvements, the rise in life expectancy has been slowing since 1992. Almost all states are moving toward being home to people who are more and more similar to one another in terms of their bodies, length of lives, living conditions, education, and understanding.

Those who tried at the turn of the twenty-first century to argue we are still in a time of acceleration now say that "whatever social acceleration may be, attempts to achieve empirical measurements of it, or of related notions, have not met with noted success."[19] So we think something is changing, faster than ever before, but don't know what it is sufficiently well (they claim) to be able to measure it. When you say, half-humorously, "Stop the world, I want to get off," you are assuming the world is still moving too fast. Once you accept that the pace of change of the world has started to slow down, what then? What happens when we can get off? How might we settle down?

Japan was the first large country in the world to slow down. In December 2018, its prime minister, Abe Shinzō, announced a new five-year target to increase the number of foreign migrants to the country by up to 345,150 people working in certain occupations.[20] The original list of skilled occupations included university professors, corporate managers, lawyers, and certified accountants, but the prime minister went on to explain that the country also needed more people to work in construction, agriculture, nursing care, shipbuilding, accommodation, food and drink manufacturing, fisheries, cleaning, casting, industrial machinery manufacturing, electronics and electrical equipment industry maintenance, and aviation.

Only a decade after the very first signs of the slowdown began to be seen, in 1978, Kawashima Tatsuhiko, then a young researcher in regional science, developed the idea of a ROXY index.[21] ROXY refers to the ratio of weighted average (X) to simple average (Y), and it measures the degree of agglomeration (coming together) or deglomeration (spreading out) in an urban system. For instance, it could be used to highlight how the population of New York was rising the most within Manhattan as more skyscrapers were built, as opposed to when the city's suburbs were extended when more trains ran through Grand Central Station beginning to arrive earlier and earlier in the day. The original ROXY paper is not easy to find online, but many later publications give details of how the index is measured, and use of it continues to reveal a great deal, even well over forty years after the method was first developed.[22]

Technically, the ROXY index is the mean population growth rate of a city when all the individual growth rates of each area are weighted by their distance from the center of the city. If the value is positive and high, it means population growth is concentrating near the central parts of the city. If it is negative and low, it means the city is spreading outward faster than it is growing in the center. If the value is near zero, this implies that not much is changing.

Figure 65 is of the timeline trajectory of just one ROXY index. It may appear at first an odd timeline to end on, but it is one of the clearest demonstrations of what a complete slowdown looks like—what the future will hold elsewhere as slowdown continues. It is not one of the originals drawn by Kawashima; it was made later by another academic, Ushijima Chihiro, and redrawn here in the style of all the other timelines in this book. It is the ROXY timeline of Tokyo—now the world's most stable mega-city. The method does not always show convergence: for instance, Finland, when tested two decades ago, was still seeing a continued spatial concentration of population toward the center of Helsinki, and a continued spiraling around between suburbanization and concentration similar to Tokyo in earlier decades.[23] However, in Japan, where the method was invented, it now appears to be showing convergence and a settling down.

In figure 65, Ushijima's timeline begins in 1920–25, when Tokyo was growing rapidly. In her timeline, you cannot see the overall rapid growth (from 3.7 million in 1920 to 7.4 million in 1940), but you can nevertheless see that the city initially grew fairly uniformly; for this time, the vertical axis value is almost at zero. In the later 1920s most growth in Tokyo concentrated toward the center of the city and so the line moves upward, but the degree to which that was occurring also began to reduce. By the 1930s the growth was still mostly central. Many high-rise buildings were being erected, but then came war, with the population falling to 3.5 million by 1945, and later came suburbanization.

In the 1940s in Tokyo there was an enormous shift of the main location of growth away from the center toward the edges; this is clearly visible in figure 65 by 1940–47. That trend, in turn, reversed, and by 1947–50 the center of the city was growing faster than the outskirts, and at the greatest relative rate yet. By 1950–55 the center was still growing almost as rapidly as the suburbs, but by 1955–60 there was a slowdown in the centralization of Tokyo, and by 1960–65 there was no greater growth in the central area as compared to the suburbs. And remember, all this time the city was still growing, with central Tokyo reaching 8 million by 1956, 10 million by 1963, 12 million by 2001, 13 million by 2008, and 13.5 million by 2015: it was growing, but both slowing and stabilizing.

Figure 65 shows that Tokyo grew rapidly in its outskirts in 1965–70 and even more so by 1970–75, but again the trend was always changing.

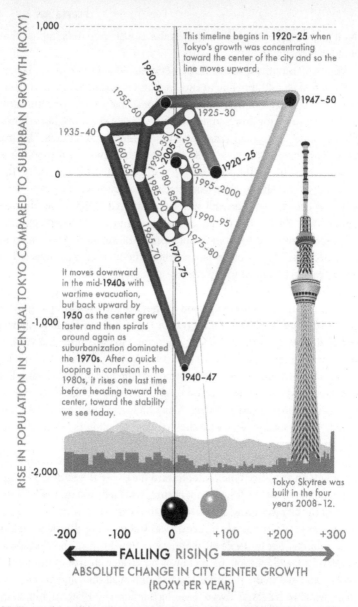

RISE IN POPULATION IN CENTRAL TOKYO COMPARED TO SUBURBAN GROWTH (ROXY)

1,000

This timeline begins in **1920–25** when Tokyo's growth was concentrating toward the center of the city and so the line moves upward.

1950–55
1955–60
1947–50
1925–30
1935–40
1960–65
1920–35
2005–10
2000–05
1920–25
1980–85
1995–2000
1985–90
1990–95
1965–70
1975–80
1970–75

0

It moves downward in the mid-**1940s** with wartime evacuation, but back upward by **1950** as the center grew faster and then spirals around again as suburbanization dominated the **1970s**. After a quick looping in confusion in the 1980s, it rises one last time before heading toward the center, toward the stability we see today.

-1,000

1940–47

Tokyo Skytree was built in the four years 2008–12.

-2,000

-200   -100   0   +100   +200   +300

← **FALLING** RISING →

ABSOLUTE CHANGE IN CITY CENTER GROWTH
(ROXY PER YEAR)

65. The spatial agglomeration and deglomeration of Tokyo, 1920–2010. (Adapted from Ushijima Chihiro, "The Urban Life Cycle in the Tokyo 60km Area and the Expansion and Contraction of City" [in Japanese], *Bulletin of Faculty of Literature, Komazawa University* 70 (2012–13): 117–35, Figure 2, http://repo.komazawa-u.ac.jp/opac/repository/all/32520/jbg070-03-ushijimachihiro.pdf.)

In fact, it never stopped changing; what you see in figure 65 is a spiral that includes the tiniest and most intricate spiral-within-a-spiral between the years 1975 and 1990. After 1990 there was again greater growth in the center; more growth there than in the outskirts by the year 2000. However, already it is clear that the line is spiraling around again and clearly heading for something—it is approaching the center of the two axes. It is heading for slowdown, for stability. Tokyo as a whole is ending its period of growth, and there will soon no longer be a question of whether the city's growth is greatest within the center, the suburbs, or the furthest outskirts.

Tokyo in particular, and Japan more widely, can be seen in many ways to be at the forefront of slowdown. Japan has changed and will continue to change rapidly, but it is an example of the end to change in things that no longer need to grow—in the number of people, the number of buildings, and in overall consumption. Culturally and intellectually we will continue to change, perhaps faster than ever before in the decades soon to come.

Let's end this book with the story of the daughter and grandson of Professor Kawashima, who created for use in the social sciences the method of measuring and graphing change that is the method used throughout this book. However, Kawashima is known to most people in Japan for a very different reason. In 1990, his daughter Kiko explained to the world's press why she would be continuing her master's studies after her engagement. She was a modern young woman, and just because she was getting married did not mean she would stop studying—even if the person she was marrying was Japan's crown prince. "Prince Fumihito likes to study catfish," she said about her fiancé. "And I like to study people and cognition."[24]

Sixteen years later, in 2006, Kiko gave birth to Prince Hisahito, the Japanese imperial family's first male heir in forty-one years. And she and Prince Fumihito began to do things a little differently: "Prince Hisahito, who attended Ochanomizu University Elementary School, is the first member of the Imperial Family in the postwar era not to enroll in Gakushuin Primary School, associated with Gakushuin University, which was established in the 19th century as a school for aristocrats."[25] Thus, even in a country living through the greatest economic and demographic slowdown, great social and cultural change is still possible, if not ever more likely. Slowdown gives us time to reflect, and time to change what really matters. It gives us time itself.

At the time of Kiko's engagement it was clear that society was undergoing a transformation in Japan in ways that had not been changed for decades (and in some ways many centuries). Even as the economy and population were rapidly slowing, social progress was accelerating. Kiko was the daughter of a modest academic; never before had someone from such a background married into the royal family. The *Japan Times* reported it thus: "The contrast with palace ways has at times approached high comedy, like the day that the solemn deputy grand chamberlain of the Imperial Household Agency, Yasuo Shigeta, arrived at the family's cramped apartment, loaded with sea bream and other engagement gifts. Miss Kawashima and the chamberlain barely had room to bow to each other."[26] Princess Kiko's son will probably be called emperor, but the imperial era is over.

We are now learning that there is more that unites us than divides us, and that cooperation frequently achieves better outcomes than competition. Creating weapons is not only wrong—in the future it will be seen as senseless. No one should have to do a job she or he knows to be pointless—or worse, harmful—simply out of economic necessity. If catfish float your boat, study catfish. We do not need more people trying to sell us what we do not need.

Hopefully, in future, we will no longer have to wind down simply to cope with having become so wound up. Emotionally, life may even become more like it was for our hunter-gatherer ancestors than our more recent forebears of the twentieth century. We do not know what will happen, but to achieve a better future we must first imagine it. Slowdown means the end of rampant capitalism. It never could last forever, based as it was on the expectation of continually expanding markets and insatiable demand, and its creation of a bizarre concentration of wealth that has made a mockery of democracy.

Great economic inequalities will be very hard to sustain during and following the slowdown. As things change less, it will become much more difficult to make money out of a shrinking and aging population who may also become savvier and harder to fool with the allure of the "new"—as well as the world's gold or its fine pearls. Most advertising aims to persuade us that we want what we do not need; we must buy it, or at the very least covet it and despair if we cannot even dream of having it. However, now that more and more people study psychology and the social sciences and have greater numeracy skills, fooling the majority will become harder and harder to achieve.

In a slower future, sleight of hand and psychological tricks will no longer work, because they will no longer be new, especially if there is less that is new because of the slowdown in technological innovation. The very worst of the old ways are now gone, and a boy with a fascination for catfish and a girl who is more interested in people and cognition can be together regardless of the families into which they were born—but only because of the slowing-down times into which they were also born.

Slowdown means our institutions—universities, schools, hospitals—and our homes—kitchens and bathrooms—will not change as much as they have, but our attitudes, in contrast, may change more quickly. Slowdown gives us time to worry more about one another and less about what we will ourselves receive in future. Slowdown means more time to question all that our grandparents never had time to question, because they were dealing with so much that was new.

Slowdown means goods lasting longer; it means less waste. It means that many of the things that we currently think of as great social and environmental problems will not be problematic in future. We will, of course, have new problems—most of which we cannot even imagine right now. And we will, of course, do things we have always done, and that we did long before the great acceleration began, throughout it, and after it—enjoying friends, fun, family. What do you hope for in the future?

Me, I'll be building sandcastles on a beach somewhere.

Epilogue

Pandemic

This book was conceived in 2014, and the final versions of all twelve chapters of the first edition were written between January and June 2019. The first edition was published in March 2020. This short epilogue, written for the paperback edition, is about what subsequently happened between March and September 2020.

THE BEGINNING OF THE END

In 2020, the human world slowed down in an unparalleled way. A billion people stopped doing most of what they normally did. Billions of others were hugely affected by that. Worldwide, by late June, half a million people had died of Covid-19, rising to three-quarters of a million by late August. That represented less than 2 percent of all deaths in the world in the first half of 2020; nevertheless, what might well become the greatest social and economic change since the Second World War had begun. Initially, most people found it very hard to adjust. Slowing down is not easy.

Pandemics occur with predictable regularity, but the timing of their individual onsets is as unpredictable as the nature of each new disease. Our reaction to the arrival of a pandemic can also vary greatly. When it is thought that the disease mostly affects only the poor, or men who are gay, or when it sounds like a disease that we are used to and which we think we understand, then we tend to be more sanguine. When the disease is new to us, when we do not know exactly how it is transmitted between people, when we have little idea of what the actual risks are, we are more fearful. In that way, this disease has been similar to when cholera first arrived in

Europe, when the populace was acutely fearful, those who could often fleeing the city to the safety of the countryside.

This epilogue concerns itself with the coronavirus pandemic for several reasons. Firstly, for many years to come, the experience of having lived
through the pandemic will be one of the defining features of our lives—
what made the times we lived through different from other times. Sec-
ondly, pandemics provide very clear examples of accelerations and slowdowns, of how a rise in deaths eventually (and inevitably) becomes a fall.
Thirdly, Covid-19 has precipitated an extraordinary amount of slowdown
itself, although, as this book explains, most of that was already occurring,
albeit less dramatically. Fourthly, the twists and turns of a pandemic matter
greatly to both the daily experience of the pandemic and its ultimate effect
on morbidity and mortality. It is those twists and turns that the method of
plotting change over time in this book reveals best.

Below we look in detail at the seven large affluent countries which were
hardest hit by the pandemic in the first half of 2020. Daily deaths cannot be
directly compared between countries, not only because of inaccuracies in
reporting, but because of different counting methods—varying from only
including hospital deaths, to perhaps also including nursing home, care
home and community deaths. A Covid-19 death might be counted as such
only following a recent positive antigen test result (though in many settings, few tests were actually done), or simply by it being a suspected cause
of death, even if it was not actually the main cause of death. However, all
these differences will probably not have significantly altered the *shape* of
the graphs drawn here. Final death tolls for almost all countries will be
revised over the next few years, but these revisions are unlikely to include
revisions to the daily figures used here, just to the overall, monthly or annual totals.

The number of deaths shown per day in the timelines in this chapter are
based on the numbers that were being reported daily by the authorities in
each state and country. In hindsight these were sometimes overestimates,
but more often at the peak they were underestimates of the actual deaths
as mortality occurring outside hospitals was often not included. For example, in the U.K. we now know from figures later released by the Office
for National Statistics (ONS) that every day between 4 April and 20 April
more than 1,000 people died with Covid-19 mentioned on their death
certificates, with the peak being 1,347 such deaths recorded on 8 April.
However, this mention of Covid-19 does not necessarily mean that there

was a positive test result for the disease; it could just have been suspected. Furthermore, Covid-19 might not have been the main cause of death. To ensure that the timelines in this epilogue are reasonably comparable, the daily initially reported data is mainly used—the numbers that scared the public at the time, but which were usually less than the even more frightening numbers released retrospectively.

On conventional graphs of the 2020 pandemic, the smaller trends are not obvious. Graphs that simply show the cumulative total number of deaths rising over time and then plateauing are the least informative of all. Graphs that show the changing daily death toll reveal a great deal more, but mostly only show when the disease peaked and just how much slower it subsided compared to the speed of its rise. The graphs shown here highlight every small detail, every twist and turn, but rely on seven-day averages so that they are not affected by weekend reporting delays. (The actual data and sources used can be found at http://www.dannydorling.org/books/SLOWDOWN/.) For consistency with the timelines shown earlier in this book and noted at the bottom of each figure, the changes shown are subsequently the average of *the day before* and *the day after* the date shown. All this smoothing removes many transient anomalies and makes the actual trends much clearer.

What matters most, in both pandemic times and in general, is the changing speed and direction of change itself. At the time of writing (early September 2020) there have not yet been any significant second waves, which will possibly arise in the coming autumn and winter in the countries discussed here—but most are unlikely to be as large as the first wave. That is to say, they will be another loop within the compass of the present graphs. We will soon learn how to live with this virus, however utterly out of control we may have felt during its first year.

CHINA

Although the coronavirus pandemic began in China, it had the least effect there in terms of mortality. This is when all large countries in the world are compared. The data from China have been questioned, but even if the number of deaths had been 100 times higher, proportionately fewer people would have died of the disease in China than in the U.S. in 2020. However, figure 66 does explain that deaths due to the pandemic may have been underestimated by around ten per day at the time when they were first announced in China.

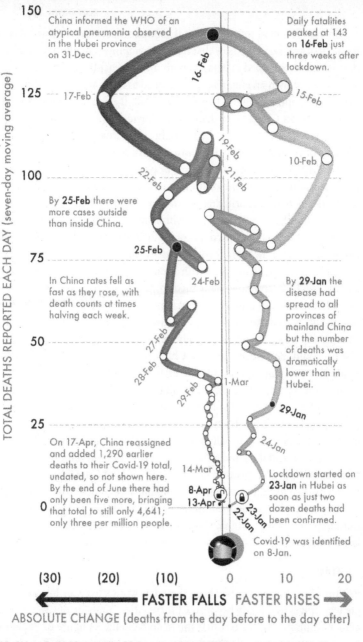

150 — China informed the WHO of an atypical pneumonia observed in the Hubei province on 31-Dec.

Daily fatalities peaked at 143 on **16-Feb** just three weeks after lockdown.

16-Feb

17-Feb

15-Feb

TOTAL DEATHS REPORTED EACH DAY (seven-day moving average)

125 —

10-Feb

19-Feb

22-Feb

21-Feb

100 —

By **25-Feb** there were more cases outside than inside China.

25-Feb

24-Feb

75 —

In China rates fell as fast as they rose, with death counts at times halving each week.

By **29-Jan** the disease had spread to all provinces of mainland China but the number of deaths was dramatically lower than in Hubei.

50 —

27-Feb

28-Feb

29-Feb

1-Mar

29-Jan

24-Jan

25 —

On 17-Apr, China reassigned and added 1,290 earlier deaths to their Covid-19 total, undated, so not shown here. By the end of June there had only been five more, bringing that total to still only 4,641; only three per million people.

14-Mar

8-Apr

13-Apr

Lockdown started on **23-Jan** in Hubei as soon as just two dozen deaths had been confirmed.

23-Jan

22-Jan

0 —

Covid-19 was identified on 8-Jan.

(30)   (20)   (10)   0   10   20

← FASTER FALLS   FASTER RISES →

ABSOLUTE CHANGE (deaths from the day before to the day after)

66. China: Covid-19 mortality, 23 January–13 April 2020 (reported each day). (Data adapted from the series provided by the Johns Hopkins University, Center for Systems Science and Engineering, accessed July 2020.)

In case you have just picked up this book and started reading this epilogue first, you need to know that figure 66 employs a method of graphing data which is explained in detail in both the first chapter and the appendix. Time is not shown on either axis, but instead as dates along a timeline. This particular graph highlights 16 February 2020, the point in time when the most people in China were dying from Covid-19 (using seven-day averages). The date drawn furthest to the right, 10 February, was when the daily number of deaths was growing most quickly, with eighteen more deaths than the day before. The point in time drawn furthest to the left, 17 February, was the time when the death rate was falling the fastest, with twenty fewer deaths that day, bringing the daily number of deaths down to 124. Within a month it was just ten, and within another month, essentially zero.

We will be debating the course of the 2020 pandemic for many years to come, including how many people actually died directly from the disease in each place, how many died with the disease but not primarily due to having caught it, and how many died from the collateral damage, such as overwhelmed health services, fear of going to hospital, the social and economic effects of lockdowns, or the consequence of not locking down fast enough. Figure 66 shows what might have been possible: how quickly the disease could have been subdued. China achieved it by the strict control of people's movement and activities, early social distancing, curfews, mass testing and supervised quarantining. But even though China was the most successful country in controlling the disease, the effect of the pandemic on its people was still enormous. The Chinese economy had been growing less quickly than it usually grew since 2017 (as figure 49 in this book illustrates), and so the pandemic hit when an economic slowdown was already under way. The greatest effect of the pandemic on China would not be the disease itself, but of how it so rapidly slowed down because of the slowdown in other affluent countries in the world that had become major trading partners with China. Global demand for goods made in China, a key factor in China's recent economic success, fell greatly.

ITALY

Within China the disease had been spread most effectively by businesspeople who travel frequently between Chinese cities.[1] Outside of China it was affluent tourists that were at first the main conduit. As figure 67 explains, it is currently thought to have been two Chinese tourists in Rome who first carried the disease to Italy; but it could just have easily been an Italian

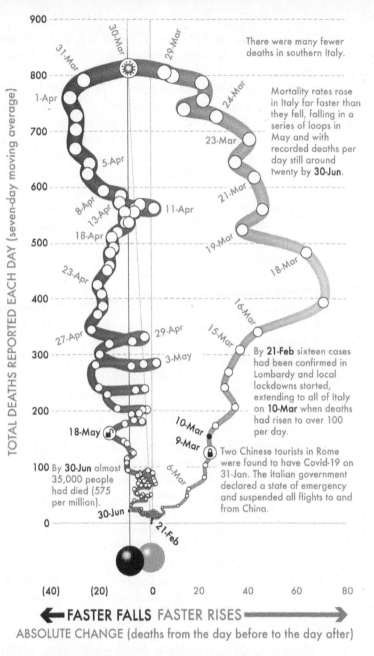

There were many fewer deaths in southern Italy.

Mortality rates rose in Italy far faster than they fell, falling in a series of loops in May and with recorded deaths per day still around twenty by **30-Jun**.

By **21-Feb** sixteen cases had been confirmed in Lombardy and local lockdowns started, extending to all of Italy on **10-Mar** when deaths had risen to over 100 per day.

Two Chinese tourists in Rome were found to have Covid-19 on 31-Jan. The Italian government declared a state of emergency and suspended all flights to and from China.

By **30-Jun** almost 35,000 people had died (575 per million).

TOTAL DEATHS REPORTED EACH DAY (seven-day moving average)

900
800
700
600
500
400
300
200
100
0

(40) (20) 0 20 40 60 80

← **FASTER FALLS** FASTER RISES →

ABSOLUTE CHANGE (deaths from the day before to the day after)

67. Italy: Covid-19 mortality, 21 February–30 June 2020 (reported each day). (Data adapted from the series provided by the Johns Hopkins University, Center for Systems Science and Engineering, accessed July 2020.)

tourist or businessperson returning from China, a student, or someone from any other group—the most likely being those that most frequently travel internationally.

International travel is not at its annual peak in January and February. Nevertheless, enough people were moving in and out of northern Italy for the disease not only to become established and widespread there, but also to spread from Italy, especially from its ski resorts, to other parts of Europe. Despite the confident claims made during the early days of the pandemic that the mutating genome of the virus meant we could track its movement around the planet with precision, we will never really know how it first got from place to place. In a way, it does not matter, because it usually then arrived a second, third and hundredth (or more) time into each place. If the first infectious traveler had not come, the disease would still have arrived. However, it was also partly chance where it struck first and worst.

Italy had bad luck. Europe had not experienced the SARS (Severe Acute Respiratory Syndrome) disease of 2002–3 other than reporting just a handful of cases and one death. In contrast, there had been over 5,000 cases of SARS in China and almost 350 deaths, with a further 300 deaths in Hong Kong. This may be the reason why the authorities in Italy did not react quite as quickly and drastically as those in China, Hong Kong and Korea (where the related disease MERS, Middle East Respiratory Syndrome, had struck in 2015). By 10 March 2020 more people were dying in Italy from Covid-19 each day than had ever died on any day in the hugely more populous China.

In Italy the number of reported deaths, even when smoothed over a seven-day period, tripled between 5 and 10 March and then tripled again in just a week before doubling again in another ten days, peaking at 814 deaths a day at the very end of March. Because the disease was by now so widespread in the north of Italy, it took much longer to fall than it had taken to rise. In Italy, unlike in China, the slowdown itself was slow. Twice (on 11 April and 3 May) it was so slow that it began to look as if the number of daily deaths was about to rise again. Thankfully, by mid-summer 2020, fewer than half a dozen people were dying each day in Italy from the disease, although that rose to just under two dozen a day in early autumn.

FRANCE

As figure 68 explains, the pandemic may have reached France as early as mid-November 2019. However, once recognized and reported, total

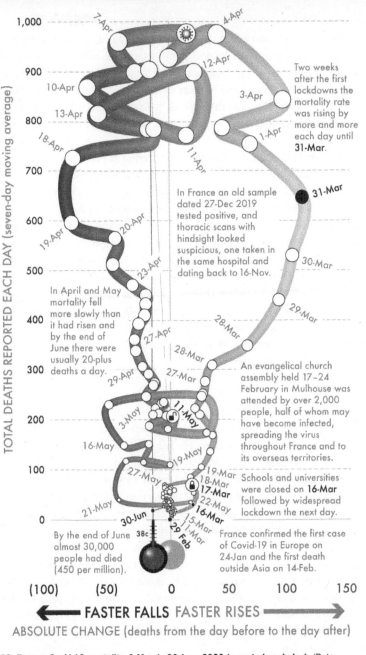

TOTAL DEATHS REPORTED EACH DAY (seven-day moving average)

1,000
900
800
700
600
500
400
300
200
100
0

7-Apr
4-Apr
12-Apr
10-Apr
3-Apr
13-Apr
1-Apr
18-Apr
11-Apr
31-Mar

Two weeks after the first lockdowns the mortality rate was rising by more and more each day until **31-Mar.**

30-Mar

19-Apr
20-Apr
29-Mar
23-Apr

In France an old sample dated 27-Dec 2019 tested positive, and thoracic scans with hindsight looked suspicious, one taken in the same hospital and dating back to 16-Nov.

In April and May mortality fell more slowly than it had risen and by the end of June there were usually 20-plus deaths a day.

28-Mar
27-Apr
28-Mar
29-Apr
27-Mar

An evangelical church assembly held 17–24 February in Mulhouse was attended by over 2,000 people, half of whom may have become infected, spreading the virus throughout France and to its overseas territories.

11-May
3-May
16-May
19-May

19-Mar
18-Mar
17-Mar

Schools and universities were closed on **16-Mar** followed by widespread lockdown the next day.

27-May
21-May
22-May
16-Mar
15-Mar
11-Mar
29 Feb
30-Jun
38c

By the end of June almost 30,000 people had died (450 per million).

France confirmed the first case of Covid-19 in Europe on 24-Jan and the first death outside Asia on 14-Feb.

(100)   (50)   0   50   100   150

← FASTER FALLS FASTER RISES **→**

ABSOLUTE CHANGE (deaths from the day before to the day after)

68. France: Covid-19 mortality, 2 March–30 June 2020 (reported each day). (Data adapted from the series provided by the Johns Hopkins University, Center for Systems Science and Engineering, accessed July 2020.)

numbers of deaths did not initially rise as quickly as they had done in Italy. France was about a week behind Italy in terms of absolute numbers of deaths being reported, but experienced the same pattern. The rise and then alarming acceleration in the number of deaths culminated, on 31 March, with 646 deaths, 111 higher than the day before. Covid-19 deaths in France peaked at 976 deaths a day in early April, and then fell only sporadically until mid-April.

By late April mortality due to the pandemic in France appeared to be subsiding less and less quickly. In early May it actually rose for a few days, fell again in mid-May, faltered again and then again in early June, not falling to below twenty deaths a day until the very end of June. By then the overall mortality rate was on a par with Italy, at around 450 people per million population having died of the disease. The number of cases was not at all trivial in France during the summer of 2020, but the number of deaths was lower as the elderly were now isolating themselves far more effectively than they were able to earlier. However, just as in Italy, when early autumn came and children returned to school from their summer holidays and the (mostly) young university students returned to campuses, cases rose a great deal, and the number of deaths increased to almost four dozen a day nationally in late September.

SPAIN

Figure 69 highlights the twists and turns of the 2020 pandemic in Spain. By now you may be finding the general pattern familiar. Covid-19 deaths rose far more quickly than they fell. For the first three weeks of March the number of deaths was rising exponentially. Total lockdown came late in Spain but before then enough measures were being taken to ensure that the daily death count peaked at the very end of March. Nevertheless, deaths per million people were ultimately higher in Spain than in France or Italy. And then, thankfully, just as elsewhere in mainland Europe, by mid-summer 2020 daily deaths fell to single figures. However, again, the number of cases rose in the autumn as people came indoors and mixed together. The number of deaths also rose, and by more than in Italy or France, but there were also reports of the late autumn rise abating. Only time will tell how and when the tail end of figure 69, the part yet to be drawn, will finally settle down. As I write in September, it has not quite reverted to where it was at the end of April.

At the end of April, 300 people a day were dying from the disease in Spain, and that figure still stood at over 30 a day at the end of May. Charting

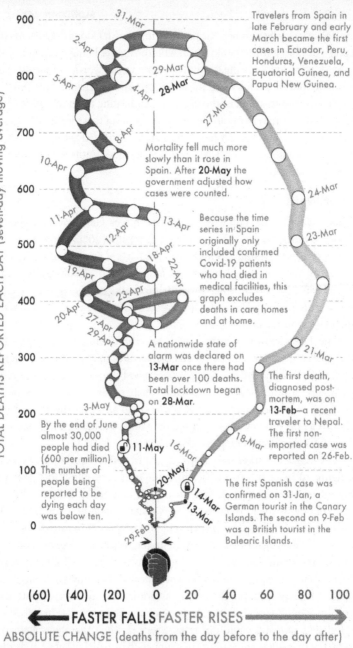

900 ········ 31-Mar ···········

Travelers from Spain in late February and early March became the first cases in Ecuador, Peru, Honduras, Venezuela, Equatorial Guinea, and Papua New Guinea.

2-Apr

29-Mar

800 ········ 5-Apr ··· 4-Apr · **28-Mar** ··········

27-Mar

8-Apr

700 ·········

Mortality fell much more slowly than it rose in Spain. After **20-May** the government adjusted how cases were counted.

10-Apr

600 ·········

24-Mar

11-Apr

13-Apr

Because the time series in Spain originally only included confirmed Covid-19 patients who had died in medical facilities, this graph excludes deaths in care homes and at home.

23-Mar

500 ·· 12-Apr ·········

18-Apr

19-Apr

22-Apr

23-Apr

400 ·· 20-Apr ········

27-Apr

29-Apr

300 ·········

A nationwide state of alarm was declared on **13-Mar** once there had been over 100 deaths. Total lockdown began on **28-Mar**.

21-Mar

The first death, diagnosed post-mortem, was on **13-Feb**—a recent traveler to Nepal. The first non-imported case was reported on 26-Feb.

200 ·· 3-May ··········

18-Mar

By the end of June almost 30,000 people had died (600 per million).

🔒 **11-May**

16-Mar

100 The number of people being reported to be dying each day was below ten.

20-May

🔒 **14-May**

13-Mar

The first Spanish case was confirmed on 31-Jan, a German tourist in the Canary Islands. The second on 9-Feb was a British tourist in the Balearic Islands.

0

29-Feb → ←

TOTAL DEATHS REPORTED EACH DAY (seven-day moving average)

(60) (40) (20)   0   20   40   60   80   100

← FASTER FALLS FASTER RISES →

ABSOLUTE CHANGE (deaths from the day before to the day after)

69. Spain: Covid-19 mortality, 3 March–30 June 2020 (reported each day). (Data adapted from the series provided by the Johns Hopkins University, Center for Systems Science and Engineering, accessed July 2020, and augmented with data from www.worldometers.info.)

the declining daily number, the timeline in figure 69 loops downwards like a plane tumbling from the sky. Even with the figures being given out by the Spanish government being smoothed over a week's worth of tragedy, there were still four moments when the falling appeared to halt and the timeline crossed over to the right of the diagram—indicating that the numbers dying each day were very briefly rising again. Three of these were in April and one was in May. The graph here uses data as corrected retrospectively by the Spanish authorities on 1 May 2020 to include deaths that should not have been omitted.

GERMANY

Among all the large countries of Europe it was Germany that kept its Covid-19 mortality rate the lowest in the first half of 2020. Initially, mortality in Germany rose much as in many other parts of Europe, and there were also cases traced back to January; but following the 22 March imposition of a national lockdown, when around 100 deaths had been recorded, the rate of increase in mortality did not rise as quickly in Germany as it did in other large European states.

Local restrictions were instigated earlier in Germany as compared to other parts of Europe and social distancing rules may well have been followed more closely. Disease control could have been easier to achieve given the nature of households in Germany—their smaller size, the comparatively less common intergenerational mix—and also how the country as a whole is a little less densely populated than other European countries, with Germany's largest city being less dominant.

The tangle of curves seen between 5 April and 26 April in the timeline in figure 70 hints at a public health battle over controlling the spread in those three weeks, when in fact the overall number of daily deaths was many hundreds lower than in Europe's other four largest countries. The much smaller tangle seen again around 3 May appears to mirror the early period, and then again around 18 May, just before the number of people reported to be dying from the disease every day in Germany fell below forty.

In total, Germany suffered far fewer deaths than any other large European country, and yet the same cascading, downward-tumbling pattern was seen. It was as if, in Europe, once the first great rise in infections had abated, you still could not relax: every so often there was a smaller event, but one still then resulting in a higher-than-usual number of deaths. By early autumn, a dozen were dying a day. The disease was endemic, if, thankfully, low level.

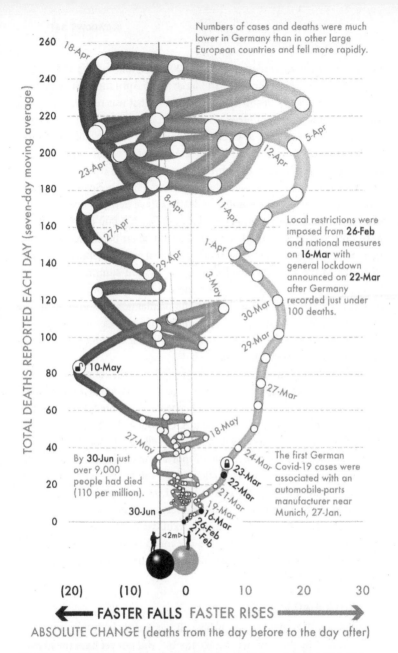

Numbers of cases and deaths were much lower in Germany than in other large European countries and fell more rapidly.

Local restrictions were imposed from **26-Feb** and national measures on **16-Mar** with general lockdown announced on **22-Mar** after Germany recorded just under 100 deaths.

By **30-Jun** just over 9,000 people had died (110 per million).

The first German Covid-19 cases were associated with an automobile-parts manufacturer near Munich, 27-Jan.

TOTAL DEATHS REPORTED EACH DAY (seven-day moving average)

260 · 240 · 220 · 200 · 180 · 160 · 140 · 120 · 100 · 80 · 60 · 40 · 20 · 0

18-Apr · 23-Apr · 27-Apr · 8-Apr · 29-Apr · 11-Apr · 12-Apr · 5-Apr · 1-Apr · 3-May · 30-Mar · 29-Mar · 27-Mar · 24-Mar · 23-Mar · 22-Mar · 21-Mar · 19-Mar · 18-May · 16-Mar · 26-Feb · 21-Feb · 27-May · 30-Jun · 10-May

<2m>

(20) · (10) · 0 · 10 · 20 · 30

⟵ **FASTER FALLS** FASTER RISES ⟹

ABSOLUTE CHANGE (deaths from the day before to the day after)

70. Germany: Covid-19 mortality, 10 March–30 June 2020 (reported each day). (Data adapted from the series provided by the Johns Hopkins University, Center for Systems Science and Engineering, accessed July 2020.)

UNITED KINGDOM

Figure 71 shows the timeline of the 2020 pandemic for the U.K. It is a slightly different shape. Between 29 March and 5 April mortality increased by around sixty extra deaths each day in a rise that was remarkably linear as compared to other countries. The numbers then oscillated in a tangle, similar to what was seen in Germany, but at a far higher daily death toll. Next, between 23 April and 11 May, the mortality count fell by around twenty fewer deaths each day, three times slower than it rose. It rose not only far higher than in Germany, but higher than in Italy, Spain and France too. It is only because the number of deaths shown here has been averaged over seven days that this timeline does not reach 1,000 deaths a day; if unsmoothed data were used, the graph would be far harder to follow, but there would be many days when both the actual and the reported number of deaths in the U.K. exceeded that figure. By mid-summer 2020 it had become clear that the U.K. had experienced the longest continuous period of excess mortality in Europe due to the pandemic.[2] However, as in the rest of Europe, although significant numbers of new cases were still being reported by then, daily mortality with mention of Covid-19 was usually under twenty by late summer 2020.

For the U.K., data released later revealed that the loop after 22 May appearing to chart a significant increase for a few days was, in fact, much less significant than previous rises, and instead represented the authorities' improvement in recording actual deaths. Of course, for each person who died, many more were severely ill, and some will have become disabled for the rest of their lives, although that proportion may turn out to be similar to those who suffered long-term effects from influenza—without enough time we cannot know. By the end of June, U.K. mortality associated with the pandemic had amounted to the highest in Europe at 650 deaths per million people. And again, as schools and universities reopened, early autumn brought a large rise in cases, but a much smaller rise in mortality. However, there was one extremely affluent country further afield that was harder hit than the U.K.

UNITED STATES

Thanks to the U.S., the U.K. probably will not end up with the worst pandemic record. By the summer of 2020 the U.S. did not yet have the highest mortality rate per million people, but the pandemic there was not in retreat as it was in all of Europe at that time. Figure 72 shows how in the U.S.

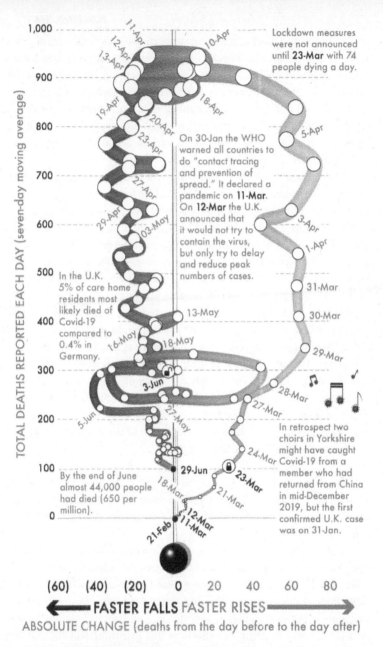

1,000

11-Apr
10-Apr
12-Apr
13-Apr

Lockdown measures were not announced until **23-Mar** with 74 people dying a day.

900

19-Apr
18-Apr

800

20-Apr
5-Apr

23-Apr
On 30-Jan the WHO warned all countries to do "contact tracing and prevention of spread." It declared a pandemic on **11-Mar**. On **12-Mar** the U.K. announced that it would not try to contain the virus, but only try to delay and reduce peak numbers of cases.

700

27-Apr

29-Apr
03-May
3-Apr

600

1-Apr

500

31-Mar

In the U.K. 5% of care home residents most likely died of Covid-19 compared to 0.4% in Germany.

400

30-Mar

13-May

16-May
18-May

29-Mar

300

3-Jun

28-Mar

27-Mar

200

5-Jun
27-May

In retrospect two choirs in Yorkshire might have caught Covid-19 from a member who had returned from China in mid-December 2019, but the first confirmed U.K. case was on 31-Jan.

24-Mar

100

29-Jun
23-Mar

By the end of June almost 44,000 people had died (650 per million).

18-Mar
21-Mar

0

12-Mar
21-Feb
11-Mar

TOTAL DEATHS REPORTED EACH DAY (seven-day moving average)

(60)   (40)   (20)   0   20   40   60   80

← **FASTER FALLS** FASTER RISES →

ABSOLUTE CHANGE (deaths from the day before to the day after)

71. U.K.: Covid-19 mortality, 7 March–29 June 2020 (reported each day). (Data adapted from the series provided by the Johns Hopkins University, Center for Systems Science and Engineering, accessed July 2020.)

at first the rise in mortality was exponential, with the numbers of deaths from 21 February to 24 March rising in a straight diagonal line leaning sharply rightward (which is what a genuinely exponential rise looks like on these graphs). The piecemeal lockdowns which took place across many U.S. states did not appear to have much effect in controlling the disease until the middle of April, after which it first appeared to fall, slightly, in severity; but many of these lockdowns and the social distancing involved were half-hearted and ended early.

The U.S. had the worst record of all the world's large affluent countries because, even when the disease began to abate locally, there were so many other places where it was still out of control. For two weeks, in mid-April, there were over 2,000 deaths every day. It could be argued that the U.S. should be considered as an amalgamation of states rather than as a single entity, but China has twenty-three provinces with populations each on average nine times that of the average U.S. state. As with the U.K., the statistics for the U.S. may not be especially reliable, but we cannot yet ascertain that as the U.S. has no ONS-like body to produce better data a few weeks later.

In late May 2020, Covid-19 deaths rose again in the U.S. to over 1,000 a day. They then fell to 600 by 20 June before again rising to over 800 a day late that month. Rates rose again in mid-July to almost 1,000 a day, and remained at above 1,000 a day for much of August and September. The timeline shown in figure 72 ends in late June 2020 because in July and August a "knot" drawn around the 1,000-deaths-a-day level would obscure the earlier picture. But it is clear that the story of the first wave in the U.S. had not finished at the time of writing.

The contrast between China and the U.S., and the contrasts within Europe, are remarkable. This is the same disease. Some countries received earlier warnings than others. None were fully prepared but, in retrospect, some were better prepared.

At a continental level, the disease had become endemic in Europe by mid-2020.[3] Even if a country could eradicate all cases, as New Zealand illustrated that summer, the disease would emerge again from outside. Nevertheless, different countries and states dealt with the problem very differently—but they all had to slow down. And they will all now have to plan for a world in which the effects of this pandemic will continue for some time to come, long after the disease itself has abated and we have learnt to live with it. It will take time for the significance of all this to sink

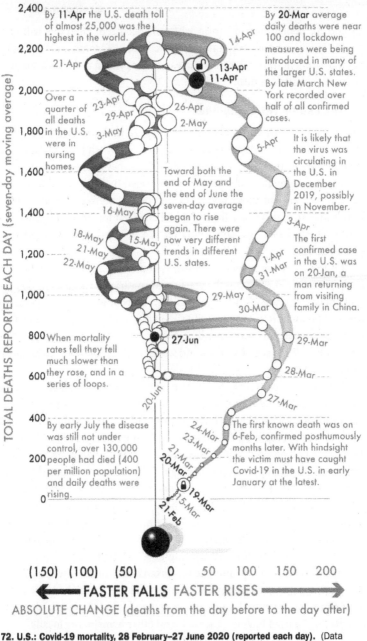

TOTAL DEATHS REPORTED EACH DAY (seven-day moving average)

By **11-Apr** the U.S. death toll of almost 25,000 was the highest in the world.

By **20-Mar** average daily deaths were near 100 and lockdown measures were being introduced in many of the larger U.S. states. By late March New York recorded over half of all confirmed cases.

It is likely that the virus was circulating in the U.S. in December 2019, possibly in November.

The first confirmed case in the U.S. was on 20-Jan, a man returning from visiting family in China.

Over a quarter of all deaths in the U.S. were in nursing homes.

Toward both the end of May and the end of June the seven-day average began to rise again. There were now very different trends in different U.S. states.

When mortality rates fell they fell much slower than they rose, and in a series of loops.

By early July the disease was still not under control, over 130,000 people had died (400 per million population) and daily deaths were rising.

The first known death was on 6-Feb, confirmed posthumously months later. With hindsight the victim must have caught Covid-19 in the U.S. in early January at the latest.

14-Apr · 13-Apr · 11-Apr · 21-Apr · 23-Apr · 26-Apr · 29-Apr · 2-May · 3-May · 5-Apr · 16-May · 3-Apr · 18-May · 15-May · 21-May · 1-Apr · 22-May · 31-Mar · 29-May · 30-Mar · 29-Mar · 27-Jun · 28-Mar · 27-Mar · 20-Jun · 24-Mar · 23-Mar · 21-Mar · 20-Mar · 19-Mar · 15-Mar · 21-Feb

(150) (100) (50) 0 50 100 150 200

⟵ **FASTER FALLS** FASTER RISES ⟶

ABSOLUTE CHANGE (deaths from the day before to the day after)

72. U.S.: Covid-19 mortality, 28 February–27 June 2020 (reported each day). (Data adapted from the series provided by the Johns Hopkins University, Center for Systems Science and Engineering, accessed July 2020.)

in, and for people to truly grasp what has occurred. Opinions will vary greatly, but as one politically-middle-of-the-road U.K. commentator bluntly put it, writing in the week before the pandemic peaked in his own country, "Liberal capitalism is bust."[4]

THE END OF THE BEGINNING

As the pandemic in Europe began to subside in mid-summer 2020, when many lockdown restrictions were still in place, 2,500 adults in Britain were surveyed about their lives and asked to tick as they wished from a list of seventeen statements that they agreed described their experience. Almost half (47 percent) of those under the age of seventy reported that there were some aspects of their lives that had changed for the better since the Covid-19 pandemic; but only a quarter (24 percent) of those aged over seventy thought so.[5]

Of these happier respondents—the people who reported at least one improvement in their lives—the reasons given varied. Half (exactly 50 percent) ticked "having a slower pace of life." Almost as many (47 percent) ticked "spending less time traveling," but the most popular reason (selected by 56 percent) was "spending more quality time with people they lived with." We are social animals and we needed to slow down to be more sociable.

Many other reasons were endorsed, and they were not all about being able to do less. Many responses concerned being free to do more of what the respondents wanted to do but previously did not have enough time for: some 42 percent reported "keeping in touch more with family or friends," 39 percent had become happier because they had "made home improvements," 37 percent appreciated "having more time to relax," but almost as many (33 percent) said that they were "doing more exercise than before." A smaller proportion (29 percent in both cases) ascribed the improvements in their lifestyle to simply "spending more time doing things that I enjoy" or "spending more time on things that matter to me"; 27 percent said that they had used the time to "learn something new." And although many might have complained publicly about being locked down, of those who said that aspects of their life had improved, a quarter (24 percent) ticked "spending more time working from home" and more than a fifth (22 percent) appreciated having "started buying [essentials and other items] more locally."

What of those aged over seventy? Only a quarter felt anything had improved. Often the restrictions on them were greater, and more often they would be living alone. And with retirement, they had already slowed down and were free to do the things that came to younger, busier people as a bonus. Overall, in June 2020, 47 percent of adults aged seventy and over said their well-being had been badly affected in the previous week, and 64 percent said that they were very or somewhat worried about the effect Covid-19 was having on their life in the U.K. Of course the risk of them dying from the disease was well over a thousand times higher than that of children or young adults.

You may be reading these words just a few months or a year or so after the pandemic subsided where you live. Nevertheless, it can be hard to remember what it felt like at the beginning and during the worst few weeks or the autumn resurgences. That is why these surveys are useful to look at now, taken while most lockdown measures were still in operation, and when many people were still dying. At mid-August, one in sixteen adults in the U.K. had not left their home at all in the previous week, so fearful were they of catching the disease. But that was a great improvement on the one in twelve that the ONS reported on 26 June who had not gone out in the week prior. Many people were initially devastated by the onset of the pandemic, despite often also listing the ways in which their lives had improved. It is very likely that attitudes in general were changing.

In that same ONS survey, but hidden away in the statistical tables, when asked "How kind or unkind do you think people in Britain were before the coronavirus (COVID-19) outbreak?," only 4.7 percent said "Very kind," 40 percent said "Somewhat kind," 29.9 percent said "Neither kind nor unkind," 17.2 percent replied "Somewhat unkind," and 3.1 percent said "Very unkind." The remainder did not know or were not prepared to answer. When then asked "How kind or unkind do you think people in Britain will be after we have recovered from the coronavirus (COVID-19) outbreak?," the number saying "Very kind" more than doubled to 10.7 percent, a further 51.6 percent said "Somewhat kind," only 18.9 percent replied "Neither kind nor unkind," and the proportion who said "Somewhat unkind" had halved to 9.2 percent, with an unchanging 3.1 percent still saying "Very unkind."[6]

We have no way of knowing if those predictions on kindness will prove accurate or not; but there was certainly a great sense that change was coming. Academics began to write more openly about the transformation from a time of having to make a profit to survive to an era when, to survive, we must no longer make profits—at least the kind of profit that is associated with growing consumption and pollution—despite so many people being worried about their jobs and income.

The slowdown that this book is about will not be caused by Covid-19, although for years to come I predict that many will say it was. The 1918 flu pandemic infected perhaps a third of the world's population and is estimated to have killed between 17 million and 50 million people worldwide (the lower figure is far more likely to be the more accurate). The death rate was highest in infants under a year old and was lowest in the 5–14 age group. Mortality peaked again in the 25–34 age group and subsequently rose significantly for those over 65 but was not as dangerous for adults as it was for babies, unless you were over 85. It devastated the workforce. It caused an economic decline possibly equivalent to a fall of 14 percent in world GDP. However, this reversed within a year. Contrast that with the 2020 pandemic in which total deaths worldwide reached 1 million by the end of September 2020—so much lower than a century earlier, especially given our global population today is so much higher and so much older. In the U.K., 89 percent of deaths with Covid-19 have been of people over sixty-five, 10 percent between fifty-five and sixty-five, and only 1 percent under forty-five years old.

So, demographically, there was dramatically more reason for the 1918 pandemic to devastate the economy, but it did so only temporarily. Today it is different: we were already in a period of slowdown, a slowdown which was happening anyway regardless of whether the pandemic had arrived in 2020, 2030 or 2040.

A LONG TIME COMING

During 2020 it began to be much more widely reported that the population of the planet would not rise to 10 or 11 billion as previously thought. Upon reassessment by a group of demographers who published their results in the *Lancet*, the global population of the planet would reach a peak of 9.7 billion people in 2064 and fall to 8.8 billion by 2100.[7]

Much of this slowdown was evident before the pandemic began, although very few people accepted that we were slowing down prior to 2020. This book is the story of the evidence that we were, and are, and will in future be slowing down for many years to come. In some ways the pandemic makes everything so much clearer as it accelerated the slowdown in just a few weeks and months; it is much harder to see change over years and decades. However, it is when you look at those much longer-term changes, as most of this book has done, that you can really see how slowdown has come about.

Viewed from the point of our short lives, this slowdown has been a long time coming. Generations immediately before us have experienced extraordinary acceleration, constant change, and even became used to that. These accelerations occurred at such a rate (demographically, economically, and socially) that a much deadlier pandemic could sweep round the world in 1918 and 1919 with apparently only short-term effect. The Russian epidemic of 1889 had little effect on rates of change; neither did the 1951 influenza pandemic, nor the 1957 or 1968 ones which were both a little less deadly than 1951.[8] But after 1968 our human world began to slowly slow, so that, when the next rapid-onset pandemic hit, just over half a century later, the effect on the lives of the majority of people was utterly different, and so Covid-19 would produce a far greater social shock than any disease had in the two centuries before.

Figure 66 explains how to read the timelines in this book. It shows you what a slowdown looks like by including two small slowdowns around the years 2000 and 2005 and then a major slowdown from 2010 onward.

In the timeline shown in figure 66, absolute change means total simple change, and YoY is shorthand for "year on year." Thus an absolute change of +0.2 is an extra fifth of a cup of coffee being drunk each day, on average, in a year, as compared to the year before. This is very different from a relative change, which depends on how many cups of coffee are being drunk in the first place. Should you be drinking two cups of coffee a day, an absolute change of 0.2 is a 10 percent relative increase. In this book the majority of timelines show absolute change because that is what matters most.

Another way to view figure 66 is to think of the line on the graph as plotting the course of a ship on the ocean. Each circle on the timeline shows where the ship was at that point in time. The further north (up) the circle is, the more is being measured, produced, made, or consumed—in this case cups of coffee drunk per day. The further south (down) the circle, the fewer cups. The further east (right) the circle, the more the quantity being measured is increasing at that point in time, and the further west (left), the more the measure is decreasing or increasing less. In the example given in figure 66, in fits and starts, the coffee drinker had become used to drinking more and more coffee per day, heading further and further north; but after 2010 something really new began, a slowdown started, and after 2012 that slowdown resulted in less and less consumption from there on, and a southward drift, although that slowdown itself appeared to have come to an end in 2020. When you are used to speeding up over time, slowing down can be a little frightening.

Position on the horizontal axes in all the timelines in this book is calculated as the rate of change from the point in time immediately before the point being considered to the point immediately after it, scaled to a constant rate such as "per month" or "per year." Occasionally this makes the most extreme point on the timeline appear to be the one before or the one after the actual extreme in the original data. However, the original data are used in any comments here in the text and within each figure.

The first and last points in any timeline usually have their rate of change calculated only from and to that point, as data for the point before and point after

1. The Slowdown

The distance between the dots indicates the speed of change in either or both quantity and degree of growth. The gap between **A** to **B** (below), for example, indicates that while there is barely any change in the quantity of coffee I drank over the one-year period between **2011** and **2012**, the rate of absolute change in my coffee consumption stagnated after a relatively fast three-year retraction into negative growth, or slowdown. By **2015** the slowdown has continued at a slower rate, having taken three years to cover the same ground between **B** and **C**, making the rate of absolute change slower.

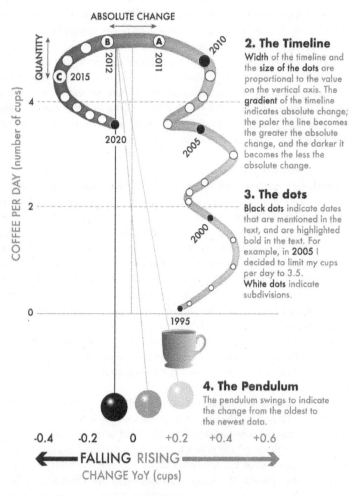

2. The Timeline

Width of the timeline and the **size of the dots** are proportional to the value on the vertical axis. The **gradient** of the timeline indicates absolute change; the paler the line becomes the greater the absolute change, and the darker it becomes the less the absolute change.

3. The dots

Black dots indicate dates that are mentioned in the text, and are highlighted bold in the text. For example, in **2005** I decided to limit my cups per day to 3.5.
White dots indicate subdivisions.

4. The Pendulum

The pendulum swings to indicate the change from the oldest to the newest data.

73. Personal coffee consumption, 1995–2020.

are not available. A website accompanying this book shows all the data used and how all the calculations were made, including highlighting in each spreadsheet when, very occasionally, interpolation is used. That website also features many more timelines than can be included here. It can be found at www.dannydorling .org—or at least until the day when that site, like all early twenty-first-century websites, no longer exists. If you are holding this as a paper book in your hand you are holding the most robust copy of these ideas.

If you want to draw timelines like these, you might want to take note of a few things that I became aware of when I first began to draw these timelines almost seven years ago:

- When using real data, always calculate the rate of change at a point in time from one point before that point (say, a year or a month before) to exactly the same distance in time after the point under consideration. The timelines become remarkably smoother when you do this. In this book the circles in most of the timelines are sized with their area roughly in proportion to the quantity under consideration, so in proportion to height on the vertical axis of each figure.
- Make sure you have very good-quality data. This technique is very good at emphasizing subtle changes, but it will also highlight any errors in your data and make them very prominent. If the image you see is too messy to understand, then try smoothing the data points over a longer time period. This is similar to using a moving average. Look at changes between years, rather than months, or between presidential elections, say, rather than single opinion polls, or compare the average of one month's worth of polls and the next. The slowdown is often slow and usually not steady, so it will not be apparent if you are using too short a time frame. This is why it is so often not noticed at all. If you don't look at the correct bandwidth, what you tend to see is a great deal of statistical noise, or very little change at all.
- Don't try to label every point on the timeline, as often points overlap. Incidentally, the world's most widely used spreadsheet package is very bad at labeling points on a connected scatterplot. Download the free add-in "XY Chart Labeler" if you are trying to draw these timelines in Excel.
- Connect the points in your graph with Bézier curves. These are often an option given in the connected-scatterplots diagrams provided in spreadsheet packages. Because pure acceleration produces a straight line, you cannot see the Bézier curves in the example drawn in figure 1 of this book, but you will see them in every other figure. It is worth thinking a little more about these curves and when they were invented, so a few words on that next. So much of what we currently know is of very recent realization because, until very recently, we were accelerating so quickly.

System

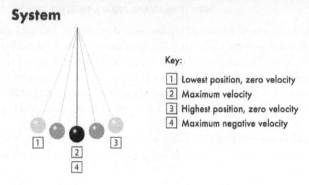

Key:

1. Lowest position, zero velocity
2. Maximum velocity
3. Highest position, zero velocity
4. Maximum negative velocity

Time series

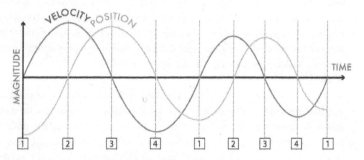

Phase portrait

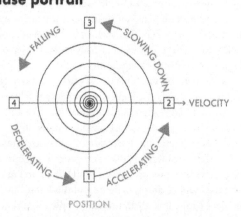

74. Three different ways of describing the movement of the slowing pendulum. (Adapted by Kirsten McClure from figure 5 in this book to show a damped pendulum whose range of movement gradually diminishes.)

The timeline is smooth in figures 2, 3, 5, and 74 in this book because behind those examples is a very simple formula determining its shape. However, most of the timelines in this book appear smooth. This is not because the underlying data reflect some similar magical hidden formula, but mainly because a smoothed curved line has been used to connect the dots: a Bézier curve. In statistical jargon, this approach to drawing timelines allows us to "remove the noise" to get a clearer picture of overall change—in other words, to see that part of the change that appears to be structural and underlying, rather than transitory and ephemeral.

We often forget just how much of what we can do, we could do only very recently. The curves used to draw the timelines in this book are named after Pierre Bézier, who was an engineer in the French car firm Renault. In 1968, he published his method, which would allow Renault to design cars with bonnets and wings that were no longer flat or crudely bent sheets of metal.[1] Before his innovation, such beautifully curved cars could not be produced.

It has been suggested that cars began to be curved in the 1950s, and better curved in the 1960s, to make some men desire them even more.[2] Almost a decade before Bézier, in 1959, another French automobile engineer, Paul de Casteljau, who was working for Citroën, had produced the algorithm that Bézier needed. It could just as easily have been de Casteljau's surname lending its name to these curves, or that of Sergei Natanovich Bernstein, who just half a century earlier developed the mathematics needed by both of these men. All of this innovation in mathematics and design has occurred in a remarkably short period of time.

When I was at school, we drew similar curves by hand using physical templates called French curves, which are now obsolete. People of my generation can easily be forgiven for thinking that the acceleration of their youth was normal. However, the Bézier curves have been here all along, just waiting to be discovered. And once discovered and used widely, they have changed our world, both in how we make objects, and in how we see what has happened and describe trends over time.

There may not be an infinite variety of new discoveries to be made in future, each as significant as the last; most of the recent changes have been just incremental, minor improvements on much greater past leaps forward. A generation before me, almost no children drew curves at school because they left school at fourteen. Just a few generations before that, there was—for the vast majority of people—no school.

Finally, and purely for completeness, figure 74 shows what figure 5 of this book would look like if a real pendulum were being shown rather than a perpetual motion one. A real pendulum, of course, slows down. The perfect slowdown produces a beautiful spiral—a miraculous spiral.

CHAPTER 1. **To Worry**

Epigraph: Song Jung-a, "South Korea's Birth Rate Falls to New Developed World Low," *Financial Times*, 28 August 2019, https://www.ft.com/content/16505438-c96c-11e9-a1f4-3669401ba76f.

1. Charles Darwin, "The Struggle for Existence," part 3 of the introduction to *Origin of Species: by Means of Natural Selection, or the Preservation of Favoured Races in the Struggle for Life* (London: John Murray, 1859). These words are from the first edition, and may differ slightly in later editions. Numerous online versions exist: https://www.gutenberg.org/files/1228/1228-h/1228-h.htm.

2. Paul Ehrlich and Anne Ehrlich, *The Population Bomb: Population Control or Race to Oblivion* (New York: Ballantine Books, 1968), 160, http://projectavalon.net/The_Population_Bomb_Paul_Ehrlich.pdf.

3. Joel E. Cohen, "How Many People Can Earth Hold?" *Discover*, 1 November 1992, http://discovermagazine.com/1992/nov/howmanypeoplecan152/.

4. See figure 64 in Chapter 12. Most of the assertions made in this introductory chapter are justified by the evidence presented later on in this book, but a few will simply be guesswork and my intuition.

5. Britain's most recent oldest person, Grace Jones, died at the age of 112 on 14 June 2019. Giuseppina Robucci, Europe's oldest, died at the age of 116 on 18 June 2019. Jeanne Louise Calment is said to be the oldest person to have ever lived, but there is doubt that she was as old as she claimed. See Tristin Hopper, "History's Oldest Woman a Fraud? Russian Researchers Claim 122-Year-Old Jeanne Calment Was Actually a 99-Year-Old Imposter," *National Post*, 31 December 2018, https://nationalpost.com/news/world/historys-oldest-woman-a-fraud-theory-says-122-year-old-jeanne-calment-was-actually-a-99-year-old-imposter.

6. Chapter 12 of this book describes the timeline's origins in Japan, where slowdown first began, and the short appendix to this book gives more details of how the timelines are drawn. Spreadsheets containing the timelines in this book (and many others) are also available at www.dannydorling.org, and they also illustrate how one can be drawn.

7. Michael Friendly, Pedro Valero-Mora, and Joaquín Ibáñez Ulargui, "The First (Known) Statistical Graph: Michael Florent van Langren and the 'Secret' of Longitude," *American Statistician* 64, no. 2 (2010): 174–84, http://datavis.ca/papers/langren-TAS09154.pdf.

8. There were very few exceptions to the runaway population growth in the year 1968. The population of Palestine was falling by 2.1 percent a year following the Six-Day War. So was that of Portugal under dictatorship (by 0.7 percent a year) and the Falkland Islands (by 0.5 percent annually). Finland was only growing by 0.1 percent a year then, the United Kingdom by 0.5 percent, France by 0.7 percent, the United States by 0.9 percent, Japan by 1.3 percent, Canada by 1.7 percent, the world as a whole (and India in particular) by 2.1 percent, Ethiopia by 2.5 percent, China by 2.8 percent, the Philippines by 3 percent, and Iraq by 3.5 percent.

9. Bob Dylan, "Idiot Wind," 1974, https://www.bobdylan.com/songs/idiot-wind/.

10. See Danny Dorling, *Population 10 Billion* (London: Constable, 2013), 338. If you ever watch *1313: Giant Killer Bees!* you may well come to believe that we have reached the end of times. It is one of the worst movies ever made. But you might also enjoy the fact that we can now parody our recent fears.

11. With colleagues I once calculated the odds of dying as a result of falling out of a tree, using mortality and hospital statistics released by the U.K. authorities. Many children receive minor injuries from falling out of trees. Hardly any die. If you are worried about your children, worry about small objects that can get stuck in their throats when they are very young; worry about drowning, even in quite shallow water; and worry about your child being hit by a car. Worry about these three things, and worry about them more than anything else. Most important, stop worrying about everything else that worries you. The chances of the terrors you lose sleep at night fretting over actually occurring to you are minuscule.

12. "There will be great storages of force for every city, and for every house if required, and this force man will convert into heat, light, or motion, according to his needs. Is this Utopian? A map of the world that does not include Utopia is not worth even glancing at, for it leaves out the one country at which Humanity is always landing. And when Humanity lands there, it looks out, and, seeing a better country, sets sail. Progress is the realisation of Utopias." Oscar Wilde, *The Soul of Man* (London: Arthur Humphries, 1900), 40, https://www.gutenberg.org/files/1017/1017-h/1017-h .htm.

13. P. D. James, *The Children of Men* (London: Faber, 1992).

CHAPTER 2. The Slowing Down

Epigraph: China Internet Information Center, "News Analysis: Experts Predict Slowdown in Greek Economy," *Xinhuanet*, 25 January 2019, http://www .xinhuanet.com/english/2019-01/25/c_137772060.htm.

1. Quoted in Roxanne Darrow, "Culinary Backstreets on the Road—The Mastic Trail in Chios," *Culinary Backstreets*, 23 September 2014, https://culinarybackstreets.com/ cities-category/athens/2014/cb-road-17/.

2. Nikos Merouses, *Chios: Physiko periballon & katoikese apo te neolithike epoche mechri to telos tes archaiothtas* [Chios: Natural Environment & Habitation from the

Neolithic Age to the End of Antiquity], Chios: Papyros, 2002), chapter 5, section 3. The population numbers are given in Maria Papaioannou's review of the book in *Bryn Mawr Classical Review* (2006), http://bmcr.brynmawr.edu/2006/2006-06-38.html.

3. Roula Ballas and Vassilis Ballas, "How Masticulture Was Created," *Masticulture,* accessed 11 February 2019, http://www.masticulture.com/about_masticulture/en/history-of-chios-masticulture.php.

4. The equation that produces the population trend shown in the timeline in figure 3, where *y* is population and *t* is year, and *e* is a Euler's constant (roughly 2.71821818), is: $y_t = 99 + e^{(1.5 \times -t/400)} \times 10 \sin(t/10)$.

5. In 2019, Eurostat reported that during 2017 the average age of women at the birth of their first child in the European Union had been 29.1, and that this ranged from 26.1 in Bulgaria to 31.1 in Italy. That age has been steadily rising toward 31.4 as I write (which is roughly 10π, explaining why 10 is in the formula directly above). See *Eurostat: Statistics Explained: Fertility Statistics,* online guide to European data, https://ec.europa.eu/eurostat/statistics-explained/index.php/Fertility_statistics. In the United Kingdom data released for England and Wales on 10 January 2019 revealed that the average age of first-time mothers was 28.8 years in 2017 and it had not risen since 2016, whereas the average age of first-time fathers was now 33.4, up from 33.3 in 2016: Kanak Ghosh, *Birth Characteristics in England and Wales: 2017* (London: Office for National Statistics, 10 January 2019), https://www.ons.gov.uk/peoplepopulationandcommunity/birthsdeathsandmarriages/livebirths/bulletins/birthcharacteristicsinenglandandwales/2017. In Tokyo, in 2017, the average age of first motherhood was 32.3 years as compared to 30.7 years for Japan as a whole: https://stats-japan.com/t/kiji/14299. In the United States, the first-time mothers of San Francisco were the oldest in 2017 at 31.9, as compared to 26 for the country as a whole, younger even than women in Bulgaria: Michelle Robertson, "San Francisco Women Have Children Later Than Anywhere Else in the U.S. Here's Why," *SFGate,* 7 August 2018, https://www.sfgate.com/mommyfiles/article/women-sf-children-mother-motherhood-later-age-13136540.php. By 2016, the United States had a bimodal distribution of births because it had become such a socially divided country with two peaks, at ages 20 and 28, as compared to a single U.S. peak a generation ago in 1980 at age 19: Quoctrung Bui and Claire Cain Miller, "The Age That Women Have Babies: How a Gap Divides America," *New York Times,* 4 August 2018. All websites accessed 13 July 2019.

6. In fact, the former British prime minister, David Cameron, made such a stupid promise and his then home secretary, Theresa May, tried to fulfill it—and failed. The American president, Donald Trump, promised to build a wall on the U.S.-Mexican border in an attempt to make the British look less stupid than the Americans who supported him. Slowdown involves realizing how very stupid we can be.

7. Here its center is set at 99 million because that is the number inserted into the formula given in note 4 above. The constants 1.5 and 400 in that formula determine

the rate at which stability is approached. This is the logarithmic spiral discovered by René Descartes in 1638 and called "miraculous" by Jacob Bernoulli in 1692.

8. G. J. Chin, "Flying along a Logarithmic Spiral," *Science,* 8 December 2000, http://science.sciencemag.org/content/290/5498/1857.3. See also "Spiral Mathematics," *Encyclopaedia Britannica,* https://www.britannica.com/science/spiral-mathematics.

9. "Not All Japanese Towns and Villages Are Atrophying: More Young Japanese Are Seeking a Rural Idyll," *Economist,* 22 March 2018, https://www.economist.com/asia/2018/03/22/not-all-japanese-towns-and-villages-are-atrophying.

10. S. Palmer, "Women Novelists Warned Early on That Village Life Wasn't All It's Cracked Up to Be," *Conversation,* 23 June 2018, https://theconversation.com/women-novelists-warned-early-on-that-village-life-wasnt-all-its-cracked-up-to-be-99884.

11. Christiaan Huygens had a much wider interest in time. In 1669 he produced the second known statistical graph, of the distribution of life expectancy by age (Michael Friendly, Pedro Valero-Mora, and Joaquín Ibáñez Ulargui, "The First (Known) Statistical Graph: Michael Florent van Langren and the 'Secret' of Longitude," *American Statistician* 64, no. 2 [2010]: 174–84, http://datavis.ca/papers/langren-TAS09154.pdf). Huygens's 1669 graph appears here: Carl Boyer, "Note on an Early Graph of Statistical Data (Huygens 1669)," *Isis: A Journal of the History of Science Society* 37, nos. 3–4 (July 1947), https://www.journals.uchicago.edu/doi/10.1086/348018.

12. Stacy Taylor, "History of the Pendulum," *Sciencing,* 24 April 2017, accessed 11 February 2019, https://sciencing.com/history-pendulum-4965313.html.

13. Sascha Reinhardt, Guido Saathoff, Henrik Buhr, Lars A. Carlson, Andreas Wolf, Dirk Schwalm, Sergei Karpuk, Christian Novotny, Gerhard Huber, Marcus Zimmermann, Ronald Holzwarth, Thomas Udem, Theodor W. Hänsch, and Gerald Gwinne, "Test of Relativistic Time Dilation with Fast Optical Atomic Clocks at Different Velocities," *Nature Physics,* 11 November 2007, 861–64, https://www.nature.com/articles/nphys778.

14. This may have been somewhat easier to do in the 1960s with the aid of new hallucinogens, although Samuel Coleridge was already using opiates back in 1797 when he wrote the poem *Kubla Khan,* subtitled *Or a Vision in a Dream. A Fragment.* The whole poem, with its "measureless spaces," makes much more sense when you have an idea of the headspace its author was in.

15. "The Phase Space and Density Function," *Wikipedia,* accessed 11 February 2019, https://en.wikipedia.org/wiki/Boltzmann_equation#The_phase_space_and_density_function.

16. Josiah Gibbs was a son of New Haven, Connecticut, and attended Yale College. The phase diagrams in this book have their origins in the use of phase diagrams in thermodynamics. Their first serious use for studying slowdown and their utility in the social sciences began in Tokyo in the 1970s and is described and referenced in the concluding chapter of this book.

17. Haynes Miller, "Linear Phase Portraits: Matrix Entry, *MIT Mathlets,* accessed 11 February 2019, http://mathlets.org/mathlets/linear-phase-portraits-matrix -entry/.

18. Krishnatej Vedala, "Empowering Caregivers with Technology," *TEDxFIU* (Florida International University) talk, 8 December 2014, https://www.youtube.com/watch?v =RVZ5L0LrlOo.

CHAPTER 3. **Debt**

Epigraph: Annie Nova, "Student Debt Continues to Grow, but There's Been a Slowdown," *CNBC,* 20 September 2018, https://www.cnbc.com/ 2018/09/20/student-debt-continues-to-grow-but-more-slowly-than-in-the -past.html.

1. I published *The Equality Effect* in 2017 and *Peak Inequality* in 2018. These two books included data showing that the growth in economic inequality was not just slowing; in most places on Earth the trend toward greater inequality had recently reversed. It is not academically fashionable to show that inequality is generally falling, but this has been the case since 2008. This is apart from the super-rich still becoming richer as I write, but their time too will come, and maybe soon. If we are indeed at peak global inequality, we will not see such obscene riches again held by so few families worldwide.

2. Statista, *Number of Higher Education Degrees Earned in the United States from 1950 to 2028,* online open access resource, accessed 11 February 2019, https://www .statista.com/statistics/185153/degrees-in-higher-education-earned-in-the-united -states/.

3. Federal Student Aid (an office of the U.S. Department of Education), *Federal Student Loan Portfolio,* accessed 11 February 2019, https://studentaid.ed.gov/sa/about/data -center/student/portfolio.

4. Melanie Lockert, "What Happens to Student Loans When You Die?" *Student Loan Hero Blog,* 18 December 2017, https://studentloanhero.com/featured/what-happens -to-student-loans-when-you-die/.

5. Danny Dorling and Michael Davies, *Jubilee 2022: Writing off the Student Debt* (London: Progressive Economy Forum, 30 October 2018), https://www .progressiveeconomyforum.com/jubilee-2022-writing-off-the-student-debt/; Michael Davies and Danny Dorling, *Jubilee 2022: Defending Free Tuition* (London: Progressive Economy Forum, 9 July 2019), https://progressiveeconomyforum.com/ publications/jubilee-2022-defending-free-tuition/.

6. Jun Hongo, "Number of Cars per Household Stagnates in Japan," *Wall Street Journal,* 18 August 2014, https://blogs.wsj.com/japanrealtime/2014/08/18/number-of-cars -per-household-stagnates-in-japan/.

7. Gil Scott-Heron, "Whitey on the Moon," *The Revolution Will Not Be Televised* (New York: Flying Dutchman Records, 1974).

8. Jeff Gitlen, "History of the Auto Lending Industry," *Lendedu,* accessed 11 February 2019, https://lendedu.com/blog/history-of-auto-lending-industry. *Lendedu* is a website aimed at enticing you to look at advertising.

9. Statista, *Light Vehicle Retail Sales in the United States from 1978 to 2018,* online open-access resource, accessed 11 February 2019, https://www.statista.com/statistics/199983/us-vehicle-sales-since-1951/.

10. Aarón González Sherzod Nabiyev, "Oil Price Fluctuations and Its Effect on GDP Growth: A Case Study of USA and Sweden" (BA thesis, Jönköping International Business School, Jönköping University, January 2009), https://pdfs.semanticscholar.org/e2dc/68b6cb8346e1bda8491b6dd490594d0e6e94.pdf.

11. Tracy Jan, "Redlining Was Banned 50 Years Ago. It's Still Hurting Minorities Today," *Washington Post,* 28 March 2018, https://www.washingtonpost.com/news/wonk/wp/2018/03/28/redlining-was-banned-50-years-ago-its-still-hurting-minorities-today.

12. Federal Reserve Bank of St. Louis, *Mortgage Debt Outstanding, All Holders (MDOAH),* accessed 11 February 2019, https://fred.stlouisfed.org/series/MDOAH.

13. Danny Dorling, *All That Is Solid,* 2nd ed. (London: Penguin Books, 2015), 236–49.

14. Daniel Thornton, "The U.S. Deficit/Debt Problem: A Longer-Run Perspective," *Federal Reserve Bank of St. Louis Review* 94, no. 6 (November/December 2012): 441–55, https://files.stlouisfed.org/files/htdocs/publications/review/12/11/Thornton.pdf.

15. International Monetary Fund, *Interest Rates, Discount Rate for United States,* provided by the Federal Reserve Bank of St. Louis and last updated 1 June 2017, https://fred.stlouisfed.org/series/INTDSRUSM193N.

16. Religious edicts against rising debt and the (consequent) amassing of great wealth are well known. It required forgetting this to see the amassing of wealth by a few as good and deserving, and the consequent amassing of debts by the many as being the result of their fecklessness and collective lack of self-control. The watering down of usury laws by the Protestant Church is one reason why the Dutch were able to become so wealthy; then the British followed suit after 1688, and the Protestant elite of the United States learned in turn from the British. Biblical edicts that there should regularly be a jubilee, in which debts are canceled, are frequently forgotten. Islam, the most recently founded of the three main Abrahamic religions, tends to be the most strict concerning the amassing of wealth through the interest paid on debt.

17. Tim Di Muzio and Richard H. Robbins, *Debt as Power* (Manchester: Manchester University Press, 2016), 20.

CHAPTER 4. **Data**

Epigraph: Justin Trudeau, "Justin Trudeau's Davos Address in Full," *World Economic Forum,* 23 January 2018, https://www.weforum.org/agenda/2018/01/pm-keynote-remarks-for-world-economic-forum-2018/.

1. Elizabeth Palermo, "Who Invented the Printing Press?" *Live Science Blog*, 25 February 2014, https://www.livescience.com/43639-who-invented-the-printing-press.html.

2. Mathew Wall, "Big Data: Are You Ready for Blast-off?" *BBC Business News*, 4 March 2014, https://www.bbc.co.uk/news/business-26383058.

3. Bernard Marr, "How Much Data Do We Create Every Day? The Mind-Blowing Stats Everyone Should Read," *Forbes*, 21 May 2018, https://www.forbes.com/sites/bernardmarr/2018/05/21/how-much-data-do-we-create-every-day-the-mind-blowing-stats-everyone-should-read/#1ad9abea60ba.

4. "History of Wikipedia," *Wikipedia*, 24 April 2019, https://en.wikipedia.org/wiki/History_of_Wikipedia.

5. Tim Simonite, "The Decline of Wikipedia," *MIT Technology Review*, 22 October 2013, https://www.technologyreview.com/s/520446/the-decline-of-wikipedia/.

6. Max Roser, "Books," *Our World in Data*, 2017, https://ourworldindata.org/books#consumption-of-books.

7. UNESCO, *Recommendation concerning the International Standardization of Statistics relating to Book Production and Periodicals* (Paris: UNESCO, 1964), 145.

8. Eltjo Buringh and Jan Luiten Van Zanden, "Charting the 'Rise of the West': Manuscripts and Printed Books in Europe; A Long-Term Perspective from the Sixth through Eighteenth Centuries," *Journal of Economic History* 69, no. 2 (2009): 409–45 (and the statistical source used by Roser in note 6 above).

9. "List of Book-Burning Incidents (Catholic and Martin Luther): The World," Wikipedia, accessed 24 April 2019, https://en.wikipedia.org/wiki/List_of_book-burning_incidents#Catholic_theological_works_(by_Martin_Luther).

10. Science Museum, "Thalidomide," *Exploring the History of Medicine*, accessed 2 September 2019, http://broughttolife.sciencemuseum.org.uk/broughttolife/themes/controversies/thalidomide.

11. Alexander J. Field, *A Great Leap Forward: 1930s Depression and U.S. Economic Growth* (New Haven: Yale University Press, 2012). See also Alexander J. Field, "The Most Technologically Progressive Decade of the Century," *American Economic Review* 93, no. 4 (2003): 1399–1413, https://www.aeaweb.org/articles?id=10.1257/000282803769206377.

12. Charles Darwin, "Laws of Variation," in *The Origin of Species by Means of Natural Selection*, 6th ed. (London: John Murray, 1888), https://www.gutenberg.org/files/2009/2009-h/2009-h.htm.

13. Tim Blanning, *The Pursuit of Glory: Europe, 1648–1815* (London: Penguin, 2007).

14. Robert Colwell, director of the Microsystems Technology Office at the Defense Advanced Research Projects Agency, as quoted in Bob Colwell, "End of Moore's Law: It's Not Just about Physics," *Scientific American*, August 2018, https://www.scientificamerican.com/article/end-of-moores-law-its-not-just-about-physics/.

15. Evangelia Christodoulou, Jie Ma, Gary S. Collins, Ewout W. Steyerberg, Jan Y. Verbakel, and Ben Van Calster, "A Systematic Review Shows No Performance Benefit of Machine Learning over Logistic Regression for Clinical Prediction Models," *Journal of Clinical Epidemiology* 110 (2019): 12–22, https://www.jclinepi.com/article/S0895-4356(18)31081-3/fulltext.

16. Christopher L. Magee and Tessaleno C. Devezas, "Specifying Technology and Rebound in the IPAT Identity," *Procedia Manufacturing* 21 (2018): 476–85, https://www.sciencedirect.com/science/article/pii/S2351978918301860.

17. Unsurprisingly, there is more than you might ever want to read about Moore's law ever so easily available: see *Wikipedia,* accessed 2 September 2019, https://en.wikipedia.org/wiki/Moore%27s_law.

18. Wgsimon, "Microprocessor Transistor Counts 1971–2011 & Moore's Law," *Wikimedia Commons,* 13 May 2011, https://commons.wikimedia.org/wiki/File:Transistor_Count_and_Moore%27s_Law_-_2011.svg.

19. The *Internet of Things* is a term that is itself going through a rapid slowdown in use and usefulness. It may mean nothing to you, depending on when you read this book. So much that we hyped as new and amazing at the start of the twenty-first century was, in hindsight, simply hype.

CHAPTER 5. **Climate**

Epigraph: Jacob Jarvis, "Greta Thunberg Speech: Activist Tells Extinction Rebellion London Protesters 'We Will Make People in Power Act on Climate Change,'" *London Evening Standard,* 21 April 2019, https://www.standard.co.uk/news/london/greta-thunberg-tells-extinction-rebellion-protesters-we-will-make-people-in-power-act-on-climate-a4122926.html.

1. Jonathan Watts, "A Teen Started a Global Climate Protest. What Are You Doing?" *Wired,* 12 March 2018, https://www.wired.com/story/a-teen-started-a-global-climate-protest-what-are-you-doing/.

2. Doyle Rice and Doug Stanglin, "The Kid Is All Right: Friday's Worldwide Climate Protest Sparked by Nobel-Nominated Teen," *USA Today,* 15 March 2019, https://eu.usatoday.com/story/news/nation/2019/03/14/climate-change-swedish-teen-greta-thunberg-leads-worldwide-protest/3164579002/.

3. Tessa Stuart, "Greta Thunberg Ups Climate Pressure Ahead of UN Summit: 'This Has to Be a Tipping Point,'" *Rolling Stone,* 29 August 2019, https://www.rollingstone.com/politics/politics-news/climate-crisis-activist-greta-thunberg-united-nations-summit-877973/, which explains that the *Malizia II* is "a 60-foot, solar- and wind-powered monohull belonging to the Principality of Monaco."

4. Thomas Boden, Gregg Marland, and Robert Andres, *Global, Regional, and National Fossil-Fuel CO2 Emissions* (Oak Ridge, TN: National Laboratory, U.S. Department of Energy, 2017), doi 10.3334/CDIAC/00001_V2017, 2017, http://cdiac.ess-dive.lbl.gov/trends/emis/overview_2014.html.

5. See "Cragside," *Wikipedia,* accessed 18 September 2019, https://en.wikipedia.org/wiki/Cragside#Technology.

6. This account and the figures I am using in this chapter are according to the latest estimates of the Integrated Carbon Observation System (ICOS): "Global Carbon Budget 2018," accessed 17 September 2019, https://www.icos-cp.eu/GCP/2018.

7. See "Monument to the First Lord Armstrong in Rothbury Graveyard," *Historic England,* accessed 4 September 2019, https://historicengland.org.uk/listing/the-list/list-entry/1371120.

8. William H. McNeil, *The Pursuit of Power* (Chicago: University of Chicago Press, 1982), 26–27.

9. Ibid., 32.

10. U.S. Bureau of Transportation Statistics, "World Motor Vehicle Production, Selected Countries," sourced from WardsAuto.com, *Motor Vehicle Facts & Figures,* accessed 20 January 2019, https://www.bts.gov/content/world-motor-vehicle-production-selected-countries.

11. Angus Maddison, 1926–2010, was a renowned economic historian. The Groningen Growth and Development Center hosts a website (accessed 20 January 2019) with much of his work, including the Maddison Project Database, which continues to update his longtime series. See https://www.rug.nl/ggdc/historicaldevelopment/maddison/original-maddison.

12. National Bureau of Economic Research, *US Business Cycle Expansions and Contractions, 1854 to 2009 List,* accessed 20 January 2019, https://www.nber.org/cycles.html.

13. Boden, Marland, and Andres, *Global, Regional, and National Fossil-Fuel CO2 Emissions.*

14. These were the goods typically won in England on the *Generation Game,* which began in Holland under a different name in 1969. In England it was a Teasmade, not an automatic coffee maker, that was the key prize. See "The Generation Game," *Wikipedia,* accessed 3 September 2019, https://en.wikipedia.org/wiki/The_Generation_Game.

15. Corinne Le Quéré et al., "Global Carbon Budget 2018," *Earth System Science Data* 10 (2018): 2141–94, https://www.earth-syst-sci-data.net/10/2141/2018/.

16. Global Carbon Project, *Global Fossil CO2 Emissions, 1960–Projected 2018,* accessed 4 September 2019, https://www.icos-cp.eu/sites/default/files/inline-images/s09_FossilFuel_and_Cement_emissions_1959.png.

17. ICOS, "Global Carbon Budget 2018."

18. Intergovernmental Panel on Climate Change (IPCC), "Global Warming of 1.5°C: An IPCC Special Report on the Impacts of Global Warming of 1.5 °C above Pre-industrial evels and Related Global Greenhouse Gas Emission Pathways, in the Context of Strengthening the Global Response to the Threat of Climate Change, Sustainable Development, and Efforts to Eradicate Poverty," 8 October 2018, https://report.ipcc.ch/sr15/pdf/sr15_spm_final.pdf.

CHAPTER 6. **Temperature**

Epigraph: Fiona Harvey, "Sharp Rise in Arctic Temperatures Now Inevitable—UN," *Guardian*, 13 March 2019, https://www.theguardian.com/environment/2019/mar/13/arctic-temperature-rises-must-be-urgently-tackled-warns-un, referring in turn to United Nations Environment Programme, "Temperature Rise Is Now 'Locked-In' for the Coming Decades in the Arctic," http://www.grida.no/publications/431 (accessed 12 October 2019).

1. Maria Waldinger, "Drought and the French Revolution: The Effects ofAdverse Weather Conditions on Peasant Revolts in 1789" (LSE working paper, 2014), https://personal.lse.ac.uk/fleischh/Drought%20and%20the%20French%20Revolution.pdf.

2. Tekie Tesfamichael, Bonnie Jacobs, Neil Tabor, Lauren Michel, Ellen Currano, Mulugeta Feseha, Richard Barclay, John Kappelman, and Mark Schmitz, "Settling the Issue of 'Decoupling' between Atmospheric Carbon Dioxide and Global Temperature: Reconstructions across the Warming Paleogene-Neogene Divide," *Geology* 45, no. 11 (2017): 999–1002, https://doi.org/10.1130/G39048.1.

3. IPCC, "Summary for Policymakers," in *Climate Change 2007: The Physical Science Basis. Contribution of Working Group I to the Fourth Assessment Report of the Intergovernmental Panel on Climate Change*, ed. S. Solomon, D. Qin, M. Manning, Z. Chen, M. Marquis, K. B. Averyt, M. Tignor, and H. L. Miller (Cambridge: Cambridge University Press, 2007), https://www.ipcc.ch/site/assets/uploads/2018/02/ar4-wg1-spm-1.pdf.

4. "Thermometer," Science Museum, 2017, accessed 18 September 2019, http://www.sciencemuseum.org.uk/broughttolife/techniques/thermometer.

5. NASA explains that it uses "a lowess smooth, i.e. a non-parametric regression analysis that relies on a k-nearest-neighbor model. In order to evaluate the function, we use a fraction of data corresponding to a ten year window of data, giving an effective smoothing of approximately five years." *NASA Goddard Institute*, accessed 3 September 2019, https://data.giss.nasa.gov/gistemp/graphs/.

6. My colleague Myles Allan and his colleagues in the Oxford University Environmental Change Institute have produced a series available here: http://globalwarmingindex.org/ (accessed 17 September 2019), which might be less influenced by one-off events such as a volcano erupting. Another series produced by Kevin Cowtan and Robert Way is used later in this chapter as a comparison.

7. This is the first generation if we work backward from generation five, starting in 2011, the point of the final acceleration, the point at which the timeline in figure 17 begins itself to take off.

8. Other writers begin Generation X in 1964. Some suggest 1962, which was the year in which Douglas Coupland first coined the term. This is the first generation to experience slowdown for all of their adult lives.

9. Wolfgang Helmut Berger, "On the Discovery of the Ice Age: Science and Myth," in *Myth and Geology*, ed. Luigi Piccardi and W. Bruce Masse (London: Geologi-

cal Society, Special Publications, 2007), 273, 271–78, http://sp.lyellcollection.org/content/specpubgsl/273/1/271.full.pdf.

10. Jason Hickel, *The Divide: A New History of Global Inequality* (London: William Heinemann, 2017), 275, 285.

11. Walmart, "Walmart on Track to Reduce 1 Billion Metric Tons of Emissions from Global Supply Chains by 2030," 8 May 2019, https://corporate.walmart.com/newsroom/2019/05/08/walmart-on-track-to-reduce-1-billion-metric-tons-of-emissions-from-global-supply-chains-by-2030.

12. Mary Schlangenstein, "Airline Shares Reach Record as Buffett's Berkshire Extends Bet," *Bloomberg News,* 15 February 2017, https://www.bloomberg.com/news/articles/2017-02-15/airlines-rise-to-a-record-as-buffett-s-berkshire-deepens-bet.

13. The oil prices used in figure 17 were sourced from *Crude Oil Prices—70 Year Historical Chart,* accessed 10 March 2019, https://www.macrotrends.net/1369/crude-oil-price-history-chart.

14. Kevin Cowtan and Robert Way, "Coverage Bias in the HadCRUT4 Temperature Record," *Quarterly Journal of the Royal Meteorological Society,* 12 November 2013, http://www-users.york.ac.uk/~kdc3/papers/coverage2013/.

15. Quotation from the source given in the paper cited directly above by Cowtan and Way and also found here, accessed 17 September 2019, http://www-users.york.ac.uk/~kdc3/papers/coverage2013/background.html.

16. Tanya Steele, chief executive, World Wildlife Fund, quoted in Damian Carrington, "Humanity Has Wiped out 60% of Animal Populations since 1970, Report Finds," *Guardian,* 30 October 2018, https://www.theguardian.com/environment/2018/oct/30/humanity-wiped-out-animals-since-1970-major-report-finds.

CHAPTER 7. **Demographics**

Epigraph: Darrell Bricker and John Ibbitson, "What Goes Up: Are Predictions of a Population Crisis Wrong?" *Guardian,* 27 January 2019, https://www.theguardian.com/world/2019/jan/27/what-goes-up-population-crisis-wrong-fertility-rates-decline.

1. David Goodheart, "Review: *Empty Planet: The Shock of Global Population Decline* by Darrell Bricker and John Ibbitson—What a Shrinking World May Mean for Us," *Times* (London), 3 February 2019, https://www.thetimes.co.uk/magazine/culture/review-empty-planet-the-shock-of-global-population-decline-by-darrell-bricker-and-john-ibbitson-people-will-disappear-5lr726vn0.

2. Jørgen Randers, "An Update of the 2052 Global Forecast Using New Data from 2011 to 2016," *Glimpse Authors' Gathering,* Cambridge, 12 October 2016, http://www.2052.info/wp-content/uploads/2016/11/2052-Jorgen-Randers.pdf.

3. I am grateful to John McKeown for pointing out to me that for their International Institute for Applied Systems Analysis (IIASA) medium projection, Lutz et al. currently suggest a global human population peak in "2070–2080." Their DataExplorer

FAQ mentions an adjustment after publication, so it now suggests a forecast peak just after 2070: Wolfgang Lutz, Anne Goujon, K. C. Samir, Marcin Stonawski, and Nikolaos Stilianakis, *Demographic and Human Capital Scenarios for the 21st Century: 2018 Assessment for 201 Countries* (Laxenburg, Austria: IIASA, 2018), 117, https://ec.europa.eu/jrc/en/publication/demographic-and-human-capital-scenarios-21st-century-2018-assessment-201-countries.

4. John McKeown, "Part 1 of a Review of Darrell Bricker and John Ibbitson, *Empty Planet: The Shock of Global Population Decline*," *The Overpopulation Project*, 11 April 2019, https://overpopulation-project.com/review-of-empty-planet-the-shock-of-global-population-decline-by-darrell-bricker-and-john-ibbitson-part-1/.

5. Danny Dorling, "We're All . . . Just Little Bits of History Repeating (Part 1 and Part 2)," *Significance*, 13 and 14 June 2011, http://www.dannydorling.org/?page_id=2255.

6. Cheyenne Macdonald, "Will the World Run out of People? Book Claims Global Population Will Start to Decline in 30 Years Despite UN Predictions—and Says Once It Does 'It Will Never End,'" *Daily Mail*, 4 February 2019, https://wwwdailymail.co.uk/sciencetech/article-6666745/Will-world-RUN-people-Book-claims-global-population-start-decline-30-years.html.

7. "Stephen Hawking's Final Warning to Humanity," *New Zealand Herald*, 28 March 2018, https://www.nzherald.co.nz/world/news/article.cfm?c_id=2&objectid=12013139.

8. Gordon Brown (former British prime minister), quoted in Danny Dorling and Sally Tomlinson, *Rule Britannia: From Brexit to the End of Empire* (London: Biteback, 2019), 78.

9. "List of Countries by GDP (PPP)," *Wikipedia*, accessed 24 April 2019, https://en.wikipedia.org/wiki/List_of_countries_by_GDP_(PPP).

10. Simon Worrall, "When, How Did the First Americans Arrive? It's Complicated," *National Geographic*, 9 June 2018, https://news.nationalgeographic.com/2018/06/when-and-how-did-the-first-americans-arrive—its-complicated-/.

11. The World Inequality Database, *Income Inequality, USA, 1913–2014*, accessed 28 March 2019, https://wid.world/country/usa/.

12. Worldmapper, *Migration to USA 1990–2017*, https://worldmapper.org/maps/migration-to-usa-1990-2017/.

13. Dara Lind, "The Disastrous, Forgotten 1996 Law That Created Today's Immigration Problem," *Vox*, 28 April 2016, https://www.vox.com/2016/4/28/11515132/iirira-clinton-immigration.

14. Yu the Great of the much earlier Hia dynasty may have ordered the first census some two thousand years before Ping, reporting 13,553,932 or possibly, if this were the number of households, 39,220,000 people. But that might all have been made up by later Han scholars, creating history: John Durand, "The Population Statistics of China, A.D. 2–1953," *Population Studies* 13, no. 3 (March 1960): 209–256, https://www.jstor.org/stable/2172247.

15. Judith Banister, "A Brief History of China's Population," in *The Population of Modern China,* ed. D. L. Poston and D. Yaukey, The Plenum Series on Demographic Methods and Population Analysis (Boston: Springer, 1992), https://link.springer.com/chapter/10.1007/978-1-4899-1231-2_3.

16. Cao Shuji, *Zhongguo Renkou Shi* [A History of China's Population] (Shanghai: Fudan Daxue Chubanshe, 2001), 455, 509.

17. AFP (Agence France-Presse), "China's Population Growth Slows," *Guardian,* 21 January 2019, https://guardian.ng/news/chinas-population-growth-slows/.

18. Bob Yirka, "Slowdown in African Fertility Rate Linked to Disruption of Girls' Education," *Phys Org,* 5 February 2019, https://phys.org/news/2019-02-slowdown-african-fertility-linked-disruption.html.

19. Danny Dorling, *Population 10 Billion* (London: Constable, 2013), 52.

20. Gladstone spoke in Parliament on Wednesday, 8 April 1840: *The Mirror of Parliament for the Third Session of the Fourteenth Parliament of Great Britain and Ireland in the Third and Fourth Years of the Reign of Queen Victoria,* 3:2461.

21. Although the potential of solar-powered irrigation in Africa is huge. Currently, on gHa (standardized hectares) and according to Global Footprint Network, China has 1.36 billion gHa, and all the countries of Africa combined have 1.48 billion gHa (John McKeown, personal correspondence).

22. Mark Rice-Oxley and Jennifer Rankin, "Europe's South and East Worry More about Emigration Than Immigration—Poll," *Guardian,* 1 April 2019, https://www.theguardian.com/world/2019/apr/01/europe-south-and-east-worry-more-about-emigration-than-immigration-poll.

23. E. Buchanan, "'Only Connect'? Forsterian Ideology in an Age of Hyperconnectivity," *Humanist Life,* 9 April 2014, http://humanistlife.org.uk/2014/04/09/only-connect-forsteran-ideology-in-an-age-of-hyperconnectivity/.

24. The first eight accession states, which joined the EU on 1 May 2004, were the Czech Republic, Estonia, Hungary, Latvia, Lithuania, Poland, Slovakia, and Slovenia.

25. Although possibly not an actual decline as the official statistics suggest the population grew by 0.64 percent that year rather than fell: Statistics Bureau of Japan, accessed 4 April 2019, http://www.stat.go.jp/data/nenkan/65nenkan/02.html.

26. Kanae Kaku, "Increased Induced Abortion Rate in 1966, an Aspect of a Japanese Folk Superstition," *Annals of Human Biology* 2, no. 2 (1975): 111–15, https://www.ncbi.nlm.nih.gov/pubmed/1052742.

27. Kyodo News Agency, "Number of Babies Born in Japan in 2018 Lowest since Records Began; Population Decline the Highest, *Japan Times,* 21 December 2018, https://www.japantimes.co.jp/news/2018/12/21/national/number-babies-born-japan-2018-lowest-since-records-began-population-decline-highest.

28. "Timeline: Australia's Immigration Policy," *SBS News,* 3 September 2013, https://www.sbs.com.au/news/timeline-australia-s-immigration-policy.

29. For the population in the air, see Dan Satherley, "Record Number of Planes in the Air at Once," *Newshub,* 2 July 2018, https://www.newshub.co.nz/home/travel/2018/07/record-number-of-planes-in-the-air-at-once.html.

30. Clara Moskowitz, "Space Station Population Hits Record High," *Space.com,* 17 July 2009, https://www.space.com/7003-space-station-population-hits-record-high.html.

CHAPTER 8. **Fertility**

Epigraph: Helen Pearson, *The Life Project: The Extraordinary Story of Our Ordinary Lives* (London: Allen Lane, 2016), 343.

1. Lee Bell, "What Is Moore's Law? *Wired* Explains the Theory That Defined the Tech Industry, *Wired,* 26 July 2016, http://www.wired.co.uk/article/moores-law-wont-last-forever.

2. Richard Wilkinson, personal communication, June 2016, May 2019.

3. For two examples from the United States and the United Kingdom, see Danny Dorling, "It Is Necessarily So," *Significance* 10, no. 2 (2013): 37–39, http://www.dannydorling.org/?page_id=3787; and Danny Dorling, "When Racism Stopped Being Normal, but No One Noticed: Generational Value Change," in *Sex, Lies, and the Ballot Box,* ed. Philip Cowley and Robert Ford (London: Biteback, 2014), 39–42.

4. Danny Dorling and Stuart Gietel-Basten, *Why Demography Matters* (Cambridge: Polity, 2017), 33.

5. Charles Booth, *Life and Labour of the People in London,* vol. 2, *Streets and Population Classified* (London: Macmillan, 1892), available in full at https://archive.org/details/b28125125_0002/page/n7.

6. Gabriel Moran, *Uniquely Human: The Basis of Human Rights* (Bloomington, IN: Xlibris, 2013), 136.

7. William Beveridge et al., *Changes in Family Life* (London: George Allen and Unwin, 1932).

8. Stephen Lynch, "How Elevators Transformed NYC's Social Landscape," *New York Post,* 8 February 2014, http://nypost.com/2014/02/08/how-elevators-transformed-nycs-social-landscape/.

9. James C. Scott, *Against the Grain: A Deep History of the Earliest States* (New Haven: Yale University Press, 2017), 86.

10. John van Wyhe, *Darwin Online,* accessed 14 July 2019, http://darwin-online.org.uk/.

11. The word *tractor* (as opposed to traction engine) first appeared in 1896. There were many prototypes. The Ivel Agricultural Motor, invented in 1901, was the first commercially successful tractor. See "Tractor," *Wikipedia,* accessed 3 September 2019, https://en.wikipedia.org/wiki/Tractor.

12. Google Books Ngram Viewer, *Nowadays 1800–2000,* accessed 14 July 2019, https://books.google.com/ngrams/graph?content=nowadays&year_start=1800&year_end=2000&corpus=15&smoothing=3&share=&direct_url=t1%3B%2Cnowadays%3B%2Cc0.

13. Innocent Senyo, "Niger Government Secures 130 Tractors to Boost Food Production," *World Stage,* 16 May 2018, https://www.worldstagegroup.com/niger-govt -secures-130-tractors-to-boost-food-production/.

14. Max Roser, "War and Peace." *OurWorldInData.org,* 2016, https://ourworldindata .org/war-and-peace/.

15. The United States experienced only the slightest of dips in births in the years up to 1955, when twenty-five births per thousand people were recorded after adjustment for those not registered, or 4.047 million births. Robert Grove and Alice Hetzel, *Vital Statistics Rates in the United States, 1940–1960* (Washington, DC: U.S. Department of Health Education and Welfare, 1968) table 19 (p. 138), table 80 (p. 876), http://www.cdc.gov/nchs/data/vsus/vsrates1940_60.pdf.

16. Max Roser and Mohamed Nagdy, "Nuclear Weapons," *Our World in Data,* accessed 4 September 2019, https://ourworldindata.org/nuclear-weapons/#note-3. Figure 5-22 is based on Steven Pinker, *The Better Angels of Our Nature: Why Violence Has Declined* (London: Penguin, 2011).

17. Statistics New Zealand, "Sure to Rise: Tracking Bread Prices in the CPI," *Stats NZ On-line,* 2011, http://www.stats.govt.nz/browse_for_stats/economic_indicators/ prices_indexes/tracking-bread-prices-in-the-cpi.aspx.

18. The term comes from the name of a fairground ride. The world's first helter-skelter is a little older, apparently appearing at a fair in Hull in 1905, although whether that is true or not hardly matters for this particular story. It will be more interesting when none appear at a fair ever again. See "Helter-skelter," *Wikipedia,* accessed 3 September 2019, https://en.wikipedia.org/wiki/Helter_skelter_(ride).

19. Kyodo News Agency, "1 in 4 Men, 1 in 7 Women in Japan Still Unmarried at Age 50: Report," *Japan Times,* 5 April 2017, http://www.japantimes.co.jp/news/2017/04/05/ national/1-4-japanese-men-still-unmarried-age-50-report/.

20. Mizuho Aoki, "In Sexless Japan, Almost Half of Single Young Men and Women Are Virgins: Survey," *Japan Times,* 16 September 2016, http://www.japantimes.co. jp/news/2016/09/16/national/social-issues/sexless-japan-almost-half-young-men -women-virgins-survey/.

21. His book was dedicated to his son, who died at age eight: David Diamond, "James Gleick's Survival Lessons," *Wired,* 1 August 1999, https://www.wired.com/1999/08/ gleick/.

22. Nicholas Gane, "Speed Up or Slow Down? Social Theory in the Information Age," *Information, Communication & Society* 9, no. 1 (2006): 35n1.

23. Danny Dorling and Sally Tomlinson, *Rule Britannia: From Brexit to the End of Empire* (London: Biteback, 2019).

24. It may have been a little earlier in Scotland, a little later in Wales. and much later in Ireland. If you feel you can, and they were British, and you are young, then maybe ask your grandparents when it was.

25. Jonathan Austen, *Save the Earth . . . Don't Give Birth: The Story behind the Simplest, but Trickiest, Way to Help Save Our Endangered Planet* (Amazon Digital Services, 2018).

26. This quote is taken from a document I received titled "PCF Bulletin 13," which was forecasting the imminent end of the world, but also noted that the next meeting to discuss it was scheduled for 14 January 2019.

27. Claude Fischer, "Made in America: Notes on American Life from American History," *Lost Children Blog,* 1 November 2011, https://madeinamericathebook .wordpress.com/2011/11/01/lost-children/.

28. The online sources can be found at *A Vision of Britain through Time (1801 to Now),* accessed 4 September 2019, http://www.visionofbritain.org.uk/unit/10001043/ rate/INF_MORT; and Office for National Statistics, *Trends in Births and Deaths over the Last Century,* accessed 4 September 2019, https://www.ons.gov.uk/people-populationandcommunity/birthsdeathsandmarriages/livebirths/articles/trendsin birthsanddeathsoverthelastcentury/2015-07-15.

29. Danny Dorling, *Peak Inequality: Britain's Ticking Timebomb* (Bristol: Policy, 2018).

30. Danny Dorling, "Infant Mortality and Social Progress in Britain, 1905–2005," in *Infant Mortality: A Continuing Social Problem; A Volume to Mark the Centenary of the 1906 Publication of "Infant Mortality: A Social Problem" by George Newman,* ed. Eilidh Garrett, Chris Galley, Nicola Shelton, and Robert Woods (Aldershot, UK: Ashgate, 2006), 223–28, http://www.dannydorling.org/?page_id=2442.

31. Office for National Statistics, *Age and Previous Marital Status at Marriage,* Historic Series, 11 June 2014, https://www.ons.gov.uk/peoplepopulationandcommunity/ birthsdeathsandmarriages/marriagecohabitationandcivilpartnerships/datasets/ ageandpreviousmaritalstatusatmarriage.

32. Choe Sang-Hun, "Running out of Children, a South Korea School Enrolls Illiterate Grandmothers," *New York Times,* 27 April 2019, https://www.nytimes.com/2019/ 04/27/world/asia/south-korea-school-grandmothers.html.

33. James Gallagher, "'Remarkable' Decline in Fertility Rates," *BBC Health,* 9 November 2018, https://www.bbc.co.uk/news/health-46118103.

CHAPTER 9. **Economics**

Epigraph: Martin Wolf, "How Our Low Inflation World Was Made," *Financial Times,* 7 May 2019, https://www.ft.com/content/1b1e0070-709b-11e9 -bf5c-6eeb837566c5.

1. H. D. Matthews, T. L. Graham, S. Keverian, C. Lamontagne, D. Seto, and T. J. Smith, "National Contributions to Observed Global Warming," *Environmental Research Letters* 9, no. 1 (2014): 1–9, http://iopscience.iop.org/article/10.1088/1748-9326/9/1/ 014010/pdf.

2. Karl Marx, preface to the first German edition of *Das Kapital,* p. 6 of the most popular public domain edition, 1867: https://www.marxists.org/archive/marx/works/ download/pdf/Capital-Volume-I.pdf.

3. See Jared Lang, *EarthWise: A New Landscape of Globalization,* a project with Danny Dorling and Peter Taylor, accessed 18 September 2019, https://www.lboro.ac.uk/ gawc/visual/lang_atlas3.html.

4. B. R. Mitchel, *British Historical Statistics* (Cambridge: Cambridge University Press, 1994).

5. Tim Brown, "Britain Goes 114 Continuous Hours without Using Coal to Generate Electricity," *Manufacturer,* 7 May 2019, https://www.themanufacturer.com/articles/britain-goes-114-continuous-hours-without-using-coal-generate-electricity/.

6. Kevin O'Sullivan, "Ireland Goes 25 Days without Using Coal to Generate Electricity," *Irish Times,* 10 May 2019, https://www.irishtimes.com/news/environment/ireland-goes-25-days-without-using-coal-to-generate-electricity-1.3888166.

7. *Maddison Project Database,* updated by Jutta Bolt, Robert Inklaar, Herman de Jong, and Jan Luiten van Zanden, 2018, https://www.rug.nl/ggdc/historicaldevelopment/maddison/releases/maddison-project-database-2018 measure: rgdpnapc—Real GDP per capita in 2011U.S.$ (suitable for cross-country growth comparisons); 2017 data added using change from 2016 according to World Bank estimates of GDP per capita, in PPP constant 2011 international $; and 2018 data added using IMF data-mapper estimate of change between 2018 and 2019 in GDP/capita at current prices: https://www.imf.org/external/datamapper/NGDPDPC@WEO/USA/DEU/WEOWORLD.

8. Joe Romm, "We Might Have Finally Seen Peak Coal," *Think Progress Blog,* 4 January 2016, https://thinkprogress.org/we-might-have-finally-seen-peak-coal-5a3e7b15cdfc.

9. Danny Dorling, *The Equality Effect: Improving Life for Everyone* (London: New Internationalist, 2017).

10. Chris Giles, "Global Economy Enters 'Synchronised Slowdown,'" *Financial Times,* 7 April 2019, https://www.ft.com/content/d9bba980-5794-11e9-a3db-1fe89bedc16e?shareType=nongift.

11. Jeremy Grantham, "The Race of Our Lives Revisited" (GMO White Paper, London: GMO Investment Management), accessed 3 September 2019, https://falconsrockimpact.com/wp-content/uploads/2018/11/the-race-of-our-lives-revisited-2018.pdf.

12. Anna-Sapfo Malaspinas, Michael Westaway, Craig Muller, et al., "A Genomic History of Aboriginal Australia," *Nature,* 21 September 2016, https://www.nature.com/articles/nature18299.

13. Grantham, "The Race of Our Lives Revisited," 4.

14. Tom Orlik, "China's Latest Official GDP Report Is Accurate. No, Really," *Bloomberg Businessweek,* 25 January 2019, https://www.bloomberg.com/news/articles/2019-01-25/china-s-latest-official-gdp-report-is-accurate-no-really.

15. Tim Cook, "Letter from Tim Cook to Apple Investors," *Apple Press Release,* 2 January 2019, https://www.apple.com/newsroom/2019/01/letter-from-tim-cook-to-apple-investors/.

16. Tim Jackson, *Chasing Progress: Beyond Measuring Economic Growth* (London: New Economics Foundation, 2004), https://neweconomics.org/2004/03/chasing-progress.

17. George Monbiot, "Goodbye, Kind World," 10 August 2004, https://www.monbiot
.com/2004/08/10/goodbye-kind-world/.

18. Drones controlled by men sitting in the United States target people on the other side
of the planet. These weapons are used not only in war, but also in countries that are
not officially at war with the United States. During his presidency, George W. Bush
ordered 57 drone strikes in Pakistan, Somalia, and Yemen. His successor, Barack
Obama, ordered 563—including one in Yemen that erroneously killed fifty-five
civilians, including twenty-one children (ten of them under the age of five) and
twelve women, five of whom were pregnant. Jessica Purkiss and Jack Serle, "Obama's
Covert Drone War in Numbers: Ten Times More Strikes Than Bush," *Bureau of
Investigative Journalism,* 17 January 2017, https://www.thebureauinvestigates.com/
stories/2017-01-17/obamas-covert-drone-war-in-numbers-ten-times-more-strikes
-than-bush.

19. Tim Jackson, "When All Parties Want 'an Economy That Works,' You Know
Neoliberalism Is Kaput," *Guardian,* 31 May 2017, https://www.theguardian.com/
commentisfree/2017/may/31/economy-neoliberalism-free-market-economics.

20. Osea Giuntella, Sally McManus, Redzo Mujcic, Andrew Oswald, Nattavudh
Powdthavee, and Ahmed Tohamy, "Why Is There So Much Midlife Distress in
Affluent Nations?" preprint (personal correspondence).

21. For what it is worth, my advice on that front is: become a parent. You will be so tired
out you will never have trouble sleeping—if indeed you are ever undisturbed again.
If that fails, write books until you are exhausted.

22. Danny Dorling, *Inequality and the 1%,* 3rd ed. (London: Verso, 2019).

23. Jenni Karjalainen, "Teaching Old Dogs New Tricks," in *Work in the Digital Age:
Challenges of the Fourth Industrial Revolution,* ed. Max Neufeind, Jacqueline
O'Reilly, and Florian Ranft (New York: Rowman and Littlefield, 2018), 286-94,
https://policynetwork.org/wp-content/uploads/2018/06/Work-in-the-Digital-Age
.pdf.

24. Anna Ilsøe, "Progressing the Voluntarist Approach," in Neufeind, O'Reilly, and
Ranft, *Work in the Digital Age,* 286.

25. "Global Unemployment Down, but Too Many Working Poor: UN," *New Straits
Times,* 13 February 2019, https://www.nst.com.my/world/2019/02/459969/global
-unemployment-down-too-many-working-poor-un. *New Straits Times* is Malaysia's
oldest English-language politics and business newspaper.

26. *Nationwide House Price Index,* accessed 6 May 2019, https://www.nationwide.co.uk/
-/media/MainSite/documents/about/house-price-index/downloads/uk-house-price
-since-1952.xls.

27. Dan McCrum, "Affordability Backwards," *Financial Times,* 19 February 2004, https://
ftalphaville.ft.com/2014/02/19/1776182/affordability-backwards/.

28. Becky Tunstall, "Relative Housing Space Inequality in England and Wales, and Its
Recent Rapid Resurgence," *International Journal of Housing Policy* 15, no. 2 (2015):
105–26, http://www.tandfonline.com/doi/full/10.1080/14616718.2014.984826.

29. "Gold Supply and Demand Statistics," *World Gold Council,* accessed 6 May 2019, https://www.gold.org/goldhub/data/gold-supply-and-demand-statistics.

30. Robert Shiller, "Speculative Prices and Popular Models," *Journal of Economic Perspectives* 4, no. 2 (1990): 59, http://www.jstor.org/stable/1942890. Note: Case and Shiller worked together for decades, but this paper was written by Shiller alone.

31. John Muellbauer and Anthony Murphy, "Booms and Busts in the UK Housing Market," *Economic Journal* 107, no. 445 (1997): 1701–27, http://onlinelibrary.wiley.com/doi/10.1111/j.1468-0297.1997.tb00076.x/full.

32. Mervyn King, "An Econometric Model of Tenure Choice and Demand for Housing as a Joint Decision," *Journal of Public Economics* 14, no. 2 (1980): 137–59, https://doi.org/10.1016/0047-2727(80)90038-9.

33. James Poterba, David Weil, and Robert Shiller, "House Price Dynamics: The Role of Tax Policy and Demography," *Brookings Papers on Economic Activity,* no. 2 (1991): 183, http://www.jstor.org/stable/2534591.

34. Bruce Ambrose, Piet Eichholtz, and Thies Lindenthal, "House Prices and Fundamentals: 355 Years of Evidence," *Journal of Money, Credit and Banking* 45, nos. 2–3 (2013): 477–91, http://onlinelibrary.wiley.com/doi/10.1111/jmcb.12011/full.

35. Matthew Drennan, "Income Inequality: Not Your Usual Suspect in Understanding the Financial Crash and Great Recession," *Theoretical Inquiries in Law* 18, no. 1 (2017): 97, https://www.degruyter.com/view/j/til.2017.18.issue-1/til-2017-0006/til-2017-0006.xml.

36. In 1997 ViewSonic, IBM, and Apple all introduced the first color liquid crystal display (LCD) monitors. We have been using much the same ever since then, as we technologically slow down. Benj Edwards, "The Evolution of Computer Displays," Vintage Computing and Gaming, 17 September 2019, http://www.vintagecomputing.com/index.php/archives/2580/vcg-anthology-the-evolution-of-computer-displays.

37. William Miles, "Home Prices and Global Imbalances: Which Drives Which?" *International Review for Social Sciences* 72, no. 1 (2018): 55–75, https://onlinelibrary.wiley.com/doi/full/10.1111/kykl.12191.

38. Zhang Qun, Didier Sornette, and Hao Zhang, "Anticipating Critical Transitions of Chinese Housing Markets," *Swiss Finance Institute Research Paper,* nos. 17–18 (May 2017), https://ssrn.com/abstract=2969801; or http://dx.doi.org/10.2139/ssrn.2969801

39. Dayong Zhang, Ziyin Liu, Gang-Shi Fan, and Nicholas Horsewood, "Price Bubbles and Policy Interventions in the Chinese Housing Market," *Journal of Housing and the Built Environment* 32 (2017): 133–55, doi:10.1007/s10901-016-9505-6.

40. Francisco Becerril, "The Sign of China's 'Rebound' May Be a Housing Bubble," *Financial Times,* 25 April 2019, https://www.ft.com/content/71d237aa-6520-11e9-9adc-98bf1d35a056.

41. International Labour Organisation, *Global Wage Report 2018/19: What Lies behind Gender Pay Gaps* (Geneva: International Labour Office, 2018), https://www.ilo.org/

wcmsp5/groups/public/---dgreports/---dcomm/---publ/documents/publication/
wcms_650553.pdf.

42. Bruce Knuteson, "How to Increase Global Wealth Inequality for Fun and Profit,"
    Social Science Research Network, 12 November 2018, https://papers.ssrn.com/sol3/
    papers.cfm?abstract_id=3282845; or https://dx.doi.org/10.2139/ssrn.3282845.

43. Ibid., n. 15. Please note—I cannot vouch for Bruce's advice (but you are unlikely to
    have billions of dollars to invest!): https://www.bruceknuteson.com/.

44. Trickle Down was a minor deity in the pantheon of the Capitalist religion. There
    were many who doubted she really existed, even at the height of her popularity
    in the early 1980s. Profit was the dominant male god of Capitalism. See Michael
    Wright and Carolin Herron, "Trickle-Down Theory Revisited and Explained," *New
    York Times,* 8 May 1983, https://www.nytimes.com/1983/05/08/weekinreview/the
    -nation-trickle-down-theory-revisited-and-explained.html.

CHAPTER 10 **Geopolitics**

Epigraph: E. M. Forster, "The Machine Stops," *Oxford and Cambridge Review,*
November 1909, http://archive.ncsa.illinois.edu/prajlich/forster.html.

1. The dates are arbitrary: 1837 was when several patents by rival inventors of the
   telegraph were filed and the first working system was used, but forms of it had been
   created earlier, and 1974 is when the word *Internet* was first used in documents on
   networking protocols. Vinton Cerf, Yogen Dalal, and Carl Sunshine, *Specification of
   Internet Transmission Control Program,* December 1974, Network Working Group,
   Request for Comments 65 (RFC65), https://tools.ietf.org/html/rfc675.

2. Most often cited as among these politicians and business elites are Ron Paul, Paul
   Ryan, and Peter Theil. But even Jimmy Wales, the founder of Wikipedia, is listed as
   having been interested in Rand. Not all information on Wikipedia is reliable information! "List of People Influenced by Ayn Rand," *Wikipedia,* accessed 2 July 2019,
   https://en.wikipedia.org/wiki/List_of_people_influenced_by_Ayn_Rand.

3. René Descartes, "Letter to Balzac," 5 May 1631, in *Selected Correspondence,* 22,
   http://www.earlymoderntexts.com/assets/pdfs/descartes1619_1.pdf.

4. W. Scheuerman, W., *Liberal Democracy and the Social Acceleration of Time* (Baltimore: Johns Hopkins University Press, 2004), 5.

5. Qiujie Shi and Danny Dorling, "Growing Socio-Spatial Inequality in Neo-liberal
   Times: Comparing Beijing and London," *Applied Geography,* forthcoming.

6. R. Smith, "London Holds off New York to Keep Its Title as the World's Number
   One Financial Centre Despite Brexit Uncertainty," *City AM,* 27 March 2017, http://
   www.cityam.com/261819/london-holds-off-new-york-keep-its-top-spot-worlds
   -number.

7. Produced by the same group: Z/Yen Group, *The Global Financial Centres Index 25,*
   March 2019, https://www.zyen.com/publications/public-reports/the-global-financial
   -centres-index-25/.

8. Jason Burke, "Kenya Burial Site Shows Community Spirit of Herders 5,000 Years Ago," *Guardian,* 20 August 2018, https://www.theguardian.com/science/2018/aug/20/kenya-burial-site-shows-community-spirit-of-herders-5000-years-ago.

9. Omar Khan et al., "A Brief Introduction to the Ancient Indus Civilization," *Harappa Blog,* 2017, https://www.harappa.com/har/indus-saraswati.html.

10. John Keane, *The Life & Death of Democracy* (London: Simon and Schuster, 2009), 1933. Keane explains that these republics recognized that "'although people were not angels or gods or goddesses, they were at least good enough to prevent some from thinking they were. Democracy was to be government of the humble, by the humble, for the humble."

11. "History of Democracy," *Wikipedia,* accessed 17 June 2019, https://en.wikipedia.org/wiki/History_of_democracy.

12. Jeremy Cushing, "Peace and Equality in the Bronze Age: The Evidence from Dartmoor Suggests That War and Rich Elites Were Unknown More Than 3,000 Years Ago," *Guardian,* 24 August 2018, https://www.theguardian.com/science/2018/aug/24/peace-and-equality-in-the-bronze-age.

13. F. H. King, *Farmers of Forty Centuries: Organic Farming in China, Korea, and Japan* (1911; repr., Mineola, NY: Dover, 2004).

14. Bill Gates, "My New Favorite Book of All Time," *Gates Notes Blog,* 26 January 2018, https://www.gatesnotes.com/Books/Enlightenment-Now .

15. Jeremy Lent, "Steven Pinker's Ideas about Progress Are Fatally Flawed. These Eight Graphs Show Why," *Patterns of Meaning,* 17 May 2018, https://patternsofmeaning.com/2018/05/17/steven-pinkers-ideas-about-progress-are-fatally-flawed-these-eight-graphs-show-why/.

16. "Meaning of *feitorias* (Portuguese)," *Wiktionary,* accessed 3 July 2019, https://en.wiktionary.org/wiki/feitoria#Portuguese.

17. Danny Dorling, *Injustice: Why Social Inequality Still Persists,* rev. ed. (Bristol: Policy, 2015), 18.

18. Timothy Hatton and Bernice E. Bray, "Long Run Trends in the Heights of European Men, 19th–20th Centuries," *Economics and Human Biology* 8 (2010): 405–13.

19. Timothy Hatton, "How Have Europeans Grown So Tall?" *Oxford Economic Papers* 66 (2014): 353 (table 2).

20. Mary Bells, "The History of Vacuum Cleaners," *The Inventors* (part of the *New York Times*), 2006, http://theinventors.org/library/inventors/blvacuum.htm: "Hubert Cecil Booth, a British engineer, received a British patent for a vacuum cleaner on August 30th 1901 and took the form of a large, horse-drawn, petrol-driven unit which was parked outside the building to be cleaned with long hoses being fed through the windows. As Hubert Booth demonstrated his vacuuming device in a restaurant in 1901, two Americans introduced variations on the same theme. Corinne Dufour invented a device that sucked dust into a wet sponge. David E. Kenney's huge machine was installed in the cellar and connected to a network of

pipes leading to each room in the house. A corps of cleaners moved the machine from house to house."

21. "Activated Sludge—100 Years and Counting," *International Water Association Conference*, June 2014, Essen, Germany, http://www.iwa100as.org/history.php.

22. Max Roser, "Human Height," *OurWorldInData.org*, 2016, https://ourworldindata.org/human-height/.

23. Lisa Trahan, Karla Stuebing, Merril Hiscock, and Jack Fletcher, "The Flynn Effect: A Meta-analysis," *Psychological Bulletin* 140, no. 5 (2014): 1332–60, https://www.ncbi.nlm.nih.gov/pmc/articles/PMC4152423/.

24. Ariane de Gayardon, Claire Callender, KC Deane, and Stephen DesJardins, "Graduate Indebtedness: Its Perceived Effects on Behaviour and Life Choices—A Literature Review" (working paper no. 38, Centre for Global Higher Education, June 2018), https://www.researchcghe.org/publications/working-paper/graduate-indebtedness-its-perceived-effects-on-behaviour-and-life-choices-a-literature-review/.

25. Hannah Devlin, "IVF Couples Could Be Able to Choose the 'Smartest' Embryo: US Scientist Says It Will Be Possible to Rank Embryos by 'Potential IQ' within 10 years," *Guardian*, 24 May 2019, https://www.theguardian.com/society/2019/may/24/ivf-couples-could-be-able-to-choose-the-smartest-embryo.

26. Tim Morris, Neil Davies, and George Davey Smith, "Can Education be Personalized Using Pupils' Genetic Data?" Preprint, 2019, https://doi.org/10.1101/645218. "Across our sample children's polygenic scores predicted their educational outcomes almost as well as parent's socioeconomic position or education. There was high overlap between the polygenic score and attainment distributions, leading to weak predictive accuracy at the individual level. Furthermore, conditional on prior attainment the polygenic score was not predictive of later attainment. Our results suggest that polygenic scores are informative for identifying group level differences, but they currently have limited use in predicting individual attainment."

27. Tim T. Morris, Danny Dorling, Neil M. Davies, and George Davey Smith, "School Enjoyment at Age 6 Predicts Later Educational Achievement as Strongly as Socioeconomic Background and Gender," at https://osf.io/preprints/socarxiv/e6c37/.

28. Hartmut Rosa and William Scheuerman, eds., *High-Speed Society: Social Acceleration, Power, and Modernity* (Philadelphia: Pennsylvania State University Press, 2008), http://www.psupress.org/books/titles/978-0-271-03416-4.html. In making this claim, the authors referenced an article (Peter Wollen, "Speed and the Cinema," *New Left Review* 16 [July/August 2002], https://newleftreview.org/II/16/peter-wollen-speed-and-the-cinema) that discussed how short shot lengths were and how they have shortened over time, but that article's research showed that they do not even halve, let alone reduce by a factor of fifty or more.

29. Greg Miller, "A Century of Cinema Reveals How Movies Have Evolved," *Wired*, 9 August 2014, https://www.wired.com/2014/09/cinema-is-evolving/.

30. The second claim made in Rosa and Scheuerman's book to support their thesis that so much was still accelerating so very quickly was the fact that the speed at which

speeches were being given in the Norwegian parliament has increased by 50 percent since 1945. It might well have done, but pithier speeches may have just become more fashionable, and longer-winded ones less tolerated. However, the very fact that a book on acceleration has to jump from vastly exaggerated claims over the acceleration rate of the cutting from shot to shot in films, straight through to even more obscure details of the verbal dexterity of Norwegian politicians, does rather suggest that back in 2008, when this book was published, and in the years immediately prior to that (when it was being written), it was becoming increasingly difficult to find evidence of acceleration.

31. Numerous surveys of sexual partnerships are conducted around the world, many introduced to try to monitor the spread of AIDS. They usually show no rise over time, often a fall, and at the extreme the rising Japanese *hikikomori* phenomenon of young adults who interact little with others. Fewer people now get married in the first place and so serial divorcing in places like the United States peaked some time ago (people on their third, fourth, or fifth marriage). There was always a practical limit to the marriage rate peak. Given that people have fewer sexual partners now than in the past, and that fewer also get married, the number of affairs can only increase if the dwindling numbers having them are becoming both ever more active, speeding up their dalliances even faster than the rising global rate of hikikomori.

32. For understanding the cabaret, see Christopher Isherwood, *Goodbye to Berlin* (London: Hogarth, 1939).

33. Office for National Statistics, *Changing Trends in Mortality: An International Comparison, 2000 to 2016*, figures 1 and 2, 7 August 2018, https://www.ons.gov .uk/peoplepopulationandcommunity/birthsdeathsandmarriages/lifeexpectancies/ articles/changingtrendsinmortalityaninternationalcomparison/2000to2016.

34. Most famously, George Edgerly Harris III was photographed outside the Pentagon putting a flower in a gun barrel in 1967. See "Be the Flower in the Gun: The Story behind the Historic Photograph 'Flower Power' in 1967," *Vintage Everyday*, 11 September 2017, https://www.vintag.es/2017/09/be-flower-in-gun-story-behind -historic.html.

35. Anna Lührmann and Staffan I. Lindberg, "A Third Wave of Autocratization Is Here: What Is New about It?" *Democratization*, 1 March 2019, doi:10.1080/13510347.2019 .1582029.

36. Its leader "stood alongside literal piss-artists"; one "candidate from the party is a pro-bono artist who makes his art by peeing in public. He has a conviction for peeing in public as the court didn't see the art in it." Daniel Boffey, "Danish Far-Right Party Calling for Muslim Deportation to Stand in Election," *Guardian*, 5 May 2019, https://www.theguardian.com/world/2019/may/05/danish-far-right-party-stram -kurs-calling-for-muslim-deportation-to-stand-in-election.

37. Sithembile Mbete, "The Economic Freedom Fighters—South Africa's Turn towards Populism?" *Journal of African Elections* 14, no. 1 (2015): 35–39, https://repository.up .ac.za/handle/2263/51821.

38. Paul Beaumont, "Brexit, Retrotopia and the Perils of Post-colonial Delusions," *Global Affairs,* 26 June 2018, 379–90, doi:10.1080/23340460.2018.1478674, https://www.tandfonline.com/doi/abs/10.1080/23340460.2018.1478674.

39. Danny Dorling and Sally Tomlinson, *Rule Britannia: From Brexit to the End of Empire* (London, Biteback, 2019).

40. Pål Røren and Paul Beaumont, "Grading Greatness: Evaluating the Status Performance of the BRICS," *Third World Quarterly* 40, no. 3 (2018): 429–50, https://www.researchgate.net/publication/329373842_Grading_greatness_evaluating_the_status_performance_of_the_BRICS/link/5c42f22d92851c22a3800547/download.

41. Eli Zaretsky, "The Mass Psychology of Brexit," *London Review of Books Blog,* 26 March 2019, https://www.lrb.co.uk/blog/2019/march/the-mass-psychology-of-brexit.

42. As reported in England in 2019, the highest child poverty rates were as follows: Tower Hamlets—56.7 percent, Newham—51.8 percent, Hackney—48.1 percent, Islington—47.5 percent, Blackburn with Darwen—46.9 percent, Westminster—46.2 percent, Luton—45.7 percent, Manchester—45.4 percent, Pendle—44.7 percent, Peterborough—43.8 percent, Camden—43.5 percent, Sandwell—43.2 percent. See "Child Poverty Is Becoming the New Normal in Parts of Britain," *End Child Poverty,* 15 May 2019, https://www.endchildpoverty.org.uk/chid-poverty-is-becoming-the-new-normal-in-parts-of-britain/.

43. Kathryn Torney, "The Religious Divide in Northern Ireland's Schools," *Guardian Datablog,* 24 November 2012, https://www.theguardian.com/news/datablog/2012/nov/24/religious-divide-northern-ireland-schools.

44. Toby Helm and Michael Savage, "Poll Surge for Farage Sparks Panic among Tories and Labour," *Observer,* 11 May 2019, https://www.theguardian.com/politics/2019/may/11/poll-surge-for-farage-panic-conservatives-and-labour?CMP=Share_iOSApp_Other.

45. Across the new 2019 European Parliament as a whole, the Mainstream Conservatives (EPP) won 179 seats; the Socialists (PES) won 152 seats; the Liberals (ALDE) won 110 seats; the Greens (EGP and EFA) won 76 seats, and the far right splintered. Two UKIP and one Democratic Unionist MEP joined a small group of "Non-Inscrits" (nonattached members)—mainly right-wing extremists, including the fascist Golden Dawn of Greece and Hungary's fascist Jobbik Party. The Conservative MEPs, now reduced to just 4, joined a group called ECR, which is dominated by the Polish extreme-right Law and Justice Party.

46. Keir Milburn, "Acid Corbynism Is a Gateway Drug," *Red Pepper,* 10 November 2017, http://www.redpepper.org.uk/acid-corbynism-is-a-gateway-drug/.

47. Erle C. Ellis, "Science Alone Won't Save the Earth. People Have to Do That: We Need to Start Talking about What Kind of Planet We Want to Live On," *New York Times,* 11 August 2018, https://www.nytimes.com/2018/08/11/opinion/sunday/science-people-environment-earth.html.

48. Danny Dorling, *The Equality Effect: Improving life for Everyone* (Oxford: New Internationalist, 2016).

49. In fact, they confirmed the slowdown was accelerating, but that is not essential here—it was predictable.

50. Just under 150 years ago, Charles Darwin could describe black people and the first inhabitants of Australia as "low," and intimate that they were uncomfortably close to gorillas. Darwin also thought that humans were about to evolve and there would be even more civilized ones than "the Caucasian." He had little idea of just how uncivilized Caucasians were or that the speed of evolution was not that fast. Lumbering old Darwin was about as good as it got, and he was often far from good, and often far from all-knowing. In his early sixties, having had a lifetime to think about it, he wrote: "At some future period, not very distant as measured by centuries, the civilised races of man will almost certainly exterminate and replace throughout the world the savage races. At the same time the anthropomorphous apes, as Professor Schaaffhausen has remarked, will no doubt be exterminated. The break will then be rendered wider, for it will intervene between man in a more civilised state, as we may hope, than the Caucasian, and some ape as low as a baboon, instead of as at present between the negro or Australian and the gorilla." Charles Darwin, *The Descent of Man, and Selection in Relation to Sex* (London: John Murray, 1871), 2:201, http://darwin-online.org.uk/content/frameset?pageseq=1&itemID=F937.1& viewtype=text.

51. Greta Thunberg, *No One Is Too Small to Make a Difference* (London: Penguin, 2019).

CHAPTER 11. **Life**

Epigraph: Quoted in Mark O'Brien and Paul Kyprianou, *Just Managing: What It Means for the Families of Austerity Britain* (Cambridge: Open Book, 2017), 187.

1. Greg Clark, "One Giant Leap: Vertical Launch Spaceport to Bring UK into New Space Age," press release, Department for Transport, U.K. Space Agency, Civil Aviation Authority, Department for Business, Energy & Industrial Strategy, Office of the Secretary of State for Wales, 15 July 2018, https://www.gov.uk/ government/news/one-giant-leap-vertical-launch-spaceport-to-bring-uk-into-new -space-age.

2. Air travel is very unlikely to be replaced by significant future space travel, although it could be slowly replaced by the "slow float to China": mass unpolluting future travel in solar-powered helium-filled zeppelins making their way on the trade winds from the United States and Europe eastward and then back across the Pacific or down to India, Africa, and across to South America and then, perhaps, Australia— but all quite slowly.

3. Leslie White, *The Science of Culture: A Study of Man and Civilization,* part 3, *Energy and Civilization* (New York: Grove, 1949).

4. Richard Wilkinson, *Poverty and Progress: An Ecological Model of Economic Development* (London: Methuen, 1983), 18.

5. William Scheuerman, *Liberal Democracy and the Social Acceleration of Time* (Baltimore: Johns Hopkins University Press, 2004), xiii.

6. "China's Slowing Pains: After Three Decades of Strong Growth, the World's Second-Largest Economy Has Been Slowing Down," *Financial Times* article series, written in 2018 and 2019, collected at https://www.ft.com/content/9903d7e2-5c43-11e9-939a-341f5ada9d40.

7. Alain Badiou, *The True Life*, trans. Susan Spitzer (Cambridge: Polity, 2017), 41.

8. Stefan Kühn et al., *World Employment and Social Outlook* (Geneva: ILO, 2018), https://www.ilo.org/global/about-the-ilo/newsroom/news/WCMS_615590/lang—en/index.htm.

9. Cyril Ramaphosa and Stefan Löfven, *Global Commission on the Future of Work* (Geneva: ILO, 2019), https://www.ilo.org/global/about-the-ilo/newsroom/news/WCMS_663006/lang—en/index.htm.

10. Steven Kapsos (head of the ILO's Data Production and Analysis Unit), *Just 10 Per Cent of Workers Receive Nearly Half of Global Pay* (Geneva: ILO, 2019), https://www.ilo.org/global/about-the-ilo/newsroom/news/WCMS_712234/lang—en/index.htm.

11. F. Engels, preface to the third German edition of *Das Kapital* (1867), p. 17 of the most popular public domain edition: https://www.marxists.org/archive/marx/works/download/pdf/Capital-Volume-I.pdf.

12. Isabel Sawhill and Christopher Pulliam, *Six Facts about Wealth in the United States*, Middle Class Memo Series, Brooking Institute, 25 June 2019, https://www.brookings.edu/blog/up-front/2019/06/25/six-facts-about-wealth-in-the-united-states/.

13. Robert Gordon, "Is US Economic Growth Over? Faltering Innovation Confronts the Six Headwinds," *Centre for Economic Research Policy Insight*, no. 6 (September 2012), https://cepr.org/sites/default/files/policy_insights/PolicyInsight63.pdf.

14. Danny Dorling, *Do We Need Economic Inequality?* (Cambridge: Polity, 2018), 130 (figure 8.1), http://www.dannydorling.org/books/economicinequality/figures-and-tables/figure-8-1.html.

15. Darrell Bricker and John Ibbitson, *Empty Planet: The Shock of Global Population Decline* (London: Robinson, 2019), 156.

16. Ian Goldin, Pantelis Koutroumpis, François Lafond, Nils Rochowicz, and Julian Winkler, "Why Is Productivity Slowing Down?" (working paper, Oxford Martin, 17 September 2018), https://www.oxfordmartin.ox.ac.uk/downloads/academic/201809_ProductivityParadox.pdf.

17. François Lafond and Daniel Kim, "Long-Run Dynamics of the U.S. Patent Classification System," *Journal of Evolutionary Economics* 29, no. 2 (April 2019): 631–44 (see figure 1), https://link.springer.com/article/10.1007%2Fs00191-018-0603-3.

18. Carolyn Cummins, "'Levels Not Seen since the GFC': NAB Calls the Retail Recession," *Sydney Morning Herald*, 14 June 2019, https://www.smh.com.au/business/

companies/levels-not-seen-since-the-gfc-nab-calls-the-retail-recession-20190613
-p51xbr.html.

19. "UK Rich Increase Their Wealth by £274 billion over Five Years," *The Equality Trust,*
13 May 2018, https://www.equalitytrust.org.uk/wealth-tracker-18.

20. "A Nation of Ferraris and Foodbanks—UK Rich Increase Wealth by £253 Billion
over Five Years," *The Equality Trust,* 12 May 2019, https://www.equalitytrust.org.uk/
nation-ferraris-and-foodbanks-uk-rich-increase-wealth-%C2%A3253-billion-over
-five-years-0.

21. Danny Dorling, *Peak Inequality: Britain's Ticking Timebomb* (Bristol: Policy, 2018).

22. Original quotation from Charlton Heston (1923–2008), playing astronaut Colonel
Taylor. "Maybe hope is a useful sentiment. After New York Magazine published an
article describing the incontrovertible deadliness of oncoming climate change—including horrific possibilities like dead oceans, cognitive decline from increased carbon dioxide and entire continents made nearly uninhabitable by temperatures too
high for the human body to counteract—waves of responses decried its irresponsi-
bility, claiming alarmism will lead to defeatism, as people become convinced there's
no altering course": Andrew Whalen, "'Planet of the Apes' Ending Is the Antidote to
Aggressively Hopeful Blockbusters," *Newsweek,* 3 April 2018, https://www.newsweek
.com/planet-apes-1968-ending-explained-50th-anniversary-870672.

23. United Nations, press release of 6 May 2019, "UN Report: Nature's Dangerous Decline 'Unprecedented'; Species Extinction Rates 'Accelerating,'" *Sustainable Development Goals,* accessed 23 June 2019, https://www.un.org/sustainabledevelopment/
blog/2019/05/nature-decline-unprecedented-report/.

24. World Wildlife Fund, *2018 Living Planet Report,* accessed 23 June 2019, http://
livingplanetindex.org/projects?main_page_project=LivingPlanetReport&home_flag
=1. For the Living Planet Index database reports on particular habitats, see http://
livingplanetindex.org/projects?main_page_project=AboutTheIndex&home_flag=1
(accessed 4 September 2019).

25. International Union for Conservation of Nature (IUCN), "Table 9: Possibly Extinct
Species," *Red List Summary Statistics,* accessed 23 June 2019, https://www.iucnredlist
.org/resources/summary-statistics.

26. Fred Liles was a long-serving member of the Independent Labour Party, which was
first formed in Bradford and later became the British Labour Party. Martin Crick,
"The Bradford Branch of the Social-Democratic Federation," *Bradford Antiquary, the
Journal of the Bradford Historical and Antiquarian Society,* 3rd ser., 5 (1991): 24–40,
http://www.bradfordhistorical.org.uk/oddities.html.

27. Explanation of the work of Gina Bridgeland and Bob Jones, who saved the banner
from being lost in the 1980s: "Banner of the East Bradford Socialist Sunday School,"
Working Class Movement Library, accessed 23 June 2019, https://www.wcml.org.uk/
our-collections/creativity-and-culture/leisure/socialist-sunday-schools/banner-of
-the-bradford-socialist-sunday-school/.

28. Anders Sandberg, "The Five Biggest Threats to Human Existence," *The Conversation*, 29 May 2014, https://theconversation.com/the-five-biggest-threats-to-human-existence-27053.

29. Anders Sandberg, "Will Climate Change Cause Humans to Go Extinct?" *The Conversation*, 29 May 2019, https://theconversation.com/will-climate-change-cause-humans-to-go-extinct-117691.

30. David Wallace Wells, *The Uninhabitable Earth: A Story of the Future* (London: Allen Lane, 2019), 4.

31. Torbjörn Säterberg, Stefan Sellman, and Bo Ebenman, "High Frequency of Functional Extinctions in Ecological Networks," *Nature*, 7 July 2013, 468–70, https://www.nature.com/articles/nature12277.

32. It is hard to know what is worth preserving and what you might think is worth preserving but which is already an almost entirely transformed landscape, fauna and flora. On the *What Is Missing* website, one personal entry on Oxfordshire concerns a nature reserve on the edge of an estate where I lived from the age of six to eighteen. The nature reserve itself is being preserved and under no threat. The woods around it are artificial, long ago planted for a king's hunting pleasure. It is now bereft of almost all its indigenous wildlife, although the fungi does well. The entry reads: "Personal Memory—Oxfordshire, UK: On a visit to England in the summer of 2017, I was given the opportunity to visit the home of Clive Staples Lewis, one of my favorite authors. Surrounding his home, there is a substantial section of forest that was part of his property when he was alive. I was told that an organization is currently attempting to acquire this land with the goal of building a large apartment complex there. The historical significance of the land is certainly one thing, but in addition, I was concerned for the wildlife upon hearing this. Many say that those woods, with their muddy forest floor, unkempt pond, and fungi growing everywhere, are not beautiful. But I would disagree, for I think that all nature is beautiful." It may all be beautiful, but some parts of it are far more valuable than others. See https://whatismissing.net/memory/forgotten-beauty (accessed 4 September 2019).

33. Amanda Goodall and Andrew Oswald, "Researchers Obsessed with FT Journals List Are Failing to Tackle Today's Problems," *Financial Times*, 8 May 2019, https://www.ft.com/content/b820d6f2-7016-11e9-bf5c-6eeb837566c5.

34. Paul Chatterton, "The Climate Emergency and the New Civic Role for the University: As We Face a Climate Emergency, Universities Must Undergo Radical Change to Lead the Way in Tackling the Crisis," *Times Higher Education*, 21 June 2019, https://www.timeshighereducation.com/blog/climate-emergency-and-new-civic-role-university.

35. Vasilis Dakos, Marten Scheffer, Egbert van Nes, Victor Brovkin, Vladimir Petoukhov, and Hermann Held, "Slowing Down as an Early Warning Signal for Abrupt Climate Change," *Proceedings of the National Academy of Sciences* 105, no. 38 (23 September 2008): 14308–12, doi: 10.1073/pnas.0802430105.

36. Vasilis Dakos, Egbert van Nes, Raul Donangelo, Hugo Fort, and Marten Scheffer,

"Spatial Correlation as Leading Indicator of Catastrophic Shifts," *Theoretical Ecology* 3, no. 3 (August 2010): 163–74, doi:10.1007/s12080-009-0060-6; Marten Scheffer, Jordi Bascompte, William Brock, Victor Brovkin, Stephen Carpenter, Vasilis Dakos, Hermann Held, Egbert van Nes, Max Rietkerk, and George Sugihara, "Early-Warning Signals for Critical Transitions," *Nature*, 3 September 2009, 53–39, https://www.nature.com/articles/nature08227.

37. Erle Ellis, "Science Alone Won't Save the Earth. People Have to Do That: We Need to Start Talking about What Kind of Planet We Want to Live On," *New York Times*, 11 August 2018, https://www.nytimes.com/2018/08/11/opinion/sunday/science-people-environment-earth.html.

38. Global Carbon Project, "Global CO2 Emissions Rise Again in 2018 According to Latest Data," press release, *COP24: 24th Conference of the Parties to the United Nations Framework Convention on Climate Change (UNFCCC)*, 5 December 2018, http://www.globalcarbonproject.org/carbonbudget/18/files/Norway_CICERO_GCPBudget2018.pdf.

39. United Nations press release, "9.7 Billion on Earth by 2050, but Growth Rate Slowing, Says New UN Population Report," *UN News*, 17 June 2019, https://news.un.org/en/story/2019/06/1040621.

40. OCED Social Policy Division, Directorate of Employment, Labour and Social Affairs, PF 2.5 Annex: "Detail of Change in Parental Leave by Country," *OECD Family Database*, 26 October 2017, https://www.oecd.org/els/family/PF2_5_Trends_in_leave_entitlements_around_childbirth_annex.pdf.

41. See Danny Dorling and Annika Kolionen, *Finntopia: What We Can Learn from the World's Happiest Country* (New York: Agenda, 2020).

42. Tony Lawson, "A Speeding Up of the Rate of Social Change? Power, Technology, Resistance, Globalisation and the Good Society," in *Late Modernity: Trajectories towards Morphogenic Society*, ed. Margaret Archer (Cham, Switzerland: Springer, 2014), doi:10.1007/978-3-319-03266-5__2; http://www.springer.com/cda/content/document/cda_downloaddocument/9783319032658-c2.pdf?SGWID=0-0-45-1490820-p176345324.

43. Thomas Rudel and Linda Hooper, "Is the Pace of Social Change Accelerating? Late-comers, Common Languages, and Rapid Historical Declines in Fertility," *International Journal of Comparative Sociology*, 1 August 2005, http://citeseerx.ist.psu.edu/viewdoc/download?doi=10.1.1.1013.4276&rep=rep1&type=pdf. See also Chapter 2 of this book.

44. William J. Goode, "The Theory and Measurement of Family Change," in *Indicators of Social Change: Concepts and Measurements*, ed. Eleanor Bernert Sheldon and Wilbert Moore (Hartford, CT: Russell Sage Foundation, 1968), 337.

45. Jamie Ducharme, "It May Not Be a Bad Thing Fewer U.S. Babies Were Born in 2018 Than in Any Year since 1986," *Time*, 15 May 2019, http://time.com/5588610/us-birth-rates-record-low/.

CHAPTER 12. **People**

Epigraph: Robin Wigglesworth, "Japanification: Investors Fear Malaise Is Spreading Globally, *Financial Times,* 27 August 2019, https://www.ft.com/content/314c626a-c77b-11e9-a1f4-3669401ba76f.

1. Hephzibah Anderson, "The 1968 Sci-Fi That Spookily Predicted Today," *BBC Culture,* 10 May 2019, http://www.bbc.com/culture/story/20190509-the-1968-sci-fi-that-spookily-predicted-today.

2. James Fulcher and John Scott, *Sociology* (Oxford: Oxford University Press, 2011), 273.

3. Calculations made by the author using figures from Angus Maddison and the UN. In 1901 global annual population growth was 1.029 percent. It peaked at 2.128 percent in 1971. Growth's fall may be more rapid than its rise.

4. Helen Pearson, *The Life Project: The Extraordinary Story of Our Ordinary Lives* (London: Allen Lane, 2016), 348.

5. Richard Clegg, *Graduates in the UK Labour Market: 2017* (London: Office for National Statistics, 2017), https://www.ons.gov.uk/employmentandlabourmarket/peopleinwork/employmentandemployeetypes/articles/graduatesintheuklabourmarket/2017.

6. Sutton Trust, *Elitism Britain, 2019: The Educational Backgrounds of Britain's Leading People* (London: Social Mobility Commission and the Sutton Trust, 2019), 6. https://www.suttontrust.com/wp-content/uploads/2019/06/Elitist-Britain-2019.pdf.

7. African Child Policy Forum, "The African Report on Child Wellbeing, 2018: A Ticking Demographic Time Bomb," Addis Ababa, Ethiopia, press release, 2 November 2018, https://africanchildforum.us1.list-manage.com/track/click?u=30fc8ce3edcac87cef131fc69&id=e9f04d0f36&e=8f9ea6f9c6.

8. Quoted in Emma Hagestadt, review of *The Examined Life,* by Stephen Grosz, *Independent,* 3 January 2013, http://www.independent.co.uk/arts-entertainment/books/reviews/the-examined-life-by-stephen-grosz-book-review-9035081.html.

9. E. Cort Kirkwood, "Immigrant Invasion," *New American,* 9 July 2019, https://www.thenewamerican.com/print-magazine/item/32664-immigrant-invasion.

10. Steven Shapin, "The Superhuman Upgrade" (a review of *Homo Deus: A Brief History of Tomorrow,* by Yuval Noah Harari), *London Review of Books,* 13 July 2017, 29–31.

11. Umair Haque, "The Three Causes of the World's Four Big Problems: Deep Transformation, or What London's Climate Change Protests Teach Us about the Future," *Eudaimonia and Co. Blog,* 22 April 2019, https://eand.co/the-three-causes-of-the-worlds-four-big-problems-e9fe49d89e3d.

12. Cesar Victora and Ties Boerma, "Inequalities in Child Mortality: Real Data or Modelled Estimates?" *Lancet,* May 2018, https://doi.org/10.1016/S2214-109X(18)30109-8.

13. Lucinda Hiam and Martin McKee, "The Real Scandal behind Britain's Falling Life Expectancy," *Guardian,* 24 June 2019, https://www.theguardian.com/commentisfree/2019/jun/24/britain-life-expectancy-health-gap-rich-poor-tory-leadership.

14. Marc Luy, "Causes of Male Excess Mortality: Insights from Cloistered Populations," *Population and Development Review,* 20 April 2004, 647–76, https://onlinelibrary .wiley.com/doi/abs/10.1111/j.1728-4457.2003.00647.x.

15. Ibid.; Jon Minton, personal communication (with thanks to him for spotting this and alerting me).

16. Gordon Marc le Roux, "'Whistle While You Work': A Historical Account of Some Associations Among Music, Work, and Health," *American Journal of Public Health* 95, no. 7 (July 2005): 1106–9, doi:10.2105/AJPH.2004.042564; https://www.ncbi.nlm .nih.gov/pmc/articles/PMC1449326/.

17. For the full lyrics and a rendition, see *Union Songs: The H-Bomb's Thunder,* accessed 4 September 2019, https://unionsong.com/u576.html Accessed 7 July 2019.

18. It is wise to use several sources. Here is one from *The World Population Review,* accessed 4 September 2019: http://worldpopulationreview.com/world-cities/istanbul -population/.

19. Tony Lawson, "A Speeding Up of the Rate of Social Change? Power, Technology, Resistance, Globalisation and the Good Society," in *Late Modernity: Trajectories towards Morphogenic Society,* ed. Margaret Archer (Cham, Switzerland: Springer, 2014), 21–47.

20. Kimura Masato, "Warning for Japan as a 'Migrant Power': Great Britain Changes Its Immigration Policy by Leaving the EU," *Yahoo Japan,* 23 December 2018, https:// news.yahoo.co.jp/byline/kimuramasato/20181223-00108781/ [Japanese].

21. Kawashima Tatsuhiko, "Recent Urban Evolution Processes in Japan: Analysis of Functional Urban Regions" (paper presented at the Twenty-Fifth North American Meetings of the Regional Science Association, Chicago, 1978).

22. Kawashima Tatsuhiko and Hiraoka Norijuki, "Spatial Cycles for Population Changes in Japan: Larger Metropolitan Areas and Smaller-and-Non-metropolitan Area," *Gakushuin Economics Papers* 37, no. 3 (2001): 227–44, https://www.gakushuin.ac.jp/ univ/eco/gakkai/pdf_files/keizai_ronsyuu/contents/3703=04/3703=04-18kawashima ,hiraoka.pdf; Kawashima Tatsuhiko, Fukatsu Atsumi, and Hiraoka Noriyuki, "Re-urbanization of Population in the Tokyo Metropolitan Area: ROXY-index / Spatial-cycle Analysis for the Period 1947–2005," *Gakushuin Economics Papers* 44, no. 1 (2007): 19–46, https://ci.nii.ac.jp/naid/110007524073/en/?range=0&sortorder=0& start=0&count=0.

23. Martti Hirvinen, Norijuli Hiraoka, and Tatsuhiko Kawashima, "Long-Term Urban Development of the Finnish Population: Application of the ROXY-index Analytical Method," *Gakushuin Economic Papers* 36, no. 2 (August 1999): 243–63, http://www .gakushuin.ac.jp/univ/eco/gakkai/pdf_files/keizai_ronsyuu/contents/3602/3602 -21hirvonen,hiraoka.pdf.

24. David Sanger, "Tokyo Journal; She's Shy and Not So Shy, Japan's Princess Bride," *New York Times,* 26 June 1990, https://www.nytimes.com/1990/06/26/world/tokyo -journal-she-s-shy-and-not-so-shy-japan-s-princess-bride.html.

25. "Prince Hisahito Tells Junior High School Entrance Ceremony of New Students' Hopes to Broaden Perspectives," *Japan Times,* 8 April 2019, https://www.japantimes .co.jp/news/2019/04/08/national/prince-hisahito-tells-junior-high-school-entrance -ceremony-new-students-hopes-broaden-perspectives/#.XMLczutKjUI.

26. Sanger, "Tokyo Journal."

EPILOGUE. **Pandemic**

1. Qiujie Shi, Danny Dorling, Guangzhong Cao, and Tau Liu, "Changes in Population Movement make COVID-19 Spread Differently from SARS," *Social Science and Medicine* 255 (15 May 2020), http://www.dannydorling.org/?page_id=7798.

2. ONS, "Comparisons of All-Cause Mortality Between European Countries and Regions: January to June 2020" (30 July 2020), https://www.ons.gov.uk/people populationandcommunity/birthsdeathsandmarriages/deaths/articles/comparisons ofallcausemortalitybetweeneuropeancountriesandregions/januarytojune2020.

3. Raj Bhopal, "COVID-19 Zugzwang: Potential Public Health Moves Towards Popula-tion (Herd) Immunity," *Public Health in Practice* 1 (2020), https://www.ncbi.nlm.nih .gov/pmc/articles/PMC7361085/pdf/main.pdf.

4. John Gray, "Why This Crisis is a Turning Point in History," *New Statesman* (1 April 2020), https://www.newstatesman.com/international/2020/04/why-crisis-turning -point-history.

5. ONS, "Coronavirus and the Social Impacts on Great Britain" (26 June 2020), https://www.ons.gov.uk/peoplepopulationandcommunity/healthandsocialcare/ healthandwellbeing/bulletins/coronavirusandthesocialimpactsongreatbritain/26 june2020.

6. Ibid. Source: Opinions and Lifestyle Survey (COVID-19 module), 18 to 21 June.

7. James Gallagher, "Fertility Rate: 'Jaw-dropping' Global Crash in Children Being Born," *BBC News,* 15 July 2020, https://www.bbc.co.uk/news/health-53409521

8. Cécile Viboud, Theresa Tam, Douglas Fleming, Mark Miller, and Lone Simonsen, "1951 Influenza Epidemic, England and Wales, Canada, and the United States," *Emerging Infectious Disease* 12, no. 4 (2006), 661–8, https://www.ncbi.nlm.nih.gov/ pmc/articles/PMC3294686/.

APPENDIX. **How to Read and Draw a Timeline**

1. Pierre Bézier, "How Renault Uses Numerical Control for Car Body Design and Tool-ing," *SAE Technical Paper* 680010 (1968), https://www.sae.org/publications/technical -papers/content/680010/.

2. Danny Dorling, *Injustice: Why Social Inequality Still Persists* (Bristol: Policy, 2015), 145.

FIGURES AND TABLES

Figures

Tables

Page numbers in italics indicate figures and tables.